THE ALAMO STORY

From Early History to Current Conflicts

J. R. Edmondson

Republic of Texas Press
Plano, Texas

Library of Congress Cataloging-in-Publication Data

Edmondson, J. R., 1950-.
  The Alamo story : from early history to current conflicts / J. R. Edmondson.
    p. cm.
  Includes bibliographical references and index.
  ISBN 1-55622-678-0
  1. Alamo (San Antonio, Texas)—Seige, 1836. I. Title.

  F390 .E32 2000
  976.4'03—dc21   99-057473
                                  CIP

Republic of Texas Press is an imprint of Wordware Publishing, Inc.
No part of this book may be reproduced in any form or by
any means without permission in writing from
Wordware Publishing, Inc.

Printed in the United States of America

ISBN 1-55622-678-0
10 9 8 7 6 5 4 3 2
2001

All inquiries for volume purchases of this book should be addressed to Wordware
Publishing, Inc., at 2320 Los Rios Boulevard, Plano, Texas 75074. Telephone inquiries
may be made by calling:

(972) 423-0090

For Shannon and Jenny

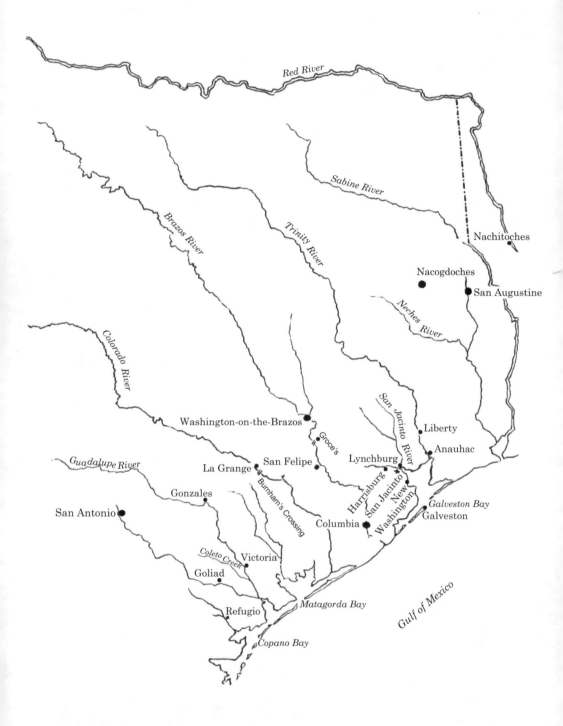

Contents

Foreword vii
Preface ix
Acknowledgements xi
Introduction xiii

Part One: The Mission
Chapter 1:   Olivares 3
Chapter 2:   Valero 17
Chapter 3:   The Head of Hidalgo 29
Chapter 4:   The Medina 38
   Myths, Mysteries, and Misconceptions 46

Part Two: Gone to Texas
Chapter 5:   The Last Filibuster 51
Chapter 6:   The Father of Texas 56
Chapter 7:   Santa Anna 64
Chapter 8:   The Constitution of 1824 70
Chapter 9:   The Hero of Tampico 76
Chapter 10: Mr. Bowie with a Big Knife 82
Chapter 11: San Saba 105
   Myths, Mysteries, and Misconceptions 118

Part Three: Revolution
Chapter 12: Tenoxtitlan 133
Chapter 13: Travis 138
Chapter 14: Anahuac 145
Chapter 15: The Raven 162
Chapter 16: Mill Creek 177
Chapter 17: Monclova 195
Chapter 18: Gonzales 208
Chapter 19: The Cannon and Victory 213
Chapter 20: Bexar 225
Chapter 21: Matamoras 247
Chapter 22: The Lion of the West 262
Chapter 23: Fannin 275
   Myths, Mysteries, and Misconceptions 291

Contents

Part Four: Thirteen Days

Tuesday, February 23, 1836:   The First Day 299
Wednesday, February 24, 1836: The Second Day 311
Thursday, February 25, 1836:   The Third Day 315
Friday, February 26, 1836:   The Fourth Day 322
Saturday, February 27, 1836:   The Fifth Day 327
Sunday, February 28, 1836:   The Sixth Day 331
Monday, February 29, 1836:   The Seventh Day 334
Tuesday, March 1, 1836:   The Eighth Day 338
Wednesday, March 2, 1836:   The Ninth Day 344
Thursday, March 3, 1836:   The Tenth Day 347
Friday, March 4, 1836:   The Eleventh Day 353
Saturday, March 5, 1836:   The Twelfth Day 356
Sunday, March 6, 1836:   The Last Day 362
The Aftermath: Remember the Alamo! 376
    Myths, Mysteries, and Misconceptions 389

Epilogue: The Battles Continue 411

Bibliography 425
Index 433

Foreword

The fall of the Alamo was arguably the greatest single traumatic episode in our country's early culture until the assassination of Abraham Lincoln on April 14, 1865. The assassination made Lincoln a martyr, and his martyrdom elevated him to iconic status. The massacre at the Alamo, nearly three decades earlier, engraved upon history an indelible memory in the collective American mind. That memory is as vivid now as it was at San Jacinto six weeks after the Alamo fell. The two buildings that remain, the Church (which defines the Alamo in photos) and the Long Barracks, stand today as silent reminders of those who lived and died there. The structures are inanimate but still very much alive.

We can't talk with those who perished at the Alamo or with the non-combatants who survived the siege. But in this book by historian J. R. Edmondson they operatively speak to us, if not in the literal sense, then surely effectively.

Edmondson offers, from an independent perspective, historical views comparable to a conductor's study of a composer's masterwork: The embedded details are there to be newly discovered by those who seek them.

In a word, it's *readable*. It is difficult to imagine a volume presented in a more professional manner than this one. It has a thesis-level substance yet it is clear enough to be accessible to anyone with an interest in history. There are volumes that can put you to sleep even after your morning coffee, but this one can keep you awake at night.

It seems no adobe brick was left unturned in the research for this book. Anyone can report facts, but Edmondson aims higher: His writing illuminates rather than decorates and shows, not the shadow but the substance of his subjects. He goes beyond simple documentation, pierces the armor, and enters the sanctum of personality and character.

The Alamo concepts and events are dramatic enough without the need of embellishment a la Hollywood. The author knows this and presents his material with extraordinary insight and a totally genuine perspective of Western history. The book is a virtual San Saba silver mine of information and fascinating details. It is riveting reading and at times assumes nearly cinematic, Hitchcock-like overtones. That it took Edmondson several years to finish this book is a testimony to his diligence and reverence for the subject matter.

This work takes its place with those of Walter Lord and others in the Alamo setting. There's no other book quite like it, so its singularity gives it its specialty. *The Alamo Story: From Early History to Current Conflicts* covers the Alamo in all its incarnations—from the historical and iconic entity to its popular cultural image. By its very immediacy, this solid book seems to enlarge and strengthen the links in the chain that binds us to our own history.

Jeffrey Dane

Preface

In the publicity for his 1960 epic motion picture, John Wayne concisely summed up the history of the Alamo—"The mission that became a fortress; the fortress that became a shrine."

This book describes the old Spanish mission San Antonio de Valero as it evolved through each of its three phases. The history of the Alamo is the story of fabulous people—Spanish, French, Mexican, *Tejano*, and Anglo-American.

Obviously special attention is given to the heroic 1836 battle that transformed the mission from a fortress to a shrine. In a very real sense that battle still rages today. It is a fluid story, dynamic, elusive, ever changing, always open to new interpretation.

But a book is static, concrete, locked in time and place. Thus neither this publication, nor any other, can ever hope to be the definitive work on the Alamo.

"When the facts become legend, print the legend," stated a newspaper reporter in John Ford's motion picture *The Man Who Shot Liberty Valance*. Perhaps too many early books on the Alamo adhered to that newspaperman's advice. Some more recent works, however, have leaned toward revisionism, challenging and occasionally taking cynical delight in debunking the traditional legends.

This book will prove harder to categorize. Sometimes the facts do overrule the legends. But often the facts and legends are more closely intertwined than is currently believed.

According to the most popular Alamo legend, late in the siege Colonel William Barret Travis drew a line in the dirt with his sword and challenged his tiny garrison to cross that line, to continue fighting—perhaps to the death—against overwhelming odds.

Some historians have disputed this story. But they can never disprove it. However, admittedly, the historical evidence supporting Travis' line remains controversial. Thus, like so many of the stories of the Alamo, it must linger in the realm of legend rather than fact.

Yet those who address the story of the Alamo essentially draw their own lines in the sand, defend their own positions, view its history from their own perspectives.

It is a powerful story, because we will always marvel at the Texian garrison that deliberately put itself in harm's way and fought to the death. Was it heroism? Or foolish, arrogant overconfidence?

We struggle to understand the Alamo defenders because in some ways they were like us, and in some ways they were not like us at all. To be sure, they were products of another time. Death was no stranger on the nineteenth-century frontier. Disease and violence were more prevalent then. Honor, ideals—and especially the fresh concept of liberty—were things for which men willingly would fight. And die.

Yet in many ways the men of the Alamo—and those who besieged it—shared basic human emotions that transcend all generations. They hoped and feared and despaired and loved. And even if they were willing to fight, they did not want to die.

It is only when we finally accept the heroes of the Alamo as mortal, flawed humans that we can truly appreciate their magnificent sacrifice.

Acknowledgements

This book owes a tremendous debt to many.

Most especially to Joseph Musso, historian and artist, who generously contributed an abundant amount of research, primary sources, and illustrations. The husband and wife team of Craig Covner and Dr. Nina Rosenstand provided knowledge, psychological perspectives, and artwork. Craig is a veritable living encyclopedia on the Alamo, and he remains one of the very few genuinely objective voices about the battle of the Alamo. Thomas Lindley, who has spent more hours than anyone else digging through dusty archives, selflessly shared his own findings and theories.

Assisting with the editing, Stacie Mercier dutifully read and reread, and reread—the typescript. Donna Donnell explored the Internet, dredging up valuable material. Artist Michael Schreck graciously permitted his new, dynamic portraits of Bowie, Crockett, and Travis to be included in this book. And artist Jo Eisenrich interrupted her overcrowded schedule to work on maps.

For other illustrations and maps this book gratefully acknowledges Kay Bost, curator of the DeGolyer Library at Southern Methodist University; Carol Roark, manager of the History and Archives Division of the Dallas Public Library; land surveyor Malcolm G. Barlow and Ms. Cindy Stringer from the Natchez Civil Engineering Firm of Jordan, Kaiser & Sessions; and artist Rod Timanus of Durham, Conneticut.

To William R. Chemerka, editor of the *Alamo Journal*, the official publication of the Alamo Society; Kevin Young, editor of the *Alamo Courier*, official publication of the Alamo Battlefield Association; and Randell G. Tarin, managing editor of the Alamo de Parras web site: Your organizations and publications greatly facilitated the research for this project.

So did those authors and historians who previously have ventured into this precarious territory, most notably Walter Lord, Dr. Stephen L. Hardin, Paul Andrew Hutton, Alan C. Huffines, Bill Groneman, and William C. Davis. Even when this book disagrees with their writings, it does so respectfully.

And there were countless others who contributed information, insights, or merely inspiration: Dr. James Batson; Dorothy Black and the Daughters of the Republic of Texas; fellow writer/historian Jeffrey Dane; V. Paul

Dickson; Gary Foreman; Dan Gaggliasso; Linda Gardner and the Vidalia, Louisiana, Chamber of Commerce; Doug Grantham; Roger M. Green; Jamie Hagwood; Joan Headley; Robert Heinonen, Dale Evans, and the Texana Living History Association; Miss Lisa Liston; Patty Miller; George Norris; Jerome Parker and Jacque Hopkins; Rudy Robbins; Mr. and Mrs. Logan Sewell; Frank Thompson; Rod Timanus; Michael Waters; Chuck and Roy Young and the late Phillip Young of Little Rock; David Zucker; and most especially the late Bernice Strong, librarian at the Daughters of the Republic of Texas Library at the Alamo.

Sincere appreciation also must be expressed to Dr. Richard Selcer, who introduced me to this project, and to my longsuffering editors, Ms. Ginnie Bivona and Mrs. Dianne Stultz.

Introduction

The urgent staccato bugle call, borne on brisk spring winds, resounded across the three-acre compound of the mission-fortress known as the Alamo. The meager garrison dashed for their stacked muskets and scrambled to their posts. From the crumbling walls they watched the enemy army approaching from the south, a thousand strong in battle formation.

West of the mission, just across the shallow, winding river, the people within the city of San Fernando de Bexar scurried about frantically, their cries of confusion and panic carrying back to the Alamo garrison. Many of the civilians grabbed whatever possessions they could carry and hustled their families out onto the chaparral prairie to the north.

The defenders of the mission-fortress grimly prepared for the hopelessly uneven conflict. Soldiers primed their muskets and held them at the ready. Artillerymen rammed charges down the barrels of their cannons. Every man wondered if he was about to die.

On this day, however, no guns would be fired; no battle would be joined against overwhelming odds. This day the Alamo's defenders would not be united in a defiant and desperate last-ditch stand.

Instead three men, holding aloft a white flag that flapped noisily in the breeze, marched out to meet the enemy. The trio had been sent by Governor Manuel Maria de Salcedo, commander of the Spanish forces defending San Fernando de Bexar, to discuss the terms for capitulation.

On this day—April 1, 1813—the Alamo would surrender. Without a shot being fired. To a rebel army fighting under a flag of freedom.

The humiliating defeat only added to the misfortune that had characterized the old mission, even before its conception more than a century earlier.

And bad luck would continue to plague the mission-fortress.

Only twenty-two years after Salcedo's defeat, the Alamo would again witness the surrender of its garrison. On December 10, 1835, Mexican forces under General Martin Perfecto de Cos relinquished the position to yet another rebel force.

And two months later a mere two hundred fifty rebels would attempt to defend the Alamo against a Mexican army numbering more than two thousand. No Alamo garrison had ever faced such overwhelming odds.

This time the Alamo would not surrender.

Part One: # *The Mission*

Chapter 1: *Olivares*

The historical record provides no birthplace or birth date for the man who would establish the most famous mission in Texas. Yet even before he marched into Texas, elderly Father Antonio de San Buenaventura y Olivares had earned a reputation as one of the most cantankerous priests in Mexico.

Olivares' mentor was the legendary Father Antonio Margil de Jesus, the guardian of the missionary college Santa Cruz de Queretaro, who consistently referred to himself as "Nothingness Itself." Despite his self-deprecating title, Margil had spent thirteen grueling years traipsing through the sweltering jungles of southern Mexico and Central America. He had established some twenty-five missions and baptized more than ten thousand Indians.

Initially Father Margil had assigned Olivares to the north central province of Zacatecas, just below Coahuila. The blistering sun had transformed Olivares' skin to splotchy, wrinkled leather, and his advanced years had turned his thinning ring of hair to gray.

In 1699 Margil dispatched Olivares and Father Francisco Hidalgo, accompanied by a squad of *soldados* under Captain Diego Ramon, to northern Coahuila. They were instructed to establish missions for the primitive tribes, hunters and nut gatherers, that lived along the Rio Grande, the great river of the north. This new assignment exhilarated Hidalgo, a veteran of Mission San Francisco de los Tejas, the first mission established in the province to the northeast.

Gold, glory, and God, essentially in that order, had motivated the founding of the missions—indeed their whole New World empire—since the time of the *conquistadores*. In 1521 Hernan Cortez, commanding a handful of Spaniards, had captured the magnificent Aztec empire and claimed the vast wealth of Moctezuma. Mexico City, the center of Spain's New World domain, rose upon the ruins of the Aztec capital Tenochtitlan.

A decade later Francisco Pizzaro, with an even smaller force, reaped more than twice as much treasure when he defeated the Incas of Peru.

Reveling in riches so easily plundered, the Spanish authorities cast their unsated gaze to the north. In 1540 Francisco Vazquez de Coronado, leading a massive expedition, rode across what would become the southwestern United States. But he found no Seven Cities of Cibola, no Gran Quivera, and returned the following year in disgrace.

About that same time, Hernando De Soto's expedition trampled through the present-day southeastern United States. When De Soto succumbed to disease, exhaustion, and frustration, his men sank his weighted body into the Mississippi River. Ironically, his greatest discovery had become his grave.

Since the explorers had found no wealth, Spain virtually lost interest in her vast northern territory. Except for some settlements along the upper Rio Grande, there would be no major ventures into that region for almost a century and a half.

Until Rene Robert Cavelier, Sieur de La Salle, stepped onto Texas soil by mistake.

In 1682 La Salle had descended the Mississippi River in a birchbark canoe, claiming for France all the lands drained by the great river and its tributaries. He christened this vast expanse *La Louisianne* in honor of the French monarch Louis XIV. Significantly, the southern extremity of this Louisiana Territory was wedged between Spanish Florida and Spain's more extensive holdings to the west. Perhaps worse, Louisiana overlapped Spain's western territory, creating a legacy of conflict that would be inherited by the United States more than a century later.

Later La Salle returned to establish a colony at the mouth of the great river. But he overshot the delta and shipwrecked in Matagorda Bay. Retreating a few miles inland, he hoisted the fleur-de-lis over a hastily constructed stockade he named Fort St. Louis.

The Spanish had learned of La Salle's incursion from captured French seamen. Don Alonso De Leon,

Rene Robert Cavelier, Sieur de La Salle

the governor of Coahuila, led an overland *entrada* to locate the French stockade.

However the Spanish proved to be the least of La Salle's problems. The coastal swamps were the domain of both malaria-bearing mosquitoes and cannibalistic Karankawas, both of whom preyed upon the French trespassers. When De Leon finally located the rotting, weed-encrusted stockade, only a few sun-bleached skeletons remained of the French garrison.

Father Damian Massanet, one of the founders of the College of Santa Cruz de Queretaro—the New World's first school for missionaries—accompanied the De Leon expedition. During the search for the French fort, Massanet encountered an unusually advanced native tribe—the Hasinai Indians of the extensive Caddo Confederation. These agrarian people hailed each other with the word "tejas," meaning friend or ally. Mistaking this general term of greeting for tribal nomenclature, Massanet described their domain as the "great kingdom of the Texas."

Soon their name would apply to the entire province.

Massanet concluded that the Hasinai were ideal subjects for Christianization. But, as with most priests, the Spanish bureaucracy frustrated him. Though designed to become self-sufficient, the missions generally required a considerable expense to establish. So did the presidios, or forts, usually constructed to protect the missions. And the garrison of *soldados* that manned the presidio remained a continual drain on the treasury. Thus the officials of New Spain rarely authorized a mission unless they expected some kind of return from their investment. Even with the missions, gold and glory, or at least political advantage, ranked as more significant factors than God.

To be sure, converting and domesticating the red man had always proven more expedient than fighting him. But such measures only were warranted if the Spanish had financial or political reason to occupy lands on which Indians resided.

La Salle's tragic incursion had created just such a situation. Returning to Mexico City, Father Massanet easily convinced the viceroy that missions and presidios would create a strategic Spanish presence to guard the disputed boundary with French Louisiana. In March 1690 De Leon and Massanet left Monclova, Coahuila, with over a hundred *soldados* and three other missionaries. They paused at Fort St. Louis long enough to incinerate the silent, rotting structures, then they continued eastward to the Neches River. There, in late May, amid the tall, fragrant pines, they established a wooden stockade mission that bore the name San Francisco de los Tejas.

Then disaster loomed. Along with God, the Spanish introduced European diseases for which the Indians had no natural immunity. When hundreds of the Hasinai fell ill, the Indians naively blamed the disease on the mission's baptismal waters, and they avoided San Francisco de los Tejas. When hundreds—and then thousands—died, the Indians rose up against the mission.

In the predawn hours of October 25, 1693, Massanet and the other priests hastily buried the mission bell and cannon. Then they set fire to the wooden structure. Massanet could not linger to watch his mission reduced to smoldering ashes. Harassed by the hostile Hasinai, he and the other Spaniards fled back to Coahuila.

The viceroy of New Spain attempted to console Father Massanet. San Francisco de los Tejas failed primarily because of its great distance from Monclova. Perhaps the priest would help establish missions among the more docile and primitive tribes along the Rio Grande in northern Coahuila. Such missions could serve as way stations helping to supply the Spanish in east Texas.

But Massanet declined. He had endured enough politics and bureaucracy. He retired back to the College of Santa Cruz de Queretaro to spend his last years teaching other missionaries.

Father Hidalgo had protested Massanet's decision to abandon the Tejas mission, and he yet longed to return to the Caddo tribes of the piney woods. Both Hidalgo and Olivares recognized that, politically, the Rio Grande missions would serve as a gateway into Texas.

They established the first mission, San Juan Bautista, on January 1, 1700, just five miles below the Rio Grande. Nearby, on March 1, they established Mission San Francisco Solano. Crusty old Father Olivares personally assumed authority over this second mission, and he promptly introduced his new Coahuiltecan charges to a celebration of Mass. Then, displaying an energy level that belied his many years, Olivares waded across the Rio Grande and hiked through the hills, seeking even more converts for his mission. Officially, however, this first intrusion did not place him in Texas. New Spain recognized a boundary line formed by the Medina and Nueces Rivers, roughly a hundred miles northeast of the Rio Grande, as the border between Coahuila and Texas.

From the outset, hostile tribes threatened the precarious existence of the two fledgling missions. Within the first year most of the Coahuiltecans abandoned San Francisco Solano, complaining that the few *soldados* could not protect them from the aggressive tribes. Olivares marched all the way down to Mexico City and demanded more troops. For once the authorities responded with uncharacteristic efficiency, dispatching a "flying company" to reinforce Captain Ramon's command. By early 1703 Ramon had established a presidio adjacent to San Juan Bautista. A community of the same name soon sprouted around the missions and fortification.

Then, for a few months, Mission San Francisco Solano prospered. Daily the tireless Olivares conducted morning and evening Mass, and between the services he joined the Indians in the cornfields. His flock swelled to over three hundred, half of whom he baptized into the Catholic faith. But before the year had passed famine set in, and the numbers rapidly dwindled.

The settlement of San Juan Bautista had grown too large too quickly. The nearby stream and surrounding fields in that arid region could not support the increased population. The priests held a counsel and decided to relocate Mission San Francisco Solano to a new site sixteen leagues west.

Gamely Father Olivares trekked west, knowing that his former converts would not follow him that great distance to the new location. In essence, Mission San Francisco Solano had been sacrificed so that San Juan Bautista might survive. Yet, determinedly, Olivares gathered some four hundred new converts into the relocated mission's new structures.

But again marauding Indians drove his new flock back to the safety of the surrounding hills. By 1706 the Indian population of San Francisco Solano had diminished to such insignificant numbers that the College of Santa Cruz de Queretaro removed Olivares from his mission.

In fact, Olivares was required back at Queretaro. To accommodate a growing Franciscan presence in New Spain, the College of Santa Cruz had authorized Olivares' former mentor, the competent Father Margil, to establish and preside over a new missionary school at Zacatecas. While Margil was founding the College of Nuestra Señora de Guadalupe, Father Olivares would serve as guardian of Santa Cruz.

It would be a short tenure. The crotchety old priest came to regard the Zacatecan school as a competitor of Santa Cruz, and a bitter personal rivalry developed between Olivares and his former teacher. But Olivares lacked the prestige to contend with the legendary Father Margil. When Olivares left Santa Cruz two years later, his fierce loyalty to his college remained as strong as his enmity toward Margil.

Olivares returned to northern Coahuila in early 1709 to find San Juan Bautista flourishing. But his own hard luck mission, San Francisco Solano, had been relocated the previous year to yet a third site—five leagues north of Bautista on the Rio Grande. Here, again, few Indians responded to the tolling of its mission bell. Olivares sensed that San Francisco Solano was doomed.

Despite his age Father Olivares knew he possessed enough ornery determination to establish one more mission. He gazed across the big river and recalled his trek to the northeast. Tribes of Indians lived on that vast frontier who had never heard the word of God.

The viceroy of New Spain also had been focusing his attention on the lands above the Rio de la Norte. He had learned that the French had established a settlement at Mobile in lower Louisiana, and they were attempting to initiate trade with the Hasinai and other Caddo tribes. Simultaneously there were rumors that the Hasinai might now be disposed toward welcoming the Spanish back into east Texas. If the latter report were true, Spanish missions and presidios could again secure the border and prevent an uncomfortable alliance between the French and Caddos. Certainly the matter bore investigation.

Captain Pedro de Aguirre received the assignment to lead a small, investigatory *entrada* into Texas. Marching at the head of fourteen *soldados*, he arrived at Bautista shortly after Olivares' return to northern Coahuila.

The old Franciscan must have perceived Captain Aguirre's arrival as a blessing from God. Olivares quickly arranged to accompany the expedition as chaplain. A younger priest, Isidro Felix de Espinosa, would serve as chronicler.

The expedition departed Bautista on April 5, 1709, and forded the Rio Grande. Within a few days they crossed the Medina and entered Texas. A short distance above the Medina they came to a broad plain surrounded by low, wooded hills. To the east, a narrow, tree-lined river meandered gently across the prairie. Just to the west flowed the crystal stream of a spring-fed creek. The local Payaya Indians called the place Yanaguana, which the Spanish interpreted as "sparkling waters."

The Spaniards named the creek "The Water of San Pedro," Father Espinosa wrote in his diary. Though he did not say so, the name probably honored Captain Aguirre's patron saint. Noting that the river had not been named by previous Spanish explorers, Espinosa added, "we called it the River of San Antonio de Padua." Presumably the river honored Father Olivares' patron saint.

Espinosa was mistaken. Eighteen years earlier, en route to Mission San Francisco de los Tejas, Father Massanet and Governor Teran had visited this same region. And they already had bestowed a Spanish name to the river.

They had arrived on June 13, 1691, the feast day of Saint Anthony of Padua, and—by incredible coincidence—they, too, had christened the area in honor of that revered Portuguese saint. Governor Teran had praised the area as "the most beautiful in New Spain."

Little had changed in eighteen years. Father Olivares noted the "rich productiveness of the soil and the plentiful water supply." More important to Olivares, near the springs stood a village of Payayas, yet another tribe of the primitive Coahuiltecan family. Father Olivares decided then that he would build his new mission among these nearly naked but generally amiable Indians at this place so emphatically destined to be called San Antonio.

The expedition needed only to proceed as far eastward as the Colorado River. There, to his disappointment, Aguirre learned from friendly Indians that the Caddo tribes remained fervently hostile toward any Spanish presence in east Texas.

The Aguirre expedition returned to Bautista on April 28. Scurrying on to Mexico City, Father Olivares approached the viceroy for the permission—and more important, the financing—for his new mission. Yet, ironically, Captain Aguirre's report worked against the old Franciscan's ambitions. Without an invitation from the Caddo, the viceroy displayed no interest in renewing any missionary work in Texas. Not even among friendly Coahuiltecan tribes along the San Antonio River.

Infuriated, Olivares resolved to take his plea to a higher authority. He made the lengthy voyage back across the Atlantic. For the next six years he pestered and pressured the Spanish government to expand the missionary program into Texas.

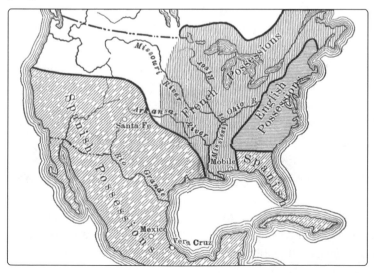

Territory claimed by Spain, France, and England in 1700.

At San Juan Bautista, Father Francisco Hidalgo remained just as frustrated with bureaucracy—and just as determined to return to the east Texas mission he had last seen in flames. But Father Hidalgo resorted to a more radical scheme to achieve his dream. For a decade the government of New Spain had ignored his requests; now he defied the government's laws. On January 11, 1711, Hidalgo dipped his quill into the inkwell and began scratching on a sheet of parchment. "Did the French Governor have any information about the spiritual and material condition of the people of the Tejas, among whom Father Hidalgo had begun to labor more than a score of years ago?" he wrote. Then he boldly inquired, "Would the Governor cooperate in establishing a mission among them?"

Hidalgo's letter energized the governor of Louisiana, Antoine de la Mothe, Sieur de Cadillac, who perceived it as an invitation. It offered the potential of developing relations—and commerce—with New Spain. Or at least the northern provinces. But the matter would have to be initiated delicately.

Cadillac turned to a dashing, forty-year-old Canadian-born explorer. Louis Juchereau de St. Denis belonged to a rare breed. The lacy silk shirts and velvet long coats of a gentleman fit him as naturally as the buckskins he wore in the backwoods. Moreover he possessed a silver tongue that had mastered Spanish and several Indian languages. With the political tact of a diplomat, the persuasiveness of a salesman, and the winning charm of a natural born confidence man, St. Denis proved to be the perfect ambassador.

Leading a company of men and a pack train crammed with everything from beaver hides to delicate linens, St. Denis rode out of Mobile in September 1713. At the Red River they paused to trade among the Natchitoches Indian villages. St. Denis appraised the strategic importance of the site. New Spain claimed the Red River as the eastern boundary of Texas; France claimed the Sabine, overlapping forty-five miles to the west, as the boundary of Louisiana.

Shrewdly St. Denis left a contingent of men at the Red River to establish Fort St. Jean Baptiste. The fort would serve as his base of operations, a trading post, and a defensive position against Spanish encroachment. Soon it would evolve into the town of Natchitoches, the first permanent settlement within the modern boundaries of Louisiana.

With twenty-five men and the pack train, St. Denis continued into Texas. Along the way he befriended and traded with various Indian tribes. He finally reached San Juan Bautista in July 1714. Cognizant that he was violating Spanish law, St. Denis boldly rode into the settlement and asked for Father Hidalgo.

Unfortunately, Father Hidalgo was away visiting the college at Queretaro. Captain Diego Ramon, who still served as commandant of the presidio, immediately arrested the trespasser. However, Ramon found the eloquent French Canadian so compelling that he had St. Denis placed under house arrest—in the captain's own residence. There, St. Denis dined off Ramon's finest silver and savored his imported Cuban cigars as they spoke of the absurdity of the Spanish law that banned commerce between their nations. There, Ramon's seventeen-year-old granddaughter, Manuela Sanchez, also fell under the spell of the cavalier adventurer. And for once, St. Denis apparently succumbed to someone else's charms. He proposed, and she accepted.

When word reached Mexico City that a French trader had been captured at Bautista, the viceroy ordered the prisoner to be conveyed to the capital. Arriving in Mexico City, St. Denis was incarcerated in the prison. But again his persuasive eloquence won over the authorities. Assisted by Father Hidalgo, who had raced to the capital from Queretaro, St. Denis finally provided a compelling argument for the Spanish to reestablish missions and presidios in east Texas. He warned the viceroy that the French already had constructed a military post, Fort St. Jean Baptiste, on the Red River—at the very border of Texas.

Spain would not legalize trade with French Louisiana, St. Denis realized. But he also knew that he could seduce the isolated Spanish settlements in east Texas into a lucrative smuggling operation with his nearby fort at Natchitoches. The tremendous distance between Mexico City and east Texas would render it virtually impossible for Spanish authorities to interfere in the contraband trade. The nearest Spanish garrison lay nearly five hundred miles away—roughly halfway to Mexico City—and it was commanded by his future father-in-law. St. Denis envisioned extending his smuggling operation all the way across Texas to Bautista.

Even if Father Hidalgo had recognized St. Denis' ulterior motives, the priest would not have cared. St. Denis, the glib adventurer from Louisiana, had reopened Texas to Spanish settlement.

St. Denis and Father Hidalgo returned to Bautista, where preparations began for the expedition to east Texas. Captain Ramon's son, Domingo, would command the expedition. St. Denis would serve as commissary officer. And, of course, Father Hidalgo would lead the missionary contingency, which included the young chronicler Father Espinosa.

The legendary Father Margil announced that he, personally, would assume authority over the east Texas missions, placing them under the jurisdiction of his new college at Zacatecas. Margil planned to accompany the expedition, but he had fallen ill and would travel to east Texas later.

Before the expedition left Bautista, St. Denis married Manuela. The wedding fiesta lasted three days. St. Denis assured his young bride he would return for her after the completion of the expedition.

Composed of twenty-five *soldados*, eleven missionaries, and herds of cattle and goats, the expedition left Bautista in April 1716. Two months later they arrived in the fragrant piney woods of east Texas. The Hasinai welcomed them with the peace pipe. On July 3 Father Hidalgo reestablished his San Francisco de los Tejas mission. Four days later Nuestra Señora de la Purisma Concepcion was established only twenty-five miles to the northeast. Meanwhile Captain Domingo Ramon began construction of a presidio, Nuestra Señora de los Dolores de los Tejas, on the east bank of the Neches River.

When Father Margil reached east Texas later that month, two more missions had already been founded. Nuestra Señora de Guadalupe de los Nacogdoches would evolve into the town of Nacogdoches. Margil personally supervised the establishment of two more missions. He located San Miguel de Linares de los Adaes east of the Sabine within the contested land claimed by both France and Spain. The last mission, Nuestra Señora de los Dolores de los Ais, would later become the town St. Augustine.

The following year St. Denis returned to Mexico to claim his bride. Not wanting to waste the trip, he escorted a caravan of contraband goods to Bautista. But the death of Louis XIV and the subsequent War of the Spanish Succession had further strained the relations between France and Spain. Despite his influential father-in-law, St. Denis again was arrested. It appeared his fabulous luck had finally played out. Spanish troops marched him south, sentenced to be forever locked away in a dark, damp dungeon in Guatemala.

But St. Denis managed a spectacular escape, stole a horse, and galloped back to Natchitoches, where he received the appointment of commandant of the post. St. Denis and Captain Ramon arranged to have Manuela sent to him at Natchitoches. There the gallant French Canadian and his young Mexican bride lived their remaining years in prosperity—one of history's few "happy ever after" endings.

Crochety old Father Olivares returned from Spain to Mexico City in 1716. Olivares knew his own time on earth was running short, but he remained driven by a compulsion to establish a mission on the San Antonio River. For four months he pled his case before the new viceroy, the Marques de Valero Baltazar de Zuniga. But now Father Olivares had learned to play the game.

Gold? The land near the San Antonio River contained fabulous mineral wealth, Olivares boldly lied.

Glory? The mission would be one of the largest and grandest in all New Spain, an invaluable way station on the Camino Real, the royal highway that extended all the way from Mexico City to the new missions in east Texas. Moreover, Olivares promised he would name the mission after the viceroy.

God? Olivares himself would provide religion for the thousands of Indian converts who gathered within his new mission's walls.

The Franciscan's tenacity and persuasiveness finally triumphed. In December 1716 the Marques de Valero agreed to provide the permission and the funding for the new mission. Olivares would relocate his failed mission, San Francisco Solano, from below the Rio Grande to the San Antonio River. Don Martin de Alarcon, the newly appointed governor general of the combined provinces, Coahuila y Texas, would lead the expedition and establish a protective presidio.

However, Governor Alarcon infuriated the impatient priest by taking more than a year to prepare for the journey. The cantankerous priest also squabbled with the governor about the quality of the *soldados* who would man the presidio. Olivares insisted that they be married men of pure Spanish blood. He did not want them molesting his Indian women.

Alarcon snorted his reply. Unlike the Franciscans, he could not recruit from missionary colleges. "In Coahuila," he announced, "there are only mulattos, lobos, coyotes, and *mestizos.*"

Finally, in February 1718, Alarcon mounted his expedition: seventy-two people—soldiers and settlers—and large herds of horses and cattle. Indignant, Olivares refused to travel with the governor-general's party.

With a bodyguard of eight soldiers, the old Franciscan made a final visit to Mission San Francisco Solano. He gathered the only two remaining Indians, construction tools, farming implements, and—very important—crop seed. And he took the registry book. San Franciso Solano, which had always been plagued by misfortune, would be the forerunner of Olivares' new mission.

Governor Alarcan reached San Antonio in late April. Father Olivares arrived on May 1 and promptly selected a site for his mission on the west bank of San Pedro Creek. True to his promise to the viceroy, he christened it San Antonio de Valero. Immediately construction began on temporary log structures.

Four days later Alarcon located his presidio three-quarters of a league up the creek at the springs. The governor could be political, too. He named it San Antonio de Bexar after the viceroy's brother, the Duke of Bexar, who had died heroically defending Budapest from the Turks. The settlement that grew up around the presidio became known as the Villa de Bexar.

Within the first year Father Olivares began to suspect that misfortune had attached itself to his new mission. While Olivares was riding across a timber bridge, his mount's hoof wedged in a gap. The animal stumbled, tossing the elderly Franciscan from its back. The fall broke Olivares' leg. Infection set in, and the old father became so gravely ill that he sent for a confessor from Bautista. But it was not yet Father Olivares' time. Miraculously he recovered, though his leg never fully healed and continued to bother him for his remaining years.

While recuperating, Father Olivares came to realize that the original site of his new mission was unsuitable. In 1719 he relocated the temporary structures to the more fertile fields on the east side of the San Antonio River.

In Europe, the War of the Quadruple Alliance had pitted Spain against France. At Natchitoches in June 1719, Lieutenant Philippe Blondel took it upon himself to attack his nearest Spanish adversaries at the nearby Los Adaes mission.

With only seven men, Blondel galloped up to the mission and captured its only occupants, a lay brother and a single *soldado*. The French soldiers began looting the buildings. When one of them entered the henhouse, a flock of clucking chickens fluttered out into the mission yard. Spooked, Blondel's horse reared and its rider fell to the ground. Blondel's injured pride would be the only casualty of what became known as the Chicken War, but the aftershocks stretched across Texas.

In the ensuing confusion the lay brother escaped into the woods. He swam the Sabine and stumbled into Mission Nuestra Señora de los Dolores. Gasping for breath, he warned Father Margil that a large French force was marching toward east Texas.

The lay brother was mistaken; the French had no intention of invading Texas. But Margil could not know that. He ordered all the missions to be evacuated.

At the presidio, Captain Domingo Ramon also chose the better part of valor. The entire Spanish presence in east Texas withdrew to San Antonio to await reinforcements. One more time Father Hidalgo retreated from his Tejas mission. This time he would not return.

Arriving in San Antonio, the priests found that Mission San Antonio de Valero consisted of thatch-roofed huts clustered around a two-story stone tower. The lower floor of the tower provided a temporary chapel, and the upper floor housed the priests. The whole structure could serve as a block-house if hostile Indians attacked.

Young Father Espinosa continued on to Bautista to hurry on the Spanish force. But a year and a half would lapse before the new governor of Coahuila y Texas, José de Azlor, Marqués de San Miguel de Aguayo, could mount an expedition. With five hundred men and six brass cannon he set out to reconquer east Texas. By then, the European war already had ended. And there had never been any Frenchmen in east Texas to defeat. Passing through San Antonio, Governor Aguayo relocated the Villa de Bexar and the presidio to the west bank of the river opposite the mission.

In 1722 Aguayo also began construction of another presido, Nuestra Señora de Loreta, to protect Matagorda Bay. The presidio supposedly stood on the site of La Salle's ill-fated Fort St. Louis. Captain Domingo Ramon assumed command of the fortification. Nearby Franciscan priests from the Aguayo expedition established Mission Nuestra Señora del Espíritu Santo de Zuniga. The mission would serve the coastal tribes, including the notorious Karankawas. (In 1749 both the mission and presidio were relocated some thirty-five miles to the east, but because of their original location, the community that developed around them continued to be known as La Bahia—"the bay.")

During their exile in San Antonio, Father Margil, Father Hidalgo, and the other Franciscans took up residence at Mission Valero. It could not have been a comfortable situation; Father Olivares still resented his former mentor. Their already strained relationship further deteriorated the following year when Margil declared his intent to establish a second mission on the river below Valero.

Father Olivares quickly petitioned Juan Valdez, lieutenant general and alcalde of the presidio and villa of Bexar, to deny Margil and his Zacatecan missionaries permission to establish a new mission. Olivares noted that

Margil's intended converts—the Pampopas, Pastias, and Suliajames—were traditional enemies of Olivares' flock.

But Margil already had circumvented Olivares. He had announced his plans in a letter to Governor Aguayo, and Aguayo had sent written orders to Valdez to allow the new mission.

Father Olivares could only fume as Margil then compounded the insult.

Spanish law stipulated that missions must be located at least three and a half leagues (seven and a half miles) apart. However, Margil measured that distance by walking along the winding river, selecting a site for his new mission on the east bank less than four miles below Mission Valero. (Later it would be relocated to a hill above the west bank, adding another mile between the two missions.) Margil established his new mission on February 23, 1720. As politically astute as Olivares and Alarcon, Margil named it Mission San Jose y San Miguel de Aguayo.

Perhaps it was the poor health brought on by his many years. Perhaps it was the throbbing pain in his broken leg. Or perhaps it was merely the distressing sight of Mission San Jose being erected to the south. In September 1720 Father Antonio de San Buenaventura y Olivares retired from Mission San Antonio de Valero. Then the cantankerous old man who had established the most famous mission in Texas history slipped back into the obscurity from which he had come.

In 1722 Father Antonio Margil de Jesus returned to Zacatecas to assume guardianship of the college he had founded. He died four years later. He is now under consideration by the Vatican for sainthood.

Although Governor Aguayo's army had restored the east Texas missions in 1719, Father Francisco Hidalgo remained in Mission Valero's two-story stone blockhouse and assumed authority of Olivares' hard luck mission.

Misfortune struck again in 1724. A hurricane leveled all the buildings, including the stone structure.

Father Hidalgo chose a new site a short distance to the north, and the construction of San Antonio de Valero began once more. This third site, just northeast of a large bend in the river, would be the mission's final location.

There it would acquire its greatest fame—and suffer its greatest defeat.

Chapter 2: *Valero*

Father Hidalgo never returned to his beloved San Francisco de los Tejas in east Texas. Ironically the mission followed him to San Antonio.

By 1730 the east Texas missions had failed. They had never fully recovered from the Chicken War fiasco. However the viceroy in New Spain did not grieve the loss of the missions. Their political purpose, at least, had been served. The border with French Louisiana had been secured, and France no longer was deemed a threat.

Three of the missions were relocated to the San Antonio region, where the missions Valero and San Jose seemed to be enjoying some success among the local tribes. Two hundred seventy-three Payaya, Pamaya, and Jarame Indians had taken up residence at Valero.

Again ignoring the regulations governing the distance between missions, Nuestra Señora de la Purisma Concepcion was constructed in 1731 on the east side of the river between Valero and San Jose.

The other two missions arrived the following year. Mission San Juan Capistrano was established on the east side of the river below San Jose. Just below San Juan, on the west bank, Mission San Francisco de la Espada became the southernmost of the five missions that flanked the San Antonio River.

Espada was the reincarnation of Mission San Francisco de los Tejas. But Father Hidalgo had not been there to greet it. He had resigned from Mission Valero in 1725. He died at Bautista the following year.

About the same time the new missions were being transplanted from east Texas, three hundred settlers from the Canary Islands arrived at San Antonio. They transformed the Villa de Bexar into a town named San Fernando de Bexar, honoring the heir to the Spanish throne destined to become Ferdinand VI.

With the arrival of the aristocratic Canary Islanders, the soldiers in the presidio moved their families across the river. A small community of huts, later called La Villita, emerged just south of Mission Valero.

At this time, in the early 1730s, the mission still consisted of temporary structures. However the first permanent buildings soon appeared. An even row of perhaps five rectangular adobe buildings, extending north to south, formed the west side of the mission complex. Here were quartered the Indian converts. These simple buildings each contained several unconnected cell-like rooms that opened eastward into arched porches providing some relief from the blistering summer sun.

An *acequia*, or water ditch, flowed just in front of these huts on its vital journey to irrigate the fields north and east of the mission.

Across the plaza to the east stood the two-story *convento*, or friary, the heart of the mission. Constructed of thick stone walls, it formed a large square of double-tiered archways enclosing a serene open yard with a well. The upper floor housed the priests. The lower floor contained the offices, the kitchen and dining area, and guestrooms for visiting missionaries. The main entrance to the convent faced the Indian quarters to the west.

Extending north on a line from the west side of the convent, the granary, too, opened west into the plaza. In the angle behind the granary and north of the convent, enclosed within a picket fence, were the workshops: a blacksmith shop, a carpentry shop, and a textile shop with twenty spinning wheels. Here, also, Indians molded adobe bricks and skilled masons chiseled the stones used in the mission's construction.

According to tradition, a permanent church, the centerpiece of every mission, was always the last major undertaking. Until then the priests and Indians worshipped in a temporary adobe chapel. On May 8, 1744, the cornerstone of the church was laid just south of the *convento*. It, too, faced west, as all mission churches were required to do. The stone walls of the church rose quickly—perhaps too quickly—for it collapsed into a pile of rubble within the year.

Again misfortune had struck Mission Valero.

Yet the 1740s and '50s reigned as Mission Valero's most successful period. During those decades more than three hundred Indians consistently resided at the mission.

Despite the fears expressed earlier by Father Olivares, no serious conflicts developed between his Indians and the tribes at San Jose or at any of the other missions. Their peaceful coexistence may have been imposed by a mutual enemy from the prairies to the north.

For centuries the primitive, nomadic Apaches had plodded wearily behind the migratory bison herds. But in recent decades Spanish horses had been dispersed among the tribes. The horse mobilized the Apaches, allowing them to range farther and faster and to become more proficient at both hunting and warfare. Mounted on horseback, they became masters of hit-and-run commando tactics, striking the missions, killing and burning and stealing more precious horses, and then disappearing into the vast expanses of prairies to the north and west, a land that came to be known as Apacheria. Sometimes Spanish troops pursued the raiders. Most often they never found the Indians.

Espada, the most remote mission, almost eight miles below the town, suffered most from Indian raids. However the Apaches also had killed several residents of Mission Valero who had been surprised away from its protective buildings. Because of the ever-present threat, such menial tasks as tilling the fields or rounding up stray cattle had become hazardous undertakings. In 1731 the Apache raiders became even more brazen, galloping inside the mission compound and driving away fifty burros.

Usually the Apaches attacked in small raiding parties. But they broke all the rules on the night of June 30, 1745, when some three hundred mounted warriors thundered into the town. Their war cries shattered the darkness, and their flaming arrows, launched into thatched roofs, transformed the town into an inferno. Panicked Bexarenos—men, women, and children —raced through a blinding hell of choking smoke and searing flame, pounding hooves and flying arrows, chilling war cries and the bloodcurdling screams of the dying. Those Bexarenos who made it inside the walled presidio prayed that the Indians would take what they wanted and then dissolve back into the prairie. Or they prayed for a quick death. Few in number and with few weapons among them, the Bexarenos could not repel a determined assault.

And this time the Apaches were determined. No longer content with hit-and-run raids, they now sought to annihilate their Spanish enemy and reclaim the Texas plains. With uncharacteristic organization, they struck the presidio from three sides, driving the desperate Spanish back from the walls.

The battle ended quickly, but not as the Apaches had anticipated. Suddenly a hundred Christianized Coahuiltecans, wielding only primitive weapons and farming implements, charged out of Mission Valero. Trampling over the wooden bridge that spanned the river, they struck the Apaches from the rear. Taken by surprise, the raiders abruptly abandoned their assault and fled into the darkness. The mission Indians had saved the town.

It would be the only time the inhabitants of Mission San Antonio de Valero ever would triumph in a military engagement.

The Apache assault on San Fernando de Bexar proved to be the tribe's high water mark. Curiously, within a few years the Apaches themselves initiated a truce. The exhilarated authorities did not probe for the ulterior motive behind the tribes' abrupt quest for peace.

On August 16, 1749, Apaches chiefs feasted in the main plaza of San Fernando with city leaders, presidio *soldados*, and mission priests. The celebration lasted three days. On the third day the Apaches lowered an indignantly protesting white horse into a deep pit dug in the center of the plaza. The braves dropped a lance, a tomahawk, and six arrows into the pit beside the trapped animal. Then, after dancing around the pit, the Apaches shoveled dirt back into the hole until the piteous whinnies had finally, permanently been muffled. If this brutal ritual offended the mission priests, they stifled their repulsion in the interest of peace. They joined the city leaders, *soldados*, and Apaches in the revelry and dancing around the grave.

The symbolism of the horse entombed with the other weapons did not elude the Spanish. The horse had served as the Apache's greatest weapon, rendering the tribe the master of the plains. The bitter irony resulted from the fact that all Indian ponies descended from the mounts brought to the New World by Cortez and the other *conquistadores*.

After that celebration, the Apaches came to Bexar not to fight but to trade. Sometimes they offered chunks of silver for the supplies they desired.

When a band of Apaches requested that a mission be established in their lands to the northwest, the Spanish officials readily concurred. A mission in Apacheria could be politically advantageous. The once fearsome tribe could be further pacified through Christianity, and the Spanish domain finally would extend northward towards its professed boundaries.

There was, of course, an even greater incentive. The Spanish had never lost their dream of finding great wealth in Texas. There had been tantalizing rumors of rich silver deposits along the San Saba River, but the Apaches had discouraged any serious efforts to locate the precious ore. Now Spanish *soldados* and prospectors could take advantage of the invitation and enter the region with the missionaries.

The soldados, prospectors, priests, and converted Indians arrived at the San Saba River in April 1757. On the south bank they hastily erected Mission San Saba de la Santa Cruz—a stockade enclosing a wooden chapel and a few crude huts. Several miles upstream, on the north bank of the river, they constructed another stockade, Presidio San Luis de las Amarillas— garrisoned with more than a hundred Spanish troops to protect both the mission and the prospectors. Because of concern about the distance between the mission and the presidio, eight *soldados* and two small cannon remained at the mission.

The Apaches gave excuses and promises, and they eagerly accepted gifts from the Franciscans, but they never moved into the mission. Unknown to the priests, a new enemy, descending from the north, threatened the Apaches more than the Spanish army ever had.

In the distant Rocky Mountains of Colorado and Wyoming, a primitive Shoshone subtribe that subsisted on nuts and roots and insects and an occasional feast of jackrabbit had learned of the wondrous, fleet-footed horses to the south. During the early eighteenth century, bands of these Indians began migrating into Texas, stealing or bartering for mounts. The horse transformed this tribe—even more than the Apaches—from an insignificant race to the greatest and most feared light cavalry in the Americas—the "Cossacks of the Plains." They pushed on southward, challenging the Apaches at their own type of warfare with a savagery Texas never before had witnessed. This new tribe came to be known by the Ute word for "enemy," *Komantcia*, or Comanche.

Apaches could be political, too. Crushed between the Spanish settlements to the south and the descending Comanche juggernaut from the north, the Apaches simply sidestepped and waited for the inevitable clash between their two mortal enemies.

The confrontation occurred just after morning Mass on March 16, 1758. Two thousand mounted Comanches, wearing animal skin headdresses, their faces painted in black and red, descended on the mission, killed some of the inhabitants, and burned the log structures.

The San Saba massacre enraged the Spanish officials more than any previous Indian atrocity. Every available Spanish soldier who could be spared from the existing missions and presidios was mustered into a punitive expedition. More than a hundred Indian scouts were recruited, mostly Apaches who eagerly volunteered to guide one foe against another. Numbering almost six hundred men and equipped with two cannon, the largest Spanish force ever assembled in Texas trailed the hostile Comanches as far north as the Red River. Then the Comanches took the offensive. The Spanish limped back into Bexar, minus their cannon and their pride.

The *soldados* rebuilt the presido out of stone and renamed it the Real Presidio de San Saba. It had become the strongest outpost on the Spanish frontier, virtually impregnable to any assault.

However the Comanches did not need to storm the presidio. As the Apaches had done at Bexar, the Comanches effectively utilized hit-and-run tactics. They burned crops and drove away horses and cattle from the outlying fields. They preyed upon *soldados* who ventured outside the gates to hunt wild game or gather wood. Worse, the Comanches ambushed the desperately needed supply trains from Bexar. With most of the garrison sick or starving, the Spanish finally abandoned the presidio. It had endured only eleven years.

Spain's misadventure on the San Saba left legends and legacies. Remnants of the smelting operation found among the presidio ruins fostered

Ruins of San Saba
presidio

tales of mineral wealth such as Father Olivares had once promised the Marques de Valero. Spanish mines, their locations quickly forgotten after the Spaniards' hasty departure, still contained wide veins of rich silver. Underground chambers concealed great stacks of processed ingots that the *soldados* could not carry in their retreat. Or so the stories went.

In fact no historical evidence ever surfaced that the Spanish had found any mineral wealth on the San Saba. But the legends would endure and tantalize, long after the Spanish or the Indians.

The legacy of San Saba perpetuated another bitter irony. The Spanish, who had easily conquered the most advanced tribes in the Americas, never achieved more than a foothold in the Texas domain of the primitive, nomadic plains Indians. With the collapse of the San Saba presidio, San Fernando de Bexar again became the northern point of Spanish occupation in Texas, a city virtually besieged by the primitive Comanches.

The Comanche hostilities accelerated construction at all the missions. At San Antonio de Valero, adobe bricks joined the Indian huts to form a western wall. Another adobe wall stretched eastward from the northern-most Indian quarters and then angled south to the granary. At the opposite end of the compound a fortified gate of stone, crowned with a cannon turret, was built into the southern wall that extended east from the lower Indian hut. This wall then turned north to join the front of the *convento,* enclosing the great rectangle.

It seems entirely feasible that the first church had been built on this line from the south wall to the convent, directly on the plaza. Indeed this southern extremity of the east wall below the convent actually may have utilized the front of the original church's foundation. However when a new church was begun in 1758—the date remains even now carved into the stone over the door—it was set back from the plaza and connected to the rear of the convent's south wall. Perhaps its builders simply chose to erect the new church behind the rubble that remained from the collapse of the first church. Why else would the new church stand so awkwardly and asymmetrically disjoined from the rectangular compound, its entrance exposed and vulnerable outside the mission's protective walls?

Later that same year, 1758, Jacinto de Barrios y Jauregui, then governor of Coahuila y Texas, visited the five missions along the San Antonio River. He reported that Concepcion, Espada, and San Juan Capistrano had completed construction of their stone churches. Concepcion had the largest and most imposing church, with two tall bell towers and a domed roof over the cross-shaped nave.

Mission Concepcion

Mission San Jose

The governor noted that Mission Valero had begun construction on a permanent church, but the Indians at San Jose, the mission that Father Margil had founded over Father Olivares' protests, still worshipped in a temporary adobe chapel.

Construction of the church at San Jose began in 1768 and continued for fourteen years. Skilled artisans decorated its facade with spectacular stone carvings. Its renaissance architectural style displayed a melding of Gothic, Moorish, and Romanesque influences. Upon its completion in 1782 it would be deemed the most beautiful church in Texas, the "Queen of the Missions."

Mission San Juan Capistrano

Speculative drawing of how Mission Valero's church would have looked upon completion.

It would be Margil's final victory over Olivares, though neither had lived to see it.

At that time, Mission Valero's church remained uncompleted. The Tuscan facade around the doorway had been decorated with exquisitely delicate stone carvings, more elaborate then the austere geometric design at Concepcion but not so ornate as San Jose. On either side of the large doorway, chiseled columns framed tall niches that held the statues of Saint Francis and Saint Dominic.

An elaborately carved shelf supported by the columns served as the foundation for the facade's second tier. A tall, rectangular window centered over the doorway opened into the church's choir loft. At either side of this window, Saint Clare and Saint Margaret of Cortona stood in niches directly above their male counterparts.

However the columns flanking these niches did not yet extend to the second level.

A proposed third tier, not yet begun, was to feature a single niche aligned above the window. From this height, Our Lady of the Immaculate Concepcion would be able to survey all that went on in the mission below.

The overall church plans generally followed the architectural design of Concepcion, with twin bell towers and a domed nave. These, also, had not yet been added. The four-foot thick stone walls rose only two-thirds of the church's intended elevation. Four rooms inside—the baptistry and confessional on either side of the entrance, both with windows looking out the front wall, and the sacristy and anteroom midway back on the left—featured vaulted roofs. However the arches that spanned the nave and the gallery supported only the sky.

That was essentially as complete as the church ever would be. Epidemics struck the hard luck mission, depleting the Indian population and preventing further construction. The priests tried to struggle on, holding services in the sacristy. But by 1793 only fifty-two Indians remained at Valero. That same year Spanish authorities delivered the mission's coup de grace. San Antonio de Valero became the first of the five missions to be secularized, its surrounding lands doled out to the few lingering Indians who dwelt there. Some of these Indians continued to reside within the mission structures; others erected new *jacales* alongside the cluster of huts just south of Valero.

Yet despite its long history of misfortune, Father Olivares' mission hardly qualified as a failure. The first and largest of the San Antonio missions, it had been the seed from which Bexar, the first and largest civil settlement in Texas had developed. And although the Indian population had rarely exceeded three hundred at any one time, during Valero's three-quarters of a century existence the priests had baptized well over a thousand Indians into the Catholic faith.

Indirectly at least, external factors had influenced the closing of the missions. For more than a century Spain and France had maintained a tense, adversarial relationship along the Texas-Louisiana border. French traders had supplied weapons to the plains Indians that preyed on Spanish settlements. On the grander scale, however, King Charles IV of Spain and Louis XV of France were distant cousins, and when the Seven Years War erupted between France and Great Britain, Charles determined that France was the lesser of two enemies. That conflict spanned the Atlantic, becoming known as the French and Indian War in North America. When Britain triumphed, Spain was compelled to forfeit Florida to the British empire. However Spain gained a much larger prize. In the secret Treaty of Fountainbleu, the French king ceded the Louisiana Territory to his Spanish cousin rather than surrender it to Britain.

Spain's North American empire now extended east to the Mississippi, even crossing the great river's lower extremity to include the Isle of Orleans, a small but vitally significant bit of real estate, which encompassed the French stronghold of New Orleans.

France, if not French influence, had been expelled from the New World, and Spain's new neighbor and former adversary, Great Britain, proved less contentious. The thirteen colonies lay east of the Appalachian Mountains. Woodland tribes occupied the wilderness west of the Appalachians. Most were former allies of the French, and they remained hostile to the British settlers to their east.

British authorities had not been impressed by the insubordinate and undisciplined colonial troops during the French and Indian War. General James Wolfe, the posthumous hero of Quebec, had described his four American companies as "the worst soldiers in the Universe." After all, the colonies had been settled essentially by dissidents, religious refugees, convicts, and fiercely independent Scotch-Irish immigrants. For the very protection of this discordant rabble, King George III issued a proclamation restricting them to the lands east of the Apalachian, away from the hostile tribes. At best this proclamation merely slowed westward expansion. Simultaneously, it added one more aggravation to a long, festering list of colonial grievances against the crown.

From the Spanish perspective, the wilderness between the Appalachians and the Mississippi served as a comfortable buffer, reducing the strategic importance of the missions and presidios in distant Texas. Aside from designating San Fernando the new capital of Texas, Spanish authorities largely ignored that province and focused their attention on New Orleans, a city founded in 1718, the same year as Bexar.

For almost a decade after secularization, the old mission remained abandoned except for the handful of Indians who still resided within its rooms. Weeds grew tall outside and inside the sun-bleached, roofless church. The adobe walls, especially the long stretch across the north end of the compound, crumbled from the rain and wind and neglect.

The town across the river fared little better. By the late eighteenth century the population of San Fernando had reached two thousand— two-thirds of the entire Spanish population of Texas. These Bexarenos were crammed into one hundred thirty-eight houses, seventy-nine of which were simple wooden huts. Even the houses of adobe or stone generally possessed only one low, musty room with dirt floors and few comforts. The Baron de Ripperda, then governor, chose to live in the town jail, presumably the most pleasant structure in the town. His wife transformed one of the cells into her birthing chamber. All the buildings stood along irregularly winding dirt streets that degenerated into bogs whenever it rained, so that a man wishing to preserve his boots had to mount his horse from his doorway.

The old presidio barracks had become uninhabitable, not even suitable for stables, according to a visiting dignitary. The outer wooden stockade had rotted away, but it was still delineated by houses that had been built against its walls on the north, west, and south sides. When the barracks finally deteriorated, the area became a military plaza. Separating it from the main plaza to the east stood the San Fernando Church, whose single bell tower rose to the highest point in the town. Though deemed modern, the church already showed signs of dilapidation.

Thus, in the waning years of the eighteenth century, San Fernando de Bexar and the abandoned mission across the river together slipped into a silent, degenerative coma under the withering south Texas sun.

The Alamo church in ruins.
Drawing by Craig Covner.

Chapter 3: ## *The Head of Hidalgo*

T he thunder of hoofbeats roused Bexar from its slumber. On December 29, 1802, a hundred cavalrymen from southern Coahuila galloped into the town, reinforcements for the underpaid and overworked *soldados* still stationed there. Behind them straggled another hundred civilians, wives and children of the *soldados*.

This new unit wore the traditional uniforms of Spanish colonial presidio troops: blue coats with red facings and black, flat crowned, flat brimmed hats with wide white bands. They carried traditional cavalry weapons: lances, sabres, and smooth bore muskets. And, traditionally, they bore an elongated Spanish name—the Second Flying Company of San Carlos de Alamo de Parras—which, also traditionally, was generally abbreviated in common usage. They would bequeath their name to the mission.

Since the presidio barracks no longer existed, commander Francisco Amangual ordered his Alamo Company to be quartered in the abandoned Mission Valero across the river. Single men like Sergeant Vicente Tarin, a widower in his mid-thirties, moved into the lower floor of the abandoned convent. *Soldados* with families took up residence in the rooms built along the western wall or in the *jacales* of La Villita south of the mission.

Valero's large courtyard would serve as a corral. The sacristy, one of the few enclosed rooms in the otherwise roofless church, was transformed into a small chapel where the *soldados* and their families could worship.

The Alamo Company had been reassigned to Bexar to help protect Spanish Texas from a new adversary that loomed to the east. Even the vast Texas prairies could not insulate Bexar from cataclysmic events that abruptly had reshaped the world.

The successful revolt of the thirteen British colonies had produced modern history's first great experiment in independent self-government. Certainly British authorities had gained a new respect for "the worst army in the Universe," although the intervention of European allies had actually assured the colonial victory. By recapturing Florida, Spain had made a modest contribution to the American cause, creating a second front against the British. The French had provided more enduring and vital support, their fleet compelling the final British surrender at Yorktown. Appropriately, France soon caught the contagious fever of revolution. From this Reign of Terror emerged a diminutive figure who would cast a long shadow.

Napoleon Bonaparte sought to extend his growing empire back into North America. In 1800, through the Treaty of San Ildefonso, he bullied Spain into returning the Louisiana Territory to France.

The defeat of the British had ended the restriction on western migration. Many Americans, especially the fiercely independent Scotch-Irish, remained as distrustful of their own new federal government as they had been of the British crown. The trans-Appalachian frontier offered free land and at least temporary isolation from federal authorities. Following in the footprints of Daniel Boone, they flooded through the Cumberland Gap and down the Wilderness Road into Kentucky and Tennessee.

The Mississippi River, which served as the nation's western boundary, quickly became a primary avenue of commerce for these western settlers. Its relentless current carried flatboats laden with goods and produce from as far away as the upper Ohio River. Below Natchez, however, the Mississippi flowed into foreign domain. Spain had previously granted the U.S. permission to use the vital port city of New Orleans. Upon learning that the fleur-de-lis again flapped above the Isle of Orleans, President Thomas Jefferson feared that Napoleon might close the city to American commerce.

Jefferson instructed the United States minister at Paris, Robert Livingstone, to present an offer for the purchase of the Isle of Orleans, and in January 1803 Jefferson dispatched James Monroe to assist Livingstone. The timing proved advantageous for the American agents. Internal problems had depleted Napoleon's treasury, and yet another war with England seemed imminent. Instead of selling New Orleans, the French emperor stunned Livingstone and Monroe by placing the entire Louisiana Territory on the block. For the price of fifteen million dollars the young nation gained some 828,000 acres between the Mississippi and the Rocky Mountains, virtually doubling its size.

However the Louisiana Purchase aggravated the tension between the United States and Spain. Napoleon had cited the Rio Grande as the southwest boundary of Louisiana, thus including Texas in the transaction. Spanish authorities argued vehemently that Napoleon could not sell what he had never possessed, and they sent battle-ready troops into east Texas to guard the border.

Then a second controversy erupted. Spain and France had never resolved the issue of the border between Louisiana and Texas. The United

States adopted the old French claim to the Sabine River; Spain still insisted that the boundary followed the Red River into present-day Louisiana. General James Wilkinson, commander of the U.S. Army in Louisiana, proposed a peaceful resolution. The land between the Sabine and the Arroyo Hondo, seven miles to the east, would be a Neutral Ground over which neither Spanish nor United States forces would have jurisdiction. Acting for Spain, Governor Simon de Herrera, commandant of the Louisiana frontier, readily acceded. Even though the boundary had not been established, the agreement at least served as an unofficial acknowledgement by the United States of Spain's claim to Texas.

For his part in the arrangement, General Wilkinson would receive a handsome reward in Spanish gold or silver. Wilkinson was a fabulously Machiavellian figure who operated as a triple agent. Even as he commanded the United States forces in Louisiana, he provided information—or misinformation, if it paid more—to both Spain and Great Britain, ultimately playing all three nations against each other. His web of deceit has never been fully unraveled.

In fact Wilkinson had no federal authority to tender such an offer. But President Jefferson also acquiesced to the arrangement. Still under pressure from Great Britain, he did not wish to subject his infant country to a war with Spain. Yet many frontier Americans felt bitterly cheated, and they kept hungry eyes turned west toward Texas.

And so, too, did General James Wilkinson.

The Second Flying Company of San Carlos de Alamo de Parras had arrived in Bexar four months before the consummation of the Louisiana

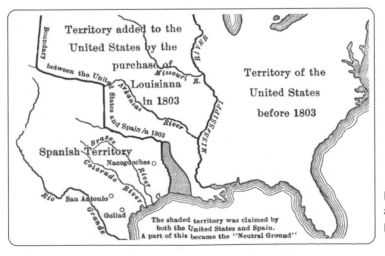

Map of English and Spanish possessions in 1803.

Purchase. Already there had been trouble with Americans trespassing into Texas.

Irish-born rogue Philip Nolan ranks as the first filibuster in Texas history. In the 1790s he made several trips into Texas to round up wild mustangs for sale back in Natchez. He also produced a detailed map of Texas, the first ever transcribed in English. Spanish authorities began to suspect that Nolan had ulterior motives, especially after the mustanger's 1799 audience with President Thomas Jefferson. Nolan's real sponsor, however, was General James Wilkinson, for whom Nolan had once worked as a bookkeeper.

In December 1800 Nolan led a party of twenty men on another foray into Texas. It would be his last. Several months later Spanish troops marched into Bexar displaying Nolan's severed ears and eleven manacled prisoners, including a resourceful eighteen-year-old-Tennessean named Peter Ellis Bean. Bean and the other captured Americans were briefly incarcerated in the Alamo before they, and Nolan's ears, were escorted on to Mexico City.

Wilkinson's machinations continued. In 1806 he dispatched Lieutenant Zebulon Pike's expedition, ostensibly to explore the headwaters of the Arkansas and Red Rivers in the southern region of the Louisiana Territory. Secretly Pike was to spy on Spanish settlements in New Mexico.

Pike achieved an immortality of sorts near the headwaters of the Arkansas when he discovered the "Great Mountain." Failing in an attempt to reach its summit, Pike guessed its altitude at 18,500 feet—an overestimate of more than 4,000 feet—and predicted that no one would ever be able to climb it.

Pike enjoyed no more success on his covert operation. Spanish troops discovered his expedition in New Mexico and arrested him for trespassing. After being detained in Santa Fe, the expedition was escorted back toward the United States. On June 7, 1807, they arrived—ragged, haggard, and hungry—at San Fernando de Bexar for a week of rest. Rather than being incarcerated, Pike's men received cordial treatment. Local authorities donated food and money. Colonel Don Antonio Cordero, then governor of the combined provinces of Texas and Coahuila, even insisted that Pike stay in the governor's residence. Apparently it had been renovated since the days when Cordero's predecessor, Baron de Ripperda, had slept in the jail.

Cordero had made other improvements as well. In 1805 he had established a military infirmary—the first hospital in Texas—in the "secularized Mission of Valero." The original infirmary beds were "made of reeds in order to avoid the dampness of the ground," but in 1807 they were replaced by thirty wooden beds. The hospital initially occupied the lower floor of the old convent building. Later it expanded to the second story after repairs to the floor and roof were completed in 1810.

Ironically the doctor serving the troops at the Alamo infirmary was a renegade American named Zervan, who had jumped a $40,000 bail in Natchez and fled to Texas. Pike described "Dr. Zerbin" in his report of the expedition: " . . . he had recently committed some very great indiscretions, by which he had nearly lost the favor of Colonel Cordero, though whilst we were there, he was treated with attention."

Pike's report also noted the station of troops across the river where the hospital was located. Pike seemed unaware that the military post had once been home to priests and Indian converts. Mission Valero had evolved into a fort. Already it was sometimes referred to as the Alamo.

The intrusions by Nolan, Pike, and others—by 1813 there were seventeen Anglo-Americans incarcerated in the Alamo's guardhouse—justified Spain's concern about its border with the United States. However a greater threat originated below the Rio Grande. The contagious fervor of independence—born in the thirteen colonies, thwarted in France—had rebounded back to the New World. In 1810 the father of Mexican independence emerged on the stage of history. Stoop-shouldered at fifty-seven years of age, his head rimmed with flowing gray hair, Father Miguel Hidalgo y Costillo seemed an unlikely champion. His passion for gambling was surpassed only by his sincere compassion for his Indian parishioners in the impoverished village of Dolores.

In the early morning of September 16, Hidalgo made his most dangerous gamble. He rang the church bells to assemble his flock, delivered a rousing speech—his immortal "Cry of Dolores"—and mustered a meager force of three hundred Indians and *mestizos* to challenge the royalist armies of Spanish Mexico. Bare feet and tattered rags served as their uniforms, and machetes and clubs as their weapons. Yet the old priest's mob quickly captured several small villages, sometimes without resistance, and then marched on the larger cities.

Hidalgo's noble rebellion, like the French Revolution before it, masked an internal class war. Mexico had a rigid caste system that denied social mobility. True Spaniards born in Spain, called *peninsulares*, comprised the elite upper class. The middle class was composed of Creoles, those born in Mexico of Spanish parentage. Indians made up the labor class. At the very bottom were the socially shunned *mestizos* of mixed Spanish and Indian blood.

The elite *peninsulares* were derogatorily called *gachupines,* or spurs, because of their relentless prodding of the lower classes. When Hidalgo attacked the wealthy mining town of Guanajuato, the *gachupines* collected their personal treasures and retreated into a fortress-like grain warehouse called the *alhondiga.* Hidalgo's vengeful mob burned through the heavy wooden doors and brutally massacred the Spaniards. "The building presented the most horrible spectacle," recalled an eyewitness. "Naked bodies lay half buried in maize, or in money, and everything was spotted in blood."

With each victory Hidalgo's popularity soared. His rabble increased to one hundred thousand men, including some two thousand trained *soldados* who had defected from the Spanish army. Many were Creoles, and there were even a few *gachupines.* The ideals of independence had begun to supplant the class conflict.

The revolutionary fever spread faster than Hidalgo's army. It possessed Jose Bernardo Gutierrez de Lara, a wealthy landowner at Nuevo Santander on the Rio Grande. Himself the brother of a priest, Gutierrez once gained an audience with Hidalgo and later pledged "my services, my hacienda, my life" to the cause.

At San Fernando de Bexar, a retired army captain named Juan Bautista de las Casas declared his support for Hidalgo and assumed control of the Alamo garrison. On January 11, 1811, he led the *soldados* in an overthrow of Governor Manuel Maria de Salcedo. The deposed governor was removed to Coahuila, where he was placed in the custody of Lt. Colonel Ygnacio Elizondo, a former Spanish officer who had switched his allegiance to the rebel cause. However, from his Coahuila prison, Salcedo managed to persuade the fickle Elizondo to rejoin the Spanish fold.

The Casas rebellion lasted a mere six weeks. It had divided the population of Bexar. Some retained loyalties to Spain. Others, like Juan Jose Maria Erasmo Seguin, the postmaster of Bexar, and Second Lieutenant Vicente Tarin, commandant of the Alamo Company, supported the cause of independence but doubted Casas' true motives. Those opposed to Casas fell in behind Lieutenant Colonel Juan Jose Manuel Vicente Zambrano, the subdeacon of San Fernando de Bexar. Their subsequent counterrevolution reinstated Salcedo at Bexar. Casas was arrested, tried for treason, and executed. As a gruesome warning to future revolutionaries, his head was impaled on a stake and mounted in the main plaza of San Fernando.

In less than six months the tide turned against Hidalgo. At Guadalajara his rabble force collapsed before the superior training and weaponry of a numerically inferior Spanish army. With only a thousand men, the old priest attempted to flee across the northern deserts. He hoped to recapture San Fernando de Bexar—already known for its anti-royalist sentiments —entrench himself within the Alamo, and reorganize his revolution within its ancient walls.

Hidalgo never made it to Texas. The fickle Colonel Ygnacio Elizondo led the royalist force that ambushed the retreating rebels in Coahuila. Captured alive, Hidalgo was executed on July 30, 1811. As with Casas, his body was decapitated. Spanish authorities sent Hidalgo's head back to Guanajuato to be impaled on a pole atop the bloodstained *alhondiga*. There the skin dried and blackened in the sun, and the long, gray hair fell away with the rotting flakes of flesh.

But Hidalgo's followers kept the revolutionary movement alive. Bernardo Gutierrez, whose land and wealth had been confiscated by the Spanish royalists, escaped across Texas to the United States. In Washington, D.C., he pled his case before Secretary of State James Monroe and President James Madison. Essentially Gutierrez espoused Hidalgo's final strategy—use Texas as a base of operations from which to revitalize the independence movement in Mexico. Gutierrez only needed a little help liberating Texas and establishing a republican government there.

Despite its great size, the United States remained a young nation standing on wobbly legs and uncertain of each step. Napoleon's war raged through Europe, and dark ominous clouds of conflict already drifted toward American shores, just ahead of an invading British fleet. With the War of 1812 imminent, could the United States risk antagonizing its western neighbor Spain, already allied with Britain against Napoleon?

On the other hand, many in the United States remained bitter that their government had not exercised its Louisiana claim on Texas. If that province were wrested away from Spain, they asserted, it would deter a British invasion from Mexico.

Gutierrez sailed to New Orleans with a promise of unofficial support. Since neither the United States nor Spain had jurisdiction over the nearby Neutral Ground, the strip had become a haven for outlaws, renegades, filibusters, mercenaries, and adventurers. Just the sort of men Gutierrez would need for an army to retake Texas.

Equally important, in Louisiana there were men—like General Wilkinson and Governor William Claiborne and U.S. Special Agent William

Shaler—with influence and money and their own designs on Texas. Augustus Magee, a tall, ambitious twenty-four-year-old West Pointer from Boston who had served under Wilkinson, resigned his commission as lieutenant to become colonel of the new Republican Army of the North.

Samuel Kemper became a captain. With his brothers, Reuben and Nathan, he had instigated the Kemper Insurrection of 1804, capturing Baton Rouge in a failed attempt to wrest West Florida from the Spanish. And six years later the brothers had participated in the more successful Rebellion of 1810, which finally accomplished their purpose.

Bernardo Martin Despallier, a Frenchman from Natchitoches, also enlisted. Despallier personally issued propaganda material that was forwarded into Texas ahead of the invasion army.

Other men joined up, some in support of the idealism of liberty, some for personal gain, some merely for the adventure, most for a combination of these reasons. In forty short days the Republican Army of the North, one hundred thirty strong, came into existence. Its overall composition probably did not differ much from the colonial forces half a century earlier that Wolfe had lamented as "the worst army in the Universe." Gutierrez served as the nominal head of this motley band of liberators, but they took their orders—when they took orders—from Magee.

Marching under a green flag, the Republican Army of the North crossed the Sabine on August 8, 1812, "determined to besiege Inferno itself." Four days later the Spanish stronghold at Nacogdoches fell without a fight. *Tejano* and Indian reinforcements flocked to the army, more than doubling its size.

Learning that governors Salcedo and Herrera were advancing from Bexar with eight hundred royalists, Magee swung south, deftly circumventing his enemy. He led his force to La Bahia, which capitulated on November 7, again without bloodshed. The republicans entrenched themselves in the old stone presidio.

A week later the Spanish army surrounded the presidio. Confident of their numerical superiority, the Spanish governors submitted terms of surrender. The Anglos would be paroled back to the United States. But the *Tejano* revolutionaries must be delivered over to the Spanish.

Facing two-to-one odds, Magee apparently agreed to the offer. Gutierrez, visualizing his own head on a pole, felt bitter betrayal for himself, his people, and their cause. To his relief, however, the Republican Army of the North ignored their commander and refused to lay down their arms.

Salcedo and Herrera's royalist force settled in for a siege that would last three months.

Magee died on February 8, 1813. The cause of his death remains an enduring mystery. Reports later circulated that he had been poisoned, or that he had committed suicide. In fact he probably died from consumption aggravated by the severe winter. However the Spanish, encamped on the open prairie, suffered far more from the icy north winds than did the fortified rebels. Enough *soldados* defected to the republican army—either for warmth or for liberty—to shift the numerical advantage away from the royalists.

Samuel Kemper assumed command. On February 19, 1813, he broke the royalist siege. Salcedo and Herrera fell back to Bexar. It was the last Spanish stronghold in Texas.

The last obstacle to the republicans' victory.

Chapter 4: ## *The Medina*

On March 25, 1813, Colonel Samuel Kemper led his revolutionaries, roughly six hundred in number, out of La Bahia toward San Fernando de Bexar. By then governors Salcedo and Herrera had regained the numerical advantage. Frantically drafting every available male into his Spanish army, they had assembled a force perhaps twelve hundred strong. But too many of these new *soldados* lacked experience, and too many sympathized with their enemy's cause.

Perhaps unwisely, Salcedo and Herrera did not entrench their men in the Alamo or behind the barricades that guarded the city. Not wishing to subject San Fernando to a withering siege or devastating battle, they marched the army out to the woodlands near Mission Espada and waited in ambush for the republicans.

In the late morning of March 29, republican scouts detected the royalist army's location, negating the Spanish element of surprise. The battle of Rosillo, as it came to be known, lasted less than an hour before the royalist line collapsed. Abandoning their weapons, the Spanish *soldados* fled back into Bexar.

Kemper did not press the advantage. He camped his battle-weary rebels at Mission Espada for the night. The next day he advanced only the five miles to Mission Concepcion. His reticence paid a premium, for during these days a substantial number of Spanish *soldados* and civilian *Tejanos* slipped away from Bexar to join his ranks, dramatically shifting the numerical advantage back to the republicans.

As with the Casas revolt, Bexar had become a city of divided and conflicting loyalties. Native Bexarenos Domingo Losoya and Francisco Ruiz joined the rebel force. Bexar's first schoolmaster, Ruiz currently served as lieutenant of the Bexar Provincial Militia. His eighteen-year-old nephew, Jose Antonio Navarro, and Navarro's older merchant brother-in-law, Juan Martin Beramendi, did not defect to the republican army, but they and many other Bexarenos actively displayed their sympathies for the rebels, further weakening Salcedo and Herrera's position.

The two governors confronted two equally unpleasant options. A last ditch stand that would devastate the city. Or ignominious surrender.

On April 1, 1813, Second Lieutenant Vicente Tarin, commandant of the Alamo Company, stood on the ancient mission walls and watched the republican army's ominous advance from the south. Tarin had been a sergeant, a widower in his mid-thirties, when the Alamo Company had first entered Bexar a decade earlier. So much had changed since then. In 1810, about the time he had received his promotion to second lieutenant, he had married Juana Isidora Leal. Her aging father, Joaquin Leal, was a prosperous cattle rancher. Both Leal and his son-in-law harbored some sympathies for the revolution, yet Tarin had actively opposed the Casas revolt in 1811. That same year his son, Martin, had been born. Now, in Bexar across the river, Juana was pregnant again. And here he stood on the Alamo walls —politically aligned with the army that would destroy him, yet bound by duty to his post. And—with all of his men—wondering if he would ever see his family again.

Then Tarin saw three men emerge from the town wielding a white flag of truce. Governor Salcedo and Governor Herrera had made their decision. They would save the city—and themselves. Tarin promptly resigned his commission to accept the rank of captain in the rebel army.

With the capitulation of Bexar, the first Republic of Texas was born. It would last only five and a half months.

According to one story, Governor Salcedo offered his sword to Colonel Kemper. The American refused to accept it, indicating that Salcedo should surrender his sword to Gutierrez. The Spanish governor had suffered enough indignity for one day. Rather than tender his sword to a traitor, he angrily plunged his blade into the ground at Gutierrez's feet. Then he turned away, ignoring Gutierrez's flash of anger.

The republican soldiers marched triumphantly into San Fernando. Even royalist Bexarenos were grateful that their city had been preserved. Conveniently suspending their allegiances, they welcomed the liberators and settled comfortably into the occupation. Kemper released the seventeen Americans and other political prisoners held at the Alamo. Salcedo, Herrera, and twelve other Spanish officials were themselves incarcerated, though in more comfortable quarters.

Gutierrez proposed that the Spanish prisoners be removed to the United States for their own protection. On April 3 a guard of sixty *Tejanos*, led by Captain Antonio Delgado, escorted the royalists out of the city. Their journey abruptly ended only a few miles later. Halting the procession,

Delgado ordered his troops to bind Salcedo, Herrera, and the other prisoners to trees. The helplessly trussed royalists watched in horror as their captors drew out knives and honed them on their boot soles. Some of the prisoners whimpered, others prayed, and others snarled their defiance right up to the instant when the keen blades sliced into their throats.

Delgado himself later accepted personal responsibility for the brutal murders. Salcedo, he claimed, had previously executed Delgado's father and brother. As with Casas, their heads had been impaled on stakes for public display.

Others suspected that Gutierrez himself had ordered the assassinations. The rebel leader denied the charge, perhaps too vehemently for the Americans. Outraged by the atrocity, Colonel Kemper, some of his officers, and a significant number of volunteers promptly marched back to Louisiana.

Politics also may have encouraged their departure. On April 6 Gutierrez issued the first Texas Declaration of Independence. It authorized him to assemble a *Junta de Gobierno*, with himself as *presidente*, to rule the new republic. Idealistic Americans regarded this self-appointed panel as a most unrepublican form of government for the republic they had just won. Other Americans were dismayed that Gutierrez had not included any Anglos in the junta.

These two factors, the brutal murders and the self-appointed government, alienated Gutierrez's supporters in the United States. They switched their allegiance to another would-be Latin liberator.

Around the first of August, Jose Alvarez de Toledo y Dubois arrived in Bexar wielding United States influence in the form of letters from U.S. Special Agent Shaler, General Wilkinson, and others. His escort even included Wilkinson's son, James. Though Toledo was Cuban born, many *Tejanos* derisively regarded him as a *gachupine*. However the junta begrudgingly recognized the disagreeable necessity of embracing him. Continued U.S. support was vital, even if its expansionist motives remained suspect. So the junta installed Toldeo as commander-in-chief of the army and, reluctantly, exiled its own creator back to the United States. Again feeling bitterly betrayed, Gutierrez left San Fernando on August 6, exactly four months after he had ascended to the presidency. His departure may have saved his life, for it spared him from the battle of the Medina, the bloodiest conflict yet fought on Texas soil.

In 1813 the Medina and Nueces Rivers still comprised the southwestern boundary of Texas. The Medina separated Texas from the province of Coahuila, which extended to the southwest. Below the Nueces, the province of Nuevo Santander stretched due south some six hundred miles along the Gulf of Mexico. Its capital, Aguayo, named for the marquis who had sponsored Mission San Jose, was located in the southern region (in the modern province of Tamaulipas). There on April 6, the same day that Gutierrez had issued his Texas Declaration of Independence, an army of over one thousand royalists began the long march north to Bexar. At their head rode stern-faced General Joaquin de Arredondo. A *peninsular*, born in Barcelona, Arredondo had risen through the military ranks in New Spain to become military commandant of Huaxteca and governor of Nuevo Santander. His ruthlessly efficient suppression of local rebel outbreaks had increased his prestige, resulting in his subsequent promotion to commandant-general of all the eastern interior provinces.

The months-long march across the barren deserts of northern Mexico proved grueling. Many in the proud Spanish army were reduced to bare feet and loincloths. At the end of the column, sharing in their husbands' miseries, trudged the *soldaderas*. Uniquely among European armies, Spain allowed these noncombatants to accompany the expeditions, to cook, mend, and serve their husbands in any other ways that would help sustain morale. Finally arriving at the Rio Grande, only one hundred fifty miles below Bexar, Arredondo rested for several weeks.

Just north of the Rio Grande, Arredondo met up with Colonel Ygnacio Elizondo, who had played significant roles in the defeat of both Casas and Hidalgo. Their combined Spanish force numbered eighteen hundred thirty-five royalist troops and eleven cannon.

The morning sun on August 18, rising into a nearly cloudless sky, foretold another dry, blistering day. When Arredondo broke camp and began his march, he was only about a dozen miles below the Medina River, less than forty miles south of Bexar.

A few miles ahead, some thirteen hundred republicans with seven cannon waited in ambush. Toledo had learned of the Spanish advance from his spies. Like Governor Salcedo before him, the new commander-in-chief of the Republican Army of the North had opted to engage the enemy away from Bexar. Colonel Miguel Menchaca—young, dashing, and impetuous—led the Bexareno faction of the republican army. Command of the Anglos had passed to Major Henry Perry, whose relative, Commodore Oliver Hazard Perry, would achieve immortality on Lake Erie one month later.

Arredondo did not know that the republican army had marched out of Bexar. However the Spanish general was shrewd enough to suspect an ambush. Accordingly Arredondo dispatched Elizondo with one hundred eighty cavalrymen to scout ahead.

Toledo's trap sprang prematurely on the Spanish cavalry. Elizondo ordered his men to fall back into the dense scrub oak at his rear. The republican army charged into the thicket in pursuit.

As Elizondo retreated in a slow, orderly manner, his couriers galloped ahead to alert the main Spanish column. Arredondo quickly dispatched one hundred fifty more cavalry to Elizondo's relief. Then he began deploying the main body of his army behind a hastily thrown up barricade of camp gear and underbrush.

Several miles away, the republicans realized that Elizondo's retreating cavalry had been reinforced. However, due to thick, putrid clouds of black powder smoke that drifted slowly through the dense thicket, obscuring their vision, the republicans mistakenly assumed that the main body of the Spanish army had arrived. Toledo advocated falling back to his original defensive position, closer to the Medina River. Menchaca, who disliked and distrusted his *gachupine* commander, argued otherwise. The fight had commenced, Menchaca dramatically announced. He would not quit until he had died or conquered. Supported by the equally rash Anglo troops, the republicans surged onward through the trees, driving the Spanish cavalry before them.

The heavy, shimmering heat drained the republican army. Grimy sweat flowed down the faces of men struggling through deep, black sand that tugged at their boots and bogged down their artillery. Thirsty and exhausted, they suddenly burst into a clearing in time to see Elizondo's cavalry disappearing behind Arredondo's makeshift barricades. The Spanish artillery immediately opened fire, its grapeshot ripping through the advancing republicans.

Later history books would report that Arredondo had cleverly lured his enemy into a vee-shaped ambush that collapsed on the republican flanks. In reality the Spanish line was straight rather than vee-shaped, and the battle had been influenced more by chance than design. For several hours the two armies blazed at a range of no more than forty yards. At one point Anglo riflemen so effectively cleared the Spanish artillerymen that Arredondo himself considered retreat.

Nevertheless the essence of the ambush legend proved true. The republican flanks finally collapsed, their impetuous charge transformed into a terrible rout. Menchaca fell. So did Bernardo Martin Despallier, the Frenchman from Natchitoches whose propaganda literature had preceded the republican army into Texas. When the gunfire finally ceased, six hundred republicans lay dead in the black sand, another hundred had been captured, and the rest were fleeing back to Bexar. The battle of the Medina had ended. But the terror had only begun.

Arredondo ruthlessly ordered the immediate execution of the hundred rebel prisoners. Then he dispatched Elizondo with two hundred cavalry to run down the fugitives from the battle.

As they fled in panicked retreat, some of the *soldados* who had previously defected from the Spanish army now deemed it a convenient time to rejoin the royalists. They abruptly turned on the retreating Anglos, slaughtering men they had earlier fought beside. Elizondo's pursuers, galloping through the forest, came upon a ghastly sight. Arms, legs, and torsos of the butchered Anglos swung from the tree limbs, blood sacrifices from these conveniently reconverted *soldados*.

Many of the refugees made it to Bexar. Major Perry and other Anglos started immediately for Louisiana. So did Toledo. Bexarenos like Francisco Arocha and Antonio Delgado, the self-professed murderer of Governor Salcedo, followed as soon as they had gathered their families from the town. Domingo Losoya may have paused at the Alamo long enough to spread the alarm. His brother, Ventura, lived with his family in the rooms at the southwest corner of the compound. His five-year-old son, Toribio, had been born there.

Francisco Ruiz and his nephew, Antonio Navarro, and Navarro's brother-in-law, Juan Martin Beramendi, hurried their families to the east. Beramendi's wife, Josefa Navarro Beramendi, had time to grab their two-year-old daughter, Maria Ursula, and little else.

Fleeing from the battle, Captain Vicente Tarin found his retreat to Bexar already cut off by Spanish cavalry. To continue into the town meant certain death as a traitor. Bitterly, Tarin spurred his horse eastward, praying that his pregnant wife, Juana, and two-year-old son, Manuel, were among the refugees already streaming out onto the prairie.

Escorted by her sister and elderly parents—and carrying little Manuel—Juana Tarin had indeed joined the flight. But she would not find her husband in the confusion. And she would not see him again for a very long time.

Colonel Elizondo's sudden arrival in Bexar cut off the retreat of other Anglos and Bexarenos. By the time General Arredondo arrived with the main army, Elizondo had taken another two hundred fifteen prisoners. Arredondo ordered forty shot, three at a time, every third day. Those prisoners he deemed "less culpable" were incarcerated, either in the Alamo's guardhouse or in the abandoned residence of Francisco Arocha. The Spanish crammed so many into the Arocha house that eight suffocated in the first night.

Nor did Arredondo show his enemies' widows and orphans any compassion. Imprisoned in a structure known as the Quinta, forced to make tortillas for the Spanish *soldados*, the women daily endured whippings and sexual abuse.

Again Arredondo dispatched Elizondo, this time with five hundred men, to track down the fugitives fleeing to the United States. The Spanish overtook the Delgado and Leal families near the Trinity River. The murderer of Salcedo was shot down and lanced in front of his hysterical family. Elderly Joaquin Leal and other captured males endured a mock trial before Elizondo, who sentenced them to immediate execution, again with their weeping families as witnesses.

During his brutal, tenacious pursuit, Colonel Elizondo condemned seventy-one men to face the firing squad, the victims all Bexarenos and therefore considered traitors to the Spanish crown. He captured more than two hundred other *Tejano* men, women, and children. But many others escaped across the Sabine, including the Beramendi family, the Navarro family, the Ruiz family, and the Losoyo family. And Vicente Tarin.

Toledo and Perry and young James Wilkinson were among the *norteamericanos* who made it to Louisiana. Elizondo pardoned the other Anglo refugees—the few lucky enough to have survived the slaughter. Then he started back to Bexar with his prisoners in chains.

He never made it back. On the return trip, a Spanish lieutenant, said to have been driven insane by the incessant bloodlust, plunged his saber into the colonel. Elizondo's subordinates continued on to Bexar with the prisoners. Arredondo again selected the men who would face firing squads. Again he sentenced the women and children to the Quinta. Upon their release weeks later, they were turned, destitute, into the streets, their homes and other property having been confiscated by the Spanish crown.

General Arredondo also disbanded the Alamo Company. In truth, there were not many *soldados* left to disband. Due to the company's conflicting loyalties, the garrison had been decimated. The royalist faction had suffered severe casualties at the battle of Rosillo. The republican supporters had been virtually exterminated at the Medina or in the subsequent purge.

Some of the survivors of the Alamo Company enlisted in a presidial guard stationed in the town. Few in number, they struggled to ward off the frequent Comanche raiding parties.

Across the river, the Alamo again stood silently abandoned.

A Spanish lieutenant, tall and handsome—only nineteen but already a two-year veteran of the Mexican revolutions—had endured the long, withering march into Texas. He had fought with enough distinction at the makeshift barricades to earn a commendation for bravery; simultaneously he had developed a contempt for his enemy—specifically the undisciplined Anglos, certainly the worst army in the universe—who had charged so recklessly to their destruction. Arriving in Bexar, he had learned well from his commander, General Arredondo, the proper treatment to be afforded to captured rebels and traitors.

It was the first time the young lieutenant had ever been in Bexar. On that sweltering August day he crossed the river and entered the Alamo. Indeed, as a mere lieutenant, he may have been quartered in that hard luck mission fortress, rather than in the more gracious accommodations in the town. There, for the first time, he would have glanced up at Saint Francis and the other statues standing like sentries in the shadowed niches on either side of the church door. And, for the first time, the blank, stone eyes of the saints would have gazed down upon him.

More than two decades later, the same four saints—warm tears of spattered blood trickling down their cold limestone cheeks—would again behold the countenance of Antonio Lopez de Santa Anna.

Illustration by Craig Covner.

Myths, Mysteries, and Misconceptions

A Name to Remember

"Alamo" is Spanish for cottonwood. A pleasantly shaded stretch of road lined on both sides with cottonwood trees, known as the "Alameda," extended just below Mission Valero on the road to Bexar. Its trees endured long after the Second Flying Company of Alamo de Parras had faded into historical obscurity. Thus many sources concluded, erroneously, that Valero acquired its more familiar name from these cottonwood trees. In fact the mission-fortress was already being referred to as the Alamo before the Alameda had been created.

The Hump

A great many paintings, illustrations, and films have depicted the distinctive bell-shaped gable of the Alamo church rising above the smoke and fury of the 1836 battle. Sometimes Texians are pictured firing from behind the arched parapet.

Historically, however, at the time of the siege, the church remained a roofless ruin, its upper profile characterized only by the irregularity of rubble. A decade later, after Texas had joined the Union, the U.S. Army took possession of the building and, rather ignominiously, transformed it into a warehouse. Army engineers constructed a wood pitched roof and—only then—added the campanulate (bell-shaped parapet) to enclose the front gable.

Now, after a century and a half, the hump has become more than an integral part of the church; ironically it has become the most identifiable aspect of the church, making it one of the most recognizable structures in the world. Line drawings of just the curved parapet alone bear such familiarity that they have served as logos for companies with Alamo in their name.

Illustration from Hiram H. McLane's 1886 play "The Capture of the Alamo:
A Historical Tragedy, in Four Acts, with Prologue."
Courtesy of the Joseph Musso Collection.

The Shrine

Pictures of the church, with its hump-shaped crown intact, have adorned countless books and postcards as well as innumerable T-shirts, coffee cups, refrigerator magnets, and virtually any other object that will take an image. Though hardly necessary, the picture is usually captioned "The Alamo." Understandably, therefore, most people regard the church as the Alamo.

In the early nineteenth century, however, the name "Alamo" referred to the entire mission compound of which the church was but one small unit. *Soldados* from the Alamo Company were not quartered in the church, but rather in the convent and in the rooms built along the outer walls. Bowie and Travis were not holed up in the church; they defended the entire perimeter.

Some historical writers have mistakenly labeled the church as "the Alamo chapel." Mission Valero did have a temporary adobe chapel where priests conducted services before the great stone church was erected. Later the sacristy in the church served as a chapel. But the church itself was never a mere chapel.

Now the church qualifies as a shrine. Under the auspices of the Daughters of the Republic of Texas, the hallowed building commemorates those who fell in the 1836 battle.

"It's So Small!"

First-time visitors often are overheard commenting that the Alamo is smaller than they expected. Size, of course, is relative. Now engulfed by San Antonio and surrounded on all sides by towering buildings, the Alamo must seem smaller than it did in the nineteenth century when it stood alone on the prairie across the river from the town.

In truth, however, the Alamo is smaller today than it was then. Only the church and a portion of the convent remain of the original mission San Antonio de Valero. Modern limestone walls enclose a compound to the east, or rear, of these buildings.

Most visitors to the Alamo are not aware that the modern perimeter does not correspond to the historical boundaries. Visitors do not realize, as they approach the front of the church, that already they are standing within the original mission compound. The historical Alamo's walls extended forward from the church, not behind it.

Busy city streets now cut through the original compound. Stand in the park between Alamo Street and Alamo Plaza Street facing east toward the church. To your right, a raised planter that bisects the park designates the location of the south wall. Here James Bowie probably died. The Alamo's gate was located at the west end of the planter, just before its termination at Alamo Street.

Behind you, the row of buildings across Alamo Street overlaps where the long west wall stood with its cell-like rooms for the Indian converts. And far to your left, past the tall, gleaming white cenotaph, across Houston Street, an old post office building intrudes over the site of the north wall where Travis fell. A walk around the historical perimeter of this three-acre compound will provide you with some healthy exercise as well as a newfound appreciation for the size of the Alamo.

But, again, size is relative. Perhaps neither the physical Alamo, nor the historical Alamo, can ever measure up to the Alamo of legend.

Part Two: *Gone to Texas*

Chapter 5: ***The Last Filibuster***

T he Republican Army of the North met decisive defeat at the Medina. The republic it created was vanquished. But Bexar and the Bexarenos were the real losers of the war. The town's population had been depleted, too many citizens dead or exiled. Many of those who remained had been reduced to abject poverty. And Arredondo's dark shadow still drifted over the houses of anyone suspected of having aided the republicans.

At thirty-one years old, Juan Jose Maria Erasmo Seguin was regarded as one of the most prominent citizens of Bexar. He had served in the lucrative position of postmaster since 1807. And he had diversified into ranching, acquiring the five leagues of land—some twenty-two thousand acres—thirty miles east of town. Originally that land had belonged to mission San Antonio de Valero. Erasmo Seguin named this vast estate La Mora. By 1810 his five *vaqueros* tended a herd of over five hundred cattle.

That same year Seguin had opposed the Casas revolt. However his independent mind and liberal philosophy often clashed with the traditional royalists. He had married Maria Josefa Becerra, the daughter of a lowly noncommissioned officer at La Bahia. She had impressed Seguin with her ability to read and write, a rare attribute on the frontier, especially among women from humble origins. Maria Josefa had given him three children, one of whom had died in infancy. Most significant would be the firstborn, Juan Nepomuceno Seguin.

Seguin and his family had not joined in the flight from Bexar. However he was accused of having conspired with the enemy. He had been on a business trip to Louisiana when the U.S. authorities there had decided to remove Gutierrez from the presidency of the new republic. They had given Seguin a letter to take back to Bexar recommending Toledo as Guterriez's replacement.

Standing before Arredondo, Seguin argued that he had been "coerced" to convey the letter of recommendation. He probably was lying, for whatever his sympathies, he, too, must have been appalled at the brutal murder of Salcedo.

Although Arredondo could not find any other evidence that Seguin had abetted the enemy, the general declared him a traitor. Arredondo removed Seguin from his office as postmaster and confiscated both his houses in the town and his large hacienda to the east. But Seguin was spared imprisonment or execution. In that sense he fared better than many other Bexarenos.

In a sense Vicente Tarin's pregnant wife, Juana, also fared better than other Bexareno women. After her release from incarceration in the Quinta, she and her two-year-old son, Manuel, were taken in by Father Jose Dario Zambrano. The pastor of the San Fernando Church—and older brother of the man who had defeated Casas—Father Zambrano retained royalist sympathies. But as the godfather of young Manuel he had a responsibility for the boy and his mother. Shortly after she moved in with Father Zambrano, Juana gave birth to a second son. In the ensuing years she would deliver at least four more children, all credited to an unholy alliance with Father Zambrano.

Her husband, Vicente, and the other Bexarenos who escaped Elizondo took up residence in Natchitoches. There they continued to advocate and promote Mexican independence.

In late 1813 General Arredondo offered a general amnesty to most of the *Tejano* refugees, allowing them to return to Bexar and reclaim at least part of their confiscated properties. However some notable families— including the Ruizes, the Navarros, and the Beramendis—were exempted from the pardon. Vicente Tarin and other Bexarenos also remained in Natchitoches, though they simply chose to reject the amnesty. Tarin, Ruiz, and others made sorties into Texas, providing weapons for the Comanches and other tribes hostile to the Spanish regime in Bexar.

During this same period the friction between the United States and Great Britain finally erupted into the War of 1812. In the fall of 1814, when the British threatened New Orleans, the Bexareno refugees in Natchitoches formed a *Tejano* company within the Eighteenth Louisiana Regiment. However they missed the climactic battle. On January 8, 1815, the day their regiment began the march to New Orleans, General Andrew Jackson defeated the British invasion force.

Arredondo returned to Monterrey where he continued to reign as commandant general of the eastern provinces. After a few years his wrath toward the Bexarenos mellowed, and he extended his clemency to all but the most adamant *Tejano* rebels. In Bexar, Erasmo Seguin stubbornly refused the pardon. He presented his grievances to the courts and in 1818 finally won exoneration. Eventually he would regain his property and his position as postmaster.

Many of the refugees in Natchitoches took advantage of the offer and returned to Bexar. Jose Antonio Navarro went home. So did his brother-in-law, Juan Martin Beramendi. His residence on the *Calle de la Soledad* also would be restored to him. Built of stone, it was regarded as one of the finest houses in Bexar. Massive hand-carved twin doors—executed by Erasmo Seguin's grandfather, a carpenter named Bartolome—opened onto the street. The rear wall backed up to the river, affording a view of the Alamo and La Villita on the opposite bank. In this house Beramendi's daughter, Maria Ursula, had been born. At last Ursula could return to the home of which she held no memory.

The refugees who remained in Natchitoches—men like Vicente Tarin and Domingo Losoya and Francisco Ruiz—would not return to Bexar until all Spanish troops had been driven from Texas. In the meantime they continued to supply muskets and rifles to the Indian tribes.

Bexar's small presidial guard never effectively deterred the frequent raids by Comanche warriors, some of them armed with contraband weapons supplied by the refugee *Tejanos*. In the fall of 1817 Governor Antonio Maria Martinez at Bexar finally detatched seventy-five *soldados* from Coahuila to reestablish the Alamo de Parras Company. Bexarenos, some of them veterans of the original Alamo garrison, also enlisted in the resurrected company, swelling its ranks. Historical precedent had already established that even large numbers of *soldados* could not defeat the Plains tribes. However the resurrection of the Alamo Company proved fortuitous. Already, far to the east, the seeds of their next major conflict had been sown.

In Florida, Seminole Indians, reinforced by vengeful Creek refugees, had been raiding into the United States and then fleeing back into the political safety of Spanish territory. In 1817 General Andrew Jackson, the hero of New Orleans, received orders to stop the forays. Old Hickory brazenly marched the U.S. Army into Florida to strike the Indians in their own swampy turf. Simultaneously he captured Pensacola and unceremoniously deposed the Spanish governor.

Spanish minister Luis de Onis protested this blatant breach of international protocol. U.S. Secretary of State John Quincy Adams responded that Spain had been derelict in governing its territory. The charge was valid. Florida had been sparsely garrisoned by Spanish troops, yet another indication that the shrinking royal treasury could no longer sustain the once great empire. Onis decided to sacrifice the more remote territory in an effort to secure his claim on another contested province. With the Adams-Onis Treaty of 1819, Spain ceded Florida to the United States. In return the U.S. agreed to forfeit any claim to Texas. The Sabine River was established as the permanent boundary between the two nations.

In Washington, President James Monroe's political opponents, men like Henry Clay and Thomas Hart Benton, strongly denounced a treaty that had signed away United States' territory beyond the Sabine. But the loudest cries of indignation rose from the settlers on the western frontier. Dr. James Long, a Virginia army surgeon then living in Natchez, raised money and a force of eighty men to liberate Texas. Long certainly possessed the appropriate credentials for a filibuster; he had married General Wilkinson's niece, Jane Herbert Wilkinson. As he marched his army through sweltering central Louisiana in the summer of 1819, Long had no difficulty recruiting opportunistic adventurers, idealistic republicans like Bernardo Gutierrez, and exiled *Tejano* refugees like Vicente Tarin.

By the time he reached the Sabine, Long's force had grown to over three hundred volunteers, a motley rabble that once again resembled the worst army in the universe. They captured Nacogdoches with no difficulty, and on June 23, 1819, a foreign army again proclaimed Texas a republic, this time with Long as president. Vicente Tarin signed his own name to the Declaration of Independence as Secretary.

Declaring Texas independence had already proven easier than maintaining it. With the rejuvenated Alamo de Parras Company stationed at San Antonio de Bexar, Long desperately needed a powerful ally.

He thought he knew where he could find one.

After being chased out of Louisiana, the notorious Jean Lafitte had relocated his piracy operation to Galveston Island. Lafitte had enough men to form another army. His ships virtually controlled the gulf. They could prevent a Spanish marine invasion. And they could import supplies for the republican force.

Most important, Lafitte reportedly had no love for Spain. Spanish vessels had been his primary prey. They had provided him with vast wealth in gold, silver, and black ivory.

Dr. Long rode to Galveston to court Lafitte. The dashing buccaneer cordially welcomed the revolutionary to his opulent residence, the Maison Rouge. There, President Long officially designated Lafitte as governor of the island. The appointment must have amused the pirate leader, who already held absolute authority over his small domain. However to Long's disappointment, Lafitte refused to involve himself in the defense of the new republic. A few years earlier Lafitte himself had entertained similar schemes. But the days for such intrigues had passed. The risk was too high, and the reward was only land. What did a pirate want with land?

Without Lafitte's help, Long's republic collapsed. In October 1819 Governor Martinez dispatched Colonel Ignacio Perez with five hundred Spanish troops from Bexar to Nacogdoches. The rebels fled back to Louisiana, the refugee Bexarenos again suffered exile, and the new president of Texas found asylum back in his native country.

Undeterred, Long tried again. In the spring of 1820 he recruited a

Jean Lafitte

second force, again including the determined Bernardo Gutierrez, and established a small fort called Las Casas at Point Bolivar, a peninsula on Galveston Bay. Though he lacked Lafitte's support, he could still hide in the pirate's shadow. This time he allowed his wife, Jane Wilkinson Long, and their three-and-a-half-year-old daughter, Ann, to join him at Point Bolivar.

Jane Long, too, would be invited to an elegant dinner at Jean Lafitte's Maison Rouge. But the pirate's days were numbered. In reality Lafitte, like Jane Wilkinson Long's uncle, had been a double agent, playing Spain and the United States against each other. Now he felt pressure from both nations imploding upon him. In May 1820 he abandoned Galveston Island and sailed away into legend. His departure left the Longs and their small army at Point Bolivar vulnerable and isolated.

News of Long's incursions enraged General Arredondo in Monterrey. The commandant general of the eastern provinces finally lost all patience with the *norteamericano* invaders. He sent explicit orders to Governor Martinez in Bexar. No more Anglos could enter Texas for any reason.

Yet already another *norteamericano* was riding across Texas—a man who would have more impact than all the filibusters combined.

Chapter 6: *The Father of Texas*

Two days before Christmas, 1820, a weary Connecticut Yankee rode through the cottonwood-lined Alameda that signaled his approach to Bexar. At fifty-five his face had been darkened by exposure, creased by hard work, and saddened by frustrated hopes. His name was Moses Austin, an appropriate name for a man who had already led one group of settlers into a new land and who dreamed of leading a second migration. For Austin, and for those who would follow him, the Camino Real was the highway to a new beginning.

Moses Austin
From copy of painting in the Jefferson Memorial Museum, St. Louis, Missouri.

His lead mines in Virginia had played out in 1796. With a wife and two infant children, and no means to support them, Austin became one of the first Anglos to gaze beyond the Spanish border for new opportunities. He had journeyed to St. Louis, then part of the Louisiana Territory, and persuaded Spanish authorities there to let him develop lead mines in southeastern Missouri. Adopting Spanish citizenship, he brought his wife, Maria, son, Stephen, and daughter, Emily—and thirty other Anglo families—into New Spain. They established Potosi, the first permanent settlement in what is now Washington County. When the Osage rose up against them, they drove the tribe from the region. But there was no conflict with the Spanish. A man of integrity, bound by his oath, Austin insured that his followers faithfully adhered to Spanish law.

By 1803, when the United States acquired Missouri in the Louisiana Purchase, Austin had become a wealthy and prominent citizen. But his fortune faltered during the War of 1812, and then he lost everything else in the depression of 1819.

But old Moses Austin was determined to start over again. And again he looked to the Spanish frontier. He did not expect to find lead mines in Texas. But he could introduce pioneering families there as he had done, so successfully, in Missouri. With Spain's permission, he could help settle their wilderness.

It had been a grueling journey of almost a thousand miles. Now hope overcame fatigue as Austin spotted the bell tower of the San Fernando church rising above the white adobe buildings across the river. He spurred his horse across the wooden bridge and trotted into the town.

Surprisingly few civilians roamed the mud streets of Bexar. A peculiar quiet emanated from the small adobe houses, many of them crumbling from neglect. San Antonio de Bexar had never recovered from Arredondo's wrath. And afterwards, it seemed, God had directed his own fury against the town. Pestilence had set in, possibly emanating from the profusion of rotting corpses. A drought killed the crops. Then the river rose and flooded the fields and town. Too many citizens had died. Too many others had fled from the poverty, the disease, and the Indian raids. And too many others remained in exile.

Austin reined in at the governor's house on the main plaza and presented himself. Governor Antonio Martinez gaped incredulously at the uninvited guest.

It made no difference that Austin had been a respected Spanish citizen. Governor Martinez would not even listen to Austin's plan. Ignoring the stammered protests, he sternly ordered Austin to depart for Louisiana immediately or be placed under arrest.

Demoralized and exhausted, Moses Austin stumbled out of the governor's house—and into the fabulous chance encounter heralded in all the Texas history books.

Incredibly, in this faraway land, Austin recognized a man crossing the main plaza. Austin had met Felipe Enrique Neri, Baron de Bastrop, only once before, years earlier, when Bastrop had received a Spanish land grant to help colonize Louisiana.

Meeting again on the plaza, they seemed very much alike—both past their prime, both fallen on hard times. But Bastrop provided a sympathetic ear to Austin's plight, and he expressed genuine appreciation for Austin's plans. More important, impoverished though he now was, Bastrop's title and position still carried influence with Spanish authorities. He had always been a good royalist. He had helped defeat the rebel leader Hidalgo. Governor Martinez, and even Arredondo, would hear his arguments.

Austin could not have found a better ally and counsel. Bastrop marched Austin back into the governor's office. *Norteamericanos* in Texas could be the solution rather than the problem, Bastrop proclaimed to Martinez. Anglo colonization had worked well in Louisiana. Settlers with wives and children, homes and communities, tended to resist conflict rather than generate it. The colonists would actually be a deterrent to the filibustering expeditions.

Otherwise Martinez need not wait for the Anglos to steal Texas, Bastrop asserted. The population already was in decline. Soon the province would revert back to an older, more traditional enemy that, for all practical purposes, had already defeated the Spanish.

It was the Comanche presence, more than anything else, that swayed the decision in Austin's favor. In the sixty years since the San Saba massacre and the defeat on Red River, little had changed. Ninety miles to the southeast, down the San Antonio River, stood the settlement known as La Bahia. And far to the east, Nacogdoches guarded the Louisiana border.

But everything in between—and north and west—belonged to the coyotes, the rattlesnakes, and, most of all, to the Indians.

In January 1821 Moses Austin left Bexar with a grant from General Arredondo himself to bring three hundred colonists into Texas. The journey home to Missouri would take months, with only hardships to overcome the tedium. But Austin was jubilant as his horse clopped across the San Antonio River bridge and past the Alamo.

Several weeks later he was attacked, not by hostile Indians, but by treacherous highwaymen. They beat him brutally, stole his horse, provisions, everything he had, and left him in the wilderness, broken and bloody. Somehow, sick from hunger and exposure, Austin staggered, stumbled, and crawled back to Missouri.

And then he died, bequeathing the colonization of Texas to his son—Stephen Fuller Austin.

The man who would become immortalized as the "Father of Texas" had been only five years old when his father had moved him to Missouri. Five years later young Stephen was sent back to Connecticut for schooling. Then two more years at Transylvania University in Lexington, Kentucky, before returning to Missouri.

Young Stephen shared his father's integrity. And he shared in his father's success. He was elected to the Missouri territorial legislature and appointed a bank director while yet in his twenties. But he also shared in his father's ruin when the banks collapsed during the Panic of 1819.

Rampant land speculation had prompted the bank failures, something the younger Austin would never forget. As penniless as his father, but with a reputation for honesty, Stephen Austin went south into the newly created Arkansas Territory.

Things almost worked out for him in Arkansas. Riding down the Southwest Trail, he acquired property on the south bank of the Arkansas River at a

Stephen F. Austin
From a miniature painting.

place early explorers had called the "little rock." Later, elatedly, he learned that the site was under consideration as the location for the new capital, something that would make Austin's land there worth a premium.

He settled further down the Southwest Trail, in Hempstead County in the southwest corner of Arkansas. In early November 1820, with uncharacteristic impetuousness, he decided to run for Congress in the first territorial election. He had filed only two weeks before the election, too late for his name to appear on the ballot in two of the five counties. Yet so great was his popularity, he placed a very close second out of six candidates. Perhaps as conciliation, in July 1820 Governor James Miller appointed him judge of the First Circuit Court.

Then things turned sour again. Little Rock did become the capital of Arkansas, but Austin's claim was contested, and the courts ruled against him. Then the Territorial Assembly reorganized the government, abolishing his judgeship.

When Moses Austin crawled back from Texas, Stephen, then twenty-seven, had no other direction in his life except west. To Texas.

Leading a small handful of settlers, the vanguard of his colonists, Austin arrived at Natchitoches in the summer of 1821. He was greeted by two prominent Bexarenos—Don Erasmo Seguin and Juan Martin Beramendi—who had journeyed from Bexar to guide Austin's party across Texas. On July 16, 1821, the Anglos and their *Tejano* guides crossed the Sabine. For the very first time Stephen F. Austin trod on Texas soil.

For more than three weeks they rode westward, Austin basking in this new land. They were only a day's ride from Bexar when they broke camp on Sunday morning August 12. Suddenly one of Seguin's *vaqueros* galloped up, waving and shouting excitedly.

Mexico had just achieved independence from Spain!

The party hurried on into Bexar. Governor Martinez assured a nervous Austin that the new government would not affect the colonization contract. Austin also met his father's friend, the Baron de Bastrop, who would serve as Austin's land commissioner. Together they worked out the terms of colonization.

At that same moment Dr. James Long and his small army of filibusters remained at the tiny fort called Las Casas on Point Bolivar. His wife, Jane, only twenty-one years old, had become pregnant again. When news of Mexican independence reached Galveston Bay, Long became agitated. Perhaps in this new climate of political turmoil he could finally wrest Texas away from Mexico. On September 19 Long led a small force of only fifty-two men up the gangplank of a ship bound for Matagorda Bay. He left Jane, daughter Ann, a young female slave named Kian, and a handful of other soldiers' families at Las Casas with the solemn promise that he would return within a month.

It was a promise he would not keep.

Disembarking at Matagorda Bay, Long's small force marched inland. They captured La Bahia on October 4. But this time Long had no avenue of escape. Four days later Colonel Ignacio Perez's *soldados* surrounded the presidio. Long and his men surrendered. Their capture stymied Governor Martinez. Were they freedom fighters, belatedly striking a nominally Spanish garrison? Or were they land pirates deserving of a firing squad? And what effect would their executions have on the future of Austin's colony, a cause for which Martinez had developed considerable enthusiasm?

Martinez finally shipped Long and his men down to Mexico City. The authorities there could sort it all out.

When news of his capture reached Galveston Bay, the other families hastily gathered up their possessions and departed for Louisiana. But despite their urgings, Jane Wilkinson Long refused to budge. She would yet await her husband's homecoming. With only her infant daughter and the young slave Kian for companions, Mrs. Long entrenched herself in Las Casas. On December 21, 1821, she bore a second daughter and named her Mary James.

Jane Long would later claim that Mary was the first Anglo child born in Texas, and many history books would perpetuate her mistaken assertion. Yet that fallacy should not diminish Mrs. Long's honorary title as the "Mother of Texas." With classic pioneer spirit and the capable aid of the slave girl Kian, she nurtured her children through the cold, lonely winter.

The "Father of Texas" did not know of the plight—or even of the presence—of the Long family when he scouted through Texas to locate the land for his colony. Austin selected the fertile coastal prairie between the lower Brazos and Colorado Rivers. Then he dashed back to Louisiana to recruit his settlers.

Austin offered specified tracts of Texas land for twelve and a half cents per acre, roughly one-tenth the going price in the United States. Even better, there would be no customs duties for seven years and no taxation for ten. But there would be official regulations. Colonists had to take an oath of allegiance to Mexico, swearing to be faithful citizens obedient to all national laws. All except one. They would not have to adopt the state religion, Catholicism. Quietly, Martinez had agreed not to enforce that legal requirement.

And since Martinez had designated Austin unofficial governor over the colonists, Austin added his own rules. "No person will be admitted as a

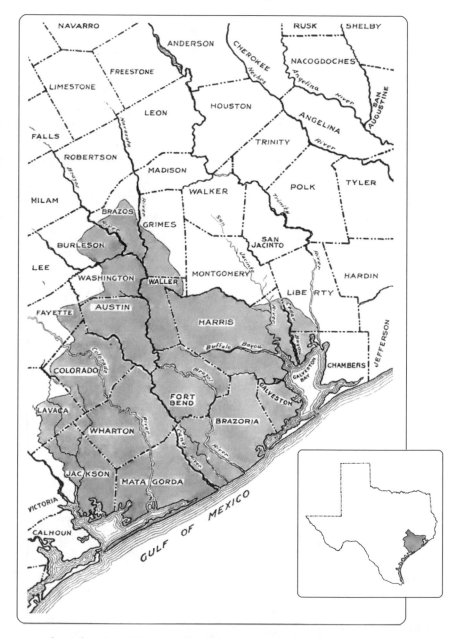

Austin's colony. The shaded portion shows the region in which
Austin's first colonists settled and indicates present counties.

settler who does not produce satisfactory evidence of having supported the character of a moral, sober and industrious citizen," he maintained.

Soon the Baron de Bastrop had filled out two hundred ninety-seven land titles, and the Old Three Hundred, as they came to be known, began drifting into Texas. Some came overland in covered wagons. Others arrived by sea.

When one group of colonists disembarked at Galveston Bay, near the small fort at Point Bolivar, they were stunned to be greeted by its emaciated female occupants. Incredibly Mrs. Long, her daughters, and Kian had survived the winter months. But Jane Long now realized, for the sake of her children, she must abandon her vigil. She followed the settlers inland, eventually to join Austin's colony.

It would be difficult for those first colonists, with money tight and provisions scarce, as they built their homes and farms and roads and towns. Then, in March 1822, Austin received devastating news. The newly formed Mexican government never had ratified his father's original contract with Spain. At this most critical moment, the very genesis of his colony, he would have to make an excruciating twelve-hundred-mile overland trip to Mexico City to plead his case.

Chapter 7: **Santa Anna**

Mexico owed its independence from Spain to Agustin de Iturbide. For six years Iturbide had led royalist forces against the remnants of Hidalgo's rebels. Then, in February 1821, he concocted his Plan of Iguala and abruptly merged with the rebels. His banner, the modern Mexican flag, symbolized the tenants of the plan. The green bar represented independence from Spain. The white bar reaffirmed Catholicism as the state religion. The red bar proclaimed the equality of all Mexicans, be they Spanish, Indian, or mixed blood. It was, at best, a compromise, but it was acceptable to all factions. With the liberal and conservative forces in Mexico united for the first time, the Spanish were quickly vanquished. Mexico had become an independent nation.

Only then were the followers of Hidalgo finally allowed to remove the old priest's head from its perch atop the *alhondiga*. After a decade nothing would have remained but a bleached skull frozen in a grisly, silent, laugh of triumph.

The Plan of Iguala did not provide for a republican form of government. Rather it placed Mexico under a limited monarchy with an elected congress. Iturbide himself, of course, would steer the country until an appropriate monarch could be found.

Stephen F. Austin's arrival in Mexico City on April 29, 1822 afforded him a ringside seat to unfolding dramatic events. On May 8 he witnessed "a night of violence, confusion, and uproar." A small band of Iturbide's *soldados* initiated the riot, charging through the streets crying "*Viva Agustin Primero, Emperador de Mexico!*" The population enthusiastically joined in the chaos, adding their own cries for Iturbide to ascend the throne of Moctezuma. Iturbide appeared on a balcony and went through the motions of trying to disperse the mob. Finally, with appropriate reluctance, he bowed to the will of the people, contingent, of course, upon the approval of congress. Then the whole city erupted in celebration. Austin must have been deafened by the echoing thunder of musket and cannon fire, and "the seven hundred bells of the city pealing from the steeples of monasteries, convents, and churches . . . . "

The congress assembled the next day and formally offered the crown to Iturbide.

Austin was still in Mexico City on July 21 when, in a lugubrious caricature of Napoleon's coronation, Iturbide accepted the crown that transformed him into Agustin I. Then the new emperor of Mexico promptly asserted his new authority, dissolving the elected congress and replacing it with a small, personally selected council.

Austin had now been in Mexico City for three frustrating months. He feared for his infant colony, for the people who had trusted him enough to leave their homes and follow him into the Texas wilderness. Yet he had accomplished nothing. A nation in the throes of rebirth had little time for the problems of a few settlers in a distant province. "In such a state of political affairs," Austin lamented, "all that a person could do who had business with the government was to form acquaintances, try to secure friends, and wait for a favorable opportunity." Having neither finances nor influential friends, Austin could only wait patiently, month after month, for his petition to be addressed. He sold his watch to buy food.

He did not languish alone. Among the acquaintances he formed were a handful of other *norteamericanos*. In fact Austin barely missed meeting Dr. James Long.

Iturbide had freed the Anglo rebels, and Long's men had returned to the United States. However Long himself had chosen to remain in Mexico City, audaciously lobbying for recognition—and reward—for his help in liberating Texas. After six months his luck ran out. On August 8, 1822, a bullet ended his quest. Some called it an accident; others said it was an assassination. Whichever, that bullet finally closed the curtain on the era of the filibusters.

The day of the *empresario* was just dawning. Other Anglos, inspired by Austin's initial success in Texas, joined in the quest for colonization contracts. Kentuckian Green DeWitt, like Austin, had lived in Missouri. Hayden Edwards hailed from Virginia. Most notable among them was General James Wilkinson, fleeing from his own duplicitous reputation in the United States. Once he had dreamed of—and schemed for—a great empire across the Sabine. Now, aged and infirm, he could only wait with the other would-be *empresarios*, hoping for just a small piece of Texas.

Finally Iturbide's council acted on Austin's petition. They approved a new contract, similar enough to the original, and on February 18, 1823, Iturbide scrawled his signature of approval on the grant contract.

But neither Stephen F. Austin, nor Agustin I, Emperor of Mexico, had reckoned on Santa Anna.

Antonio Lopez de Santa Anna y Perez de Lebron was born in Jalapa, Vera Cruz, February 21, 1794, into an affluent Spanish colonial family. A disruptive troublemaker in school, he joined the royalist army at the age of sixteen, the same year Father Hidalgo's "Cry of Dolores" echoed through Mexico.

He proved himself to be an effective soldier, displaying courage and decisiveness in battle. In February 1812 he received a promotion to second lieutenant, then, later that year, to first lieutenant. When he marched with Arredondo into Texas, he would garner a commendation for bravery at the bloody Medina.

And Santa Anna watched attentively as the rebel prisoners at Bexar fell before Arredondo's firing squads.

Santa Anna had grown to manhood in the army. He stood a bit taller than most Mexicans, with handsome features marred only by a slightly bulbous nose (that would swell grotesquely in his later years). Certainly the ladies found Lieutenant Santa Anna strikingly attractive in his uniform—and, too often, out of it.

Lithograph of Santa Anna during the Alamo period.
Courtesy of the Joseph Musso Collection.

Even as his military career was in ascendancy, Santa Anna's personal indulgences contributed to a self-destructiveness that would recur throughout his life. His passion for the *señoritas*, and perhaps for a few *señoras*, may not have jeopardized his career, but his passion for gambling did. He lost heavily. He recklessly forged Arredondo's signature to company drafts, embezzling army funds to cover his debts. And he was caught.

He also displayed another recurring trait, a remarkable

resiliency not only to survive, but to bounce back. He conned the regimental surgeon into reimbursing the misappropriated money. Still, the incident cost Santa Anna his sword and all his personal possessions. And it left a blemish on his record. But he retained his military rank and, in 1816, he even received a promotion to captain.

If Santa Anna had learned ruthless efficiency from Arredondo, he learned political opportunism from Iturbide. Ever since the Texas campaign, he had pursued rebel troops around Mexico. Iturbide had already presented his Plan of Iguala and defected to the rebels, but Santa Anna remained in the royalist army. One morning he won a stunning, almost bloodless victory over a large rebel force. "Obeying my natural inclination, I more often than not resorted to persuasion, rather than to arms," Santa Anna recalled in his autobiography. "By these means, I managed to bring about the surrender of the insurgents—more than two thousand armed and mounted men—who agreed to live in peace and to be obedient to the government."

Learning of the victory, the Spanish commander forwarded Santa Anna a promotion to lieutenant colonel that same afternoon. But Santa Anna already had received a better offer; the rebels would make him a full colonel if he joined their army. "Ah, the painful moment of decision. . . remains fixed forever in my memory," remembered Santa Anna. "But through this awesome struggle, this moment of trial, my patriotism overcame all other emotions."

Like Iturbide, Santa Anna defected. However his switch in allegiance had been influenced by more than the promotion. Santa Anna already sensed the surge of public sentiment supporting the Plan of Iguala. The Spanish would lose this fight, and it was time to join the winning side.

Thereafter, Colonel Santa Anna used his natural inclination for persuasion to lure other royalists to the rebel cause. But General Arredondo, Santa Anna's former commander, remained true to the Spanish Crown. He escaped to Cuba.

After Iturbide's transformation into Agustin I, he promoted Santa Anna to brigadier general. The promotion rewarded Santa Anna's military service to Mexico. Then Agustin gave Santa Anna commandancy of the province of Vera Cruz. That appointment at least got the twenty-eight-year-old Santa Anna out of Mexico City where his courting of Agustin's sixty-year-old spinster sister had been an embarrassingly blatant attempt to win even more favors from the emperor.

Santa Anna responded to his new honors with a nauseatingly praiseful letter to Agustin in which Santa Anna credited himself and his regiment as "the first who offered our lives and persons to conserve the respectable existence of Your Majesty and the crown which you so worthily obtained, remaining as we are constant subordinates who will shed our blood for the most worthy Emperor."

In reality Santa Anna had already sensed another shift in public sentiment. Agustin's dissolution of the elected congress had angered too many Mexicans. "The people strongly favored a regency with lawmaking by means of representatives," Santa Anna recalled. "I myself, favored such a system, and I let my opinions in support of it be known." The faint scent of revolution drifted with the warm breeze across Mexico.

Santa Anna recognized the stench—and did not find it unpleasant. But he bided his time, waiting for the tempest that would follow. In the meantime he gambled and wenched in Vera Cruz, and he used his position to acquire a large, plush estate in his hometown of Jalapa.

In Mexico City, Agustin heard complaints from the Vera Cruz population about the corrupt behavior of their commandant. And the emperor also heard rumors that Santa Anna was preaching discontent with the monarchy. Something had to be done, but it would have to be done delicately. For all his faults, Santa Anna wielded powerful influence.

The emperor himself traveled to Jalapa to meet with the general. They sat at a table in Santa Anna's hacienda, talking like old comrades. And then Agustin suggested that Santa Anna accept a new position in Mexico City.

To Agustin that seemed the best solution. Get Santa Anna away from the disgruntled Vera Cruz populace. Put him where Agustin could keep an eye on him.

Santa Anna played along. He could hardly refuse a request from the emperor. He could only buy himself some time. He told Agustin that he would be honored to relocate to Mexico City. But first he must conclude some affairs in Jalapa.

Agustin seemed satisfied.

Then an aide to the emperor wandered into the room. Seeing the two men seated at the table, the indignant aide exploded in Santa Anna's face. "In the Emperor's presence one should always stand at attention!"

Agustin saw the flash of anger in Santa Anna's eyes. As he himself rose to leave, Agustin tried to mitigate the unfortunate confrontation. "I await you in Mexico, Santa Anna, to make your fortune for you." Then Agustin returned to Mexico City to confront other problems of state, including Stephen F. Austin and the other *norteamericanos* clamoring for Texas land.

But back in Jalapa, Santa Anna's dignity had been offended. The time had come, again, to shift with the prevailing winds. He had been awakened "to the true nature of absolutism," he remembered bitterly in his autobiography. "I immediately resolved to fight against it at every turn and to restore to my nation its freedom."

Following Iturbide's example, Santa Anna produced his own manifesto, the *Plan de Casa Mata*, demanding reinstatement of the elected congress. The plan emerged as the rallying point for the republicans who opposed Agustin. In truth Santa Anna had no use for republicanism. He later conceded that at the time he wrote the *Plan de Casa Mata*, he did not even know the meaning of the word "republic." Upon learning the definition, he admitted that having been raised under a monarchy, he could not favor such an extreme political change. But for the moment the republicans were useful to him, and he to them.

Chapter 8: **The Constitution of 1824**

On February 18, 1823, Agustin approved Stephen F. Austin's colonization contract. Anxious to see if his colony had survived his ten-month absence, Austin made immediate arrangements to leave for Texas on February 23.

Then republican forces rallying behind Santa Anna's *Plan de Casa Mata*—but led primarily by Vicente Guerrero—besieged Agustin's government. Austin postponed his departure, again to become an unwilling witness to Mexican history. With his empire crumbling, the emperor abdicated on March 19. And, as Austin feared, the newly created republican congress immediately nullified all acts of Agustin's government. Austin had no choice but to resubmit his contract to the new government.

Fortunately, during his long stay in Mexico City, Austin had impressed a great many prominent men. Rather than a single Baron de Bastrop coming to his rescue, a host of respected Mexicans appeared before the new congress, praising the integrity and humble nobility of the soft-spoken *norteamericano*. The congress singled Austin out for prompt attention and granted his contract in mid-April. The other Anglo voices calling for Texas land would have to wait for a general colonization law.

After almost a year's absence, Stephen F. Austin returned to Texas. Hunger, disease, and Indian raids had depleted his colonists. Some settlers had died. Others had given up and returned to the United States. But others had remained. The colony had survived. Now Austin could assume his role as its leader. In July he selected a ford on the west bank of the Brazos as the site for his headquarters, San Felipe de Austin. Simultaneously he directed his attention to filling the vacancies and completing his contract for three hundred colonists.

The new political environment in Mexico encouraged the last of the diehard *Tejano* refugees—men like Vicente Tarin, Francisco Ruiz, and Domingo Losoya—to return to Bexar. The historical record does not relate what must have been an intriguing reunion between Tarin and his wife, Juana—when Tarin discovered that she had given birth to four illegitimate children while under the care of Father Zambrano. Perhaps Tarin embraced the children as his own. Later civil records listed Tarin as their father.

Because Tarin and Ruiz had established close relations with the Indian tribes to whom they had sold weapons during their exile, the new Mexican government determined that both men were uniquely qualified to serve as Indian agents. In 1822 they secured a significant treaty with the Lipan Apaches.

Tarin passed away shortly afterwards. The year of his death is not known, but the 1826 census would list his wife as a widow. Ruiz transferred back to military duty, eventually being placed in command of the Alamo Company. Tarin's first son, Manuel, enlisted as a private in the company. So did Domingo Losoya's nephew, Toribio. Toribio's enlistment in the Alamo Company seemed especially appropriate, for he had been born in the Alamo on April 11, 1808.

Back in Mexico City the congress kept busy. In recognition of his relentless efforts to liberate Mexico, Bernardo Gutierrez was named governor of Tamaulipas, the newly created province that butted against the southern tip of Texas at the Nueces River. Later Gutierrez became commandant general of the eastern interior provinces, the very post once held by his nemesis, General Arredondo.

Santa Anna, Arredondo's lieutenant who had defected to the rebel army, posed a delicate problem for the Mexican congress. While some republicans gratefully acknowledged his aid in overthrowing Agustin, most did not trust the motives of the young general. The congress dispatched him to the distant Yucatan peninsula, but Santa Anna found the heat stifling. Then the congress brought him back to Mexico City to command army engineers, but Santa Anna became so bored with the assignment he retired from the army. Returning to his estate in Jalapa, he slipped back into temporary obscurity.

Santa Anna was a patient man. He would wait for the winds to shift again.

Agustin was not so fortunate. The former emperor had been exiled to Italy. In July 1824 he tried to slip back into Mexico, only to be arrested and promptly marched before a firing squad.

In October 1824, after eight months of drafting, the Mexican congress concluded its federal constitution. Dr. Lorenzo de Zavala helped draft the document, and his was the first signature attached to it. Erasmo Seguin, who had helped guide Austin to Bexar, represented Texian interests at the constitutional convention. The congress had patterned the constitution after the United States constitution with one obvious exception—Catholicism was acknowledged as the state religion and none other would be tolerated.

The constitution combined Texas and the neighboring province of Coahuila to the southwest into one state called Coahuila y Texas. If some colonists were rankled that their capital had been relocated from Bexar to Saltillo, in the far southwest corner of the combined province, the liberal aspects of the constitution more than compensated. Besides, for all practical purposes, the Anglo settlers answered to Austin in San Felipe.

Learning of the constitution, Austin promised his colonists that the new republican

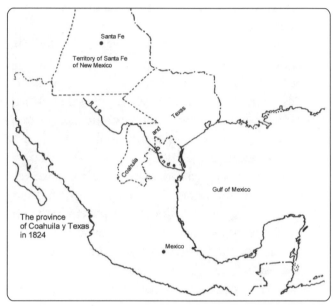

Mexican government would be fully organized within a year. "In the meantime, fellow citizens, we have nothing to disturb our tranquility here unless we willfully create confusion and discontent among ourselves," he wrote, adding, "I am responsible to you, to the world, to my honor, and to my God that no difficulty or embarrasment can or ever will arise unless produced by your own impatience or imprudence."

The Constitution of 1824 also included a general colonization law, influenced by Austin's friend Erasmo Seguin, that guaranteed private contracts between colonists and *empresarios*. However contracts became void after six years if less than one hundred settlers had located in the new colony.

In accordance with this law, Austin, who had already fulfilled his first contract, received a second contract allowing him to bring another five hundred settlers into Texas.

With the overbearing commitment he felt toward both the Mexican government and his original colonists, Austin became even more rigid about the quality of his settlers. He expelled "some bad men." Of the new colonists, he demanded "the most unequivocal and satisfactory evidence of unblemished character, good morals, sobriety and industrious habits." He listed restrictions: "No frontiersman who has no other occupation than that of a hunter will be received—no drunkard, no gambler, no profane swearer, no idler."

As a result of his careful scrutiny, Austin was later able to boast, "The settlers of this colony taken en masse are greatly superior to any new country or frontier I have ever seen, and would lose nothing by a comparison with some of the oldest counties of many of the southern and western states."

All new settlers still had to become naturalized Mexican citizens, and the new colonization law mandated that they also adhere to the state religion. That one requirement troubled Austin. He himself was Protestant, and he remained loyal to the United States concept of freedom of religion. Fortunately the local priest in San Felipe was a liberal—and colorful—Irish transplant named Father Muldoon. After formally converting the new arrivals to Catholicism, the priest agreeably turned his head, ignoring whatever religion the settlers actually worshipped. Austin's colony began to fill up with what became known as "Muldoon Catholics."

The colonization law finally opened the door to the other *empresarios*. Green DeWitt received a grant to settle four hundred colonists, mostly from Missouri. DeWitt selected the fertile Guadalupe River valley west of Austin's colony. Construction of his headquarters, Gonzales, began in December 1825.

Haden Edwards' colony in the eastern woodlands overlapped an already established population. The grant included the town of Nacogdoches and nearby land upon which Cherokees, displaced from the United States, had settled.

General James Wilkinson never received his grant. Broken in health and spirit, he died in Mexico City in 1825.

There were other *empresarios*, but they all acknowledged Austin's seniority. And his integrity. As a man of peace, Austin towered above a violent frontier. He preferred rational, political negotiation to armed confrontation, even with the neighboring Indian tribes. But negotiation did not always work, and Austin knew that men sometimes had to defend themselves, their families, their homes, and their lands. He assured his colonists that if conflict became necessary, "you will not find me backward in prosecuting it." As early as 1823 he had organized—and personally financed—a small militia to protect against hostile Indians. This ranging company would be the forerunners of the legendary Texas Rangers.

Austin delivered a severe judgement against the cannibalistic Karankawas. After enduring numerous depredations from the coastal tribe, Austin assembled a force of colonists that virtually annihilated the Karankawas.

Austin's colony experienced few problems with the most feared of all Texas Indians. The Comanches generally roamed to the north and west. However Green DeWitt had placed his colony in harm's way, well within the indefinite boundaries of Comancheria. Gonzales lay closer to San Antonio de Bexar than it did to San Felipe de Austin.

Gonzales was barely half a year old on July 2, 1826, when sixty Comanches thundered up its dusty streets. They killed a settler named John Weightman, set fire to the buildings, and stole all the horses. The colonists fled on foot to San Felipe.

Later DeWitt's settlers returned to the east bank of the Guadalupe and rebuilt their town. To help protect the new community, Antonio Saucedo, then *jefe* (political chief) of the Department of Bexar, presented the citizens of Gonzales with a cannon. A relic of the Magee-Gutierrez filibustering expedition, it was a small, insignificant-looking piece of artillery. Its bark literally exceeded its bite.

But a spark through its touchhole would later ignite the Texas Revolution.

Such a war must have been inconceivable to Austin in the 1820s. "The policy which the Mexican Government has uniformly pursued towards the settlers of this colony, has been that of a kind and liberal and indulgent parent," he wrote. "Favors and privileges have been showered upon us . . . . "

Yet the first serious threat to Anglo-Mexican relations arose as early as December 16, 1826. The colonists in Hayden Edwards' east Texas grant became disgruntled over conflicting land claims with earlier *Tejano* settlers. Seizing the Old Stone Fort in Nacogdoches, Edwards' followers proclaimed their colony to be the independent Republic of Fredonia.

It would last only six weeks. Austin and his own colonists and settlers from DeWitt's colony displayed their own loyalty to Mexico by joining the Mexican force, led by Lieutenant Colonel Francisco Ruiz, that chased Edwards and his people back into Louisiana.

Yet Austin noted that some of his own colonists "growled and grumbled and muttered" about authority. Their complaining had "not arisen from moral depravity," he insisted.

On the contrary it arose from a principle which is common to all North Americans, a feeling which is the natural offspring of the unbounded republican liberty enjoyed by all classes in the United States; that is, jealoucy of those in office, jealoucy of undue encroachments of personal rights, and a general repugnance to every thing that wore even the semblance of a stretch of power.

Austin's observation virtually defined the Scotch-Irish mentality, so prevalent in the southern and western states from which most Texian emigrants had originated. The tension could only worsen as more settlers migrated into Texas.

Because of the time restraints imposed upon their contracts, some of the *empresarios* began advertising their grants in the United States, billing Texas as the "Land of Milk and Honey."

Austin himself joined in the promotion. Whether or not he believed the legends, he designated the old San Saba presidio as the site of a lost silver mine on an 1829 map and again in an 1831 brochure, both of which were distributed in the United States.

Texas hardly needed such propagandizing. Americans had already contracted "Texas Fever." "G.T.T.," carved into the doors of hundreds of abandoned cabins, served as a simple, universal message to neighbors —and especially, to creditors—that the former inhabitants had Gone To Texas.

After fulfilling his second contract, Austin himself would receive two more grants. Ultimately he would introduce some twelve hundred Anglo families into Texas. But they constituted only a fraction of the total number of emigrants. In the decade of the 1820s, the *Tejano* population remained constant around thirty-three hundred, most residing in Bexar and La Bahia, now becoming known as Goliad. But during that same ten years more than twenty thousand colonists arrived in Texas, their settlements dotting the map from the piney woods southwest along the coastal plain.

Such a burgeoning, dispersed population would prove difficult for Austin to monitor. Worse, the fence he straddled between his colonists and the government became increasingly uncomfortable as revolution and counter-revolution swept through Mexico.

Chapter 9: *The Hero of Tampico*

Elected by the Mexican congress in 1824, former rebel leader Guadalupe Victoria served as the first president of Mexico. And he held a second historical distinction. For the next half century no other president would complete a full term of office.

The turmoil and unrest that forever seemed to characterize Mexican politics erupted again in 1828. The liberal federalists, who vehemently opposed a strong central government, comprised one of the two competing factions. Their leaders included Vicente Guerrero, another prominent rebel hero of Mexican independence; Gomez Farias, co-author of the Constitution of 1824; and Dr. Lorenzo de Zavala, who had spent time in a Spanish prison for promoting his liberal views.

The conservative centralists—supported by the aristocracy and the clergy—aligned themselves behind men like Anastacio Bustamante and Manuel Mier y Teran. Ideologically the centralists favored monarchy—or at least a dictatorship. Bustamante served as the commandant general of the eastern interior provinces, the same position the ruthless Arredondo had held during Spanish reign, and there were some similarities in their characters.

Vicente Guerrero became the federalist candidate for the election of 1828. The centralists put forth a moderate candidate, General Gomez Pedraza, secretary of war.

Intriguingly, the candidates and their parties also represented rival factions of freemasonry. Most federalists were Yorkinos, adherents of York rite masonry, while the centralists were Escocesses, loyal to the Scottish rite masons. (Freemasonry had been popularized in Mexico by the United States ambassador Joel Poinsett, who would be the source of the English name for the winter blooming *noche buena* flower.)

Although Guerrero was the most popular of the presidential candidates, Pedraza won by the slim margin of one electoral vote in the legislature. Despite rumors that the election had been fixed, Guerrero conceded defeat.

Antonio Lopez de Santa Anna did not.

Although a centralist at heart, and even a member of the Scottish rite masons, Santa Anna sensed an opportunity for self-aggrandizement—always more important than any personal philosophies. He wrote in his autobiography:

> Depression and desperation followed Pedraza's election. Revolution was the natural result.
>
> At the time of the election, I was in charge of the government of Vera Cruz. Nothing that I could do to preserve order in this grave situation was sufficient. I knew that revolution was inevitable!
>
> In order to spare the lives of the people and to quell the whirlwind of revolution, I adhered to the pleadings of the people that Vicente Guerrero be declared President of the republic.
>
> Pedraza's partisans declared me "outside the law," but it took me only three months to put down their attacks.

Initiating revolutions had worked before for Santa Anna. But this time he overextended himself. In Mexico City Pedraza ordered the arrest of anyone even suspected of abetting the rebellion. The federalist leader Dr. Lorenzo de Zavala, no stranger to political incarceration, was arrested and locked in the Acordada jail. Then Pedraza's generals marched on Vera Cruz. Santa Anna fled into the Oaxacan Mountains with the centralist armies locked in pursuit.

But again Santa Anna's luck held.

From his cell in the Acordada jail, Zavala's oratorical skills won over both his jailers and the local militia. At the head of this impromptu army, Zavala stormed the National Palace. When the centralist armies in Oaxaca learned of the assault, they abandoned their hunt for Santa Anna and marched

Lorenzo de Zavala

back to Mexico City. But they were too late. President Pedraza already had fled to the United States.

In January 1829 the Mexican congress elected the popular federalist Vicente Guerrero as the new president. Centralist leader Anastacio Bustamante was chosen as his vice-president.

In San Felipe, Stephen F. Austin realized that the federalists would be more sympathetic to the Texian colonists. Since the clergy had opposed Guerrero's election, Austin especially hoped that the president would be lenient on the enforcement of the Catholic religion in Texas. It was a futile hope. The general who had bravely engaged the armies of Spain would not, as president, challenge the power of the Church.

Religion remained a sensitive issue in Texas. Most of the American colonists revered the freedom of religion guaranteed by the U.S. Constitution, which—Austin politely reminded them—had no jurisdiction in Mexican Texas. For now his settlers still would have to hide behind Father Muldoon's casual approach to Catholicism.

As president, Guerrero inherited a young nation deeply mired in debt. Tied to that was the temptation—faced also by his predecessors—to alleviate that debt by selling Texas to the United States. The U.S. had never lost its hunger for Texas. Many Americans still maintained that the United States had been cheated out of the province. Land speculators coveted the vast potential of the region. And politicians realized that the acquisition of Texas would help maintain a desired balance of power between the free and slave states. As early as 1824 the Mexican ambassador in Washington, Jose Anastasio Torrens, observed that the United States' appetite for Texas was "without limits." In 1827 President John Quincy Adams authorized Ambassador Poinsett to offer one million dollars for Texas, but President Guadalupe had steadfastly refused. Two years later President Andrew Jackson raised the bid to five million dollars. To the relief of the nervous centralists, Guerrero also declined.

Suddenly the fear of losing Texas was overshadowed by a threat to the entire nation. In July 1829 General Isidro Barradas landed twenty-seven hundred Spanish troops on the eastern coast of Mexico near Tampico in an effort to reclaim Mexico for the crown. The invasion reverberated all the way up to Texas, where Austin complied with the government request to muster the local militias into a state of readiness.

But the modest invasion force would never get that far north. Santa Anna smelled opportunity again.

"The invaders passed through the territory under my control, and I was seized with patriotic fervor," Santa Anna recalled. "I knew that the honor of leading the defense of my country lay in my hands."

Commanding three thousand *soldados*, Santa Anna marched out to combat the banners he once had defended. But tropical diseases already had defeated Barradas' army. By the time Santa Anna arrived, one-third of the Spanish were dead, and most of the rest were so stricken with fever that Barradas had no option but surrender. "When fortune smiles on Santa Anna, she smiles fully," Santa Anna conceded after the capitulation. Of course his official reports embellished the conflict and glorified his own role as the savior of Mexico.

"As is the custom in Mexico, cheers and ovations greeted the conquering hero at every turn," Santa Anna wrote in his autobiography. He received a promotion to the rank of general and was lauded by the public as the "Hero of Tampico."

But Santa Anna had adopted another title for himself. Before he had left Vera Cruz, an aging French soldier had advised him, "This campaign may do for you what Napoleon's Egyptian campaign accomplished for him." After the victory at Tampico, Santa Anna would herald himself as the "Napoleon of the West."

During the Spanish invasion, the Mexican congress resorted to emergency measures, awarding war powers to President Guerrero, which essentially transformed him into a dictator. This abuse of the constitutional balance of powers alarmed the Anglo colonists in Texas. The situation worsened immediately when the president utilized his new authority to aggravate another sensitive nerve of the Texians.

On September 15, "to celebrate in the year of 1829 the anniversary of our independence with an act of justice and national beneficence," President Guerrero issued an edict abolishing all slavery in Mexico.

In that sense Guerrero was ahead of his time. Abolitionism in the United States was yet in its infancy, with most supporters of the movement advocating a gradual end of the "peculiar institution." The fiery William Lloyd Garrison would not emerge until early the next decade to demand the immediate termination of human bondage in the U.S.

In fact Guerrero naively had been manipulated into the edict by the centralist faction in his government. The repeated efforts by the United States to purchase Texas had alarmed the centralists, and they were further distressed by the burgeoning migration from the United States into Texas. Since slavery virtually did not exist elsewhere in Mexico, the only negative impact of the abolition would be to curb—perhaps diminish—the Anglo population in that northern province.

The edict reeked of hypocrisy. Even though the institution of slavery did not exist in Mexico, the rigidly enforced traditional caste system denied the social mobility afforded in the United States and colonial Texas to everyone but slaves. The plight of the Mexican lower classes—the peons, Mayans, and *mestizos*—was not dissimilar to enforced slavery.

In Texas approximately eleven hundred slaves were dispersed among the twenty thousand Anglo colonists. As in the southern United States, most Texians did not own slaves, could not afford slaves, and did not need slaves. But they respected the right to own property guaranteed by the colonization laws of Texas. And slaves qualified as property.

Austin was so fearful of the colonists' repercussions that he tried to suppress publication of the edict. But rumors swept across Texas, generating a panic.

"In the Name of God what Shall we do?" John Durst of Nacogdoches wrote Austin. "We are ruined forever Should this measure be adopted."

Austin chose his own words carefully. The people of Texas would defend the Constitution of Mexico "and with it their property."

For the first time the Texas colonists seemed on the brink of revolt.

Meanwhile, Ramon Musquiz, the sympathetic *jefe* of the Department of Bexar, implored Jose Maria Viesca, the governor of Coahuila y Texas—and the brother of Guerrero's minister of relations, Agustin Viesca—to write to the president. Governor Viesca explained the importance of the Texas economy to the development of the state, implying the importance of slavery to the economy and suggesting that the edict might cause serious disturbances in the region.

On December 2 Minister of Relations Agustin Viesca wrote back to his brother:

> . . . having considered how necessary it is to protect in an efficacious manner the colonization of these immense lands of the republic, [President Guerrero] has been pleased to accede to the solicitation of Your Excellency and declare the department of Texas excepted from the general disposition comprehended in said decree.

Immediately Austin strove to mitigate all the tensions. In a letter to a Mexican authority he wrote, " . . . there was never the slightest break in the good order of this colony on account of the decree of September 15, because these inhabitants have placed the most blind confidence in the justice and good faith of the government. . . . "

And to his brother-in-law, Austin beamed, "This is the most munificent government on earth to the emigrants—after being here one year you will oppose a change to Uncle Sam. . . . "

Though he could not know it, Austin had won only a temporary respite. Another revolution loomed in Mexico, and once again the rules affecting Texas would be changed. In the meantime there was the never-ending task of monitoring the constant flow of emigrants from the United States.

Though Austin had continued to screen his own colonists, he had limited control over the quality of settlers that migrated into other *empresarios'* grants. And many of the new arrivals disturbed Austin. Single men unencumbered by responsibility. Men of dubious morals fleeing either debt or their own bloodstained pasts. Adventurers and exploiters who did not affiliate with any of the established colonies.

Men like James Bowie.

Chapter 10: ## *Mr. Bowie with a Big Knife*

Alexandria, Rapides Parish, Louisiana, 1826.

James Bowie burst into the salon at Bailey's Hotel. Through the waves of stale cigar smoke that drifted across flickering lanterns, he spotted Major Norris Wright. The sheriff of Rapides Parish sat at a table, playing cards with friends. And talking. So far as Bowie was concerned, Major Wright had done enough talking.

Bowie stormed across the room to confront Wright and his allies. "It was [Bowie's] habit promptly to settle all difficulties without regard to time or place, and it was the same whether he met one or many," recalled friend William H. Sparks. "At the same time he was self-possessed and conspicuously cool."

Bowie stared across the table, his thin lips compressed, only the flash in his eye revealing his anger.

Was it true, Bowie demanded? Had Wright been maligning Bowie's honor?

Wright did not reply. Allegations of Bowie's fraudulent land claims had become a frequent topic of conversation in central Louisiana. Wright had merely expressed his scorn more loudly than others.

Bowie had no patience for Wright's sanctimonious criticism. It was well known that Wright had fabricated the votes that got him elected parish sheriff in 1824.

The antagonists shared only a disposition towards knavery. In a frontier that provided an unparalleled opportunity for social mobility, both James Bowie and Norris Wright had manipulated laws to achieve their ambitions.

But there all similarity ended. Bowie, at six feet or a little more, towered over Wright and, indeed, most other men of his time. Bowie weighed around one hundred eighty pounds, "about as well made as any man I ever saw," recalled his oldest brother, John. "Taken altogether he was a manly, fine-looking person, and by many of the fair ones he was called handsome."

Bowie's face possessed distinctively acute features. His mane of brown hair, tinged with red, formed a widow's peak on his high forehead. His nose was straight, almost pointed. In the style of the day he wore sideburns that descended behind high cheekbones toward a cleft chin. His deep set eyes, his most prominent feature, were brownish gray, about the color of tempered steel—and just as piercing.

If Bowie had the physical advantage, Wright had the more fearsome reputation. He was said to be a crack shot with a dueling pistol, perhaps the "best shot in the parish." Caiaphas Ham, a close friend of the Bowie brothers, recalled:

> It was said of [Wright] that he would say hard things of gentlemen in order to induce them to challenge him, thus securing to himself the right to choose the weapon. He was credited with having, in this manner, engineered several "affairs of honor," and of having killed his man in each.

In contrast no historical documentation exists that Bowie had ever fought a duel or killed anyone. In fact his adversaries, including Major Wright, regarded him as an uncouth backwoodsman rather than a gentleman. Therefore, according to the strict code that regulated dueling, they deemed Bowie an unworthy opponent to face on the field of honor.

Since social protocol denied Major Wright the privilege of shooting Bowie in an honorable fashion, Wright apparently decided to resolve the matter then and there in Bailey's salon. He never responded to Bowie's question. Instead he rose from his chair, drew a pistol from under his coat, and pointed it at Bowie's breast.

Bowie grabbed an empty chair and held it up as a shield. Except for a clasp knife kept in his pocket for general use, Bowie had brazenly initiated the confrontation without a weapon.

Even the sheriff of Rapides Parish could not justify shooting an unarmed enemy in front of witnesses. The two men stood in that position for several long moments, a tableaux frozen on the very edge of history—and legend. Then Bowie abruptly, impatiently, raised the chair over his head to strike.

James Bowie portrait by Joseph Musso.

And Wright pulled the trigger of his pistol.

The retort thundered within the room, almost drowning out the clatter of the chair as it bounced on the floor. Incredibly, despite the close range, James Bowie still stood.

"When fired by anger [Bowie's] face bore the semblance of an enraged tiger," remembered Caiaphas Ham.

"When aroused as fierce as the hunted tiger," agreed Sparks.

Wright glimpsed into that same ferocious expression for only an instant. Then the tiger lunged.

Wright fell back. Bowie landed on top, straddling Wright's chest, his knees pinning Wright's arms to the floor. As one of Bowie's powerful hands clamped around Wright's throat, his free hand dug under his coat. Withdrawing the clasp knife, Bowie tried to open the blade with his teeth. Wright wrestled an arm free and clawed at Bowie's face, desperately grasping for the knife. Wright's friends tugged at Bowie's coat, struggling to separate the combatants.

The knife fell to the floor, unopened. Bowie felt himself being hoisted off of his enemy. At the last instant before he was jerked away, Bowie sank his teeth into Wright's hand.

Some of Bowie's friends entered the hotel in time to witness the climax of the fight. They quickly carried Bowie up the stairs to a hotel room. Wright's companions observed a trail of blood proceeding up the steps. They assumed that Bowie had been mortally wounded by the major's pistol shot.

But that was a dangerous assumption to make. James Bowie was a hard man to kill.

In fact, Wright's pistol ball, possibly deflected by a silver dollar in Bowie's vest pocket, only had inflicted a painful bruise on Bowie's left side. The blood had come from a tooth that Bowie had dislodged when he bit Wright.

Bowie knew that he and Major Norris Wright would meet again. When that day of reckoning arrived, Bowie would not again afford Wright the advantage he had just enjoyed.

Bowie had little confidence in the clumsy, single-shot pistols of his era.

But he had an old hunting knife.

It looked like an ordinary butcher knife. The blade, about eight or nine inches long, had been forged from a file. Wood scales comprised the handle. Bowie had worn the knife whenever hunting in the backwoods and bayous. His brother John recalled that Wright's attack had so enraged

Bowie "that he had a neat leather scabbard made for his hunting knife, and affirmed that he would wear it as long as he lived, which he did."

The "neat" scabbard would be the knife's only concession to respectability. A gentleman of that day, clad in top hat and tail coat, might supplement his pistol with a refined English dirk or push dagger, mounted in ivory and coin silver, hidden in his vest pocket. Or with the ever-popular sword cane. But he would regard a crude butcher knife as a most inappropriate accouterment.

Yet Bowie adopted the knife. With it "Big Jim" Bowie would literally carve his name in the pages of history.

In spirit if not design, James Bowie's knife descended from the fierce Scottish dirks. With the claymore and the bow, these long knives helped William Wallace defeat the British at the battle of Stirling Bridge in 1297. Only a few miles and seventeen years later, similarly armed Scots under Robert the Bruce won their independence at Bannockburn. Since it was in this same area—Stirlingshire on the edge of the Scottish highlands—that the Bowie clan flourished, it can be assumed that James Bowie's ancestors had fought for the freedom of Scotland. Perhaps these battles had been the origin of the Bowie clan motto: *Quod Non Pro Patria.*

"What not for country!"

Intriguingly, the traditional Bowie coat of arms depicts a shield bearing a diagonal band with three buckles. A lion rises behind the shield holding aloft a dagger.

The Bowie family tree included the viking warrior Bue the Thick, said to have sprung from Odin himself, and Eocha Bui, or King Eugene IV, who reigned over Scotland from 605 to 621. In 1581 James VI provided a house and garden in Cowper to "Jereme Bowie, Master of the King's Wines." Jereme named his son, James, in honor of the king, and James inherited the prestigious position upon his father's death in 1597.

There were other honorable Bowie ancestors, men who served as burgesses and constables and magistrates. And there were scoundrels. In 1602 a John Bowie led a raid on lands owned by the sheriff of Moray. Eight years later authorities arrested a William Bowie for "striking his dirk into Alaster Reach."

The blood of heroes and rogues mingled in the veins of Big Jim Bowie.

His grandfather, also named James, sailed to Maryland in 1742. An earlier Bowie migration, dating from 1705, had established a flourishing colony in Prince George County. But grandfather James did not remain with them. After three years he migrated to North Carolina, married Sarah Whitehead, and the couple eventually settled in Georgia.

They christened their first son Rezin, after Sarah's father, who himself had been named for a warrior king of Israel. When the American Revolution broke out, young Rezin Bowie fought with Francis Marion, the "Swamp Fox." Wounded at the battle of Savannah, he was nursed back to health by Elve Ap-Catesby Jones, the illiterate daughter of a Welsh emigrant. As so often happens, the patient developed an emotional attachment for his nurse, and her ministrations became more than professional. They married on March 8, 1782. Typically for that time, their union would produce a large brood—at least ten children—two of whom would die in infancy.

Rezin personified the typical American frontiersman. He possessed that pioneer spirit that compelled so many of his generation to migrate into the trans-Appalachian wilderness, ever venturing beyond the fences of other settlers seeking greener pastures, better hunting, and more individual freedoms. His son John Jones Bowie, who was born in 1785, before the family left Georgia, remembered:

> My father was passionately fond of the adventures and excitements of a woodsman's life, and as the country improved and opened, population increased, and the refinements of civilization encroached upon the freedom of his hunting-grounds, he retired to wilder regions, where he could enjoy those sports and stirring adventures peculiar to a frontier life.

Rezin's first stop would be Elliot Springs, in the north central part of what would soon become Tennessee. There, on September 8, 1793, Elve delivered a son named Rezin Pleasant Bowie.

Early the next year Rezin Sr. moved the family north across the border into what was then Logan County, in the newly created state of Kentucky. There, Rezin operated a mill on Terrapin Creek. And there, in the spring of 1796, James Bowie was born. His name perpetuated the Bowie tradition of honoring King James VI of Scotland. But it also conformed to a practice—commonplace in that day—of bestowing Biblical names on children. That practice would be continued with the birth of Stephen a year or so later.

Then civilization encroached again. But now Rezin was running out of U.S. territory. To the west across the Mississippi River, Missouri remained part of the great Louisiana Territory—then nominally a Spanish possession.

Three and a half decades had passed since France had ceded Louisiana to Spain, yet most of the land remained uninhabited. Except by the Indians.

Before Spain had transferred Louisiana back to France the inscrutable James Wilkinson obtained Spanish permission for Anglo settlers to enter Missouri. That most famous of all pioneers again led the way. Old Daniel Boone moved to the Missouri boot heel in 1799. When asked why he was leaving Kentucky, he replied, "Too many people! Too crowded! I want more elbow room." It was exactly the kind of answer Rezin Bowie would have given. In 1800 he followed Boone into the boot heel, settling on land near New Madrid. It is very possible that Rezin introduced his family—including a very young James Bowie, cowering behind his mother's dress—to the legendary Daniel Boone.

Other Kentuckians came—too many, too quickly. In only three years Rezin again needed more elbow room. In 1803, the same year President Thomas Jefferson purchased the Louisiana Territory, Rezin took his family south, finally settling near Opelousas in St. Landry Parish.

James and his brothers grew to manhood there, just over a hundred miles from the Spanish Texas border. His mother, Elve, proved to be a remarkable woman. According to family historian Walter Worthington Bowie of the Maryland clan, after Rezin Sr. was arrested for shooting a squatter, Elve Bowie armed herself with a brace of pistols and broke her husband out of jail.

Even more to her credit than this legend, Elve Bowie overcame her own illiteracy, taught herself to read and write, and then passed that knowledge on to her sons. The boys also learned to work their sums well enough to keep track of their monies, at times substantial, at times nonexistent. The Bowie brothers were by nature gamblers, wagering their fortunes—and sometimes their lives—on schemes, enterprises, and adventures.

Rezin P. Bowie, two and a half years older than James, may have participated in the first of the Bowie brothers' great exploits. His grandson, John Seybourne Moore, later claimed that Rezin "followed Kemper to Texas."

If Rezin did participate in the Magee-Guterriez expedition, he was back in Louisiana to confront a new conflict that loomed much closer to home.

The War of 1812 had been raging for two years, but even the British capture and burning of Washington City in September 1814 had failed to arouse the pioneer families on the southwestern frontier. To many backwoodsmen, the very government that had granted their liberty remained the greatest threat to that freedom.

By November, however, a British invasion force was threatening New Orleans. The war had come to Louisiana. General Andrew Jackson, fresh from his defeat of the Creek Indians at Horseshoe Bend, raised the call for volunteers as he marched to defend the Crescent City.

This time Rezin definitely enlisted in the Louisiana militia. And so did his eighteen-year-old brother James.

The Treaty of Ghent, signed Christmas Eve, 1814, officially ended the War of 1812. However word of the peace did not arrive in New Orleans in time to prevent the January 8, 1815 British assault against the city's cotton bale defenses. Nor did Bowie's Louisiana regiment arrive in New Orleans in time to help Jackson repel the British force. But before he was mustered out, a wide-eyed James Bowie enjoyed his first exposure to the opulent Crescent City with its fabulous diversity of international cultures and sensual pleasures.

Bowie's brief military career also brought him into contact with men who would play significant roles in his future. He befriended Samuel Wells of Alexandria, who had been a sergeant in the Louisiana militia. And Bowie forged a lasting bond with fellow adventurer Warren D.C. Hall of Natchitoches, a veteran of the Republican Army of the North.

Perhaps Bowie had met Vicente Tarin, Domingo Losoya, and other Bexareno refugees serving in the volunteer company from Natchitoches. Most intriguingly, Bowie may have been introduced to Juan Beramendi, who later would welcome Bowie into his family.

Bowie also may have encountered the notorious buccaneer Jean Lafitte, now a hero since he had helped defeat the British. And Bowie may have met an army surgeon from Virginia named Dr. James Long.

Although James Bowie had missed the big battle, his brief tour of duty served as a rite of passage. He returned to Opelousas only long enough to bid his parents farewell. Then he acquired his own land some twenty-five miles to the north along Bayou Bouef in southwestern Avoyelles Parish. Accustomed to hard work, Bowie applied his muscles to a lumbering operation, clearing the dense forests and selling the timber. "He was young, proud, poor, and ambitious, without any rich family connections, or influential friends, to aid him in the battle of life," John remembered.

Bowie also had inherited his father's love of the wilderness. Bowie's long rifle supplied the dinner table with wild turkeys and raccoon meat, but he favored another method of hunting the larger game that roamed the backwoods. Armed with a lariat and a hunting knife he galloped through the trees after deer and wild cattle. Roping the animals provided better sport than shooting them, and dispatching his lassoed prey with a knife saved on shot and powder.

He also lassoed wild mustangs and rode them in impromptu rodeos for the entertainment of his neighbors. John Bowie even claimed that James roped and rode alligators.

"I don't see why he shouldn't have ridden them," alligator authority E. A. McIlhenny later told Bowie researcher J. Frank Dobie. "I used to." So perhaps there is truth to that Bowie legend.

Older brother Rezin also had enjoyed the hunt, until his sight began to fail. He soon relocated to Avoyelles Parish with his wife, Margaret, and infant son, again named James. Younger brother Stephen married Mary Ann Compton and settled in neighboring Rapides Parish. And John, the oldest brother, resided in nearby Catahoula Parish. The four brothers shared an intense bond, a reflection, perhaps, of their Scottish clan heritage.

In the summer of 1819 Dr. James Long marched his army from Natchez across central Louisiana towards Texas. Bowie's adventurous friend Warren D.C. Hall enlisted. Possibly James Bowie did, too. However if Bowie accompanied Long, he, like Rezin, did not remain for the final defeat. Court records placed him in Avoyelles Parish in early October, about the time Colonel Ignacio Perez's *soldados* were marching against Long's rebels in Nacogdoches.

Within a few months James Bowie was back in Texas, meeting with Lafitte on Galveston Island, and brothers John and Rezin were with him. They were about to engage in the Bowies' first great scheme—smuggling slaves into Louisiana.

The slavery issue had vexed the United States Congress since 1776. In fact most Americans had no need for slaves, and the small percentage who were slaveowners generally possessed only a house servant or a few field hands.

But the agrarian south had fostered a plantation culture in which the majority of land belonged to a very small elite faction whose economy depended largely on the cheap labor that slavery provided. Significantly, members of this landed gentry usually represented their states in the U.S. Congress where they battled relentlessly against a growing abolition movement.

In 1808 Congress enacted a law prohibiting the importation of any new slaves into the United States. Thereafter, new stock would have to come from the loins of existing slaves. But even with some of the aristocratic planters sowing their own seeds, the supply could not keep up with the demand of an expanding nation. As so often happens, the prohibition generated a thriving black market.

Along with the silver, gold, and other booty that Lafitte's pirates delivered to Galveston were large numbers of slaves. Lafitte readily offered his captured blacks to smugglers at a fraction of their market value in the United States.

But the smugglers gambled on a high stakes game. If they took their slaves by ship from Galveston, they risked discovery by custom officers at the coastal ports. Or betrayal, later, when they tried to market the slaves. Louisiana law stipulated that recovered contraband slaves be sold at public auction, half of the sale price going to the benefit of the parish, the other half as a reward to the informers. Since most slaves sold for over a thousand dollars, a reward of five hundred dollars or more per slave created substantial incentive to betray the smugglers. The penalties for smuggling slaves included lengthy sentences on vile prison labor farms—or execution.

The overland route from Galveston provided even greater perils. There were hostile Indians and Spanish patrols alert for Anglo intruders since Dr. Long's failed expedition. And though the dense, moss-draped bayous offered concealment, the silent, sluggish black waters were fraught with natural dangers.

The Bowies knew the odds, and they knew the bayous. They chose the land route. John remembered that on their first venture they bought forty slaves, "at a rate of one dollar per pound, or an average of $140 for each negro."

The brothers managed to sneak the slaves into Louisiana without incident. Then came the brilliance of their scheme. They promptly turned the contraband slaves over to the local authorities. Since they themselves were the informers, the Bowies could outbid other buyers at the subsequent auction, knowing they would recoup half their cost. Then, with legal title, they could sell the slaves anywhere in the United States.

The Bowies continued the operation for about a year. The local authorities must have been suspicious. But since they, too, profited from the operation, they had no incentive to stop it. Though illegal, the operation hardly seemed immoral. Everyone—the parish, the planters, and especially the Bowies—benefited. Everyone except the slaves. Arguably even they were better off working on plantations than rotting away in Lafitte's cells.

John Bowie wrote, "We continued to follow this business until we made $65,000, when we quit, and soon spent all our earnings."

And that characterized the Bowie brothers better than anything else. Gamble everything on a dangerous venture, make some money, and spend it quickly.

Family friend William H. Sparks explained the Bowies' somewhat ambivalent sense of ethics: "They despised a petty thief, but admired Lafitte; despised a man who would defraud a neighbor or deceive a friend, but would without hesitation co-operate with a man or party who or which aspired to any stupendous scheme or daring enterprise without inquiring as to its morality."

Lafitte's departure from Galveston ended the slave smuggling operation. James promptly turned to another stupendous scheme. He began dabbling in land speculation. Some of the land he acquired and sold carried legitimate title. And some of it—perhaps a lot of it—apparently did not.

The thousands of wilderness miles, so recently shuffled from Spain back to France and then to the public domain of the United States, lent themselves to such shenanigans. And it seemed so easy to do, with little risk or overhead. Simply manufacture a fake Spanish land grant, complete with fictionalized names, preferably for uncontested land in the public domain. Submit the forged claim to the harried district land offices for approval. Then, when legitimate title had been established, sell the land for almost pure profit. Again everyone profited—except the victim of the fraud, the United States government.

The slave operation had been illegal—but not immoral. The land scheme seemed immoral—but not illegal. Land fraud was so new the government had not yet enacted any statutes against it. Therefore the only real risk was that the land office might discover the forgeries and deny the claims.

Historian William C. Davis speculated that Bowie practiced land fraud on an epic level, audaciously submitting false claims for some 65,000 acres, more than a hundred square miles spread out across Louisiana, and, later, another 60,000 acres in the Arkansas Territory. Certainly James Bowie was audacious, and he lived his life on an epic scale.

Davis based his estimates on speculation, and he conceded that critical documents had been lost. Moreover he suspected Bowie of masterminding transactions in which James' name never appeared. Only John J. Bowie's signature, along with some of the most prominent names in early Arkansas history, adorned the fraudulent Sampeyreac grants in the Arkansas territory.

However, frustrated land officials in nineteenth-century Louisiana obviously believed that James Bowie was operating behind hired front men. Martin Despallier, whose father had been killed at the battle of the Medina, was named as a Bowie accomplice. "Despallier is the person who has the reputation of having made the claims known in our state as the Bowie claims," one land official wrote.

Bowie may have operated on too epic a scale in this instance. The very bulk of forged titles stymied officials all the way to Washington, and the so-called Bowie claims festered in bureaucratic limbo, finally clogging the courts for years to come.

Rezin Sr. passed away in 1821. Though his sons, especially James and Rezin, had inherited his love for the outdoors, the brothers had not retained their father's reclusiveness. John noted that James was "very successful in securing a fair portion of the friendship of the better class of the people."

Caiaphas Ham, who had met Bowie in those years in Avoyelles, agreed. "He would go to great lengths to assist his friends, and acquired great influence over them," Ham wrote, adding that a gentleman endowed with these qualities wins popularity.

Certainly James possessed a charismatic personality, but then so did John and Rezin. In 1824, despite the increasing notoriety attached to the "Bowie claims" in Louisiana, John won the Catahoula seat in the state legislature. Two years later Rezin joined him as a representative from Avoyelles. And by 1834 John had relocated to Helena, Arkansas, where, even after the "Bowie claims" there had been proved fraudulent, he would be elected to the Arkansas legislature.

A decade earlier James Bowie had moved from Avoyelles to Alexandria in neighboring Rapides Parish. The town included two banks, a weekly newspaper called the Louisiana *Herald*, a handsome parish courthouse, and "a number of lawyers and physicians, and many very respectable citizens," wrote Timothy Flint, a transported New England minister.

Old Reuben Kemper—brother of Samuel, who had led the Republican Army of the North when it captured Bexar—also lived in Alexandria. He had derived some esteem for his role in liberating west Florida. But the term "gentleman" fit him somewhat awkwardly. He once sliced off an adversary's ears and displayed them, pickled in wine, in his brother's tavern. Such frontier savagery was a bit extreme for Bowie, yet he probably identified with the rowdy old war-horse and backwoodsman entrenched among such southern gentility. Even more so because Kemper, like Bowie, was engaged in a frustrating battle to get monies owed him by the United States government.

During the Florida conflict Kemper had given his note for $11,850 to a rebel arms dealer, Enrique de la Francia, for weapons to be used in the insurgency. In 1814, with west Florida officially recognized as part of Louisiana, the U.S. government had assumed all such debts. Yet a decade had lapsed, de la Francia had died, and Kemper had yet to receive any federal compensation. With accrued interest, he now owed the de la Francia estate more than twice the original amount.

Bowie preferred to spend his winters in New Orleans. While there in January 1826, he encountered Jose de la Francia, brother of the late arms dealer who had supplied weapons for the Florida insurrection. Equally frustrated by the delays, de la Francia appointed Bowie his agent to recover the money that the government yet owed for the weapons. It justified a trip to Washington, where Bowie could investigate why both their claims had become mired in the bureaucratic morass.

Bowie sailed from New Orleans on February 13, 1826. Arriving in Washington, he arranged an audience with Louisiana representative William L. Brent. It was rumored that Brent himself had profited from forged titles. Certainly Brent did not seem dismayed by Bowie's notoriety. Rather Brent appreciated Bowie's charisma—and his prominent following in Louisiana. The congressman promised to look into both the de la Francia and the Bowie claims. He also may have suggested that Bowie should consider a political career, possibly assuming Brent's seat in Congress.

Confident that he had an important ally in Washington, Bowie returned to Alexandria in the summer. Only to stare into the muzzle of Major Norris Wright's pistol.

" . . . Bowie was not long confined to his room by the wound," wrote Caiaphas Ham. Even better, a few of Bowie's claims somehow finally got approved. Enthusiastically he strapped on his hunting knife in its neat new leather scabbard and galloped out of Alexandria. On August 2, 1826, General Walter H. Overton wrote to Senator Josiah Stoddard Johnston:

> Mr. Bowie, notorious for his land titles, came from Washington the warm and devoted friend of Brent, he had been riding through Catahoula, Washita, and other parishes ever since his return and he has acquired an influence since you left us that astonishes those that have witnessed its progress. His success in these land titles have led the mob to believe that he is endowed with more than human energy and ability and he is

already spoken of as the successor of Brent and I understand has already announced himself; he wields the Cunys and Wells in this Parish besides many others of less note. . . .

Bowie's primary supporters, the Wells and Cunys, ranked among the most affluent families in Louisiana. Bowie had known Samuel Levi Wells III as a sergeant in the Louisiana militia during the New Orleans campaign. With his brothers—Montfort, Thomas Jefferson, and James Madison—the Wells clan comprised the second generation of a prominent plantation dynasty. Their father, Samuel Levi Wells II, one of the original pioneers of the region, had became the largest landowner in central Louisiana and had served in the state House of Representatives.

Bowie's relationship to the Wells family may have entailed more than mere friendship or politics. Decades later Rezin's granddaughter, Mrs. Elve Sonait du Fosset, would claim that James had become engaged to Miss Cecelia Wells, an orphaned cousin of the Wells brothers.

It was past due time for James Bowie to take a wife. Most men married young in that era; Bowie was now in his late twenties. All of his brothers were married. But it would have to be a long engagement. Bowie was engaged in too many schemes and enterprises to get married immediately.

Dr. Richard Cuny and his hotheaded brother, Sam, were first cousins of the Wells family and equally wealthy. Wearing the finest clothes, Bowie traveled in their circles, attended their parties, and befriended their friends. "He was social and plain with all men," John recalled, "fond of music and the amusements of the day, and would take a glass, in merry mood, to 'drive dull care away'; but seldom allowed it to 'steal away his brains,' or transform him into a beast."

Archibald Hotchkiss, who would meet Bowie in Texas, recalled that "When he gave his friend his hand it was a pledge of fidelity never to be broken by him." That sense of loyalty dictated that the enemies of Bowie's friends became his own enemies. And the Wells and Cunys had powerful enemies. Beneath its tranquil facade, Alexandria was torn apart by a feud as tumultuous as the waters that cascaded through the rapids.

A feud that only could be resolved with blood.

Opposing the Wells and Cunys—and Bowie—were a band of relative newcomers to Louisiana that included Major Norris Wright and Colonel Robert Alexander Crain.

Robert Crain seems to have been the catalyst of the feud. To his supporters—and he had many—he was "the personification of chivalry."

However his detractors regarded him as an unscrupulous villain who preferred to pay off his debts with a challenge to combat. And like Major Wright, he enjoyed a formidable reputation as a duelist. Dr. John C. Rippey, related by marriage to the Wells clan, died on the field of honor because he refused a personal note in lieu of cash that Crain owed him.

Crain also reneged on a note to Richmond Edmond Cuny, the father of Sam and Richard. The elder Cuny elected not to challenge Crain and had to sell off some slaves to make the note good. That humiliation cemented the hatred between Sam Cuny and Crain.

The feud extended to politics. On the national level, the established planters such as the Wells and Cuny brothers supported Henry Clay's emerging Whig party, whereas Crain and his allies were staunch Jacksonian democrats.

Local politics further aggravated the conflict, especially after Wright's 1824 victory in the sheriff's election, despite charges that he had "manufactured a few votes."

By identifying himself with the Wells' interests, Bowie initiated his personal enmity with Major Wright. The sheriff used his influence to stifle a bank loan that Bowie had requested.

In the local elections of January 1827, Bowie's friends scored more significant victories. Samuel Wells defeated Norris Wright for sheriff, and Sam Cuny gleefully bested Robert Crain's bid for brigadier general of the militia.

But General Sam Cuny was not yet through with Colonel Crain. On May 7 Crain and some friends rode past Cuny's plantation en route to the courthouse. Suddenly Cuny emerged from his house with a rifle, the ferocity in his expression signaling his intent. Someone passed a shotgun to Crain. The two men fired almost simultaneously. Crain's shot missed, but Cuny's rifle ball ripped through Crain's left arm. Crain recovered from the wound, vowing to shoot Cuny on sight.

Ultimately, it would take that most heinous breach of chivalry, an attack on a woman's honor, to bring the feud to its gory climax.

During the late spring a female patient told Dr. Thomas Maddox an unseemly rumor about Mary Sibley, a sister of the Wells brothers. Maddox imprudently related the story to others, generating a scandal that titillated all of Alexandria that summer.

Inevitably Samuel Wells arranged to meet Maddox on the field of honor. At noon on September 19, they would exchange pistol shots on the first sandbar above Natchez, Mississippi.

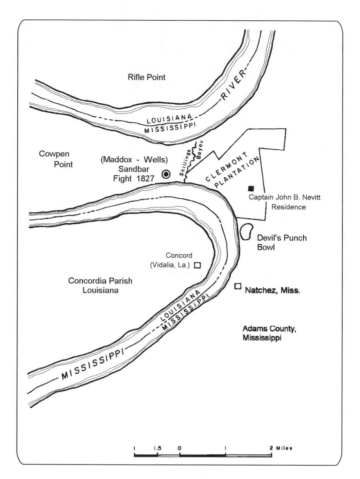

Map of sandbar fight.
Courtesy of Malcolm Barlow; Jordan, Kaiser & Sessions Engineering.

The Maddox party, including Colonel Crain and Major Norris Wright, arrived in Natchez several days early. Crain, acting as Maddox's second, arranged for Dr. James A. Denny of Natchez to serve as Maddox's physician, always a necessary precaution. Denny recalled, "It was mentioned to me at the time, that the opposing party were extremely hostile, and it was expected that if Mr. Wells should fall in the duel, a general attack would be made on Dr. Maddox and friends." Fearing this attack, Denny recruited two more doctors to attend the duel. All the physicians were warned to go armed "to prevent the rencontre that was feared in the event of the death of Mr. Wells." No one in the Maddox party knew which of Wells' friends would accompany him to the sandbar, but Crain remarked that he would shoot General Cuny "the first time they met."

In fact Wells had asked Major George C. McWhorter, an attorney from South Carolina, to act as Wells' second and Dr. Richard Cuny to be his physician. Jefferson Wells followed his brother on the journey from Alexandria. So did the two men that the Maddox party feared most; General Sam Cuny and James Bowie. Prior to the duel the Wells party stayed at the Alexander House in Vidalia, across the river from Natchez.

The Maddox faction spent the days preceding the duel at Captain John B. Nevitt's twelve-hundred-acre plantation, Clermont, located just a mile above Natchez. From Nevitt's house they could see down the steep wooded bluff to a great bend in the river—and to the shimmering white sandbar on its northern bank.

Wednesday, September 19, 1827, was "clear, dry and warm," Captain Nevitt wrote in the daily journal he kept. At 10:30 that morning a total of eleven armed men rode from Clermont down to the river.

It took them an hour to reach the southeast end of the sandbar. They saw an empty boat beached at the opposite end of the beach and knew that the Wells party had already arrived.

By previous arrangement only the principals and their seconds and physicians could be on the field. Leaving the rest of their party with the horses in the trees, Dr. Maddox, Colonel Crain, and Dr. Denny walked out into the sand.

Samuel Wells, Major McWhorter, and Dr. Cuny emerged from a willow grove at the northwest end of the sandbar. Crain looked past them and recognized James Bowie, Jefferson Wells, and, worse, General Sam Cuny lingering back in the shade. Their proximity disturbed him; he was not reassured when Dr. Cuny promised, "They will not approach nearer."

Initially everything went according to the ritualistic code of honor. Both physicians engaged in the futile exercise of trying to dissuade the principals from their fight while the seconds measured off the distance and loaded the pistols. Both Crain and McWhorter had brought a boxed pair of fine dueling weapons.

A few minutes after noon Wells and Maddox stood eight paces apart in the center of the sandbar, their pistols primed and ready. On verbal command they aimed. They fired. And they both missed.

Neither Wells nor Maddox were experienced duelists, and, in truth, neither were particularly enthusiastic about the affair of honor in which they now engaged. Once they had been friends; now, even as political adversaries, they did not possess the animosity that existed between Colonel Robert Crain and General Sam Cuny—or Major Norris Wright and James Bowie.

Yet fate had selected Samuel Wells and Dr. Thomas Maddox to represent their opposing factions, and the code of honor stipulated at least two exchanges of fire. Major McWhorter supplied them with a second set of loaded pistols, and one more time they prepared to kill each other like gentlemen.

And again they both missed.

Colonel Crain had already reloaded the first pair of pistols, in case there would be a third exchange of fire, but Wells and Maddox decided their honor was satisfied. They shook hands, forgiving past transgressions and sharing an almost intoxicating relief that they both had survived injury or death. Major McWhorter and the two surgeons, Dr. Denny and Dr. Richard Cuny, warmly congratulated each other that no blood had been shed.

Wells proposed that the gentlemen should all retire into the willow grove and take a glass of wine. Colonel Crain objected immediately: "No, Mr. Wells, you know that I can not meet certain gentlemen that are there, but let us go down to the river to our friends and drink and bury the hatchet."

"Agreed, Sir," Wells nodded cordially.

Maddox and Dr. Denny led the way. Crain retrieved the loaded pair of pistols and followed in company with Wells, McWhorter, and Dr. Cuny.

The rest of the Maddox party had witnessed the proceedings from the trees at the southeast. Nevitt carried a shotgun and most of the others had one or two pistols each, tucked under their coats, in case the predicted battle had erupted. Now seeing the approach of the reconciled parties, someone suggested they should leave the guns behind and go out and meet the gentlemen in a less hostile attitude. Major Wright argued that they should remain where they were. He, too, was apprehensive about the three men in the willows across the sandbar. Especially James Bowie. Nevertheless Nevitt propped his shotgun against a tree and started out onto the beach. The others followed, more reluctantly. They retained their pocket pistols and sword canes.

Seeing Major Wright and his other friends stepping out into the sunlit beach, a mere hundred yards away, Crain's own fear waned. He would be safe in their company.

But suddenly he spotted General Cuny, James Bowie, and young Jefferson Wells darting from the trees in a path that intercepted his own. They stopped ten feet in front of Crain, isolating him from his allies. Surrounded by men he perceived as enemies, Crain felt his fingers tighten around the grips of the two loaded pistols he was carrying.

Recklessly ignoring Crain's pistols, General Sam Cuny demanded that he and Crain should settle their own affair then and there.

Crain stepped back, his pistols leveled. Dr. Richard Cuny immediately stepped in front of his hotheaded brother while Samuel Wells grabbed the general's shoulders. Wells exclaimed that it "was not the time nor place for the adjustment of their difference."

Sam Cuny nodded slowly. Assuming that they had averted the conflict, Samuel Wells and Dr. Cuny turned away.

At that moment Crain saw Bowie "preparing his pistol for me, or I believed so from his manner. . . . " Crain did not wait to find out. He fired one pistol at Bowie, then spun and fired the second at General Cuny, who had already drawn his own pistol. Cuny fell, the femoral artery in his left thigh ruptured. He would bleed to death in minutes.

Crain knew his first pistol ball had struck Bowie, yet somehow Bowie still stood. His face contorted into its tiger's rage, and he exclaimed, "Crain, you have shot me, and I will kill you if I can." And then Crain saw that big blade slide out from its neat scabbard under Bowie's coat.

Crain stumbled back and hurled an empty pistol at Bowie "which struck him on the left side of the forehead." Stunned by the impact, blood draining from the ugly gash, Bowie dropped to his knees. Crain turned and raced for the woods.

Major Norris Wright had barely emerged from the trees when the shooting started. He muttered, "Gentlemen, this is what I expected." Drawing his pistol he charged forward, followed by the others.

Shots echoed across the sandbar. Maddox and some of the men ran for cover. But Norris Wright saw, again, that he had Bowie at a disadvantage. Still dazed and nearly blinded by the blood that flowed into his eyes, Bowie faced his nemesis. He rose awkwardly, stumbled a few paces, and fell behind a leaning snag protruding from the sand. Nearly six feet high but less than a foot in diameter, it did not provide much cover. Wright leveled his pistol as he deliberately advanced on Bowie.

Someone heard Bowie call out that he was unarmed, "but that if [Wright] was a man to shoot. . . . "

Wright obliged, but the pistol ball buried itself harmlessly in the narrow snag. He discarded the pistol and drew another from under his coat.

Major McWhorter passed a pistol to Bowie. Dr. Denny interjected, "This must be stopped, Sir, this must be stopped!" He pushed past McWhorter and grabbed Bowie from behind in an effort to prevent the next exchange of shots.

Wright fired his second pistol at Bowie. The ball amputated one of Dr. Denny's fingers as it passed through the lower part of Bowie's breast.

Shrieking, Denny took flight. A stray pistol ball grazed his thigh as he raced for the surrounding woods.

Wright drew a gleaming sword blade from his cane. Bowie, despite his wounds, raised the pistol McWhorter had given him and fired. The ball struck Wright in the side. From the trees Crain heard Wright exclaim, "The damned rascal has killed me!"

Wright was wounded—Bowie even more so—and only the pure hatred flashing in their eyes and the adrenalin pumping into their spilling blood kept them fighting. Bowie struggled back to his feet. Captain Nevitt saw Bowie and Wright advance on each other, "Mr. Bowie with a large knife, and Major Wright with a sword cane." Bowie deflected the sword point into his arm and plunged his own blade into Wright's shoulder. Wright staggered back.

At that instant one of Wright's friends fired on Bowie. Struck in the thigh, Bowie crumpled.

Again Wright had the advantage. He and a friend named Alfred Blanchard rushed forward and plunged their sword canes into Bowie's prone body. Somehow, incredibly, James Bowie struggled to a sitting position. He slashed Blanchard across the abdomen, driving him back. Then, desperately, Bowie grabbed for the collar of Wright's coat and pulled Wright forward—off-balance—down. With all his waning strength Bowie drove

The Sandbar Fight. *Illustration by Joseph Musso.*
The Alamo Journal, Feb. 1988, No. 60.

the knife upwards, burying it almost to the hilt in Wright's chest. Wright died instantly, without a sound, his limp body draping across Bowie. Both of them collapsed back into the sticky, bloodstained sand.

Dr. Maddox appeared on the field carrying his shotgun. Samuel Wells turned to him, yelling, "Doctor, for God's sake don't do any further damage, for it is all over."

It was all over. Death had ended the personal enmities between Crain and Cuny and between Bowie and Wright.

Immediately the doctors began attending to the fallen, each side offering assistance to the other. Samuel Wells helped bind Alfred Blanchard's wound; he would survive. Colonel Robert Crain helped carry Bowie's bloodied body into the shade.

In a letter written the day after the fight, Samuel Wells reported, "Bowie is shot through the lungs and thigh, and stabbed in seven places, the faculty generally are of the opinion that he will not recover."

The September 21, 1827 edition of the Natchez *Ariel*, the first newspaper to report the melee, agreed with that prognosis. The *Ariel* did not even know Bowie's first name; it referred to him simply as "Mr. ____ Bowie," adding that he was "not expected to recover."

But once again James Bowie would prove that he was a hard man to kill. And his knife had been baptized in blood.

Of such things are legends made.

Thereafter, the *Ariel*—and newspapers around the country—would know the name James Bowie. And of the weapon that bore his name.

Ironically Samuel Wells died less than a month after the sandbar fight. Indirectly, perhaps, he had been a victim of the battle, for he succumbed to a fever he had contracted in Natchez.

It took several months for Bowie to recover from the wounds he had received on the sandbar. In the late winter of 1828 he set out on another trip to Washington. En route he spent the bitter cold night of March 11 in Natchez playing cards with Captain John Nevitt. Although the two had probably met for the first time on opposite sides of the sandbar, they had become friends.

In Washington Bowie again called on Brent, but nothing more had been accomplished on either the Bowie or the de la Francia claims. Brent probably urged Bowie to be patient. However, at this point, Bowie was short of both patience and money. But he had a new reputation. Everyone had heard stories of the sandbar fight. Even Secretary of State Henry Clay. Apparently Bowie gained an audience with Clay, and, presumably, Clay also promised to look into the matters. Certainly the "Great Compromiser" later claimed he knew Bowie. Clay described him as the "greatest fighter in the Southwest."

On Bowie's return from Washington in early July he again stopped at Natchez long enough for Nevitt to pay off a forty-dollar debt, possibly Nevitt's loss in the previous game.

Then Bowie made an exploratory trip to Texas. It had changed dramatically since Mexico had achieved independence from Spain and opened it to Anglo colonization. Clearly fertile opportunities existed here that Bowie had overlooked.

At San Felipe de Austin, the unoffical Anglo capital, Bowie visited Noah Smithwick's blacksmith shop, knife in hand. Smithwick remembered:

> The blood-christened weapon which had saved its owner's life twice within a few seconds was an ordinary affair with a plain wooden handle, but when Bowie recovered from his wound he had the precious blade polished and set into an ivory handle; the scabbard also being silver mounted. Not wishing to degrade it by ordinary use, he brought the knife to me in San Felipe to have a duplicate made.

Later that year James moved down to join Rezin, Stephen, and his mother, Elve, on the brothers' new Acadia plantation, encompassing some twenty-one hundred acres on Bayou La Fourche near Thibodaux. There they would grow sugar cane and establish one of the first steam-powered mills in Louisiana. James, Rezin, and Elve lived in houses constructed virtually adjacent to each other. If the story is true about Jim's engagement to Cecelia Wells, he obviously planned to move Miss Cecelia into his home after their wedding.

The ceremony never took place. On September 7, 1829, Cecelia died of a fever in Alexandria. Rezin Bowie's granddaughter, Mrs. Elve Soniat du Fosset, wrote that Cecelia had passed away "just two weeks previous to the day set for the wedding."

Bowie may have consoled himself in Natchez. Captain Nevitt's journal records five December nights that he, Bowie, and others played brag late into the evening. Dr. Denny joined them for a couple of nights. So did Bowie's new friend, an attorney named Angus McNeill. On Monday, December 21, the last night Bowie was mentioned in Nevitt's journal, they ate an oyster supper before sitting down at the gaming table. And Bowie probably raised a glass or two—or more—to 'drive dull care away.'

Nothing, it seemed, had worked out for him in Louisiana. Smallpox had killed twenty-seven slaves at Acadia, jeopardizing the crop, and creditors were circling around the plantation. Cecilia and her cousins, Samuel Wells and Samuel Cuny, were gone. The two Sams had been the foundation of Bowie's political support in Louisiana. William Brent had been defeated in Washington, leaving many of Bowie's land titles and the de la Francia claim, yet mired in the bureaucracy.

For James Bowie, the approach of the new year signaled the time for a new start. In a new place.

In that sense James Bowie was not unlike so many others who migrated to the Mexican province of Texas. He just carried a big knife. And a bigger reputation.

James Bowie rode away from the Acadia plantation on January 1, 1830. Caiaphas Ham accompanied Bowie, Ham's later chronicle providing an account of their journey and subsequent adventures.

Entering Texas, the two men stopped briefly at Nacogdoches, "where we made the acquaintance of the principal inhabitants," Ham recalled. Then they continued west to the Brazos River, where they visited what Ham modestly referred to as "Jared Groce's farm."

A native Virginian, Groce had established a prosperous plantation in Alabama before enlisting as one of Austin's Old Three Hundred. In 1821 he had literally transported the plantation culture to Texas, arriving with fifty wagons, at least as many slaves, large herds of livestock, and the first cottonseed to be planted in Texas soil. In 1828 he constructed the first cotton gin in Texas. Reputedly the wealthiest man in the province, Jared Groce qualified as the sort of man whose friendship Bowie would nurture.

Again the old Bowie charm worked. Groce graciously opened his home to the famous hero of the sandbar fight.

Bowie and Ham stayed with Groce for a month. During that time Bowie gained an appreciation for the potential that cotton offered an enterprising newcomer in Texas. He proposed to construct a cotton mill in the province, and Groce expressed interest in financing the project.

Thirty miles south lay San Felipe. When Bowie and Ham arrived there it consisted of some thirty rough hewn log structures with clapboard roofs haphazardly flanking both sides of a half-mile stretch of road. There were two hotels, the newspaper office of the *Texas Gazette*, a few stores, Noah Smithwick's blacksmith shop, and a couple of saloons.

Austin headquartered out of a double log cabin with an open "dog trot" separating the two rooms. When Bowie presented himself, Austin must have recognized the name. And the notoriety. To Austin, Bowie's reputation, unlike his knife, bore a double edge; land speculator and knife-fighter. As to the former, Austin still blamed land speculation for the panic of 1819 that ruined his father, and he yet believed that such men could only be detrimental to Texas.

And then there was the big knife that Bowie wore. It symbolized, memorialized, even romanticized violence. Recently Austin had seen too many violent men drifting into Texas. Hot-tempered aristocrats eager to avenge any breach of honor with a challenge to mortal combat. And drunken rowdies who bragged of their savage, rough and tumble, no-holds-barred fights to the finish.

To his credit, Bowie could claim only one kill. Although that occurred on a field of honor, Bowie himself had never participated as a principal in a duel. And, in his refined clothes, displaying the gentility of Natchez and New Orleans, he hardly qualified as a common ruffian or cutthroat. Yet with his cool, soft-spoken manner punctuated by those penetrating eyes, James Bowie seemed infinitely more dangerous than other men.

Stephen F. Austin should not have liked James Bowie. But whatever his initial reservations, Austin cordially received Bowie. Soon he, too, supported Bowie's cotton mill proposal. Such an enterprise would be good for Texas.

Groce funded the long trip to Saltillo, where Bowie could acquire the necessary permits for his project. Groce's son, daughter, and son-in-law, an attorney named William H. Wharton, would accompany Bowie and Ham, providing whatever assistance they could. Austin supplied the passports and letters of introduction to prominent citizens in Bexar.

The party rode west through Gonzales, the westernmost Anglo town, nestled on the sleepy Guadalupe River. Then on to San Antonio de Bexar.

As they approached the town along the shady Alameda, Bowie must have noticed the crumbling, weed-encrusted ruin off to his right. But he probably paid little attention to the mission now known as the Alamo. His destiny there would wait. There was still time for more stupendous schemes, more daring enterprises.

Chapter 11:   **San Saba**

"**O**n reaching San Antonio the excursionists were treated with great consideration, courtesy, and hospitality by Gov. Beramendi, Col. Seguin, and others," Caiaphas Ham remembered. Big Jim Bowie's charm worked as well on *Tejanos* as on Anglos. Both Beramendi and Seguin took to the *norteamericano* with the *cuchillo grande*. Beramendi expressed interest in investing in the cotton mill. Both he and Seguin provided Bowie with critical letters of introduction to the authorities in Saltillo, most notably Beramendi's brother-in-law, Jose Antonio Navarro, who now represented Texas in the legislature.

"Our sojourn in the 'war-worn city' was very pleasant," Ham continued. It must have been especially pleasant for James Bowie, for as Ham succinctly noted, "...Bowie fell in love." The object of his affection was Beramendi's eighteen-year-old daughter, Ursula. At the age of two she had survived the flight to Louisiana to escape Arredondo. Now in the full bloom of womanhood she possessed the necessary attributes to stir Bowie's blood: passionate youth, refined Castillian beauty, poised charm and grace, and—perhaps most of all—a family with a great deal of influence and affluence.

However, as always with Bowie, romance would have to wait. His party left Bexar, crossed the Rio Bravo at Presidio de Rio Grande, and continued southwest to Monclova. Then a "laborious and fatiguing" trek across arid desert to Saltillo. Ham recalled, "We made the mountain city with joyous feelings, and indulged freely in drinking and bathing."

Bowie's joyous feelings continued. He won over Navarro and the other authorities in Saltillo and received his charter for the cotton mill. Even better, he saw new opportunities for land speculation. The government offered league grants of Texas land—63,360 acres—to Mexican citizens, but many could not afford the nominal purchase price. Bowie persuaded more than a dozen newfound *amigos* to apply for the grants with the understanding that Bowie would pay for and acquire ownership of the land. The government did not require immediate compensation, and, best of all, everything was legitimate.

Then somehow things got even better. In September, Beramendi was appointed vice-governor of Coahuila y Texas, and he brought his family to Saltillo. It now seemed like a very good time for Bowie to pay court to Ursula. While they were in Saltillo—or else when Bowie accompanied the Beramendis on the long journey back to Bexar—he proposed marriage. According to Spanish tradition, Señor Beramendi accepted. And, also according to tradition, he requested a dowry agreement.

Bowie made a quick trip back to the United States. In Natchez he deposited $20,000—funds apparently raised from Groce, Beramendi, and other investors—with his attorney, Angus McNeill, the capital to be used for the cotton mill enterprise. In Louisiana Bowie liquidated all his assets, legitimate or otherwise, and raised all the cash he could. Then back to Bexar where, on April 22, 1831, he presented his soon-to-be father-in-law with the dowry contract.

Bowie claimed his net worth at $222,800, but he had padded the financial statement a bit. He included $30,000 from brother John's Arkansas land scheme, a fraud in which James may or may not have been involved. And Bowie claimed $32,800, the entire amount, with current interest, owed Jose de la Francia by the U.S. government, although Bowie was entitled only to a percentage. (Within two years the Supreme Court would negate the Arkansas claims, and the U.S. Congress would not compensate de la Francia until 1848.)

Bowie also had included $45,000 from the sale of his share of Acadia, and the balance came from other land sales, which may or may not have been as legitimate. However he probably had received more notes than actual cash. But even if money was tight, he only owed Ursula $15,000, in cash or land according to the dowry agreement, and the contract allowed him two years to pay her.

Señor Beramendi was satisfied. On April 25, 1831, James Bowie married Maria Ursula de Beramendi in the San Fernando Church.

Bowie promptly borrowed $1,879 from his father-in-law and another $750 from Ursula's grandmother, Josefa Ruiz Navarro, using the money to finance a honeymoon to the United States. He and Ursula took a schooner to New Orleans where the big, legendary adventurer and his beautiful young Latin bride were reportedly "the observed of all observers." Bowie proudly displayed Ursula to his family. Then back to Texas.

Everywhere they went they generated comments such as the statement recorded by Captain William G. Hunt:

> I first met Colonel Bowie and his wife at a party given them on the Colorado on Christmas Day, 1831. Mrs. Bowie was a beautiful Castilian lady, and won all hearts by her sweet manners. Bowie was supremely happy with her, very devoted and more like a kind and tender lover than the terrible duelist he has since been represented to be.

If it was, for Bowie, a marriage of convenience, by all accounts he loved Ursula very much. And her family, and the other Bexarenos, reciprocated his affection. Ursula's cousin Juana Alsbury—who would play a much more prominent role later on—described Bowie as "a tall, well-made gentleman, of a very serious countenance, of few words, always to the point, and a warm friend." It was a familiar description, significant only in that it had been provided by a new *Tejano* relative. Juana added, "In his family he was affectionate, kind, and so acted as to secure the love and confidence of all."

Certainly Bowie had won Beramendi's confidence. Beramendi treated Bowie more as a son than a son-in-law. After the couple had resided for three months in a house rented from a Bexareno named Yturio, Beramendi provided them with land and a home near Mission San Jose. There, against the wall of the old mission, Bowie established his cotton mill.

Texas had worked its magic on James Bowie. Everything was coming together for him. Then, abruptly, he risked it all on another stupendous scheme—a daring enterprise that just might make him richer than all the land dealings in Louisiana, Arkansas, and Texas combined. If he did not lose his life. Or his scalp.

James Bowie would attempt to reclaim the lost Spanish silver of the San Saba.

Legends of the lost silver mines along the San Saba River had persisted for almost a century. With their fabled veins of pure ore—and hidden chambers of minted bullion—the mines remained concealed somewhere near the ruins of the abandoned presidio that had been established deep within Apacheria. Now it was the Comanches and their allies who jealously guarded the secret. Only the bravest, or most foolhardy, treasure hunter would have trespassed in their domain.

Yet, according to Caiaphas Ham, James' brother Rezin had not only braved the Indians, he already had found the mine. Ham wrote:

It was visited by Rezin P. Bowie, at a date previous to 1831. It was not far from the fort. The shaft was about eight feet deep; the bottom was reached by means of steps cut in a live oak log. Bowie used his tomahawk in getting possession of some ore. He carried it to New Orleans, had it assayed, and it panned out rich.

An ancient inscription seems to support Ham's claim. The words carved into the stone gate of the old presidio, originally read, "Bowie con sua tropa [Bowie and his men] 1829."

Rezin himself did not confess to having found the mines, at least not in his surviving account of the San Saba expedition. But he did specify that the mines were "a mile distant" from the presidio.

Caiaphas Ham also would play a significant role in the silver mine venture. By 1831 the Comanches had become uncharacteristically docile. Like the Apaches before them they rode into Bexar to trade for supplies. Ham befriended one band of Comanches led by a chief named In-cor-roy and arranged to have himself adopted into the tribe. "My desire was to know something of them, and of the country they wandered over," Ham wrote, adding that he wanted to "buy good mares to carry to Louisiana."

Initially James Bowie opposed Ham's endeavor, but reluctantly Bowie helped him acquire the trading material he would need: gunpowder, balls, knives, tobacco, brass rings, and a pack horse to bear the merchandise.

Ham rode off with the nomadic Comanches, hunting and trading for mares as they roamed through their wilderness. He reported an especially intriguing incident.

One fat warrior was frequently my hunting companion. He pointed to a hill, and said—"There is plenty of silver on the other side—We will go out by ourselves, and I will show it to you. If the other Indians find out I have done so they will kill both of us."

But the Comanches broke camp the next day and drifted on. Ham never saw the other side of the hill.

After four months among the tribe, Ham received an urgent correspondence from Bowie announcing that the Mexican government intended to renew its war with the Indians. "If you are found among the Comanches you will be killed with them," Bowie wrote. "Come in at once."

Ham must have shared this information with In-cor-roy. The chief and twenty-five warriors escorted Ham and the mares he had acquired back to Bexar. Simultaneously, as a conciliatory display of good faith to the Mexican authorities, the Indians returned other horses stolen from settlers along the San Antonio River.

Back in Bexar Ham realized that he had been manipulated by the Bowie brothers. Rezin had arrived in town. He and James were mounting an expedition to recover the lost treasure of the San Saba mine. They needed Ham, needed his knowledge of the terrain and, most of all, needed his friendly relations with the Comanches.

Governor Beramendi helped finance the venture. He extended his personal guarantee that Ham's mares would be cared for at his ranch until the expedition's return. "This left no excuse for refusing to go," Ham conceded.

Ramon Musquiz, the *jefe*, or political chief, of Bexar also sanctioned the mission. James Bowie advised him, "some benefit might result therefrom both to the community and myself."

Along with Ham, the Bowies' recruited Thomas McCaslin, whom James described as the "foreman of my mechanics." Robert Armstrong, David Buchanon, James Coryell, Matthew Doyal, and Jesse Wallace also enlisted. A Mexican servant named Gonzales and a young mulatto slave named Charles rounded out the expedition.

On November 2, 1831, Bowie kissed his young bride goodbye and tried to reassure her fears. Then the nine men and two servant boys, leading pack horses, rode out of Bexar. Ursula had good reason for concern. Even if the Comanches remained friendly, there were other tribes eager to hang white scalps from their lodge poles.

The Texians rode northwest, through Bandera Pass, across the Llano River, toward the distant San Saba hills. Two weeks passed without incident. Then the expedition encountered a small group of friendly Comanches who were returning more stolen horses to Bexar. They warned Bowie that a war party of one hundred sixty-four Tawakonis, Wacos, and Caddos were stalking the white men, planning to take their horses, their possessions, and their scalps.

Bowie knew the importance of a defensive position. Without cover his small party had no chance of survival against one hundred sixty-four Indians. The Plains tribes had developed a strategy that too often had proved very effective against European trespassers caught in the open. One group of braves would charge, compelling the white men to discharge their weapons. Then, before the rifles and muskets could be reloaded, the main body of Indians closed in for the kill.

Indians were less enthusiastic about attacking a fortified position. Generally they would probe for weaknesses before launching an assault. Good cover could buy the Texians some time. It might even buy them their lives.

Bowie elected to try for the presidio.

Rezin Bowie remembered, "The fort surrounds about one acre of land, under a twelve feet stone wall." It was, in fact, much too large a perimeter for nine men and two servant boys to adequately defend. However, Rezin explained, "Within the fort is a church, which, had we reached before night, it was our intention to have occupied to defend ourselves against the Indians."

Had they reached it, James Bowie might have become famous for making a last ditch stand in yet another Spanish church.

But they did not make it.

"Throughout the day we encountered bad roads, being covered with rocks, and, our horses feet being worn out, we were disappointed in not reaching the fort," recalled Rezin. With darkness closing in around them, the men sought a defensive position.

The best they could find consisted of a grove of live oak trees, "some thirty or forty in number, about the size of a man's body," Rezin remembered. A smaller grove stood a short distance to the north. James Bowie assigned three men there, "so as to prevent the enemy from taking possession of it, and thereby have an advantage over us." A creek flowing about thirty-five yards to the west provided water and a natural barrier against an enemy charge. To the east lay "open prairie, interspersed with a few trees, rock, and broken land." A high hill, some sixty yards to the northeast, dominated that horizon.

They hobbled their horses, placed sentries, and prepared for an uneasy night.

At this point, according to James Bowie, they were three miles north of the San Saba River. Rezin claimed they camped six miles from the presidio. Ham later wrote, "We traveled over the ground twice afterward, and agreed upon twelve miles as the correct distance."

The restless night passed slowly but quietly. However the next morning, even as the men climbed into their saddles, someone raised the cry.

"Indians!"

One hundred sixty-four warriors advanced out of the east. A single dismounted Indian walked ahead of them, his face close to the ground, following the white men's tracks. They were only two hundred yards away when they heard the cry from the trees ahead. Immediately the Indians emitted a loud war whoop and began stripping down for battle.

Bowie's men swung from their saddles. Some of them secured the horses and pack animals in the center of the grove while the rest crouched behind trees, their long rifles primed and held at the ready.

Rezin decided to attempt to negotiate with the Indians. Considering the overwhelming odds, compromise seemed preferable to combat.

Rezin stepped brazenly out into the open, his pistol tucked in his belt and the shotgun, which he favored because of his nearsightedness, pointed to the ground. David Buchanon followed. The two men began walking towards the warriors. One of them thought he knew enough of the Indian language to invite their chief forward to treat with the white men.

Some of the Indians responded in broken English, "How de do? How de do?"

Encouraged, Rezin and Buchanon advanced to within forty yards of the Indians.

Back in the grove, James Bowie noticed some of the warriors slipping behind the hill to the northeast. Bowie stepped from the trees to warn his brother to return.

Suddenly a mounted Indian at the head of the braves raised a scalp into the air. At that signal a dozen shots rang out. Buchanon spun to the ground, his leg shattered. Rezin leveled his shotgun, blasted with both barrels, and then snapped off a pistol shot. Then he heaved Buchanon onto his back and raced back for the trees.

The Indians discharged a second volley of shots. Two more balls grazed Buchanon. Others whipped harmlessly through Rezin's hunting shirt.

Eight of the warriors broke from the main party and dashed after the two fleeing white men. With Buchanon's added weight, Rezin could not outrace them. He could hear their whoops drawing ever closer. But already Rezin had neared the trees. James Bowie and his men had charged from the grove, their rifles blazing. Four Indians crumpled to the ground. The rest hastily retreated, and the main body withdrew behind the hill to the northeast.

Gasping, Rezin staggered up to his comrades and passed Buchanon to outstretched arms. The white men fell back into the shadowy cover of the trees. They bandaged Buchanon's wounds as best they could and left him in the center of the grove. Then, reduced to eight riflemen, they reloaded and waited.

Five minutes passed.

Suddenly the Indians surged over the hill, their yells mixed with the retort of their rifles. The Texians picked their targets and returned fire.

A chief appeared at the crest of the hill, urging his men to rush the grove. He sat "perfectly composed" upon his horse, as if defying the white men's marksmanship.

Bowie shouted, "Who is loaded?"

"I am," replied Ham.

Ham aimed. Fired. The rifle ball ripped through the chief's lower leg and into his horse's flank. The animal sank to the ground. The chief extricated himself, hopping around on his one good leg, trying to protect himself with his rawhide shield.

By then Bowie and others had reloaded. The painted symbols on the Indian shield provided no magic against the Texian rifle balls that tore through it and into the chief's body.

A half dozen or more Indians closed around the fallen chief's body. They lifted it and carried it back behind the hill. The rest of the warriors followed. Texian rifle balls dropped a few of the retreating braves.

Bowie's men scarcely had time to reload before the warriors charged

From "The Bowie Knife Hero" in *Frank Leslie's Popular Monthly*, October 1882. *Courtesy the Joseph Musso Collection.*

back over the hill, shouting and shooting. This time Indian bowmen had joined the attack, arching their arrows into the trees. The Texians fired back as rapidly as they could prime their weapons.

Then a second chief appeared at the crest of the hill. Again Bowie called, "Who is loaded?" Nobody was. Young Charles, the mulatto slave, rushed up and handed Buchanon's rifle to Bowie. It had not been discharged since the fight began. Bowie sighted down the barrel and squeezed the trigger.

The chief toppled from his horse. Again a half dozen Indians raced to their fallen chief and carried him back behind the hill.

At almost that same instant a volley of rifle fire erupted from the creek behind the Texians. Several horses reared, jerking against their ropes, emitting a high-pitched whinny as rifle balls pierced their flesh. Matthew Doyal fell, shouting that he had been wounded. The ball had passed through his left breast but missed any vital organs. Thomas McCaslin darted over to where Doyal clutched his wound.

"Where is the Indian that shot Doyal?" McCaslin demanded. Then he spotted a Caddo in the shallow creekbed. McCaslin raised his rifle. The Caddo fired first. McCaslin emitted a death groan as he sank to the ground, a dark red hole through the center of his body.

Now Robert Armstrong raced to McCaslin. "Damn that Indian that shot McCaslin," Armstrong cursed. "Where is he?"

Another Caddo popped up and fired. The ball slammed into the forestock of Armstrong's rifle, lodging against the barrel. Armstrong ducked for cover.

Some fifteen Caddos had slipped into the creek behind the grove. "These were the severest of our foemen," James Bowie remembered. The Texians shifted into a dense thicket that provided them with a better perspective on the creek bed. They eliminated the Caddo threat "by shooting the most of them through the head," Rezin recalled, "as we had the advantage of seeing them when they could not see us."

Meanwhile other Indians had encircled the grove, sniping from behind rocks, brush, and solitary trees scattered across the plain. Such sparse cover proved inadequate, for Rezin bragged that the Texians "brought half a dozen down with every round." Rezin added:

> . . . we had a fair view of them in the prairie, while we were completely hid. We baffled their shots by moving six or eight feet the moment we fired, as their only mark was the smoke of our guns. They would put twenty balls within the size of a pocket handkerchief, where they had seen the smoke.

One Texian apparently did not move fast enough. An Indian ball tore through a bush and struck James Coryell in the arm. Fortunately the bush had slowed the projectile; the ball only penetrated to a depth equivalent to its own diameter.

The sniping continued for two hours. Around 11:00 A.M the Indians resorted to a more deadly strategy. With the wind blowing from the west, Indians ignited the dry prairie grass across the creek, sending flames and smoke roaring towards the Texian position. However the wind faltered, and the conflagration failed to jump the creek.

The Indians resumed their sporadic sniping. Bowie instructed the two servants, Charles and Gonzales, to construct a barricade. Keeping low, the boys dragged tree limbs and rocks.

About 4:00 P.M. the wind shifted, suddenly gusting from the north. Immediately the Texians realized they were vulnerable to another prairie fire. So did the Indians. Robert Armstrong spotted a brave torching the grass by the creek above them. Armstrong's rifle shot dropped the Indian. But already the prairie was ablaze, the roaring flames leaping ten feet into the smoke-filled sky, the raging inferno sweeping directly towards the Texians.

The Indians charged onto the prairie behind the curtain of fire, shooting through the flames. Bowie's men held their fire. The shower of sparks flying ahead of the blaze transformed every man's powder horn into a potential bomb. To uncap their horn risked a deadly explosion. Thus the Texians were restricted to the one shot in their rifles—and two desperate choices. "We must either be burnt up alive, or driven into the prairie among the Indians," Rezin declared, "and, to make it more awful, their shouts and yells rent the air—they, at the same time, firing upon us about twenty shots a minute."

Bowie's men anticipated an attack under cover of the smoke. Rezin wrote that the Texians came to a determination "to give them one fire, place our backs together, draw our knives and fight them as long as any one of us was left alive."

However the warriors did not charge. Instead, confident the flames would destroy the white men, the Indians utilized the barrier of smoke to drag their dead and wounded from the field.

As the blaze approached, the Texians grabbed blankets, deerskins, bear hides, and buffalo robes and attacked the inferno itself. Their boots smoldered. Their clothes singed. Their lungs were filled with thick smoke. Their burning eyes drained tears onto faces blackened by soot-stained sweat. Yet they beat down the flames.

The diminished blaze danced through the grove. Six panicked pack mules snapped their ropes and galloped off. Much of the thicket burned away. But again the warriors did not press their advantage. Squinting through the smoke, Bowie saw that the Indians had withdrawn to a pond about a half-mile distant.

With most of their natural cover burned away, the Texians strengthened their breastworks. Bowie's knife, with which he had prepared to make a last stand only moments earlier, now dug into the ground for rocks and dirt to pile onto the barricade. So did its namesakes, wielded by the other Texians. Occasional random shots whizzed by harmlessly.

James Bowie recorded that the battle ended about 6:30 P.M. "only one shot being fired by them after 7 o'clock, which was aimed at one of our men who went to obtain water."

As darkness fell, the Indians withdrew to a safe distance three hundred yards from their entrenched enemy and encamped for the night. The exhausted Texians savored their first respite after almost twelve continuous hours of combat. They had lost one man killed—the engineer, Thomas McCaslin—and three others wounded. Several horses had been shot and six pack mules had run away. Yet Bowie's report suggested that his men still had fight in them.

> We had agreed to attack the enemy while they were asleep, but when we reflected that we had only six men able to use their arms, and that the wounded would have to remain unprotected, we thought it more advisable to remain in camp, which we had now fortified with stones and timber, so as to make it quite secure against further assault.

Rezin recalled that they continued working on their makeshift fortification "and succeeded in getting it ten feet higher by ten P.M." The distant Indians serenaded their labors with the eerie wailing of the warriors crying over their dead. Not anticipating another attack until morning, the Texians filled all their canteens and skins with water, then settled into slumber.

Caiaphas Ham took the last watch. He spotted one of the escaped pack mules, retrieved it, and tied it to a tree. Across the prairie the death songs continued to resonate in the night. Then, an hour before dawn, he heard movement in the Indian camp. Ham quickly roused the Texians. Again they prepared for battle, rifles primed as they squinted into the waning darkness.

They heard a single gunshot. Rezin later presumed that the Indians had killed one of their chiefs, "it being also a custom to shoot any of their tribe that are mortally wounded."

The dawn revealed no Indians on the prairie. James Bowie reported that the war party had retreated to the northeast. Rezin wrote that the

Indians "set out with their dead and wounded to a mountain about a mile distant, where they deposited them in a cave in the side of it."

Two of the Texians ventured out to where the Indians had camped the night before. They counted forty-eight bloody spots in the grass where dead and wounded warriors had lain the night before. (Ham would later hear from Comanches that the war party had lost fifty-two killed and many more wounded.)

James Bowie could only hope that such losses had compelled the Indians to give up the fight. With only six effective riflemen left, he could hardly repel another determined attack. Or, with their limited supplies, endure a protracted siege.

Nor could Bowie retreat. He did not have enough horses or pack mules to evacuate all their men and equipment. Besides, the wounded were not yet in a condition to travel. Rezin noted that his brother "attended to them faithfully." The other Texians passed the morning hours strengthening their stone walls.

Around noon—James Bowie remembered 11:00 A.M., Rezin 1:00 P.M.—thirteen warriors rode back into sight. Rezin wrote, "As soon as they discovered we were still there and ready for action, and well fortified, they put off."

The reappearance of the Indians inspired James Bowie to erect a flagpole. Perhaps he attached a crude, hastily fabricated banner to it. Perhaps it was a Mexican tricolor signifying the expedition's official sanction by the authorities in Bexar. Whichever, the flag that waved over the Texians' makeshift stone fort now served as a brazen symbol of open defiance.

Bowie also kept a fire burning day and night, hoping to attract some friendly Comanches.

Meanwhile the Comanches who had warned Bowie had continued on to San Antonio de Bexar with their contraband horses. There they reported that the Texians had been pursued by a war party that outnumbered the whites fifteen to one. Surely Bowie and his men had been killed. The news must have devastated young Ursula. And the entire *Tejano* population of the town joined her in mourning.

On the cool night of December 6, 1831, a small group of men staggered from the darkness into San Antonio de Bexar. Most of them trudged along on sore feet. Others slumped forward on the back of stumbling horses. "There was not one of the party but had his skin cut in several places, and numerous shot-holes through his clothes," noted Rezin.

Prominent Texas Ranger John S. "Rip" Ford, who had included Caiaphas Ham's account among his own papers, provided his own melodramatic conclusion to the story:

> Some of them were recognized; a shout went up; it was repeated, it spread from street to street, from house to house. Stout men quivered with excitement; tears of joy dimmed bright eyes. Fearless men rushed forward to grasp in friendship and admiration the hands of citizens who had approved themselves heroes in a contest demanding the exercise of courage, prudence, endurance, and all the qualities adorning the soldier and the patriot. "Bowie's party have returned —they have won a glorious victory" was the cry. House after house was illuminated. The people in their heart of hearts decreed them a triumph—and well they deserved it.

Neither James nor Rezin, nor Ham nor Ford, described what must have been a poignant reunion between Bowie, returned from the dead, and his young bride still clad in widow's black.

The San Saba battle greatly enhanced James Bowie's reputation. Once again he had proven himself a hard man to kill. And now he had established himself as a leader of men in combat.

Historian James T. De Shields added to the veneration, describing Bowie's San Saba fight as "without a parallel on this continent; certainly a more skillful and heroic defense against such fearful odds was never made on Texas soil."

But De Shields was mistaken. James Bowie was yet destined for the most heroic defense in Texas history.

Myths, Mysteries, and Misconceptions

Bowie: The Man and the Myth

With his namesake weapon, James Bowie slashed through the boundaries separating fact from folklore, inundating both the man and his namesake weapon in a dense fog of mythology that only now is beginning to dissipate. Indeed, the vast majority of material published about Bowie perpetuates legend rather than chronicling fact. At the annual meeting of the Alamo Battlefield Association in March 1997, historian William C. Davis, author of *Three Roads to the Alamo*, announced, "The real mystery of the Alamo is not how Davy Crockett died, but rather how Jim Bowie lived."

The same dilemma does not exist with Bowie's contemporaries such as Austin, Houston, Crockett, and Travis. When they were born, where they were born, where they went, and what they did, can be readily traced. Yet Bowie's biographers often have faltered from the outset. The date of his birth has never been ascertained. (Raymond Thorp, in his book *Bowie Knife*, provides the date April 10, 1796, but he gives no reference for this information. Other sources have dated Bowie's birth from 1795 to 1799.)

Until recently four states—Georgia, Tennessee, Kentucky, and Louisiana—claimed the honor of being Bowie's birthplace. Not until 1989 did Bowie historian Joseph Musso unearth the documentation that substantiated Bowie's birth in Logan County, Kentucky, nine miles northwest of present-day Franklin. (In 1869 this land was transferred from Logan to Simpson County.)

Actually, Bowie's birthplace should never have been an issue. In October 1852 *DeBow's Review* published an article by John Jones Bowie, entitled "Early Life in the Southwest—The Bowies," that focused specifically on his more famous brother. John stated that James was born in Logan County, Kentucky, "in the spring of 1796" (though not necessarily on April 10). Though obviously biased toward James, the brief article

is generally accurate in those areas in which John had personal knowledge. John even described the brothers' slave smuggling operation and
alluded to James' land speculation. But the article omitted any reference
to forged titles or land fraud, something in which John himself had been
deeply involved.

Beginning about the time John's article was published—and continuing throughout the nineteenth century—romanticized stories about
James Bowie began finding their way into the national press. Often these
stories were pure melodrama, with Bowie rescuing some naive planter's
son or damsel in distress, Bowie's blade defeating the villain in a climactic battle.

In truth, no historical documentation has surfaced that proves that
James Bowie ever wielded a knife other than at the sandbar fight. Yet virtually all Bowie biographies right up to Clifford Hopewell's 1994 effort,
James Bowie: Texas Fighting Man, have treated these knife duels as historical fact.

In a sense Bowie inadvertently contributed to his own mythology.
Throughout his life, he left a frustratingly sparse paper trail. Where history failed, the legends prevailed.

The decades surrounding the turn of the century provided some sincere attempts at chronicling Bowie. Best by far was the 1887 account
written by Caiaphas Ham, who had befriended Bowie in Louisiana and
accompanied him to Texas. Again it contains a very pro-Bowie slant.
Also Ham was eighty-four when he penned it, and such late reminiscences are usually suspect. Yet Ham retained a remarkably keen
memory. If James Bowie ever wrote of his first altercation with Norris
Wright at Bailey's Hotel, or of the subsequent sandbar fight, the documents have not surfaced. But Bowie related these events to Ham, and
Ham's vividly descriptive narrative is as close as we can come to Bowie's
own perspective.

About that same time accounts by Rezin Bowie's grandchildren, John
Seybourne Moore and Mrs. Eugene Soniat, found their way into the
press. Neither had ever met their Great-uncle James, and though their
hand-me-down family traditions contain some intriguing scraps, they are
already tainted by the popular mythology.

The same can be said for the accounts provided by two descendants
of the Maryland Bowies, at best distant relatives of James. In 1899 Walter
Worthington Bowie published a genealogical history, *The Bowies and
Their Kindred*. Despite his best efforts, Mr. W. W. Bowie's brief biographical sketches in his chapter on the Louisiana Bowies contained too many

errors to be reliable. For instance he has James Bowie born at Elliott Springs, Tennessee, in 1795. Miss Lucy Leigh Bowie's 1916 monograph, "Famous Bowie Knife, its History and Origin," retains that same error and many more. Ironically, Miss Bowie completely disputes the validity of John Bowie's account. "I have carefully gone over it several times item by item and every statement I find untrue," she wrote. "It is probable that John J. Bowie never knew of the article." Most likely Miss Bowie's rejection of John's account stemmed from his reference to slave smuggling, which had become a much more sensitive issue in her day.

Most late-twentieth-century Bowie biographies have simply repeated the errors and, too often, embellished the myths found in these early accounts.

Where Was the Sandbar Fight?

The participants in the sandbar fight specifically placed it on the first sandbar above Natchez on the Mississippi side of the river. Though dueling remained a popular pastime with the Southern gentry, the practice had been outlawed by the state legislatures (ironically composed of the very gentlemen most prone to engage in affairs of honor). However since no federal statute existed against dueling, the participants would "cross the river," or at least cross state lines, defend their honor, and then the survivors would cross back, knowing they would not be extradited.

The sandbar fight did not remain on that beach in Mississippi. Walter Worthington Bowie located the fight "on a little island in the Mississippi River opposite Natchez," and, again, Miss Lucy Leigh Bowie repeated that error.

By the mid-twentieth century the fight had completed its journey across the river to Louisiana, when Raymond Thorp (*Bowie Knife,* 1949) popularized the notion that the battle took place on the Vidalia sandbar. This misconception became so prevalent that the state of Louisiana erected a historical marker in Vidalia commemorating the fight. The marker is gone now, but some writers who should know better still describe Bowie's fight on the Vidalia sandbar.

Around 1930 the Army Corps of Engineers dredged a new channel, called Giles Cut-off, that straightened the river above Natchez. Ironically, the original site of the sandbar fight now exists on Giles Island on the Louisiana side of the river, just above Vidalia, although the land is still owned by the state of Mississippi.

Bowie's Lovers: Sybil and Judalon

Since so much of the alleged history published about Bowie was, in fact, fiction, it is hardly surprising that fictional novels about Bowie would often achieve historical credibility. In *Three Roads to the Alamo* (1998) noted historian William C. Davis wrote, "Vague stories later surfaced of [Bowie's] dalliances with a Creole girl named Judalon de Bornay [and] an Acadian woman named Sibil [*sic*] Cade . . . ." However Mr. Davis could find no census records to support their existence. That was hardly surprising. He was looking in the wrong place for these ladies.

Sybil Cade was a fictional character who first appeared in Monte Barret's 1946 novel *Tempered Blade*. The equally fictional Judalon de Bornay made her debut in Paul Wellman's 1951 novel *The Iron Mistress*. Virginia Mayo portrayed her in the movie of the same title released the following year.

Horace Shelton, not the first or last writer to confuse Bowie fact and fiction, listed both women as Bowie's historical lovers in his November 1951 publication *Under Texas Skies*. Virgil Baugh also ignored their fictional origins and listed Sybil and Judalon as "rumors" in *Rendezvous at the Alamo* (1960). Clifford Hopewell, in *James Bowie: Texas Fighting Man* (1994), wrote that Bowie was "reported to have had hectic affairs" with them. Appropriately, perhaps, Sybil and Judalon both returned to their fictional origins in the 1998 novel *Bowie*, by Randy Lee Eickhoff and Leonard C. Lewis.

The First Bowie Knife

Although an integral part of the James Bowie saga, the Bowie knife itself spawned legends and became as enigmatic and as controversial as its namesake master. More than a dozen men have been credited with its invention; accordingly there exist a broad diversity of descriptions and dimensions; and at least as many men claimed to have acquired the knife. At least part of this confusion can be reconciled by the understanding that there was not one Bowie knife. After the fame of the weapon had been established in the sandbar fight, James Bowie acquired subsequent Bowie knives. (However no knife in existence today can be positively identified as having come from James' scabbard.)

So did Rezin, who capitalized on the knife that bore his family name by presenting Bowie knives to close friends and influential acquaintances. (It is one of Rezin's presentation knives that is exhibited in the Bowie display case in the Alamo shrine.)

And so did almost everyone else, though the term "Bowie knife" had not yet been confined to its popular image—wide cross-guard and clipped, or concave, point—but applied rather generically to a diversity of knife patterns. In June 1836 the *Red River Herald* observed that after the sandbar fight, "All the steel in the country was immediately converted into Bowie Knives." Blacksmiths, gunsmiths, and surgical instrument makers diverted their attention to the public's appetite for Bowies. Sheffield, England, then the world's leading producer of fine cutlery, heard the clamoring all the way across the ocean and began churning out Bowie knives; it has been estimated that more than seventy-five percent of all Bowies carried on the American frontier were manufactured in Sheffield factories.

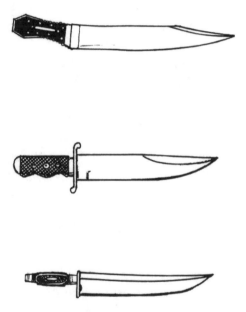

The day of the Bowie knife had come. Many of them were exceptionally ornate, mounted in nickel or coin silver with etched blades and handles of ivory, ebony, and mother-of-pearl. And, in name if not design, they had all evolved from a plain weapon—yet forged in controversy—that Bowie wielded on a Mississippi sandbar.

If James Bowie ever wrote a single word about the original Bowie knife, that document has not surfaced. Unfortunately, even those who saw the knife could not agree about its dimensions.

Caiaphas Ham remembered it had been forged from a flat file. "When finished it was not more than twelve inches long, handle and all." A foot long knife possessed a maximum blade length of eight inches.

"The length of the knife [blade] was nine and one-quarter inches, its width one and a half inches, single edge and blade not curved," wrote Rezin Bowie.

"[It] was an ordinary affair with a plain wooden handle," recalled

Three Bowie knives of the 1830s. The top one, with its coffin-shaped hilt, is generally attributed to James Black of Washington, Arkansas. The escutcheon plate bears the intriguing etching, "Bowie No. 1."

Henry Schively of Philadelphia made the second Bowie knife.

The third knife was made by Daniel Searles of Baton Rouge. A knife of this pattern that once belonged to Rezin Bowie is displayed in the Alamo shrine.

Noah Smithwick. "The blade was about ten inches long and two broad at the widest part." Smithwick penned his memoirs many years later, and the blade had probably grown with the legend.

Eyewitnesses at the sandbar fight simply referred to it as a "large knife" or a "butcher knife."

The origin of that knife remains equally controversial. Even Bowie's brothers could not agree. Rezin claimed he made the knife himself. He later wrote:

> Colonel James Bowie had been shot by an individual with whom he was at variance; and as I presumed that a second attempt would be made by the same person to take his life, I gave him the knife to be used as occasion might require, as a defensive weapon.

Curiously, Rezin's grandchildren contradicted their grandfather by asserting that Rezin's blacksmith, Jesse Clifft, actually forged the knife under Rezin's supervision.

John Bowie and Caiaphas Ham both credited the knife to a blacksmith from Kentucky named Lovell Snowden.

Simple odds and common logic sway the argument slightly in Snowden's favor. Rezin, who capitalized on the Bowie knife's fame with his presentation knives, claimed to have given his hunting knife to James after the altercation with Wright. However, James Bowie was thirty years old when he and Wright tangled in Bailey's Hotel. Raised in the bayous and backwoods of Louisiana, Bowie certainly would have possessed a hunting knife of his own. Both John Bowie and Caiaphas Ham acknowledged that James acquired the Snowden knife some years before the incident with Wright.

Ironically, for all his schemes, James Bowie apparently never sought to profit from the one item he had transformed into one of the most popular commodities in the country.

When Did Bowie Settle in Texas?

Most previous accounts describe Bowie migrating to Texas in 1828. This popular misconception stems from a misreading of a June 26, 1828 entry in the Book of Baptisms of San Fernando Parish Church. Some historians misconstrued the handwritten name as "Santiago Buy." In fact it reads "Santiago Rox," born in South Carolina, with parents named James and Juana. Historian Robert L. Tarin Jr., descendant of Vicente Tarin, has ascertained the existence of a South Carolinian named James Ross who immigrated to Texas at that time.

James Bowie visited Texas in 1828, and perhaps again in 1829, but he did not settle there until 1830.

San Saba Silver

As with his knife and the sandbar fight, James Bowie's quest for the lost silver mines became the stuff of legends.

According to the most popular legend, Bowie got himself adopted into a Lipan Apache tribe hoping to learn the location of the lost Spanish mine. For nearly a year he lived among the tribe, often fighting side by side with them against their sworn enemy, the Comanches. A jealous and antagonistic Lipan warrior called Tres Manos (Three Hands) resented Bowie and suspected his motives. However, Bowie won over the old chief Xolic and presented him with a silver mounted rifle. Defying tribal law, Xolic revealed the location of the hidden treasure to Bowie.

Bowie promptly returned to Bexar and mounted his expedition to recover the silver. Xolic died, and Tres Manos became chief, swearing vengeance against Bowie. They faced each other in the climactic San Saba battle where Bowie killed Tres Manos.

This story was published in John Warren Hunter's 1905 *Rise and Fall of the San Saba Mission*, though obscure earlier versions may exist in late-nineteenth-century newspapers. However the historical record contradicts this legend. The three eyewitness accounts to the San Saba fight (by James and Rezin Bowie and Caiaphas Ham) clearly establish that the Apaches were not the Indians that attacked the Texians. Nor do any of the three accounts make any reference to Xolic or Tres Manos. In fact no historical documentation has yet surfaced to prove that either Apache chief ever actually existed.

Moreover, Bowie's movements in the months preceding the San Saba fight are well documented; no eleven-month gap exists in which he could have disengaged himself from civilization to live with the Apaches. Most likely the legend is a corruption of Caiaphas Ham's sojourn among the Comanches.

Yet the legend of Xolic and Tres Manos persists and has been retold in many variations. A tableau in the Lone Star Brewery's Hall of Texas History, a wax museum originally constructed for the 1968 Hemisfair, depicts Xolic and Bowie (his trademark knife in his hand) standing inside the lost mine complete with bats, a skeleton, and stacks of minted silver bars.

According to one fanciful version of the legend, the Apaches had placed a curse upon the silver. Although Bowie had learned its location, he would never be able to claim its wealth, and the secret would die with him in the Alamo.

Where was the San Saba Indian Battle?

James Bowie wrote, "the ground upon the San Saba offering no position for protection, we went about three miles north of the river and there selected a grove wherein to camp for the night." Rezin Bowie claimed that the Texian camp was six miles from the San Saba presidio. Caiaphas Ham argued for "twelve miles as the correct distance." Matthew Doyal told J. Marvin Hunter that "the party had reached a creek only two or three miles east of the old mission ruins ("Bowie's Battle Ground on the San Saba," *Frontier Times*, February 1939).

Many years later a circular rock breastworks found on Calf Creek, about twenty-five miles east of the presidio, became known as "Bowie's Fort." That was good enough for Texas. The state placed a historical marker commemorating the battle on nearby State Road 42.

But the state may have been hasty. Another circle of stones and timber found on Jackson Creek, only six miles east of the presidio, more closely conforms to the location according to Rezin Bowie's account.

And "an old battle ground near the head of Celery Creek," three miles north of the presidio, matched what Matthew Doyal told J. Marvin Hunter. Hunter quoted the reminiscences of Mrs. Mary A. Nunally of Thorp Springs, Texas, which she penned around the turn of the century:

> We moved to Menard County in the fall of 1864, and set-
> tled at Bowie Spring, where the former James Bowie had a fight
> with the Indians five miles from Menardville and three miles
> from the old Spanish fort. My father found a sabre on the battle
> ground, and made a graining knife out of it. Celery Spring was
> up the valley from where we lived; it ran about a hundred
> yards and sank in the head of the creek, then came on down
> and made Bowie Spring. It ran out of a cave, the water was
> about a foot deep and very clear and sparkling; it ran on down
> to the San Saba River near the old Spanish fort.

Yet other treasure hunters insisted they had found Thomas McCaslin's grave near Silver Creek, eight miles west of the presidio and three miles north of the river.

The San Saba River

H. A. Desmond, in his booklet *My Search for Las Almagres Mine Later Called the Bowie Mine* (1976), attempted to reconcile some of these different sites by suggesting a series of engagements between Bowie and the Indians.

According to Desmond, Bowie had already recovered the silver and was racing back to San Antonio. "The Indians overtook the fleeing men about two and a half miles short of the San Saba River about seven miles west of the ruins of the Mission San Luis de las Amarillas..." Desmond wrote, and although he does not mention Silver Creek by name, he has placed Bowie in that immediate vicinity. There, taking refuge in a thicket, the Texians erected a "barricade of brush and rocks." Thomas McCaslin was killed in the ensuing battle and "buried in a shallow grave on the spot."

Then according to Desmond, under cover of darkness Bowie's men "moved quite a distance southeast, erected a second barricade, and fought the Indians again. Here Desmond speculates that Bowie buried the silver along with the body of a fallen Indian.

Then, again after dark, the Texians slipped away. "Soon they came to a large spring at the head of a creek," wrote Desmond, apparently describing what is now called Bowie Creek, and "the party followed the creek until it flowed into the San Saba River." They continued down river until the war party again caught up with them. "From this thicket near Calf Creek, they fought the last skirmish with the Indians," Desmond concluded.

Perhaps Desmond had heard this story. Perhaps he concocted it. While it does incorporate several of the alleged battle sites, the account lacks any historical basis.

But perhaps Bowie and his men did not want to provide a historical basis for what really happened on the San Saba. Some have speculated that the Texians deliberately left conflicting reports to protect the site of the lost silver mine.

The Alamo Well

A "legend" of more recent origin suggests that Bowie not only found the San Saba treasure, he brought it with him to the Alamo.

"I could never understand what would possibly motivate 189 men to stand up to between 1,000 and 8,000 men climbing over the walls," Frank Buschbacher stated in the *San Antonio Light* (August 22, 1992).

And why, Buschbacher wondered, did Santa Anna even bother with the Alamo, a post denounced by most historians as having no strategic importance?

Buschbacher claimed to have gotten the answers from Maria Gomez—variously described as a curator and prophetess—in Culima, Mexico. Señora Gomez claimed she had never been to the Alamo. However, she told Buschbacher that she knew the Texians had stashed a treasure in the Alamo's well.

Buschbacher concluded that Bowie had transported the San Saba silver to the Alamo. To Buschbacher, that gave the Texians a comprehensible reason to defend the old mission—and Santa Anna a justification to besiege it. But after the battle, Santa Anna did not find the bulk of the treasure where Bowie had hidden it in the Alamo's well.

Buschbacher persuaded the Archaeology Department at St. Mary's University in San Antonio to excavate the site of the well. However skeptical they might have been about a legendary lost treasure, the university archaeologists eagerly accepted the excuse to dig around the Alamo, knowing that any artifacts they found would constitute a historical treasure.

The excavation, which finally began in February 1995, received national exposure on the television program *Unsolved Mysteries*. Unfortunately the Alamo well dig proved to be as anticlimactic as the opening of Al Capone's vault. Only some small shards and corroded fragments were recovered.

The San Saba silver had eluded yet another treasure hunter.

James Bowie—Highwayman?

J. Frank Dobie got the story in 1927 from Aaron Moss, whose father, Matthew, claimed to have known Bowie in San Antonio ("How Jim Bowie Got His Silver," reprinted in *Gold* magazine, 1970 Annual).

A generation later C. F. Eckhardt heard basically the same story from Ralph A. Doyal, whose grandfather, Matthew, had fought beside Bowie in the San Saba fight (*The Lost San Saba Mines*, 1982).

Dobie wrote:

> Jim Bowie, as Aaron Moss's father used to tell it, was the town drunkard in San Antonio when the elder Moss knew him, but generally was always in funds from the sale of silver bullion. Every few months he would disappear from his haunts for a few weeks and come back with more bullion, always explaining that he had a silver mine up San Saba way. Finally he explained the mystery of the bullion to Moss and invited him to join the next expedition.

But according to the story told by the younger Moss, his father and Bowie did not go to a lost mine. Instead they hijacked a Mexican mule train carrying bullion to the United States.

Eckhardt related a similar story. He also reported that the Bowie brothers lived off "bar silver, which they allegedly got from a secret Indian mine...." But again, according to Eckhardt, the silver did not actually originate in a mine. The San Saba story that Ralph Doyal heard from his grandfather, Matthew, "differs radically from the accepted version," Eckhardt wrote:

> The purpose of the expedition, according to Matt Doyal, was not to hunt for a lost mine, scout for Indians, examine land, explore the country, or any of the other reasons given by historians, but rather to steal three or four mules from a Mexican silver train.

However J. Marvin Hunter, publisher of *Frontier Times*, knew old Matthew Doyal personally and cited Doyal as an "authority" for Hunter's article, "Bowie's Battle Ground on the San Saba" (*Frontier Times*, February 1939). "[Doyal's] account of the battle coincides with that given by Rezin P. Bowie," Hunter wrote.

Did Doyal tell Hunter one story and his grandson, Ralph, another? Or did Ralph Doyal read Dobie's earlier account about hijacking silver mule trains and, for some reason, attribute that story to his grandfather?

The weight of historical evidence suggests the latter. First, the story that James Bowie ever lived off silver bullion, though repeated in both these accounts, lacks any historical basis. Rather, in the hard times, Bowie lived off Beramendi wealth and influence. He had married his "silver mine."

Second, no reports have surfaced that Mexican pack trains of silver were repeatedly robbed during the years Bowie lived in Texas. In fact, both Dobie and Eckhardt concede that they cannot document that the Mexicans ever transported silver bullion overland across Texas in those years. Specifically to avoid the threat of highwaymen and hostile Indians, Mexican authorities were much more inclined to ship bullion by sea.

James Bowie, the son-in-law of Vice-Governor Beramendi—and who was writing official reports to Ramon Musquiz, the political *jefe* of Bexar—never robbed Mexican mule trains. In 1831 he went looking for a lost mine. He probably never found it. But one hundred sixty-four Indians found him.

And the Bowie legend grew.

Part Three: *Revolution*

Chapter 12: *Tenoxtitlan*

"The affairs of Texas are understood by only you and me, and we alone are able to regulate them," Brigadier General Manuel de Mier y Teran—scholar, soldier, and patriot—once wrote to his friend Stephen F. Austin. Both men sought to preserve Texas as a Mexican province. However Mier y Teran did not understand Texas—or its stubbornly independent colonists—as well as he thought he did. Tragically, his efforts to retain Mexican control over Texas would ignite a long fuse that would sputter relentlessly toward the powder keg of conflict.

Mier y Teran had been born in Mexico City in 1789. Soon after graduating from the College of Mines in 1811, he joined the fight for independence from Spain. He subsequently served in the first constituent congress in 1822, and two years later he was promoted to brigadier general in the Mexican army.

In 1827 President Guadalupe Victoria appointed Mier y Teran to lead the *Comision de Limites*. Specifically, Mier y Teran was to determine the U.S.-Mexican border between the natural boundaries afforded by the Red and Sabine Rivers. He also had been instructed to garner information on the natural resources of the region and to accumulate data concerning the inhabitants—especially Indians and the Anglo-American colonists.

For two years Mier y Teran traveled through Texas in a silver mounted coach. During that period President Victoria retired from office and President Pedraza's election was overturned by revolution.

Mier y Teran returned to Mexico in 1829, just in time to join Santa Anna in the defeat of the Spanish invasion at Tampico. Santa Anna proudly recalled, "I was promoted to General of Division and acquired the emblems of rank, which were pinned on me by General Manuel de Mier y Teran."

The most historically significant aspects of the report Mier y Teran submitted on his Texas expedition focused on the Anglo colonists who greatly outnumbered the *Tejano* natives. Mier y Teran conceded that he had not sensed any revolutionary tendencies among the colonists. But he expressed great concern that the Anglos had refused to assimilate into the Mexican culture. They had resisted Catholicism and continued to practice, although sometimes discreetly, their Protestant religions. And they had retained their English language, teaching it in their schools rather than Spanish. With Texas dominated by a United States population, practicing a United States lifestyle, on the southwestern border of the land-hungry United States, its future as a Mexican territory seemed very tenuous. "Either the government occupies Texas now, or it is lost forever," Mier y Teran concluded.

Such a report might not have alarmed the old federalist warrior President Vicente Guerrero. He had become passive and lethargic in his latter years. Too lethargic for the centralists. Vice President Anastacio Bustamante promptly disposed of the president through the traditionally expedient method of rebellion. Guerrero joined the sad roster of former Mexican leaders whose political career terminated in front of a firing squad. Bustamante declared himself president, though he exercised the absolute powers of a dictator. General Mier y Teran succeeded him as commandant general of the eastern provinces.

The newly enthroned centralists reacted vigorously to Mier y Teran's report. The result was the Law of April 6, 1830. Bustamante rewarded Mier y Teran by appointing him Federal Commissioner of Colonization with authority to oversee the instigation and enforcement of the new law.

It would be a thankless and frustrating job. Mier y Teran had sought only to "Mexicanize" Texas. He had recommended that new military garrisons be established to help maintain the three-way peace between the *Tejanos*, colonists, and Indians. More important, Mier y Teran intended the forts to serve as anchors, attracting new settlements of industrious Mexican and European immigrants who would offset the Anglo majority.

However, the centralists had turned Mier y Teran's recommendations into a law certain to antagonize the Anglo settlers. The centralists decided to man the military garrisons, at least in part, with convict soldiers. They would enforce the harsh provisions of the new law: repealing unfulfilled *empresario* contracts; prohibiting the introduction of new slaves; and worst of all, sealing the border to any further immigration from the United States. As a soldier, Mier y Teran could only comply with his orders.

The Law of April 6, 1830 created a stir across Texas. Austin managed to keep a tight rein on his colonists, curbing any talk of insurrection, as he wrote directly to Mier y Teran for verification. Almost apologetically, Mier y Teran assured Austin that only the colonies with fewer than a hundred setters would have their contracts suspended. Thus Austin and DeWitt, at least, could continue their operation. And Mier y Teran promised that he would order his garrison commanders in Texas not to provoke either the colonists or the Indians. Beyond that there was little he could offer, but it was enough for the moment to allow Austin to mitigate the crisis—if not the tensions.

In keeping with his philosophy of "Mexicanizing" Texas, Mier y Teran selected traditional Mexican names for the new garrisons. Anahuac, named for an ancient Aztec capital, would be established in 1831 at Galveston Bay. It was the best natural harbor in Texas, near enough to Louisiana to effectively guard the United States border, and conveniently centered between the Anglo settlements that stretched from Nacogdoches down the coastal plain to Gonzales. Anahuac also would serve as the first port in Texas to collect customs, since the colonists' seven-year duty-free exemption had expired.

Velasco, named after a Mexican general, would be the custom port at the mouth of the Brazos. Fort Teran, named for the general himself, on the Neches River below Nacogdoches would guard the border, controlling illegal immigration and smuggling.

But first would come Tenoxtitlan. General Mier y Teran had preserved his most ambitious designs for this post. He would locate it midway on the "upper road" between Nacogdoches and Bexar, and he planned to man it with four hundred *soldados*, rendering it a stronghold "impregnable to attack by the North Americans." Immigrants from Mexico and Europe settled in the security of its walls, and the community would grow and prosper. "In my opinion this point, if it is developed, will in time become the capital of all Texas," Mier y Teran predicted.

He could hardly wait to get this dream capital realized. No time to send troops up from Mexico. On April 24, 1830, he dispatched orders to Lieutenant Colonel Francisco Ruiz, commander of the Alamo Company, to establish and garrison the new post of Tenoxtitlan.

In his youth Ruiz had battled Indians raids and Spanish royalists. From his protracted exile in Natchitoches he had traded weapons to the tribes he had once fought so that they could continue his war against the Spanish. But now the old warrior was forty-seven years old and feeling every year of his age. Yet dutifully he obeyed his orders. On June 25 he led his cavalry company, a hundred men with an ox cart and a mule train, out of the Alamo's gate and away from Bexar. Private Manuel Tarin rode with the company. So did Private Toribio Losoya. With their departure, the namesake mission that had served as their barracks again fell into disuse and abandonment.

Ruiz did not find a suitable site on the upper road. With their machetes and axes, his men hacked their way through the steaming underbrush along the river, until Ruiz discovered a second river crossing. Here, on the west bank of the Brazos, twelve miles above the road and one hundred miles above San Felipe, the Alamo Company laid out Tenoxtitlan.

Mier y Teran had wanted the fort constructed of stone, but stone was not readily available in the river bottoms. Instead logs would be used for the buildings, only the first of many disappointments that Tenoxtitlan would provide Mier y Teran.

Ruiz completed the compound by the fall of 1830, and his *soldados* moved from their temporary shelters into the fort. A few weeks later more than fifty immigrants arrived from Tennessee in their covered wagons. Major Sterling C. Robertson, who led the emigrants, flourished a colonization contract. One of the Tennesseans, Dr. Thomas Wooton, graciously offered to treat some *soldados* who had taken ill.

Ruiz knew that the unfulfilled colonization grants had been revoked by the Law of April 6, 1830. Therefore these North Americans had entered Texas illegally. It was his duty to expel them. But Ruiz saw little difference between the centralist regime and the Spanish royalists he had once battled. Like many *Tejanos* he despised the Law of April 6, 1830 almost as much as the Anglo colonists.

"I cannot help seeing the advantages which, to my thinking, would result if we admitted honest, hard-working people, regardless of what country they came from, . . . even hell itself," he wrote.

Ruiz offered the temporary shelters his *soldados* had just abandoned to the Tennessee colonists. In the meantime he could delay their expulsion by writing to Mexico for specific instructions.

It took three months for the anticipated orders to arrive from Mexico City. "Turn them over to the Military Commandant of the Town of Nacogdoches so that he may transport them without fail to the other side of the Sabine."

Ruiz pondered for a moment, then scribbled a letter back. He had only heard about these Tennesseans. He had not actually seen them and did not know where they were. Nor could he try to find them, because his horses were in such a "fatal" condition.

Ruiz's duplicity saved the Robertson Colony. But he had only partially lied in his letter. His horses truly were in poor condition. So were his men.

The promised reinforcements that would boost his force to four hundred *soldados* had never arrived. Nor had the settlers. Nor had additional provisions. Shortly after establishing Tenoxtitlan, he had written, "We are already running short of soldiers, and soon the supplies will begin to play out."

The shortage of soldiers resulted primarily from desertions. Private Manuel Tarin deserted twice. Both times he was recaptured, but he received nothing worse than a reprimand. With so few men, Ruiz could not afford to incarcerate or execute anyone.

Then the supplies finally played out. The *soldados* of the Alamo Company had to forage through the swampy Brazos bottoms for sustenance. In the summer of 1832, the commander at Anahuac pleaded for reinforcements to help quell an uprising. Ruiz sadly responded that he had no *soldados* to spare; his men were out somewhere scrounging for food.

"I cannot find the words to describe the present condition of my garrison," Ruiz lamented. "Suffice it to say that my lot is a very sad one, and I do not know what will become of this establishment."

The answer came soon. Ruiz himself collapsed from illness, and on August 22, 1832, he feebly ordered the company to return to the Alamo. Private Toribio Losoya was returning to the place of his birth and, though he could not know it then, the place of his death.

Ironically, Tenoxtitlan, intended as a barrier to further Anglo immigration, would linger for several decades as a modest Anglo settlement.

In 1832, the same year that the Alamo Company pulled out of Tenoxtitlan, a bachelor from Georgia named Eliel Melton arrived in the settlement. He had entered Texas three years earlier and worked as a merchant in the tiny community of Nashville-on-the-Brazos. Within a few years destiny would send him to the Alamo to join Losoya and the rest of the motley garrison under the command of a twenty-six-year-old attorney named William Barret Travis.

Chapter 13: *Travis*

Twelve-year-old Berwick Travis exhaled slowly and fought back tears as the court in Loudon County, Virginia, rendered its decision. His petition had been denied. Despite his charge that Robert Watson had violated their agreement, young Berwick must remain his indentured servant for another nine years.

This minor courtroom drama occurred in 1763. Seven centuries earlier a Norman knight, said to be Berwick's ancestor, crossed the English Channel and helped King William defeat Harold's Saxons at the Battle of Hastings. After the Norman Conquest, the knight claimed Tulketh Castle, near Preston, England, as his prize. His name, as it appeared on both the Battle Abbey Roll and his epitaph at Preston, was simply Travers.

But names evolved, especially in early America, and perhaps young Travis was descended from Travers. To be sure, servitude in the Virginia backwoods, sleeping in the corner of a crude log cabin, was far removed from being master of a castle. But with a knight's determination Berwick Travis endured the next nine years. Then he promptly moved down to the wilderness along the Saluda River in South Carolina.

His first name also evolved. Over the years Berwick became Barrick and then, finally, Barret.

Travis possessed a strong work ethic. He acquired a fair amount of land and managed to save some money. At the time of his death in 1812, he was worth over four thousand dollars, a respectable showing for an honest backwoods farmer who had started with nothing.

Barret Travis had named his wife, Ann, and second son, Alexander, as the executors of his estate. Barret had chosen Alexander over his older son, Mark, because of Alexander's unquestioned integrity. In 1809, at the age of nineteen, Alexander became a Baptist preacher, riding a small circuit to the pioneer churches in the vicinity. By the time of his father's death three years later, he had already acquired a formidable reputation. In later years he won further acclaim for helping to establish churches and schools.

In contrast his older brother, Mark, though a hard working farmer, generally was regarded by the family as "something of a rounder." Sometime prior to his June 1, 1808 marriage to Jemima Stallworth, Mark Travis fathered an illegitimate son named Taliaferro. To his credit, Mark accepted responsibility, and he and Jemima adopted the child as their own. (In fact Taliaferro's mother was never identified. Therefore the possibility exists that Jemima herself was the mother, though traditionally she is regarded as Taliaferro's stepmother.)

In 1809 Jemima gave birth to their first legitimate child. William Barret Travis was born at his parents' modest farm some four miles from the Red Bank Baptist Church, in what was then Edgefield (later Salud) County. Historians quibble over his exact birth date; it was either August 1 or August 9. The inscription in the family Bible identified him as William B. Travis, the middle initial obviously honoring his paternal grandfather.

The more affluent Bonham family lived four miles away. They had a son, James Butler, two years older than William Barret. Legend, without historical documentation, describes the two boys as close friends during their early years, though Taliaferro actually was closer in age to young Bonham. Certainly James Bonham and William Travis became acquainted, possibly during services in the old wood frame church, and they may have played together during the social activities that attracted all the families living in pioneer communities.

While cavorting in their youthful innocence, neither William Barret Travis nor James Butler Bonham could envision that they would meet their destinies together. In a distant Mexican province called Texas. In another sort of church called the Alamo.

Their fateful reunion would come after a long separation. When William was nine years old, Mark Travis loaded what possessions he could fit into a wagon, abandoned everything else, and joined the westward migration. Jemima and her youngest children rode in the creaking wagon. William and Taliaferro trudged alongside. They followed the Federal Road across Georgia, forded the Chattahoochee River, and entered Alabama. Mark Travis settled his family in Conecuh County in the lower part of the state.

On December 3, 1821, the state legislature recognized the aptly named frontier community of Sparta as Conecuh's first county seat. Only five days later Sparta Academy was established, with Alexander Travis serving as a trustee. There, William Travis, who would later compose some of the most dramatic correspondence in American history, received his first formal schooling.

He was an avid student. The curriculum extended beyond the basic "Three R's" to Greek and Latin and philosophy. Perhaps the romantic literature of Sir Walter Scott and the popular young gothic poet George Gordon, Lord Byron, made the strongest impression on the young scholar. Scott's chivalrous knights in shining armor may have reminded Travis of his own alleged ancestor, Travers of Tulketh. However Travis' later life would emulate more closely the classic Byronic hero—a defiant, brooding protagonist haunted by some dark, mysterious sin from his past.

Travis decided to further his education at the academy of Professor William H. McCurdy, located in Claiborne, thirty miles to the west. Nestled on the east bank of the Alabama River, Claiborne had become the county seat of the newly formed Monroe County. Yet it had no courthouse. The two-story, white frame Masonic Hall, perched on the high bluff above the river, provided space in its lower floor for all court proceedings. Nor was there a Baptist church in town, so the Baptist preachers—including circuit riding Alexander Travis—also held their services in the Masonic Hall.

The river traffic had made Claiborne a boomtown with a population rapidly approaching one thousand. Here Travis, still in his late teens, saw elegantly attired gentlemen and ladies riding in fine carriages. And here, also, he saw the dark side of civilization, the saloons and brothels and gambling houses.

In some respects Caliborne was but a smaller, poorer version of Natchez, where James Bowie's fame had been launched on a bloodstained sandbar. Similarly Claiborne would provide the first defining moment in Travis' life, not in combat, but in courtroom drama.

Already he had rejected his father's profession. Travis had been to the city, and he would never go back to the farm. He was proud, he had ambitions, and dirt did not figure into his future—neither as farmer, nor planter, nor land speculator.

A friend later remembered that Travis "hungered and thirsted for fame—not the kind of fame which satisfies the ambition of the duelist and desperado, but the exalted fame which crowns the doer of great deeds in a good cause."

First he tried teaching, either at Professor McCurdy's Academy or at Claiborne Academy. Or perhaps they were one and the same; the records remain unclear. Alexander Travis may have encouraged this pursuit. At the very least Travis sought to emulate his uncle's prestige.

However Travis' career in education lasted less than a year. Certainly he enjoyed wearing the clothes of a gentleman. But he came to realize that the respect he desired would take years to earn. And the money he craved would never materialize. Then, as now, teaching was not a lucrative profession.

In that one sense, at least, Travis was like Bowie. He was in a hurry to make his fortune. But Travis' Baptist upbringing would never allow him to engage in the great schemes that Bowie had perpetrated. Even so, like Bowie, Travis was willing to take risks. Only a lack of funds kept him away from the gambling tables.

And away from the whorehouses. Here the sins of the father clashed with his uncle's reverence, for Travis found his sexual urgings often in conflict with his religious background.

There was one significant result of his brief career as a teacher—Rosanna E. Cato. She was one of his students, the daughter of a farmer, and only three years younger than Travis. Hopelessly smitten, he referred to her as "the beautiful Miss Cato." She apparently liked what she saw. Travis had blue eyes, light, reddish-brown hair, and what one acquaintance described as "a fine Saxon face." At nineteen years old, he had matured into a big-boned man who stood about five feet, ten inches tall—not so tall as six-foot James Bowie—certainly not a giant like six-foot, two inch Sam Houston—but still above average height for that time. Travis and Rosanna talked of getting married just as soon as he was able to support a family.

Now Travis was more impatient than ever. He already had chosen a new profession that he felt sure would garner him wealth and prestige. He would be a lawyer. However that endeavor necessitated that he devote at least a year to "reading law"—serving an apprenticeship—under a practicing attorney.

Claiborne had plenty of lawyers, but Judge James Dellet reigned as the most prominent. Like Travis, he had migrated from South Carolina to Alabama in 1818. The next year he was elected to the first of three terms in the Alabama House of Representatives and served as its first Speaker. In later years he was destined to become a U.S. Congressman. In the interim years he engaged in private practice and served as a circuit court judge.

Uncle Alexander's influence probably persuaded Dellet to accept Travis as a pupil. Travis must have appreciated the honor of having as a mentor so formidable a figure as Dellet. Travis reviewed cases and ran errands. But reading law provided no income, and his lust for Rosanna grew.

Impetuously he initiated a second career as a newspaper publisher and editor, establishing the weekly *Claiborne Herald* on May 16, 1828. "Thou shalt not muzzle the ox that treadeth out the corn," read the paper's motto.

Since Travis had no capital to invest and no credit, he apparently acquired the building, press, and equipment by merely assuming the debt of a defunct newspaper. In fact, at least three newspapers had already failed in Claiborne, but Travis' impatience—and arrogance—overruled caution. Though he was now in debt, the newspaper provided him a respected job and a modest income.

In the sultry evening of October 26, 1828, nineteen-year-old William Barret Travis married Rosanna, then sixteen years of age. The family Bible dates the arrival of his son, Charles Edward Travis, as August 8, 1829.

Early in 1829 Travis passed his bar examination. He had studied under Dellet for less than a year, an unusually brief period, which suggests he had immersed himself in the law. His feat was even more remarkable considering that he was simultaneously editing and publishing his newspaper. The February 27, 1829 issue of the *Herald* proudly proclaimed: "William B. Travis has established his Office for the present at the next door above the Post Office, where he may be found, at all times, when not absent on business."

He borrowed fifty-five dollars to get his practice started.

William B. Travis, Esq., continued to strive for the community's respect. In the summer of 1829 he joined the Masonic Lodge, after embellishing his age by one year to be eligible for admission. Perhaps to make himself appear more mature, he had grown a red beard.

On January 3, 1830, he received a commission as adjutant in the local militia, popularly known as the "Monroe Cavalry."

But by now he had overextended himself. It showed in the *Herald*. As typographical errors and missed deadlines became more frequent, advertisers and subscribers faded away.

His legal practice fared no better. Acquaintances brought him minor cases, but even they took their most important legal work to Dellet and the other established attorneys. The problem may have stemmed from Travis' personality more than his ability. He reportedly possessed a brusque manner, a short temper, and a limited sense of humor that he most often displayed through practical jokes that offended more often than they amused. Even Dellet skipped over Travis and recruited a recently arrived attorney, about Travis' age, as a legal partner. Usually Travis was hired to collect unpaid debts for a paltry five percent commission. In the meantime, he himself was borrowing more and more to support his family and keep his businesses afloat. And when the notes came due, there was never enough money to pay them.

"He was unquestionably an honest man, but debt will weigh down the loftiest soul, and humble the brightest intelligence," remembered a fellow attorney who knew Travis only casually. "Never have I seen a more impressive instance of depression from debts."

Travis' schedule left little time for his wife and son, a frequent source of marital discord. The stress from the accumulating debts must have aggravated his already sour disposition and further strained his relationship with Rosanna. Men mired in such desperation often spiral downward, squandering what little income they have for the briefest respites from their gloom. Never much of a drinker, Travis probably did not resort to the bottle to drive dull care away. But he may have visited the gambling houses in futile attempts to beat the odds. Or the whorehouses where painted and perfumed ladies could feign the sympathy and love absent from his marriage. Such self-destructive behavior can only be surmised, but it seems consistent with Travis' character.

Rumors later circulated about Rosanna's infidelity. She got pregnant again. Speculation subsequently arose as to whether Travis was the real father. Perhaps some justification existed for the gossip about her morality. On the other hand Rosanna made a convenient scapegoat for Travis' family and supporters—and for the later white-washers of Texas heroes.

In March 1831 William Barret Travis trudged along Main Street to the white, two-story Masonic Hall. Not for a Lodge meeting. Nor for a Baptist service. He was going to court, acting as a defense attorney in the most important trial of his brief career.

Because he was also the defendant.

The worst of it was that his own mentor, James Dellet, represented the plaintiffs who were suing for the collection of their unpaid notes.

Travis must have mulled over his strategy prior to the hearing. He knew that trying to wriggle out of his financial responsibilities would not endear him to the community, and that pained him. But his clever ploy just might impress Dellet. More important, it might keep Travis out of debtor's prison.

Travis remained seated as Dellet reviewed the charges. And he remained seated when the time came for him to respond. Legal precedent, he asserted, held that minors were not responsible for any debts they incurred. He had been under twenty-one when he had signed most of the notes before the court today. Therefore he could not be held accountable for the debts.

Travis was citing a legal tradition known as the "infancy" law, though he probably avoided that term. Dellet did not avoid it. Ordering Travis to stand and approach the jury box, Dellet presented the tall, stocky, bearded infant to the jury.

The jurors howled, completely humiliating young Travis. And then, of course, they found him guilty. Even as another court, long ago, had ruled against his grandfather.

But young Berwick Travis had abided by the court decision. William Barret Travis, Esq., had other ideas. When they came to escort him to debtor's prison, they would find that he had "Gone to Texas."

He confided in Rosanna. He had no money to leave her, but her family was hardly poor. They would look after her and Charles and the new baby when it arrived. In effect Travis had condemned her as a wife deserted to share in his public humiliation. But he said all the proper words. He still loved her. He would send for her and the children as soon as he was established in Texas.

Then, in the night, he climbed onto his large black horse and slipped out of Claiborne into the dark, surrounding woods. The difficult overland trip required two months. In May 1831 twenty-one-year-old William B. Travis arrived in San Felipe, proclaiming himself to be a twenty-two-year-old lawyer.

And single.

The abandonment of his family, or at least of his son, would be the mysterious, haunting sin from his past. Now he needed only one more element to complete the transformation into a classic Byronic hero—a cause in which he could prove his defiant courage.

> *When a man hath no freedom to fight for at home.*
> *Let him combat for that of his neighbors;*
> *Let him think of the glories of Greece and of Rome.*
> *And get knocked on his head for his labors.*
>
> *To do good to mankind is the chivalrous plan,*
> *And is always as nobly requited;*
> *Then battle for freedom whenever you can,*
> *And, if not shot or hanged, you'll get knighted.*
>
> —George Gordon, Lord Byron

Chapter 14: *Anahuac*

Anahuac, May 1832

The *soldado* on sentry duty at the new military post of Anahuac suddenly snapped alert. His long musket poised, he squinted into the night. "*¿Quién es?*" he called out tersely.

"*Amigo*," came the soft response.

A tall man wrapped in a black cape, his hat shadowing his face, quietly emerged into the dim light. He approached the gate and handed a letter to the guard. Then the tall man silently faded back into the warm, humid darkness from which he had come.

The sentry delivered the communication to Colonel Juan Bradburn, commandant at Anahuac. The letter contained an ominous warning. A hundred armed men had mustered just across the Sabine in Louisiana—a scant forty miles away. They were preparing to attack the Mexican garrison at Anahuac.

The letter bore the signature "Ballou." Bradburn probably recognized the name of one of Lafitte's pirates and presumed it was a pseudonym. But he had no reason to doubt the validity of the warning.

Colonel Juan Bradburn had become the most hated Anglo American in Texas.

His parents had christened him John Davis Bradburn at the time of his birth in Virginia forty-seven years earlier. While he was still young his family joined the great migration through the Cumberland Gap into Kentucky.

During his mid-twenties something lured him to Natchitoches and instilled him with enough local popularity to be selected a lieutenant in the Louisiana militia—in the same regiment as the Bowie brothers and the Bexareno refugees.

Immediately afterwards Bradburn served as a sergeant major in a new filibustering force raised by Henry Perry. They sailed to the Texas coast and established a headquarters, called Perry's Point, in northeastern Galveston Bay on a bluff thirty feet above the mouth of the Trinity River.

Interminable months passed—then a year—as rebel leaders bickered on strategy and targets. Finally Bradburn joined Perry and the other Anglos who cast their allegiance behind a Spanish-born liberator, Francisco Xavier Mina, who planned to reinforce the revolutionaries in Mexico.

Some three hundred fifty rebel troops followed Mina up the gangplank onto eight ships. They sailed down the coast, past the Rio Grande, to the mouth of the Santander River. But the filibusters encountered unforeseen difficulty recruiting Mexican supporters to their ranks—ironically because Mina himself was a Spaniard—a *gachupin*. In August 1817 most of the rebels were massacred when the Spanish stormed their stronghold at Fort Sombrero. Only Bradburn and a handful of others escaped annihilation.

Bradburn remained in Mexico where he soon attached himself to rebel leader Vicente Guerrero. Then, curiously, Bradburn switched his allegiance to the royalists, emerging as a colonel in the army of Agustin Iturbide. When Iturbide himself joined the fight for Mexican independence, Bradburn continued to support his commander and again fought against the Spanish. Thus, after Mexico had won its independence, former republican filibuster John Davis Bradburn had evolved into Colonel Juan Bradburn, devoted centralist and trusted aide of Emperor Agustin I.

When Iturbide abdicated and the liberal federalists came to power, Bradburn discreetly stepped back into the shadows. Then the centralists reemerged under President Bustamante, and Bradburn offered his services to General Mier y Teran.

Mier y Teran liked what he saw. Although a Mexican officer loyal to the current regime, Bradburn was an Anglo and therefore should be acceptable to the colonists and appropriately sympathetic toward them. Moreover, Bradburn's own filibustering experience made him familiar with Galveston Bay.

On October 4, 1830, Bradburn received orders to establish a fort and town, to be called Anahuac, on Galveston Bay. Bradburn already knew the ideal spot—Perry's Point.

Three weeks later Bradburn arrived at the base of the bluff with three officers and forty men. Six of the *soldados* were convicts, paroled from prison after volunteering to serve in Texas. They would be expected to perform the most strenuous labor involved in the construction of the new post.

Mier y Teran had instructed that the fort be built of brick, but with winter looming, the *soldados* hastily erected a single log building, one hundred fifty feet long and twenty feet wide. Bradburn located his quarters at one end, the guardhouse at the other, and the barracks in the center. He also had two large kilns, the size of rooms, constructed to fabricate the bricks he would need for the fort. But as soon as the kilns became operational, Bradburn sold the bricks, at five dollars a ton, to settlers moving onto the bluff. By March 1831 a community had emerged comprised of some twenty houses, seven stores, and one doctor named Nicholas Labadie. By June the town of Anahuac could boast a population of three hundred, some lured from nearby Anglo settlements, others newly arrived European immigrants.

By that time one hundred seventy *soldados* occupied the wooden quarters, and Bradburn finally began construction on the permanent brick fort. His garrison, generally idle during the months when the kilns had produced bricks for the town, suddenly found themselves ordered to perform long hours of strenuous labor, the regular *soldados* sweating alongside the handful of convict troops. Worse, Bradburn demanded perfection, and he made them rebuild anything that did not meet his high expectations. It was too much for some of the *soldados*, especially when their pay from Mexico arrived late. Desertions depleted the ranks. Even Bradburn's subordinate officers, unaccustomed to frontier duty, griped about the extent of nonmilitary work.

Mier y Teran had specified that Bradburn must not provoke the Anglo colonists. Rather Bradburn should reassure them that the fort would provide protection and help promote prosperity. But Bradburn soon proved as unpopular with the settlers as with his own *soldados*.

The colonists knew that the seven years of duty-free shipping had expired. In fairness to Bradburn, they probably would have resented any officer—Anglo or not—sent among them to initiate the collection of customs. But Bradburn also came to enforce the hated Law of April 6, 1830. He had established a military garrison in their midst, garrisoned—at least partially—by convict troops. The colonists readily attributed all local thefts to the occupying troops. A visitor to Anahuac that year described the *soldados* as "men of a most depraved character... as cowardly as they were wicked and ignorant."

Had he been endowed with honor, patience, and political tact, he eventually might have won over the colonists. But Bradburn did not possess such qualities. Rather than earning the colonists' respect, he demanded their immediate compliance. He responded to their criticisms with petty displays of authoritarianism. His arrogance only further aggravated the colonists.

When General Mier y Teran visited Anahuac in November, he became alarmed at the anti-Mexican sentiment, especially in the nearby community of Liberty, which *Tejano* officials had established as the seat of government for the encompassing Atascosito District. Mier y Teran attributed much of the dissent to a profusion of lawyers—a "plague of locusts"—who practiced in Liberty. It was bad enough that most Anglos traveled "with their political constitution in their pockets." Lawyers were even worse—generally more knowledgeable, more arrogant, and more prone to inciting unrest.

Mier y Teran must have realized that he was responsible, at least in part, for the two primary points of discord: the Law of April 6, 1830 and Colonel Juan Bradburn. But already the breach had grown too wide to be mended by mere diplomacy. Again Mier y Teran perceived the necessity of stern measures to control the colonists.

He mulled over the matter until after his departure for Monterrey. Or perhaps he merely wanted to avoid the outrage his new orders certainly would generate. Sitting in his shadowed quarters on the United States schooner *Topaz*, he dipped his quill into the inkwell and scratched his instructions on parchment to be sent back to Anahuac. Bradburn was to remove the seat of government from Liberty to Anahuac, effectively placing the local civil authority under military rule.

A second order specifically targeted the attorneys. Mier y Teran reasoned—accurately—that few, if any, of the Liberty lawyers possessed a Mexican license. It could only be obtained at the provincial capital of Saltillo, a long, arduous, and expensive journey from Liberty. Mier y Teran stipulated that anyone in the Atascosito District engaged in the practice of law must show his Mexican license to Bradburn.

On this one point, at least, Mier y Teran had been accurate. Bradburn's greatest threat came from attorneys—especially one young, newly arrived lawyer named William Barret Travis.

Travis arrived in Anahuac during the summer of 1831, just about the time of his twenty-second birthday. Another young lawyer, Patrick Churchill Jack, probably accompanied Travis on the journey from San Felipe. They would become close friends and law partners.

Most of the other attorneys in the Atascosito District lived in Liberty, but Travis and Jack took up residence in Anahuac. They were near enough to practice law before the *ayuntamiento* (town council) at Liberty. More importantly, the new customshouse at Anahuac would require legal paperwork, and paperwork required lawyers.

Travis' first clash with Bradburn arose over the issue of slavery. The Atascosito District lay below Austin's colony and therefore was subject to the abolitionist clause of the Law of April 6, 1830. This provision actually encouraged slaves in nearby Louisiana to escape their plantations and seek asylum at Anahuac. Bradburn welcomed the runaways and offered them sanctuary. Then he promptly put them to work on the construction of his fort, replacing the *soldados* who had deserted his garrison. Their new situation hardly seemed an improvement over their Louisiana bondage, but few slaves would be willing to face the severe punishments that awaited captured runaways.

In the fall of 1831 William Logan, agent for an Opelousas, Louisiana, plantation owner, confronted Bradburn and demanded the return of two runaway slaves. Bradburn refused. He smugly advised Logan to present the matter to the Mexican embassy in Washington. Before returning to Louisiana, Logan hired the new young lawyer William Barrret Travis to deal with the matter.

Travis, too, gained an audience with Bradburn. Travis could not argue from any position of strength, but he probably asserted that slaves qualified as legal property, and even the Mexican government had guaranteed protection of private property. This time Bradburn responded that the two slaves in question had enlisted as *soldados* and had requested Mexican citizenship. Travis' notorious temper may have erupted, but there was nothing he could do. For the moment. But Bradburn later would recall, "One matter which caused me much trouble and brought down the hatred of the community against me was the protection I gave to two escaped slaves."

A winter descended on the Texas coast as cold as the relationship between Bradburn and the Anglo colonists. Despite the slave labor and despite the arrival of new troops that raised the garrison strength to over two hundred *soldados*, the fort remained unfinished.

Several concurrent events rapidly escalated the tensions. After returning to Monterrey on the schooner *Topaz*, Mier y Teran commissioned Captain Nicholas Rider to take Colonel Domingo de Ugartechea and his troops and supplies back to Texas. Mier y Teran had ordered Ugartechea to establish Fort Velasco, the new customshouse at the mouth of the Brazos.

Rider's American crew knew that the *Topaz* also carried three thousand dollars. In February 1832, as the schooner neared Galveston, a squall blew into the gulf. It provided the opportunity the crew had been awaiting. As the ship rolled on the rough sea, they advised the *soldados* to take shelter below decks. Then the crew barred the hatches, trapping the Mexican troops in the ship's hold. When Captain Rider confronted the mutineers, they simply cast him into the tall, lunging waves. Then the crew prepared the ship's rowboat. Once the storm had subsided, they planned to scuttle the *Topaz*, letting the hungry ocean swallow all witnesses and evidence of their crime.

But the crew had underestimated the resourcefulness of the *soldados*. They managed to escape the ship's hold and overpower the mutineers. When the *Topaz* reached Anahuac, Ugartechea turned the manacled Anglo crew over to Bradburn. Then the ship completed its voyage to the Brazos.

The prisoners insisted that they were innocent; the *soldados* themselves had perpetrated the mutiny and then blamed the crew. In the hostile climate that Bradburn had generated, many colonists naively accepted the story. They accused Bradburn of being too willing to believe the Mexican account of the mutiny, and they resented his locking up American sailors. Town residents frequently visited the guardhouse, offering sympathy and food to the incarcerated crew.

To make matters worse for Bradburn, about that same time two of his convict *soldados* stayed too long in the town tavern. Stumbling back to the fort, they reportedly committed that most grievous affront to Southern chivalry—the molestation of an Anglo woman.

On April 26 a small mob formed. First they turned their wrath against an Anglo male who allegedly had seen the assault and failed to intervene. They tarred and feathered the hapless witness and paraded him around on the traditional log. Then the rabble marched to the fort and demanded that Bradburn surrender the two *soldados*. Secure behind his assembled troops, their bayonets fixed, Bradburn refused. The men backed away, but the disturbances continued late into the night. "The town of Anahuac was so excited that it was necessary to call out the troops at two o'clock in the morning to stop disorders stemming from this incident," Bradburn remembered.

Travis is not specifically mentioned as a participant in the disturbance. But considering his thirst for approval from his community, he may well have been one of the instigators.

He almost certainly helped organize the May 1 meeting that created a local militia. Travis had been in Texas almost a year. He had made friends in the region, men like Nicholas Labadie, the town doctor; Warren D. C. Hall, Bowie's old comrade-in-arms; *empresario* David G. Burnet, who would later serve as the provisional president of the Republic of Texas; Colonel James Morgan, a wealthy plantation owner and businessman; and Monroe

Edwards, a clerk at Morgan's store. Some of them affectionately called him "Buck" Travis. But he yet lacked the charisma, the popularity, and the prestige to lead men. The assembly passed over him and selected his friend and partner Patrick C. Jack as militia captain.

The colonists advised Bradburn that the militia had been formed to protect them from Indian raids. Bradburn knew better. His *soldados* would protect the colonists from Indians—except that there had been no hostile tribes in that region since the virtual extermination of the Karankawas. This militia had been formed to protect the colonists from Bradburn and his troops.

Moreover, Bradburn could not ignore the fact that the organization of a militia violated Mexican law. He dispatched his *soldados* to arrest Patrick Jack. Jack was incarcerated, not in the guardhouse with the *Topaz* mutineers, but instead on a schooner anchored in the bay.

The arrest of Jack ignited Travis' short temper. Now it had become personal. Yet, again, Travis could do nothing against Bradburn's authority. Nothing official.

It fell to another lawyer—a largely forgotten giant of Texas history popularly known as "Three-Legged Willie"—to affect Jack's release. He had been born Robert McAlpin Williamson twenty-six years earlier in Georgia. At the age of fifteen he had been crippled by an illness that paralyzed his right leg at a ninety-degree angle bent back at the knee. He attached a wooden appendage to the knee, wore custom tailored trousers that accommodated his three legs, and joined the Georgia bar at the age of nineteen. Shortly afterwards he left for Texas, settling in San Felipe. There he supplemented his legal income by establishing a newspaper called the *Cotton Plant*—with more success than Travis had enjoyed in Alabama.

Williamson's infirmity did not impair his skills as a horseman. When he heard of Jack's arrest, he galloped down to

Robert McAlpin "Three-Legged Willie" Williamson

Anahuac and hobbled into Bradburn's office. There he simply announced that he would kill Bradburn if Jack was not released.

Bradburn immediately ordered his *soldados* to free the imprisoned lawyer.

Perhaps something about "Three-Legged Willie" had cowed Bradburn. Or perhaps Bradburn had begun to realize how precarious his situation had become. Even as the Anglo colonists united against him, he had received disturbing reports from Mier y Teran that the federalists had launched a new rebellion against the centralist regime in Mexico.

If Bradburn had hoped that Jack's release would ease the tensions at Anahuac, he soon was disappointed. He still held the *Topaz* mutineers in his guardhouse. On May 10 the *New Orleans Louisiana Advertiser* printed a letter charging that Bradburn had unjustly incarcerated innocent American sailors and brutally denied them adequate food and medication.

The letter further noted that Bradburn was providing asylum for runaway slaves from Louisiana.

It was signed "An American Citizen."

An arriving schooner probably delivered a copy of the newspaper to Bradburn. It could only have added to his mounting distress that now bordered on paranoia. Now he must fear not only the local colonists, but also intervention from the United States. Thus he was suitably primed, a few days later, when the night sentry presented him with the letter from "Ballou" which had been delivered by the tall man in the black cape.

Bradburn could not doubt the validity of the letter's warning. A hundred armed men, just across the Sabine in Louisiana, preparing to attack the Mexican garrison at Anahuac. Bradburn hastily dispatched patrols to scout to the east.

The patrols all returned with the same report. They had not seen any armies. Nor did any of the settlers along the Sabine have any knowledge of an armed mob.

Bradburn exhaled slowly. The letter had been a hoax. But his relief transformed into fury. Who had perpetrated the insidious prank? Then, suddenly, he knew. The whole plot reeked of William Barret Travis.

No historical evidence supports Bradburn's conclusion that Travis was responsible. Many people knew of the situation in Anahuac and could have penned the letters. But Travis certainly qualified as a primary suspect for the anonymous "American Citizen" who had written to the *New Orleans Louisiana Advertiser*. The letter would have been in retaliation for Jack's arrest and for Bradburn's refusal to release the slaves. After all, Travis still represented the slave owner's agent, William Logan.

And Travis could have continued the antagonism by penning the "Ballou" letter. Indeed Travis himself probably had been the tall man in the dark cape who delivered the letter to the sentry.

In a literal sense Travis' quill always would prove more potent than the cavalry saber he had yet to don.

Bradburn promptly dispatched his *soldados* to arrest Travis. They found him in his legal office with Patrick Jack. Jack followed the procession back to the fort. This time it was Jack's turn to remonstrate against the arrest of his friend and partner, undoubtedly demanding that Bradburn release Travis or face an insurrection. But this time intimidation did not work. Bradburn had had enough of lawyers. He ordered Jack incarcerated in the guardhouse with Travis, and he threatened other protestors—including Jack's brother, William H. Jack of San Felipe—with the same fate.

Perhaps the only man who might have been able to avert the impending catastrophe was not then in Texas. Stephen F. Austin was serving in the legislature in Saltillo. In his absence other honorable men did what they could.

Colonel James Morgan raced to the fort and pledged all of his extensive holdings as bail. At Velasco, Colonel Ugartechea concluded that Bradburn had overreacted. He dispatched Lieutenant Ignacio Dominguez to Anahuac to encourage Bradburn to relinquish the prisoners to civil authorities. Father Michael Muldoon, the ever-cooperative priest at San Felipe, offered himself in exchange for Travis and Jack. But Bradburn stubbornly rebuffed all these efforts to defuse the crisis. Let the revolution begin.

It almost did, right there in Anahuac in the latter part of May 1832. Bradburn informed his prisoners that he would send them to Matamoras to stand trial before a military court. Travis realized that he would have little chance of vindication in a military court already predisposed to his guilt as a traitor fomenting sedition. Here was a bitter irony. Having fled Alabama to escape debtors prison, he now faced a more dismal future rotting in a distant Mexican dungeon.

Colonel Morgan arranged for a slave woman named Harriet to bring food and fresh clothing to the prisoners. (Morgan later would be implicated in a tenacious Texas legend regarding another of his slaves, Emily, who would be celebrated, inaccurately, as the "Yellow Rose of Texas.") Harriet also passed notes between Travis and Monroe Edwards, Morgan's store clerk, plotting an escape attempt. Unfortunately the guards intercepted one of the communiqués, and Bradburn subsequently had Edwards confined with his friends.

Fearing that the colonists would attempt a rescue from the guardhouse, Bradburn ordered his *soldados* to transform the stronger and more secure brick kilns into a prison. Then two cannon were rolled into position at the entrance to the kilns. The entire garrison mustered out to escort the prisoners on the short march. Perched on a fence, Dr. Labadie was among the civilians who witnessed the procession. Labadie called out words of reassurance to Travis. Help was on the way, Labadie shouted brazenly.

Travis responded with a gallant bow. He had finally won the community respect he had always craved, and he knew it. Then the points of bayonets brutally prodded him forward.

He was shoved into one of the kilns. The thick iron door clanged shut, enveloping him in a sweltering, oppressive gloom.

However Dr. Labadie had been correct. Efforts already were underway to rescue the prisoners. All of Texas reverberated from the hoofbeats of riders calling for men to assemble at Lynch's Ferry on the lower San Jacinto River. During the first week in June groups of armed colonists marched determinedly toward Anahuac. John Austin, a distant relative of the *empresario*, led some thirty men from Brazoria where he served as *alcalde*. A contingent from San Felipe fell in behind their former *alcalde* Francis W. (Frank) Johnson. Soon more than a hundred men had assembled at Lynch's Ferry, only a few miles west of Anahuac. Warren D. C. Hall was there. So was "Three Legged Willie" Williamson. In the militia tradition of electing their own officers, the men voted Frank Johnson as their leader. Hall was selected second-in-command.

Learning of the approaching rebel force, Bradburn dispatched his entire contingent of cavalry—all nineteen of them—to scout out the enemy. The cavalry company soon blundered into the entire Texian force, and the Mexicans quickly surrendered. Without a shot being fired, the Texians had won the first engagement.

Bradburn had created the very rebellion he had feared. At the same time his own situation became more precarious. His outer ramparts remained unfinished. His ever-fluctuating garrison had been reduced, mostly by desertion, to eighty men. He had anticipated the arrival of the schooner *Martha* from Matamoras, with reinforcements and payroll for the garrison at Anahuac. Yet when it docked in early June, the ship carried no money and only two political prisoners, Lieutenent Colonel Felix Maria Subaran and his sergeant. A communiqué from Mier y Teran provided a dismal explanation. The rebellion in Mexico was going badly for the centralists. "General Teran had told me that I could not expect aid in men or money because of the revolution in the interior," Bradburn remembered. Subaran and his sergeant were federalist sympathizers whom Mier y Teran had banished to Fort Teran.

Bradburn desperately needed men and elected to keep the two new arrivals at Anahuac, even appointing Subaran as deputy commander. Bradburn maintained that, federalists or not, they were loyal Mexican soldiers who would fight against a provincial rebellion. "And I was not wrong," he later noted.

On June 10 the colonist force, now swelled to over one hundred fifty volunteers, reached Anahuac. As the men took shelter in the nearby buildings, Frank Johnson, John Austin, and a few others approached the fort under a flag of truce. Bradburn admitted them into his headquarters.

The Texians curtly expressed their demands. They had come for the prisoners. In exchange they would release the captured Mexican cavalry. Otherwise they would reduce the fort by storm and then rescue the prisoners.

Although facing two-to-one odds, Bradburn again refused to be intimidated. He rejected the terms. Johnson and the other Texians promptly stomped out to rally their men for the attack.

Random gunfire signaled the approach of the Texian assault force. But the advance was halted—not by the two cannons mounted and waiting in front of the kilns—but rather by the view behind the artillery. The Texians could see Travis through an open kiln door. He was seated on the ground, his wrists bound to his knees. Mexican *soldados* stood around him, their muskets trained on him, the gleaming points of their bayonets poised only inches from his body.

Patrick Jack and Monroe were similarly trussed and threatened.

Then Bradburn called out that the prisoners would be shot immediately if the Texians did not withdraw.

Isolated in his dark, makeshift cell, Travis had been oblivious to the unfolding events until moments earlier when the *soldados* had burst into the kiln with their ropes and muskets. The daylight flooding through the doorway must have blinded him at first. Now that rectangle of brilliance stretching across the kiln floor acted like a spotlight. It illuminated the defiant hero in Travis. He was armed only with words, but Travis could manipulate words as skillfully as Bowie wielded his knife. He shouted to the Texians to "blaze away upon the fort." He would rather "die like a man" than serve as a hostage to Bradburn's tyranny.

As often happens in hostage situations, the lives of the captor and his victims were irrevocably intertwined. Sorely outnumbered and commanding a force characterized by low morale and dubious commitment, Bradburn's shield, his last defense, were the prisoners. To order their execution would precipitate his own.

The Texians emphasized that very point as they retreated back into the town. To wait.

The next day some of the Texians reconnoitered around the fort. A skirmish erupted. One Texian and five *soldados* fell. Again the blood of conflict stained Texas soil.

Bradburn could not afford to lose any of his troops. Moreover the fort was not equipped to endure a protracted siege. On June 12 he advised the Texians that he would surrender the prisoners within twenty-four hours. However there were two conditions that had to be met immediately. The captured Mexican cavalry must be released, and the Texians must withdraw to Turtle Bayou, north of Anahuac.

Some of the Texians suspected treachery, but Johnson decided to comply. He released the cavalry. They were, after all, of nominal value to him. Although he had attempted to trade them for Bradburn's prisoners, he had never threatened them, never attempted to barter with their lives. Moreover, they required food and guards—both of short supply. Then he withdrew his men to the bayou.

At least most of them. Militia were never known for discipline. Some thirty men stubbornly refused to evacuate the town.

That was all the excuse Bradburn needed—if he really needed an excuse—to violate the agreement. Not only did he then refuse to release Travis, Jack, and Monroe, he trained his artillery on the town. Citizens and would-be soldiers scattered for the prairie when the cannon opened fire.

Bradburn had bought himself some desperately needed time. Time to strengthen his fortifications. Time to gather reinforcements. He dispatched couriers to the other Mexican garrisons in Texas, and his force soon doubled in size to one hundred sixty *soldados*.

At Tenoxtitlan, Lieutenant Colonel Francisco Ruiz, commander of the Alamo Company, could spare no men. His starving command had scattered, scrounging for food. But then Ruiz probably did not try very hard to assemble his garrison. Like most *Tejanos*, he had little fondness for Bradburn and the centralists.

However Colonel Jose de las Piedras, the commandant at Nacogdoches, was a centralist officer. He mustered another hundred *soldados* from Nacogdoches and Fort Teran and began marching to Bradburn's relief.

Bradburn had proclaimed—and he honestly may have believed—that he was fighting against an Anglo rebellion whose goal was to separate Texas from Mexico. Certainly a few of the Texians already shared that sentiment, and, ironically, Bradburn probably swayed a few more in that direction. But the majority of Texians encamped at Turtle Bayou were colonists who perceived themselves as loyal Mexican citizens. They had been forced into armed opposition, not against Mexico, but against a corrupt agent of the Mexican government.

Of course most of the Texians regarded President Bustamante's centralist government itself as corrupt. Therefore the current federalist revolution afforded the colonists a convenient political justification for their actions. On June 13 they drafted a document known as the Turtle Bayou Resolutions. The document condemned the "present dynasty" for violating the Constitution of 1824. The colonists were not Anglos attacking a Mexican fort, but rather they were Mexican citizens who had pledged their "lives and fortunes" in the fight for the "correct interpretation and enforcement of the constitution and laws." Thus the Texians officially allied themselves with the federalist revolution.

After helping to draft the Turtle Bayou Resolutions, John Austin raced back to San Felipe with a copy of the document. His mission was twofold: rally other Texian colonists to the cause, and secure artillery for a siege on Anahuac. A contingent of men formed up at San Felipe and set out for Anahuac, dragging one cannon along with them.

Austin found a hundred more recruits—and three more cannon—at Brazoria. He also secured the services of the schooner *Brazoria*. Transporting the cannon by boat down the Brazos and along the coast would be easier and quicker than the overland route.

The only problem was the Mexican garrison at Velasco guarding the mouth of the Brazos. Previously Colonel Ugartechea had expressed reservations about Bradburn—even encouraging Bradburn to release his prisoners to civilian authority. But Ugartechea, a centralist, could hardly sanction a Texian assault on Anahuac. Though outnumbered by nearly two-to-one odds, he refused to parley. The Texians would have to fight their way past Velasco.

The first real battle between Texian colonists and the Mexican army commenced after dark on June 26, 1832. Austin led two-thirds of his force in a land assault against Velasco's stockade walls while the three cannon mounted on the *Brazoria* engaged in an artillery duel with the fort's big guns. Both sides fought determinedly; both sides suffered dead and wounded. But by the next day the Mexicans had expended their ammunition. Austin allowed Ugartechea to surrender with honor. The *soldados* retained their side arms and were paroled back to Mexico.

In a sense, Ugartechea had won. His artillery had damaged the *Brazoria* to such an extent that the schooner could not deliver the cannon to Anahuac. But by then it did not matter. The crisis at Anahuac had ended.

When Colonel Piedras from Nacogdoches reached Anahuac on July 1, he faced two grim realities. First, the Texians outnumbered the Mexican forces. Second, the colonists had politically outmaneuvered him by shrewdly declaring themselves part of the national federalist revolution.

Piedras had no great fondness for the Texian colonists. He believed that the centralists eventually would triumph in Mexico and then sterner measures could be forced on the rebellious Texians. But for now, he concluded, the most effective way to restore peace—and hopefully undermine the passion for revolution—would be total appeasement. Thus instead of reinforcing Bradburn, Piedras relieved him of his command.

Though neither man knew it, General Mier y Teran in Mexico had realized, belatedly, the necessity of the same action. On June 29 he had scribbled a communiqué ordering Bradburn's removal. It would be one of Mier y Teran's last official actions. He did not share Piedras' confidence that the centralists would triumph. And his efforts to subjugate the Anglos in Texas had only enflamed them. Dismayed and depressed, on July 3 Mier y Teran strolled behind the Church of San Antonio in Padilla, Tamaulipas. It was the place where Emperor Iturbide had been executed. There, General Mier y Teran plunged his body down upon his own sword.

On the previous day, July 2, Piedras released all of Bradburn's prisoners, including Travis and the *Topaz* mutineers locked in the guardhouse. Travis had been imprisoned for more than a month and a half, for most of that time in the brick kilns. The long days and nights in the confined, sweltering darkness had made him harder and stronger. And more bitter.

The prisoners were remanded to the custody of the civil authorities at Liberty to stand trial for sedition. The colonists, of course, could find no legal grounds to justify a trial, not even for the murderous mutineers. Officially vindicated, Travis now could flavor his victory with vengeance.

Justifiably fearful of an outbreak of the contagious fever of rebellion back in Nacogdoches, Piedras left Anahuac on July 8. Travis and Jack arrived shortly afterwards. Bradburn, as frightened as he was humiliated, remained cloistered in the fort. Certain that Travis or one of the other Texians would assassinate him, he demanded a sentry outside his quarters.

It is doubtful that Travis would have resorted to cold-blooded murder, but he must have relished, even encouraged, Bradburn's terror.

On July 11 Travis and Jack brought a keg of whiskey into the town square and extended a magnanimous invitation to their former captors. Most of the Mexican garrison, including the federalist officer Colonel Subaran, attended the unexpected celebration. The drunken revelry continued late into the night. By the time the keg ran dry, Travis and Jack had persuaded almost all of the *soldados* to join Subaran in the rebellion against the centralist regime.

Now Bradburn could not even trust the *soldados* in the fort. "From the moment I surrendered the command, my life was continuously in danger despite there being a guard at my door," he recalled. "At night my enemies, directed by Travis, who now had control of Anahuac, would sneak up to my quarters, which made me decide to leave."

On the night of July 13 Bradburn secured a horse and galloped off into the darkness to the east. Fearful of being followed by Travis and the other vengeful Texians, he cautiously avoided the main trails and traveled "incognito." Along the way to Louisiana he passed numerous Anglos forging into Texas. They advised him they were going "to help our brothers drive the Spaniards out of Texas." Bradburn noted that a judge who lived on the Rio Matan bragged that he could easily enlist four thousand men for the campaign.

Even after he arrived safely in New Orleans on August 6, Bradburn found himself still haunted by Travis. Ten days earlier the *Louisiana Advertiser* had published an inflammatory letter from Travis, penned on July 8. The letter described the recent events at Anahuac and Velasco, obviously portraying Bradburn as a tyrant and proudly proclaiming that the "Mexicans have learned a lesson."

"Americans know their rights and will assert and protect them," Travis had written. Their constitutional and sacred guarantees were not "things to be broken and trampled under foot." Travis did not specify which national constitution he was citing.

With public sentiment against him, Bradburn soon sailed for Mexico. He arrived in time to distinguish himself in battle against the federalist rebels, and Bustamante promoted him to brigadier general. In Bradburn's official report on the Anahuac disturbances, prepared for the commandant general of the eastern interior provinces, Travis' name held a position of prominence among the cited Texian rebels for "when the time and opportunity come to punish the settlers."

Bradburn asserted, "from what I already know from the time that I spent in command in Texas, it is necessary to have a sizeable force to reduce the settlers and the inhabitants of said district to obedience to Mexican laws because until now they have only observed Anglo-American laws."

In fact, a sizeable Mexican force already had descended on Texas.

Referring to federalist officer Colonel Subaran, Bradburn had written, "every Mexican loves his country when it is threatened by foreign enemies." Colonel Jose Antonio Mexia was another federalist who conformed to that description. Hearing rumors of an Anglo rebellion to separate Texas from Mexico, Mexia detached himself from the war against the centralists. He boarded his four hundred troops on five ships and sailed up the coastline to reassert Mexico's authority over Texas. At Matamoras he picked up a passenger. Having concluded his term in the legislature at Saltillo, Stephen F. Austin was going home.

Austin had been informed of the events at Anahuac through correspondence, and he had come to regard Bradburn as an arrogant tyrant, "half-crazy" part of the time and "incompetent" to command. During the voyage Austin described to Mexia the Texian perspective on the events at Anahuac.

Mexia's fleet reached Brazoria on July 16. Texian leaders, including John Austin, Francis W. Johnson, and Robert Williamson, met with Mexia and extended a cordial greeting. They assured him of their commitment to the Constitution of 1824, and, as evidence, they displayed the Turtle Bayou Resolutions.

Perhaps significantly, William Barret Travis was not among the men who met with Colonel Mexia. Although the majority of Texian colonists were sincere in their allegiance to Mexico, a small, zealous faction argued for independence. Even if Travis had not yet revealed his true convictions, already some men suspected that he—perhaps understandably, after his long, brutal incarceration—adhered to the separationists.

Mexia was satisfied that the Texian colonists had become federalist allies in the revolution against the centralists. After six days he sailed on to Anahuac. There, Colonel Subaran and the garrison boarded the ships to return to Mexico, where their services were more desperately required. The hated fort was abandoned. Shortly afterwards, someone put the torch to it.

The duel of egos between Colonel Juan Davis Bradburn and William Barret Travis had propelled Texas into the Mexican civil war. Here then occurred one of the great ironies of Texas history. The Texians had declared themselves as allies of the federalist rebels. The federalists were known as *santanistas,* in honor of the general who initiated and led the revolt.

His name was Antonio Lopez de Santa Anna.

Chapter 15: ## *The Raven*

"Throughout the entire nation there rose a cry of indignation against the cruel and shameful treachery of the enemies of General Guerrero," Santa Anna remembered. Of course he could not remain indifferent to the demands of his fellow citizens. So in 1831 the "Hero of Tampico" had emerged from his villa to challenge the "hard-hearted and self-satisfied" centralist leaders. Again raising the cry of revolution, he hastily captured the customshouse at Vera Cruz, conveniently appropriating the collected funds for himself.

President Bustamante's regime tried to terminate the rebellion quickly. General Jose Calderon, commanding a "strong division," was dispatched to Vera Cruz. But again Santa Anna's luck held. Malaria decimated Calderon's army, allowing the "Napoleon of the West" another easy victory.

"It was now too late to turn back the tide," Santa Anna wrote, "the issue would be decided with guns!"

He formulated his Plan of Vera Cruz to justify the revolution, organized his army at Orizaba, and began his advance on Mexico City. The northern provinces readily joined in the revolt, fighting as *santanistas* against the centralist forces. Both sides won and lost battles as the civil war endured into the next year.

By the summer of 1832 the rebellion had spread up into Texas. To Anahuac. To Velasco. And then, as Colonel Piedras himself had feared, to Nacogdoches.

As with Mier y Teran and Bradburn, Piedras' own fears had largely provoked the conflict. After his return from Anahuac, Piedras had tried to abort any chance of rebellion by disarming the colonists in and around Nacogdoches. His order for the surrender of weapons only enraged the settlers. Even worse, rumors circulated that Piedras had encouraged the east Texas tribes to attack any colonist factions that resisted his authority.

The Texians hastily organized their own militia, again declaring for Santa Anna and the federalists. By late July riders were galloping through the nearby settlements appealing for help. Volunteers at St. Augustine and in communities along the Neches and Sabine grabbed for their hunting rifles and scatterguns.

It all made Stephen F. Austin very nervous. Though he, too, favored the *santanistas*, he had serious reservations about the participation of his colonists in the revolution. If the centralists triumphed, the Texians would face repercussions even more severe than the Law of April 6, 1830. Even if the federalists won, their leaders might misconstrue the conflicts generated by the impetuous Anglo colonists.

Having just returned from the legislative session at Saltillo, Austin found himself confined to the pressing matters at San Felipe. But he needed someone he could trust to act as a troubleshooter at Nacogdoches. Someone who had not committed himself to either faction in the civil war. Someone respected by *Tejano* and Texian alike. Someone with the natural ability to lead men.

Austin sent a rider galloping off to advise Big Jim Bowie that "his services were greatly needed."

James Bowie had staggered back from the San Saba Indian battle on December 6, 1831. Such a narrow escape might have discouraged some men from venturing back into the Indian dominated northern frontier of Texas. But by January Bowie was planning another expedition.

At least he would take more men this time, especially since he specifically intended to engage the Indians. His mission, authorized by the political chief Ramon Musquiz, was to deter recent Indian raids by striking "the Toahucanoes and other hostile nations." The Tawakonis were, of course, the principle tribe responsible for the attack on Bowie's San Saba expedition, and their removal would expedite future silver mine ventures.

Bowie recruited twenty-six volunteers. In late January they rode northwest out of Gonzales.

This time there would be no dramatic battles. After two and a half months of "fruitless search" from the headwaters of the Colorado to the upper Brazos, Bowie found nothing but traces left by a half dozen hostiles. In his official report to Musquiz, penned on April 23, 1832, Bowie concluded that the well-armed Cherokees and other eastern tribes had driven the Tawakonis to a "Section too far distant for our discovery."

The wandering expedition managed to revisit the San Saba and engage in a bit of prospecting. "I also spared no pains in Extending my Examinations to the mineral character of the Country, in hopes that Something might be discovered that should prove advantageous & beneficial to that section of Country," Bowie explained to Musquiz. "I will forward you the different Specimens of mineral that I was able to collect."

No assay records exist of the mineral specimens that Bowie collected. However in mid-July he had mounted yet a third prospecting expedition. Then he received the urgent dispatch from Stephen F. Austin.

Bowie climbed into the saddle and rode off to Nacogdoches.

He arrived the evening of August 2, just hours too late to prevent the conflict from erupting. Earlier that same day the militia, nearly three hundred strong, had marched into the town. Piedras, commanding about the same number of *soldados*, refused an offer to either surrender or declare for Santa Anna. When the guns roared, both forces took refuge in the town's buildings, and the battle raged from house to house.

Nightfall brought a reprieve from the fighting. Piedras took advantage of the darkness and slipped his troops into the woods outside of town. Then the Mexicans began a retreat to the south.

Their departure was not discovered until sunrise. While some Texians debated the best course of action, Bowie took command of the situation. He assembled a force of twenty men and galloped off in pursuit. His riders easily circled the lumbering Mexican army.

When Piedras' force approached the Angelina River, a volley of rifle fire erupted from the thick timber on the opposite bank. Squawking birds fluttered into the sky ahead of a rising cloud of pungent smoke. A Mexican sergeant crumpled into the water. The rest of the *soldados* fell back into the trees.

Then Bowie dispatched a messenger into Piedras' camp demanding surrender or annihilation. Bowie was bluffing, of course, gambling on the Mexicans' ignorance that they outnumbered his force by more than ten to one. But Bowie was a natural gambler who had wagered his own life more than once.

But Piedras could gamble, too. Again he stubbornly refused to surrender. However his officers fell for the bluff. A captain named Francisco Medina led a mutiny against their commander. Piedras stoically relinquished his sword and command, and Medina agreed to disarmament and surrender.

Big Jim Bowie had done it again. But then, for Bowie, more and more, the incredible seemed commonplace. With minimal troops, in a minimal amount of time, he had resolved the crisis in favor of the Texians. And by inflicting minimal casualties he had mitigated the conflict into an insignificant event unlikely to arouse Mexican antagonism. In fact Bowie supplied them with food and provisions, prompting Captain Medina to thank Bowie for his consideration.

Below Texas the centralist forces were faring no better than Piedras. Bustamante finally capitulated on December 23, 1832. He accepted exile in London. President Gomez Pedraza, the previously exiled president, returned from the United States to complete Bustamante's term of office. But everyone knew who held the real power in Mexico—and who almost certainly would win the pending elections and assume the office of president in April.

"My entire ambition is to exchange the sword for the plow," announced Santa Anna. "If any hand again disturbs the public peace, Mexicans, do not forget me: I shall return to your call and we will make the world see that tyrants and oppressors cannot stay in the Mexican Republic."

Once more he coyly stepped back into the shadows, retiring again—but only briefly—to his villa in Vera Cruz. His moment was so near he could already savor its sweet taste. He was the Hero of Tampico, the Napoleon of the West, and soon he would be the eagle who soared over all of Mexico.

Ironically, on December 2, 1832, another eagle, circling above the Red River, had welcomed a lone horseman onto Texas soil. A man the Cherokees called the Raven had come to meet his destiny.

Big Jim Bowie was not accustomed to looking upward into a man's eyes. But Sam Houston, at thirty-eight—three years older than Bowie—also stood a good two inches taller. Houston actually measured about six feet two inches from the soles of his feet to the crest of his receding brown hair. In that era, however, his height would have been the equivalent of the six feet, six inches, often attributed to him in legend. And his massive, bear-like physique, held erect in a military bearing, contributed to the impression that he was a giant. He bedecked his huge frame in a

Early daguerreotype of Sam Houston
Courtesy the Joseph Musso Collection.

gaudy blend of cultures: a white beaver plantation-style hat with a low crown and wide brim, an Indian blanket tossed over a coat of velvet or buckskin, beaded moccasins, or tall boots adorned with Spanish spurs.

These two men—both large and both larger-than-life—may have crossed paths before, perhaps as early as January 1828, in New Orleans. However the historical record does not confirm their meeting until December 1832, at San Felipe. Bowie had arrived on business. Houston was passing through en route to San Antonio de Bexar. Bowie offered to guide him.

Even if they had not previously met, Sam Houston certainly had heard of James Bowie. Houston probably carried a variation of a Bowie knife in his sash. And Bowie would have heard stories about Houston. On the road to Bexar they probably traded biographies, cutting through the already accumulating legends that had become attached to both men. It would be the beginning of an enduring friendship.

Houston had been born on March 2, 1793, in Rockbridge County, Virginia, to a prominent, if not especially prosperous, family. His father, Major Samuel Houston, passed away in 1806. The following year his mother, Elizabeth, moved the family west, settling near Maryville in the eastern part of Tennessee.

Although a passionate reader, young Sam was too restless, too impetuous, to endure formal schooling. Nor did the mundane tasks of working the farm or clerking in the family store appeal to him. At the age of fifteen he ran off to the nearby Cherokee village. Adopted into the tribe, he lived among them for the better part of three years. Chief Oolooteka bestowed the name *Colonneh*—the Raven—on the husky, sandy-haired youth. From then on the Cherokees would be Houston's surrogate family, but he developed a general empathy for all tribes, a perspective that would generate troublesome conflicts and contradictions for the rest of his career.

Such as when the Creek Indians massacred the settlers at Fort Mims and allied themselves with the British.

In 1813, as a third lieutenant in the United States Army, Houston fought under General Andrew Jackson against the Creek Indians. His blood brother Cherokees served as army scouts. With youthful exuberance Houston had boasted to his family and friends in Maryville that they would hear of him before the campaign was over.

On March 24 the Creeks made their last stand behind a wooden stockade that stretched across the neck of a large peninsula on the large Horseshoe Bend of the Tallahoosa River. Just after noon a bugle signaled the army's advance against the Indian breastworks. Houston drew his sword and motioned his company forward into a hail of musket balls and arrows. Through the gun smoke Houston saw Major Lemuel P. Montgomery at the head of the army. Montgomery reached the Indian fortifications first, scrambled to the top, then toppled back—dead. His name would be memorialized as the capital of Alabama.

Then Houston was scaling the breastworks. He flung himself over the top and landed in the frenzied midst of the enemy. He stood a head taller than the surrounding Indians, and he hacked furiously with his sword as they closed in around him. He felt a blow to his thigh, saw the protruding arrow shaft, felt the warm blood trickling down his leg. He crumpled, his flashing sword still deflecting their spears and tomahawks.

But now other soldiers were dropping over the ramparts. The Indians fell back. Houston collared a passing lieutenant and ordered him to extract the arrow. The barbed point ripped through muscles and tendons and flesh. Blood spurted from the ugly gash. Houston hobbled back to find the military surgeons, grimacing in both agony and frustration as the battle raged behind him.

The doctors treated his wound as best they could, but they expressed concern over the amount of blood he had already lost. Yet Houston insisted on returning to the battle. Old Hickory himself rode by and ordered Houston to stay out of the fight.

By evening the remaining Creeks had fortified themselves in a formidable covered redoubt. When they refused Jackson's offer to surrender, the general called for volunteers to storm the redoubt. To his surprise, Third Lieutenant Sam Houston limped forward.

Maryville would hear of him yet.

Houston wounded at Horseshoe Bend

For the second time that day, Houston led a charge. This time he did not make it into the redoubt. Two Creek musket balls tore into his right shoulder and arm, spinning him around, slamming him to the ground. More precious blood drained from his body. The doctors gave him little chance for survival.

But as with James Bowie, the near fatal wounds that Sam Houston suffered would launch his fame. Andrew Jackson had witnessed the gallantry displayed by the youthful giant. When Houston recovered, Jackson became both a father figure and mentor, guiding Houston into a rising political career that paralleled Jackson's own ascendancy to the White House.

Adjutant general—and later major general—of the Tennessee militia. Attorney general for the district of Nashville. United States Congressman from the Ninth Tennessee District. And then, in 1827, governor of Tennessee.

In January 1828 Houston joined Jackson in New Orleans for a weeklong celebration held on the thirteenth anniversary of Old Hickory's

Andrew Jackson

greatest military victory. A parade on January 7 initiated the festivities, followed by a grand ball the next night. Recuperating from his injuries at Horseshoe Bend, Houston had missed the Battle of New Orleans, but as the governor of Tennessee he probably attended most of the social events that continued until January 15.

It was then that Houston just might have met the celebrated James Bowie, recently recovered from his own wounds in the already famous sandbar fight. A land transaction deed places Bowie in the Crescent City on January 12. Though not a Jackson supporter, as a veteran of the New Orleans campaign, if not the actual battle, he certainly attended some of the festivities.

The year 1829 proved to be pivotal. Andrew Jackson was inaugurated president of the United States. As Jackson's protege, Houston's own political prospects skyrocketed. So did his passions. On January 22, 1829, thirty-five-year-old Sam Houston married nineteen-year-old Eliza Allen.

Eleven weeks later she moved back to her family's home in Gallatin.

Neither party would ever address the cause of their separation. Houston would only assert, "The lady is blameless."

However the ensuing scandal drove Houston from the governor's mansion—and from any ambitions he may have entertained about the presidency.

Broken and despondent, Houston took refuge with Chief Oolooteka and the Cherokees, now relocated in the Indian Territory that would become Oklahoma. Rejecting the white society that had pained him so, Houston adopted the Cherokee culture and clothing, and he even took a Cherokee wife, Tiana Rogers. Together they operated a trading post called Wigwam Neosho. Throughout this time Houston continued to brood, too often finding sanctuary in the bottle. The Cherokee came to know him as the "Big Drunk."

During his periods of sobriety, however, Houston acted as an Indian agent. In December 1831, still bedecked in traditional Cherokee garb, Houston accompanied a Cherokee delegation to Washington. While they were there, William Stanbery, a representative from Ohio, made allegations before Congress that Houston had been involved in a fraudulent Indian rations contract.

On the night of April 13 Houston encountered Stanbery on a dark Washington street. Proclaiming Stanbery a "damned rascal," Houston struck him repeatedly with a cane whittled from Hermitage hickory. Stanbery managed to draw a pistol, shoved the muzzle against Houston's chest, and pulled the trigger. The hammer "snapped" harmlessly. Houston jerked it away. Now even more enraged, he added insult to injury by raising Stanbery's legs and thrashing his rear end.

Stanbery subsequently pressed Congress to arrest Houston. Francis Scott Key, most notable for the national anthem he had penned during the War of 1812, acted as Houston's attorney. The month-long proceedings generated intense public interest, most of it sympathetic to Houston. At the climax Houston delivered a lengthy, patriotic oration that obviously owed a debt to Key. The packed galleries exploded in applause. A woman tossed a bouquet at his feet.

Ultimately Houston received an official reprimand and a five-hundred-dollar fine.

"I was dying out and had they taken me before a justice of peace and fined me ten dollars it would have killed me," Houston later recalled, "but they gave me a national tribunal for a theatre, and that set me up again."

Perhaps even more important, Houston had reestablished his relationship with Jackson. The president remitted the five-hundred-dollar fine for "divers good and sufficient reasons." Earlier Jackson had provided Houston with money to buy more suitable clothing for the trial. When Houston shed his Cherokee buckskin jacket for a frock coat, he effectively returned to the white man's world. But he would never shed his empathy for the Indians.

Sam Houston

He returned only briefly to Wigwam Neosho. He gave Tiana title to the trading post, the surrounding fields, and two slaves. Then he was "Gone to Texas." He would never see her again.

Officially Sam Houston entered Texas as a United States Indian agent to report on the native tribes. But hardly anybody believed that was the real reason he came to Texas. Rumors circulated that Houston had plotted to conquer Texas with a Cherokee army and declare himself emperor of the republic. Or that President Jackson, frustrated that his efforts to purchase Texas had been rebuffed, gave Houston secret instructions to foment rebellion and bring Texas into the United States. In reality, Jackson had secured a promise that Houston would not engage in any enterprise injurious to either his country or his own reputation.

Certainly Houston entertained some ambitions about Texas. But he also may have been enticed by the promise of easy profits through land speculation. Or perhaps, like so many others, he just needed a place to start over.

The true reason for Houston's arrival in Texas remains as much an enduring mystery as the cause for his separation from Eliza Allen.

At Bexar, Bowie and Houston parted company. Houston went to parlay with the Comanches. Bowie continued on to Saltillo. His father-in-law already was there, filling the office of the recently deceased governor of Coahuila y Texas, Jose Maria Letona.

And Don Juan Beramendi needed James Bowie.

The revolution had ended, and Antonio Lopez de Santa Anna had been elected the next president of Mexico. Yet the civil war had left Saltillo veiled in the dark shadows of distrust, highlighted only by volatile emotions. Centralists and federalists alike had fortified their haciendas, and many feared venturing beyond their guarded walls.

In this precarious environment, Beramendi was endorsing a movement, popular with both *Tejanos* and moderate Anglo colonists, to relocate the capital to Monclova, more than a hundred miles closer to the Texas border. Beramendi needed Bowie, both for the physical protection afforded by his *cuchillo grande*, and for the charismatic influence Bowie wielded just as skillfully.

Bowie reached Saltillo on February 7, 1833. Largely through the lobbying efforts of Beramendi and himself, the legislators finally voted to move the capital to Monclova.

Ursula had not heard from her husband since his departure. On April 4 she wrote from San Antonio, "My dear Bowie."

"I have received letters from papa and in all of them he talks to me of you," she noted, chiding her husband for not having written personally. On "another subject that holds me without my will," she mentioned two impatient *Tejanos* demanding repayment of funds they had advanced to Bowie when he and Ursula were in New Orleans. Bowie had passed the sum on to Angus McNeill, probably to purchase machinery in Boston for the cotton mill. "Here they have another way of thinking," Ursula wrote, delicately admonishing Bowie that her people were not accustomed to the wheelings and dealings of the Anglos.

She and her family were planning a trip to Monclova, apparently to meet Don Beramendi there. Ursula concluded, "all the family is in good health and salutes you and receive thou the heart of thy wife."

She signed the letter, "Ursula Veramendi de Bowie," spelling her last name with a "V," a practice adopted by the family in the 1830s. Though it is only speculation, a logical explanation exists for this spelling transition. In that era, the Spanish "B" was pronounced like a "V." With the influx of Anglo settlers into Texas, the Beramendis may have found it more convenient to spell their name phonetically—Veramendi.

Ursula probably sent the letter to Saltillo, which means that Bowie did not receive it. By April 1 he had ridden into San Felipe to witness a convention called for that date.

It was the second convention held by the Texian colonists. The first dated back to October 1832. Bowie had missed that one, but it hardly mattered. The same issues were being resurrected.

His new friend Sam Houston was back in San Felipe, too. Houston had returned to Nacogdoches in time to be elected the town's delegate to the convention. As Houston later wrote, he "took up residence among his new constituents, who had extended him so generous a greeting."

And he had written to President Jackson, claiming to possess information that "may be calculated to forward your views, if you should entertain any, touching the acquisition of Texas by the Government of the United States." Houston asserted that "nineteen-twentieths of the population of the province" desired annexation. That estimate displayed more wishful thinking than reality. Even Nacogdoches, near the United States border, was not so radical, and the majority of colonists across Texas still professed their loyalty to the Mexican Constitution of 1824.

Yet Houston clearly had allied himself with the most radical Texians, and he expressed their sentiment. "She [Texas] has already beaten and repelled all the troops of Mexico from her soil," Houston continued. "She can defend herself against the whole power of Mexico, for really Mexico is powerless and penniless."

On these points he was mistaken. Though in debt, Mexico was hardly powerless. And Mexican *soldados* yet remained on Texas soil. San Antonio de Bexar was garrisoned by troops, including the Alamo Company still quartered in the old mission-fortress. And a smaller force occupied the formidable presidio at La Bahia.

Houston also advised Jackson of the impending convention. He expected it to "form a State Constitution."

William H. Wharton, the son-in-law of wealthy plantation owner Jared Groce, presided over the convention. Watching the proceedings, Bowie realized that the relocation of the capital to Monclova might be a temporary measure. The primary issue before the convention was separation from Coahuila. The Constitution of 1824 had united Texas and Coahuila only until the population of the former justified its reestablishment as a separate province. Certainly with a current population exceeding forty thousand, that requirement had been met. And certainly the colonists had proved their loyalty to Santa Anna and the federalists. Now, with Santa Anna supporting a return to the Constitution, many Texians felt justified in petitioning Mexico for separation from Coahuila.

As Houston had predicted, the delegates were so confident that the Mexican congress would approve separate statehood they wanted to submit a state constitution with their petition. They appointed the ex-governor of Tennessee to chair the committee that drafted the constitution.

And there were other requests in the petition, most notably the repeal of the immigration clause of the Law of April 6, 1830, further exemption from tariffs, and the right to maintain local militias for protection against hostile Indians.

Stephen F. Austin, who had presided over the October convention, only gave the opening address at the week-long second convention. The proceedings made him uncomfortable. Of course he sympathized with the issues being presented. So did Ramon Musquiz, the political chief of the Department of Texas. But Musquiz had refused to send a delegate from Bexar to either convention. He regarded them as illegal assemblies exercising powers "that belong exclusively to the state." He believed that many of the colonists desired not only separation from Coahuila, but also separation from Mexico. Like Houston, Musquiz's views had been influenced by a small minority of radical Texians. Yet Austin feared that other Mexican officials would share Musquiz's perspective.

Austin was correct.

On April 1, the first day of the convention, Antonio Lopez de Santa Anna assumed the office of president of Mexico. Santa Anna wrote " . . . the foreigners who have introduced themselves in [Texas] have a strong tendency to declare themselves independent of the republic, and that all their remonstrances and complaints are but disguised to that end." Yet in the same letter he conceded:

> The interest of the nation requires a kind policy toward these people, for they have done us good service, and, it must be confessed, they have not on all occasions been treated with justice and liberality. That they have grounds to so feel towards our government is derogatory toward the honor of the republic. . . . Moreover, it is possible for them to become so exasperated as to make it impracticable to restore order among them without much trouble.

Santa Anna had profited from the incidents at Anahuac, Velasco, and Nacogdoches, and it almost sounded like he had learned from them. Yet the man in whose name all Mexican troops had been driven from Texas now advocated the military reoccupation of the region.

Despite Austin's misgivings, the convention recognized that he was still the most logical choice to deliver the petition to the Mexican congress. Once again the long journey to Mexico City loomed before Austin.

James Bowie also faced a long journey. Finally back at his home in Bexar, he made preparations for a trip to the United States. All the recent news from there had been distressing. His younger brother Stephen had died on January 29 of bilious pleurisy, leaving a widow and two orphans. The United States Supreme Court had ruled against the fraudulent Arkansas land claims that bore John's name. And Rezin's staggering debts at the Acadia plantation had forced him to declare insolvency. Even worse, Rezin's eyesight had finally failed. He wanted to visit two eye specialists, Dr. Valentin Mott in New York and Dr. Joseph Parrish in Philadelphia. But he would need someone to escort a blind man on such an extended trip.

He needed his brother James Bowie.

It seemed Bowie was there for anyone who needed him. Anyone except for the one person in his life who loved him most. He had been away from San Antonio, and Ursula, for almost half of the two years of their marriage. Seasoned pioneer wives on the frontier might be inured to such extended absences, but not the refined young daughter of the governor of Texas y Coahuila. Yet in her total devotion to Bowie, Ursula endured the loneliness with silent stoicism. Always waiting for his return. Praying he would return.

However this journey eastward hardly merited concern. This time Bowie was not galloping into harm's way. Bowie kissed Ursula goodbye and told her to convey his respects to Don Veramendi when she saw him in Monclova. Then Bowie rode east to meet Rezin in Louisiana.

The Bowie brothers traveled northeast. The efforts of one or both of the doctors succeeded in partially restoring the sight in one of Rezin's eyes. Perhaps that enabled him to write the account of the San Saba Indian fight published in the August 17, 1833 edition of *Atkinson's Saturday Evening Post and Bulletin*. Also while in Philadelphia the brothers probably called on Henry Schively, a cutler and surgical instrument maker at 75 Chesnut Street. Rezin, at least, acquired a large knife from Schively, and the intriguing possibility exists that James did also.

They also visited Boston regarding the cotton mill machinery. While in that city, James may have sat for a portrait by the noted artist George Peter Alexander Healy. According to family tradition, Healy painted the portrait of Bowie still in the possession of Rezin's descendants. Historical records place Healy in Boston from the fall of 1830 until March 1834.

By late September the brothers had returned to Louisiana. After parting from Rezin, Bowie called on his friend and business associate Angus McNeill, at Natchez.

Bowie had almost died at a sandbar near Natchez, only six years earlier. Upon his return he was nearly slain again, this time by a foe that even his great knife could not intimidate: a mosquito.

James Bowie from portrait attributed to artist George Peter Alexander Healy.

Cholera and malaria had both ravaged the lower Mississippi that year. It was the latter that laid Bowie prostrate in one of McNeill's beds. For days he suffered the chills and delirium. Convinced for the first time that he actually might die, on October 31, 1833, he feebly dictated his will to Natchez attorney Felix Huston.

He left Ursula only some jewelry he had recently purchased for her. He did love her, in the only way James Bowie could love a woman, more than he had ever loved any other woman. He had always been gentle and attentive. "My dearly beloved wife," he had called her. He longed to see her, to hold her, one last time.

But he had already provided for her with his dowry, at least that portion of it which was valid. Besides, her family had wealth.

Most of Bowie's estate would go to his impoverished and nearly blind brother, Rezin, and to Stephen's orphans. He also stipulated the repayment of certain outstanding debts.

Bowie managed to scrawl his signature on the document and laid back to await his death.

Then his fever broke. His body began to heal. James Bowie conquered malaria as effectively as he had defeated Indians, Mexicans, and arrogant Southern aristocrats.

In the meantime the cholera epidemic that had skipped over Bowie swept on through Texas. It killed more than eighty residents at the tiny community of Brazoria. John Austin and both of his children perished. Samuel May Williams, the secretary of the *ayuntamiento* at San Felipe, barely survived and sent some medicine on to his friend Jose Antonio Navarro, in Bexar.

By then the plague had pushed southward across the Rio Grande, blanketing northern Mexico with the terrible cramps, diarrhea, vomiting, and fatal dehydration.

Monclova was devastated. Five hundred and seventy-one people died there in the first half of September. The parish priest was nearly overwhelmed, trying to administer last rites and record all the dead. The cholera played no favorites. The priest's list of fatalities included the young and the elderly, the peons and the wealthy.

Even the former governor of Coahuila y Texas—and his family.

The news reached Bexar sometime in the latter part of September. On September 26 Don Jose Navarro dipped his quill in the inkwell and wearily scratched a letter back to Samuel Williams in San Felipe. Navarro thanked Williams for the medicine. Then he continued.

> When you told me about the awful cholera, it is very sad to realize that this which is inexplicable hurts me as well. On my part, it has been a misfortune that my brother Veramendi; my sister, Josefa, his wife; and Ursulita Bowie have died in an awful way in Monclova.
>
> I have lost my special brother-in-law in Veramendi and Texas has lost a good son; a faithful and interested friend . . . .
>
> Bowie no longer has a wife and I hope some way he will be told of this news.

A letter reached Bowie around mid-November. It hit him harder than Robert Crain's pistol ball, pierced deeper than Norris Wright's sword cane. McNeill feared Bowie would plunge into a fatal relapse. However, Bowie's body struggled back to health.

But something inside of him had died.

Chapter 16: *Mill Creek*

"**I** felt an intense desire to be worthy of the high confidence placed in me by the people as I took over my presidential duties," remembered Santa Anna. "When there suddenly appeared an army under the command of Gabriel Duran, proclaiming 'Religion and Rights,' I knew that I must suppress this revolt at the very outset."

The revolution continued. But now the pendulum of power had swung to the opposite extreme, and the centralists had become the rebels.

"I swear to you that I oppose all efforts aimed at destruction of the Constitution," Santa Anna announced, " and I would die before accepting any other power than that designated by it."

When Santa Anna marched the army out of Mexico, he left Vice-President Valentin Gomez Farias in control of the congress. Farias had been the leader of the federalist revolt in the province of Zacatecas. In the name of reform, Farias and the new legislators proposed rabidly liberal laws that struck vindictively at the three mainstays of Mexican conservatism—the privileged, the military, and, most critically, the Catholic Church.

Suddenly ecclesiastical offices were to be appointed by the government rather than the church. Monks and nuns would be permitted to retract their sacred vows. The size of the army would be reduced—and so would the *soldados'* pay.

The federalists had transformed the revolt into a holy war, with the centralists pledging to "defend at all hazards the religion of Christ and the rights and privileges of the church and the army." Farias should hardly have been surprised when he learned that the president's force had defected to the centralist rebels. Santa Anna himself had been betrayed to the enemy.

"General Duran informed me that if I would accept the dictatorship, he would be the first to obey my command," Santa Anna wrote in his autobiography. "In disgust, I replied: 'The President of the Republic, duly elected by the legislature, cannot be made a rebel!'"

In reality Santa Anna wanted nothing more than to become dictator of Mexico. He would have the support of the army, the church, and the elite class. All he needed was to dispose of Farias and the new federalist legislature without turning public sentiment against him. And if the centralist rebels could manage that while he was their prisoner, no blame would be attached to him.

Wittingly or unwittingly, Santa Anna had left Farias vulnerable, with no regular forces to protect the new government. However, when the centralist rebels threatened Mexico City, Farias managed to assemble a volunteer army of six thousand civilians to repel the attack.

When the coup failed, Santa Anna conveniently escaped from the centralists and returned to Mexico City. He dutifully took command of the new volunteer army and marched out in pursuit of the rebels.

Then the cholera hit. It depleted both forces. General Duran died. The centralist revolution stalled.

"I have never witnessed such horrible scenes of distress and death," Stephen F. Austin wrote. He had arrived in Mexico City on July 28, 1833, again to be a witness to history. Again he heard church bells, but this time they mourned for the dead, the dying, and the bereaved. The streets seemed deserted except for the silent funeral processions and the creaking carts piled high with human carcasses. Austin estimated that more than eighteen thousand would die before the disease had run its terrible course. He very nearly was one of them.

"I was taken about 3 o'clock P.M. with excessive purging of a white mucos character, great pain in bowels, cold feet, legs, hands, all, pains over the body—" he wrote Samuel Mays, "in about ¾ of an hour I was relieved by a fine perspiration which I think saved my life for others have died in less than an hour whose symptoms were similar to mine."

Austin survived, but not even he could appreciate the political impact of the plague.

With Santa Anna away from the capital, Austin met with acting president Farias and the new congress. Despite his own reservations, Austin delivered an emotional plea in support of the colonists' petition, especially the request for separate statehood.

The colonists remained loyal to the Republic, Austin maintained, but the inability of Coahuila to adequately govern them had created a dire situation:

> Texas is today exposed . . . to being the sport of ambitious
> men, of speculators and reckless money-changers, of sedi-
> tious and wicked men, of wandering Indians who are

devastating the country, of adventurers, of revolution, of the lack of the administration of justice and of confidence and moral strength in the government. In short, for the want of government that country is already at the verge of anarchy.

...in such case the probability is great that the government of the North would take possession of Texas in order to preserve order upon their frontiers, as it did in the case of the Floridas.

All this and incalculable other evils would be avoided by establishing Texas as a state.

He would not get an immediate reply. The cholera drove congress into adjournment. Once again Austin could only wait. And write letters home.

"If the heroes of the Cross [the centralists] get the upper hand, it is difficult to say what they will do as to Texas matters," Austin advised his brother-in-law, James F. Perry, on September 11. "But there is not prospect that they will succeed at present...."

And Austin received letters. Perry's young daughter, Mary—a favorite niece of Austin's—had died of the cholera. So had many Texian friends. The tireless Austin tired—and slipped into despondency.

Then the Mexican congress finally reconvened—and took no action on the Texas petition. Austin became uncharacteristically impatient. He wrote Perry on October 2:

I shall wait but a short time longer. I am tired of this government. They are always in revolution and I believe always will be. I have had much more respect for them than they deserve. But I am done with all that.

Then he scripted a second letter to the *ayuntamiento* at San Antonio de Bexar, urging it to circumvent the federal government and help establish a state government for Texas separate from Coahuila. Austin asserted, "there is now no doubt that the fate of Texas depends upon itself and not upon this government; nor is there any doubt that, unless the inhabitants of Texas take all its affairs into their own hands, that country is lost."

The letter reached Bexar at the end of the month. Although most Bexareno members of the *ayuntamiento* desired statehood, they feared political repercussions and sternly reprimanded Austin for his "exceedingly rash" proposal. "It is certainly very regrettable that you should breathe sentiments so contrary and opposed to every good Mexican, whose constitution and laws prohibit in a positive manner this class of proceedings, as you very well know," the council wrote back, advising Austin to "rethink yourself and do not provoke a new motive for disturbance, which . . . must be more injurious to the colonists than to anyone else, and particularly to yourself."

By then the congress had finally begun deliberations over the Texas petition. And Santa Anna returned, triumphant, from the revolution, having regained control over what was left of the Mexican army. He met personally with Austin and promised favorable treatment for the colonists. However the president speculated that Texas yet needed a larger population before it could achieve statehood. In the interim, Santa Anna offered to send troops back in to protect the settlers from the Indians. Austin politely refused.

Austin had already admonished congress that "it is useless to try to subject or regulate Texas by military force."

"Austin in Mexico," William Barret Travis noted succinctly in his diary on September 3, 1833.

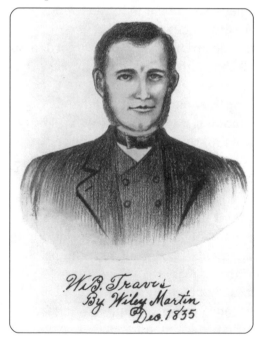

Pencil sketch of William Barret Travis by Wiley Martin.
Courtesy DeGolyer Library

Following his misadventures in Anahuac—which nevertheless brought him a fame that benefited his professional ambitions—Travis had relocated to San Felipe de Austin in the late summer. The town already bristled with so many attorneys that in comparison the "plague of locusts" at Anahuac and Liberty seemed like a modest swarm. But despite its rustic demeanor, San Felipe ranked as the political capital of Anglo Texas. And Travis' newfound celebrity and above-average education provided him an edge that soon whittled out its own niche.

He no longer needed a beard to make him appear older, and after his release from the

Anahuac brick kilns, he probably had enjoyed a good shave along with a bath. However he retained the long chin whiskers, not yet called sideburns, that were fashionable in his era.

Travis kept a combination diary/ledger/record book into which he faithfully recorded, in abbreviated phrases, the significant events of each day—both business and pleasure—and the monies (often in IOUs) that he received or spent. Only the entries from the end of August 1833 through June 1834 survive—other volumes apparently having been destroyed in the 1836 fire that consumed San Felipe. However those ten months provide an intriguing glimpse of colonial Texas—and an often intimate insight into the life of a man yet to become a legend.

His terse writing style did not lend itself to emotionalism, but Travis could express dramatic feelings in a word or two. On the same day as his reference to Austin, he noted, "Rec'd letter from R. E. Travis—*malo.*"

"R. E. Travis" denoted his wife back in Claiborne. Roseanna still believed that when Travis became settled he would send for her and Charles and Susan Isabella, the daughter he had never known. But Travis had come to enjoy his free, mobile bachelor existence. The thought of being tied down by marriage—especially to Roseanna, whose fidelity he may have questioned—became increasingly distasteful.

Even so he wrote her back that day, apparently still professing his love. But he knew the sham could not last.

As with everyone else in Texas at that moment, his immediate concern was the cholera. On September 6 Travis recorded that his friend Eli Holly was dying. "McQueen and myself sat up with him," Travis wrote.

Holly succumbed the next day, leaving nine orphans back in Alabama. Travis attended the funeral on September 8 and then penned a letter to Alabama "communicating the news of his death to his children."

Old William Pryor, one of Austin's original Three Hundred, died the following evening, and again Travis had "sat up" with him.

With Alabama flooding his thoughts, Travis resolved to erase his debts in Claiborne as diligently as he redeemed his gambling notes. "Made an arrangement with [Henry] Sewell to go to Alabama & buy my paper [IOUs] for me," Travis wrote. "I am to pay him in property here—He said he would charge me only what he would have to give for the notes."

On September 12 Travis noted, "The Alcalde made a decree appointing me attorney to the absent heirs of El Holly dec'd." That appointment and other pending matters required Travis to journey to Brazoria.

After a three-day trip on a borrowed mule, Buck Travis arrived on Saturday, September 21. He took a room in the boardinghouse operated by Jane Long. Later he called on fellow attorney R. M. Williamson, now one of the most respected lawyers in Texas. "Three-Legged Willie" had become a close friend—a rarity in Travis' life.

That night he engaged in perhaps his second favorite vice and lost $27.25 at the faro table. He had to borrow fifteen dollars from Williamson to carry him over.

On Thursday Travis awoke feeling "unwell." His spirits soon improved and he returned to the faro table and lost nine dollars. Then he engaged in his favorite vice, and as always he recorded it in his diary in Spanish: "*Chingaba una mujer que es cincuenta y seis en mi vida.*"

In Travis' defense, his limited Spanish may have accounted for the somewhat vulgar term he used for making love. Then as now, such crude expressions are often the first ones learned. Travis may have chosen the crude verb deliberately, for it was hardly couth to brag, even to himself, that she was the fifty-sixth woman in his life. It was an impressive record, one that dwarfed his father's indiscretions, but which in turn paled compared to the three hundred-plus conquests of Lord Byron. However, whereas Byron's dalliances ranged across populated Europe, Travis lived on a frontier where single women were scarce. His numbered conquests must have included females of both Anglo and *Tejano* heritage, lonely widows, and eager prostitutes whom he compensated at the going rate of one dollar or peso.

He would never send for Rosanna.

On September 27 Travis paid Mrs. Long $7.50 for his six-day stay, climbed onto his borrowed mule, and started back for San Felipe. He would continue to visit Brazoria on business so frequently that Mrs. Long eventually reduced his lodging to the daily rate paid by her full-time boarders.

Travis' law practice continued to prosper and he began investing in land.

And he still gambled, losing more often than winning. He did not confine his wagers to games such as monte, faro, and euchre. In December he bet ten dollars and a hat of equal value that his close friend Robert Williamson would defeat merchant Silas Dinsmore in the election for *alcalde* of San Felipe. Travis campaigned energetically for Williamson but remained on friendly terms with Dinsmore.

The election was held December 8. When the final tally was released December 15, Williamson had won the position. Travis claimed the ten dollars but refused the hat. On that same date Travis also recorded, "Gen'l Houston in town."

And there were still the women, the liaisons still always denoted in Spanish. "*Chingaba la Susana que is 59*," he wrote on November 7. On December 2 his diary referred to another tryst with an unidentified—and unnumbered—companion. She may have been a repeat performance, and Travis never counted his conquests again.

A week later he visited Dr. J. H. C. Miller and purchased a vial of medicine. His diary did not explain the problem, but it obviously persisted. The following week Travis acquired more medicine from Dr. Miller.

And then, perhaps for the first time since he had arrived in Texas, Travis found himself attracted to a woman on more than just a physical level. The object of his affection was a Miss E. Henry. On December 16 he arranged to escort her to a Christmas Eve Ball at Connell's inn.

Three days later Travis stayed at the home of Mosely Baker outside San Felipe. It rained heavily into the night. By the following day, December 20, the banks of Cummings Creek overflowed. Travis decided to remain at Baker's for another night. He lost $3.25 playing poker with other guests at the house. But if he was unlucky at cards, Travis' luck at romance held out. He wrote in his diary, again resorting to that crude term, "*Chingaba la C.*"

The next day Travis fabricated a raft, but he still could not ford the flooded creek. Or maybe he did not try hard enough. He stayed at Bakers another night and noted, again in Spanish, that he gave "*la C*" one dollar, presumably for the services she rendered.

At the Christmas Eve Ball Travis observed that he had two rivals for the hand of Miss Henry. On Christmas Day he sent her a present of two bottles of cologne and a package of cinnamon. The following night he looked for her at a party hosted by Major Ira Lewis. To Travis' disappointment he learned that Miss Henry already had left.

He soon found out why. She had accepted a marriage proposal from A. C. Westall. It was to be a short engagement. They would be wed on New Year's Eve.

"Rain—& cold—disagreeable," Travis wrote in his diary on December 27. The weather mirrored his mood. It also reflected the demeanor of a client for whom Travis translated a bond. James Bowie, still grieving over the loss his wife, had returned to Texas. Certainly Travis knew of Big Jim Bowie's reputation, but this probably was their first encounter.

The holiday season must have been an especially difficult time for men to be alone without loved ones. Bowie likely sought out another solitary figure, Sam Houston. Together they may have resorted to John Barleycorn to drive dull care away.

Alone and melancholy, Travis might have considered seeking temporary solace in the arms of a local prostitute, but he rejected the notion. His brief courtship with Miss Henry had awakened that human need for genuine love—compassion rather than passion. That evening he returned to the Lewis residence for dinner.

And there another guest, Miss Rebecca Cummings, caught his attention.

They must have met before. Since her mother's death in early 1832 Rebecca had lived with her brother John at his inn on Mill Creek, and Travis occasionally visited there. But Rebecca never had merited an entry in Travis' diary until this evening. Travis gratefully accompanied her to another party later that evening.

Two days later, New Year's Eve, he graciously attended the wedding of Westall and Miss Henry. Then he went home by himself. He lit candles and settled back into the still silence with a borrowed book.

On December 7, 1833, after four draining months in Mexico City, Stephen F. Austin finally received an official reply to the colonists' petition. Congress had repealed the hated anti-immigration clause from the Law of April 6, 1830. That alone was a major concession for the Texians. Other provisions in the petition were being favorably considered. However the issue of separation from Coahuila had been indefinitely tabled.

Three days later Austin finally started back for Texas, planning once again to preach contentment for what the colonists had won—and patience regarding the rest.

Santa Anna also departed the capital. This time the stench of death and the wail of mourners had alerted him to the shifting political winds. Congress' persistent attack on the church could not have been more ill timed. The cholera had created a religious revival in Mexico. Seventeen years later Bayard Taylor, an American journalist visiting Guadalajara, noted that the faithful still held "solemn religious festivals" within the majestic cathedral in remembrance of the terrible cholera epidemic of the 1830s. And, truly, the priests and nuns who bravely ministered to the sick and dying were the real heroes of the plague. Some Mexicans superstitiously speculated that the cholera was God's punishment for the federalist assault on the church. Santa Anna wrote:

> One faction [of the government] was endeavoring to confiscate the property of the church and to deny to the clergy its rights and ancient privileges. The public was dismayed by these actions and opposed violently any usurpation of the clergy's rights. Obeying the dictates of my conscience and hoping to quell a revolution, I declined to approve the necessary decree to put these edicts into law.

Having won the gratitude of the church, Santa Anna feigned illness. He shrewdly withdrew to his villa at Vera Cruz, allowing Farias to become acting president—and to continue making the political mistakes that would deliver absolute power to Santa Anna.

Then Farias made a most critical mistake. He received a packet from Bexar containing both Austin's letter advising the formation of a state government and the *ayuntamiento's* response. Incorrectly presuming that Austin was promoting the independence of Texas, Farias ordered the arrest and imprisonment of the greatest *norteamericano* ally Mexico ever had.

Oblivious of the warrant, weary old Stephen F. Austin arrived in Saltillo on January 3, 1834. He made a courtesy call on the military commandant, who immediately placed him under arrest and dispatched him, under guard, back to Mexico City. En route Austin wrote to the *ayuntamiento* in San Felipe, requesting that his letter be published for all colonists to read.

He described his arrest and the reasons for it, but, characteristically, he advised the colonists that he did not blame the Mexican government.

> I give the advice to the people there that I have always given: keep quiet, discountenance all revolutionary measures or men, obey the state authorities and laws so long as you are attached to Coahuila, have no more conventions, petition through the legal channels, that is, through the *ayuntamiento* and chief of department, harmonize fully with the people [*Tejanos*] of Bexar and Goliad, and act with them.

The letter expressed Austin's sincere sentiments. Yet he must have hoped that, upon seeing its publication, the Mexican government would be lenient toward him.

He learned otherwise when he arrived back in Mexico City on February 13. Without benefit of hearing or trial, he was immediately incarcerated in a fifteen foot by fifteen foot cell in the ancient Inquisition dungeons. There were no windows. A tiny skylight in the ceiling provided so little illumination that he only could read during the middle hours of brightly sunlit days. For the next three months, Austin would be locked in the damp darkness, held in total isolation—except for two visits from Father Muldoon, San Felipe's liberal Irish priest, who had recently transferred back to Mexico City.

"News of the Repeal of the Law of the 6th of April 1830—Joyous intelligence!" William Barret Travis scribbled into his diary on January 13, 1834. The victory almost justified his own incarceration at Anahuac.

Almost.

Yet, curiously, Travis' diary did not mention Austin's arrest and imprisonment, to which Travis must have been more sympathetic than most others in Texas.

His immediate concern in January focused on his son, Charles Edward.

9 January

Thursday—Recd letter from R. E. Travis—answered same
—She is willing to give up my son Charles to me. I directed
him to be sent to Brazoria to the care of Mrs. Long.

On the following day Travis arranged for his friend and one-time fellow prisoner Monroe Edwards to fetch Charles Edward from Alabama. Travis did not request Susan Isabella. He may have felt it best that the daughter remain with her mother. Or Travis still may have questioned whether Susan actually was his child.

For some reason Edwards never retrieved Charles. Neither did William P. Huff, whom Travis engaged on March 3 "to bring out Charles Edward Travis who is now in N. Orleans with his mother."

Perhaps Rosanna had second thoughts. Clearly Travis' letters no longer deluded her with false affirmations of love. Perhaps she even attempted to use young Charles as a hostage either to win back her husband's affection or to punish him. She would not finally bring herself to file for divorce until September, and then she retained Judge James Dellet to represent her.

Travis loved his son and missed him very much. He occasionally wrote to Charles, though the son could not have been old enough to read the letters himself. Unfortunately, none of these letters exist today. They must have resonated with the passion generally absent from his diary—a passion that would resurface in letters Travis later would write from the Alamo.

In the absence of his son, Travis directed his paternal emotions at the children he encountered. He bought shoes for the child of one friend. Mrs.

Dilue Rose Harris recalled an incident from her youth when Travis sent books to her and her sister. Sometimes Travis doled out money to young people he met.

And he gave generously to charities. He could afford to. No longer a debtor, he had clients who owed him money.

Two other considerations garnered Travis' attention in the early part of that year. On February 5 he was elected secretary of the *ayuntamiento*, replacing Samuel Williams. *Alcalde* Williamson probably influenced the election, assuming he was helping his friend Buck. In fact Travis seriously questioned whether he wanted the responsibility. But on the following day he decided in favor of the regular paycheck and political prominence afforded by the job. One of Travis' first duties as secretary was to validate the claim of Major Sterling C. Robertson, the *empresario* whose colonists had been saved from expulsion by Colonel Francisco Ruiz of the Alamo Company.

And then there was Rebecca Cummings, the woman Travis could not erase from his mind. He visited her on February 16 and later reported that his "proposals [were] agreeably received." Presumably he had explained about his situation with Rosanna. Perhaps they had discussed marriage after his divorce was finalized.

But then on February 21 he apparently sought the company of a lady of the evening named Mary. He must have felt guilty about betraying Rebecca. He inscribed in his diary, "*No pudiera* [I could not]." Even so he gave Mary fifty cents, half the going rate.

He planned to see Rebecca again on March 9, undoubtedly sporting the new white hat he had purchased just a week earlier. But the heavy rains drove him back. "—waters all swimming & prairie so boggy—could not go—*The first time I ever turned back in my life.*"

Two days later Travis tried again to see Rebecca. He rode out to the Chesney farm on the opposite bank of Mill Creek and paid Mr. Chesney fifty cents to keep his horse. Then Travis challenged the current to meet his lover. He made it to the opposite bank, but then, with the daylight fading, he became lost in the woods. However his story had a happy ending. He wrote, "arrived at Cummins' in the night—&c—&c—&c—&c—&c."

Despite the implied evening of passion, the following day Rebecca apparently displayed some reservations. Travis described their relationship that day as "Intrigue—Bargain & management—successful." It may have helped that he did some legal work for her brother, probably gratis. He also gave Rebecca a breast pin. In exchange, he claimed a lock of her hair.

That night Travis again stayed at the inn. The next morning, March 16, Rebecca gave him a ring. Perhaps it was the same "cat's eye" ring that Travis would take with him to the Alamo. Then he retrieved his horse by canoe and returned to the business of the *ayuntamiento*.

But he could not stay away from Mill Creek. He was back on March 20. It was a playful day, and they frolicked in the brisk creek waters. Travis mentioned a "good ducking" and a "narroe escape." The evening took a more serious tone. They talked about Roseanna, a subject that must have bothered Rebecca. Travis displayed a bitter letter he had received from the woman he now referred to as his former wife. Rebecca expressed understanding, sympathy, and love. In Spanish, Travis wrote in his diary, "I have good fortune in my love affair with Miss C."

He spent the night there and enjoyed a second pleasant day "*in la sociedad de mi inamorata.*"

Then business kept him away for more than a week. The libidinous urge that Travis never could resist returned on March 26, and there was no time to gallop out to Mills Creek. In the Spanish he always used to describe such activities, Travis wrote that he paid one peso to "S" for—. He finished the sentence with a single word of self-denunciation, "*malo.*" This time his conscience had kicked in too late.

Two days later his diary explained why he might have been acquiring the vials of medication. "*Venerao mala.*" He misspelled *venerea*, but the man who had counted fifty-nine conquests apparently had contracted the disease then commonly referred to as the pox.

The most common treatment was mercury, the lethal liquid metal applied externally. It could not cure the disease, but it apparently helped heal the sensitive sores.

Travis did not let his medical problem interfere with his social life. He rode back to Mill Creek on April 1. Perhaps Rebecca had heard rumors of Travis' philandering because she gave him a cold reception. But once again he won her over, noting in his diary that the conclusion was "*muy calliente.*" Even so, he conceded that they arrived at a simple understanding, presumably about his relations with other women.

Back in San Felipe on April 7 Travis purchased another vial of medication from Stewart's store. Five days later he went back to Cummings' inn "& staid all night —&c." Rebecca proved very affectionate and rewarded him with "*muchas carizias*" (many caresses). They recuperated the next day, pleasantly fishing in the creek.

Another vial of medicine on April 16; another visit to Rebecca three days later. They talked seriously about their future together, agreeing to marry as soon as Travis' divorce had been finalized. They also may have talked seriously about something else. When Travis visited Stewart's shop on April 21, he purchased a vial of mercury for Rebecca and sent it on to the inn.

A week later Travis recorded exhilarating news. Until that time Texas had been divided into two political districts, the departments of Bexar and Nacogdoches. In March the Texas friendly legislature at Monclova had created a third political division, subdividing the Department of Bexar and creating from its eastern region the new Department of Brazos. Concentrated around Austin's colony, the Department of Brazos afforded the citizens of that area more voice in self-government.

Map showing Departments of Texas

Governor Agustin Viesca instructed the *ayuntamiento* at San Felipe to present a slate of candidates for political chief (*jefe*) of the new district. On April 28 the *ayuntamiento* offered three names. Travis' friend and fellow radical, Robert Williamson, the *alcalde*, naturally headed the list. The second candidate was a diametrically opposed centralist sympathizer named James H. C. Miller.

The third name on the slate was William Barret Travis.

Whether or not Travis won the position, his mere nomination displayed his increasing political prominence. But again Travis played reticent. He wrote to Ramon Musquiz, the *jefe* at Bexar, "I have no desire to be employed in the position of Chief; but if I were named I should comply with all the laws and orders of the government to the best of my ability." Apparently Travis wanted the position badly enough to try to portray himself as more moderate than his reputation as a firebrand suggested.

Travis was "joyously received" when he returned to Rebecca on May 7. Perhaps she was celebrating his nomination.

Then his workload kept him away until the end of the month. When he opened the *ayuntamiento's* mail on May 14, he read that his friend David G. Burnet had received an appointment as district judge at San Jacinto. But there was even more exciting news. The Monclova legislature had opened up vast amounts of unoccupied lands in Texas and Coahuila to be sold at public auction—open to foreigners. Travis hastily wrote Burnet that same day, describing the new legislation as "the most important law ever passed by the state gov't."

On May 31 he paid Rebecca another visit. Again she was angry. Presumably she had heard more lascivious rumors. But Travis assured her, perhaps honestly, that he had behaved himself. At least his diary had not recorded any indiscretions for over two months. "Hell—love L-v-e triumphed over slander &c—" he recorded.

Nearly three weeks passed before he called on her again. He spent the night of June 20 at Cummings inn and merely observed, "*buena*."

Two nights later, back in San Felipe, he had a presumably illicit "Adventure with Miss T &c—" Undoubtedly the story got to Rebecca before Travis did on June 25. But once again his glib tongue—or her willingness to forgive—overcame his transgressions. "—reconciliation—happy &c—" he noted.

It was his last reference to her, although their relationship continued along its rocky path. Travis' diary concluded the next day with one last entry, describing random living expenditures and dry professional matters. Curiously the surviving volume of the diary included very little of the fiery rhetoric which would characterize Travis.

Most Texians had been mollified by Austin's accomplishments in Mexico City, especially the reopening of the borders to immigration, as well as the Monclova legislature's establishment of the Department of the Brazos and the impending land auctions. As a period of quiet prosperity embraced

Texas, radical politics had slipped into the background. The colonists seemed to be heeding Austin's warning of moderation so literally that Austin himself began to fear that he had been forsaken.

On May 9 Austin was released from the claustrophobic darkness of his solitary confinement and finally afforded quill, ink, and paper. "I have no idea when I shall be at liberty," he wrote his brother-in-law, James Perry. "I think that all depends upon the report of Almonte. . . ."

Reportedly the offspring of the revolutionary priest Padre Jose Maria Morelos and an Indian woman named Brigida, Juan Nepomuceno Almonte had been born on May 15, 1803. Upon learning of the birth of a son, Padre Morelos allegedly ordered the boy to be taken to the mountain, *"¡Al monte!"* the origin of his surname. Instead Morelos sent young Juan to be educated in the United States.

A leader in the revolt against Spain, Padre Morelos was captured and executed in 1815. Almonte subsequently returned to Mexico and supported Vicente Guerrero's struggle for independence. He won enough prestige to

Juan Nepomuceno Almonte
Courtesy The Institute of Texan Cultures

be included in the 1824 legation to England and helped draft the Republic of Mexico's first commercial treaty with a foreign nation. Almonte had enjoyed some prestige in the new Mexican Republic. Although appointed minister of war under President Anastacio Bustamante, Almonte later turned against the centralist leader and joined the federalist movement. In January 1834, following the arrest of Austin, acting president Farias dispatched Almonte to make an inspection tour of Texas and, especially, to ascertain whether the Anglo colonists were plotting revolution.

Almonte remained in Texas through the summer, preparing an extremely detailed report. He spent a considerable amount of time with his father's old comrade-in-arms Colonel Peter Ellis Bean, who certainly contributed insights to the report. Almonte noted:

> The population of Texas extends from Bexar to the Sabine River, and in that direction there are not more than twenty-five leagues of unoccupied territory to occasion some inconvenience to the traveler. The most difficult part of the journey to Texas is the space between the Rio Grande and Bexar, which extends a little more than fifty leagues, by what is called the Upper Road, and about sixty-five leagues by the way of Laredo. These difficulties do not arise from the badness of the road itself, but from the absence of population, rendering it necessary to carry provisions, and even water during summer, when it is scarce in this district.

Only two years later Almonte would learn firsthand the difficulties of moving an entire army across that barren region.

He concluded that:

> . . . Texas must soon be the most flourishing section of the Republic. There is no difficulty in explaining the reason for this prosperity. In Texas, with the exception of some disturbers, they only think of growing the sugar cane, cotton, corn, wheat, tobacco; the breeding of cattle, opening of roads, and rendering the rivers navigable.

Except for "some disturbers," Almonte had not found a great movement for independence from Mexico. Yet even those disturbers, whose ranks included men like William Wharton, Robert Williamson, Sam Houston, and William Barret Travis, were not unsympathetic to Stephen F. Austin's plight, even though they differed from his politics of moderation. In mid-July Robert Williamson in his capacity as *alcalde* at San Felipe, aided by Travis as secretary of the *ayuntamiento,* composed a letter to the Bexar *ayuntamiento* —to be conveyed on to Mexico City—calling for Austin's release. Williamson portrayed Austin as the honorable representative of the people, nobly delivering their petition despite his own reservations. Any blame should be attached to the Texians, who still lamented their "unnatural connexion [*sic*] with Coahuila."

Although Austin received support from his political opponents in Texas, he faced a more severe threat from unscrupulous speculators in the United States who perceived him as a block to the acquisition of Texas and the fortunes that could be derived from its rich lands. Colonel Anthony Butler, the United States ambassador to Mexico, so regarded Austin. En route to his new post, he had passed through San Antonio de Bexar in 1829. Bexar *jefe* Ramon Musquiz recalled that Butler had confided the primary object of his mission was the purchase of Texas.

Butler, who seems to have represented the interest of land speculators more than those of his own government, still had not accomplished his purpose five years later. He rejoiced over Austin's imprisonment, proclaiming:

> [Austin] is unquestionably one of the bitterest foes of our government and people that is to be found in Mexico and has done more to embarrass our negotiations upon a certain subject than all the rest of the opposition together; and I am very sure that he was the principal cause of my being defeated in the last effort to obtain a cession of Texas.

Consequently, Austin received no official assistance from the United States ambassador. Worse, Butler and his cronies may have been behind the rumor—and even promoted the notion—that Austin would be sentenced to a California penal colony for ten years.

In fact Austin was moved, first to the Acordada on June 12 and later to the Diputacion prison on the main plaza of the city.

"I believe that uncertainty was the greatest torture Colonel Austin endured," wrote George Hammeken, an American in Mexico City who had befriended Austin.

"I am suffering, but the evils of Texas are remedied," Austin himself declared. "This idea consoles me for my misfortunes and enables me to bear them firmly."

Neither Austin nor his colonists could appreciate that the prosperity and political solitude currently enjoyed by Texas was merely the tranquil lull immediately preceding the deadly tempest.

Santa Anna rode the advance winds. During his first year as president, he had managed to be away from the capital for all but about three months, allowing Vice President Gomez Farias and his federalist legislature to blunder their way into oblivion with their excessive reforms.

With discontent sweeping the nation, Santa Anna conveniently recovered from his ailment. On April 24 he returned to Mexico City to reassume the presidency. Many of the liberals suspected Santa Anna's motives. However Farias surrendered the government without conflict and retired from office with his hands clean of money and blood.

Supported by the military and a grateful clergy, nothing stood in Santa Anna's way. In his autobiography he recalled:

These careless reforms of the Congress caused turmoil among the people. In Cuernavaca a *Plan* was issued and swiftly accepted by all the states. Under this *Plan*, the President was granted extraordinary powers.

The centralist-backed *Plan de Cuernavaca*, issued May 23, 1834, proclaimed Santa Anna the sole defender of the Mexican Constitution, finally transforming him into the dictator he had always wanted to be. " . . . it is very true that I threw up my cap for liberty with great ardor, and perfect sincerity, but very soon [I] found the folly of it," he later admitted. "A despotism is the proper government for [the people of Mexico]. . . . "

He sprang into action. In the name of religion Santa Anna denounced reform, repealed liberal legislations, dismissed the congress, and deposed all governors and state legislatures that opposed him. Then, following the example of his former commander, Iturbide, he carefully handpicked his own government. But he stopped short of declaring himself emperor. Still pretending allegiance to the Constitution that he had effectively dismantled, Santa Anna asserted in his autobiography, " . . . once more the government gained the people's confidence and was able to preserve the peace."

This time prison bars had obscured Stephen F. Austin's view of the political coup that would alter the history of both Texas and Mexico.

Chapter 17: **Monclova**

Santa Anna's sudden transformation into a dictator generated aftershocks that rumbled across Texas. And the two men most frequently found at the epicenters of contention were William Barret Travis and James Bowie.

According to the popular, romantic tradition, Bowie became a reclusive alcoholic after the death of his wife. The tradition is wrong. Certainly Bowie now had more than "dull care" to drive away. Not only had he lost his beloved Ursula, but her father's death had removed the financial security on which Bowie had relied. On occasion he did apparently drink to excess. Significantly, however, there would be few documented instances when he was described as being drunk, and most of those allegations were made by political adversaries years after Bowie's death.

Nor did he become reclusive. Instead he remained as mobile as ever. His friend Captain William Lacey described Bowie as a "roving man—sometimes searching for mines, sometimes fighting Indians, sometimes speculating in lands, and always a gentleman from bottom to top."

Beginning in March 1834, Bowie accompanied Lacey on an extended exploration of the Trinity all the way up to present-day Tarrant County (a full decade and a half before the United States Dragoons would establish a tiny frontier outpost there called Fort Worth). Land speculation probably prompted the expedition, though they also may have searched for lost mines along the way. The northern wilderness afforded a high risk of Indian attack, which made Bowie a good man to have along. However, Lacey did not describe any altercations.

The Bowie magic remained. "He was like Barnum's show—wherever he went everybody wanted to meet him," Lacey recalled.

Bowie rarely laughed, an indication that he was still brooding over his loss, but Lacey described him as generally pleasant, even cheerful at times. "He was not in the habit of using profane language, and never used an indecent or vulgar word during the eight months I passed with him in the wilderness."

On the detail of the time passed, Lacey's account errs, perhaps owing to the faulty memory of the aged narrator, or possibly attributable to an incorrect transcription of his account. Eight *weeks* would have been ample time to explore the upper Trinity, and after two months Bowie definitely was back in San Felipe.

He had heard of the Monclova legislature's generous land offers. Since he was primarily responsible for the movement of the capital to Monclova, Bowie was eager to profit from the land sales. At San Felipe Bowie teamed up with William Wharton and a few other land speculators. William Barret Travis filled out the necessary passports for their long journey.

Travis did not win the election as *jefe* of the Department of Bexar. In fact no election was held. For whatever reason, Governor Agustin Viesca disregarded the slate of candidates and appointed Henry Smith of Brazoria to the post.

Henry Smith

A forty-six-year-old Kentuckian who had migrated to Texas in 1827, Smith had worked as both schoolteacher and surveyor. And he had been politically active. One of the Texian leaders during the Anahuac difficulties, he had been severely wounded during the capture of Velasco.

Yet he was a curious choice for the highest political position any *norteamericano* ever had held in the Mexican province of Texas. Travis and Williamson may have taken some consolation from the fact that Smith shared their radical philosophy. However the new Anglo *jefe* lacked any vestige of political skills. Obnoxiously stubborn and tactless even to his allies, he utterly vilified anyone who disagreed with him.

Although the Department of Brazos remained headquartered at San Felipe, Smith refused to budge from his Brazoria residence. When letters arrived at San Felipe addressed to Smith, Travis, as secretary of the *ayuntamiento*, could only forward them to Brazoria and wait a frustrating week or more to learn what information the correspondence contained. This delay proved to be more than an inconvenience in those uncertain times after Santa Anna had assumed absolute power. The Monclova legislature had denounced the dictator. The centralists at Saltillo recognized an opportunity and quickly created a separate government sympathetic to Santa Anna. Suddenly Coahuila y Texas had two competing capitals.

Travis found a more compatible *jefe* in Juan Nepomuceno Seguin, the twenty-eight-year old son of prominent Bexareno Don Erasmo. Seguin had been politically active since 1823, when he had helped operate his father's post office while Don Erasmo served in the Coahuila legislature. In 1825 Juan had married Maria Gertrudis Flores de Abrego, the daughter of a prominent ranching family. They quickly started a family that would ultimately include ten children.

In December 1833 Seguin was elected *alcalde* of San Antonio de Bexar. The following summer Ramon Musquiz, suffering from poor health, retired as political chief of the Department of Bexar, and Seguin served as ad interim *jefe* until December.

Seguin shared Musquiz's federalist views but retained none of his political conservatism. As a young man he had witnessed the horrors of Arredondo's purge. In the following years Bexar had stagnated and drifted into decline. Then came Austin and

Juan Nepomuceno Seguin
Courtesy Texas State Library and Archives Commission

the colonists, and with them came an era of prosperity for Texas. Seguin had developed more confidence in the *norteamericanos* than in the unstable Mexican government—especially now that it had fallen into the clutches of Antonio Lopez de Santa Anna.

With the combative militias from Saltillo and Monclova generating a civil war, Seguin joined the radical Texian colonists calling for separation from Coahuila. He certainly communicated his views to Travis, who in turn scripted a letter prodding Smith in the same direction. Revolution and discord had deprived the Texian colonists of both state and national government, Travis wrote. "We are subject legally and constitutionally to no power on earth, save our sovereign selves." The letter displayed Travis' true sentiments. He was advocating independence from Coahuila, but his argument worked equally well in support of independence from Mexico.

Travis hardly needed to waste such rhetoric on Smith. By November 1834 the *jefes* of both the Bexar and Brazos departments were calling for a convention to declare the independence of Texas from Coahuila.

Texas simply ignored both men. Henry Rueg, the usually radical *jefe* of the Department of Nacogdoches, did not join with them. *Ayuntamientos* throughout the colonies argued against the wisdom of pressing the matter at this time.

After all, Mexico City had granted most of the colonists' requests.

Why provoke Santa Anna to reclose the border to new immigration?

Such an extreme action might jeopardize Stephen F. Austin, still a prisoner in the capital.

All were valid arguments, yet Travis recognized an underlying universal truth. The Texians were doing too well. Trying to console Smith, who typically had taken the rejection of his convention as a personal rejection, Travis wrote, "as long as people are prosperous they do not desire a change."

Even Travis' most radical friends—men like Francis White Johnson—had retreated from their earlier convictions. Johnson was regarded as being among the most ardent of the firebrands. The native Virginian had come to Texas in 1826. A surveyor, he had laid out the town of Harrisburg. Later he served as *alcalde* of San Felipe before being elected commander of the volunteer Texian force that tried to rescue Travis and the other prisoners held by Bradburn at Anahuac.

But at the moment Frank Johnson was disparaging the new conventions, he was focused on his own prosperity. Shortly afterwards he left San Felipe to join the land speculators amassing at Monclova.

He was there by December, to join Wharton and Samuel M. Williams and other land hungry *norteamericanos*—including several who, like Johnson, would become leaders in the Texas Revolution.

Dr. James Grant had arrived from his home near Nacogdoches. A forty-one-year-old Scot, he had been a member of the Coahuila y Texas legislature in 1832 before acquiring an *empresario* contract in the province of Tamaulipas.

Benjamin Rush Milam from Kentucky also had received an *empresario* grant, but the Law of April 6, 1830 had prevented him from fulfilling his contract. That was only one incident in a life more often characterized by failure than success. He had first come to Texas in 1818, joined a filibustering expedition, and landed in a Spanish prison. Finally released after Mexico had achieved independence, Milam enlisted in the Mexican army and advanced to the rank of colonel. But he had sought his fortune through *empresario* contracts and mining operations that never seemed to pay off. Now in his late forties, Milam saw in the Monclova land sales one more opportunity to achieve his dream.

And then, of course, there was James Bowie, the man with fame but no fortune, in the capital he had helped create. He must have realized the bitter irony that the town where Ursula and her family had died now afforded him his greatest opportunity.

The Monclova legislature embraced them all when it convened March 1, 1835. With a faction in Texas calling for separation from Coahuila, with Saltillo fighting to regain the capital, and with Santa Anna in power, the legislators knew their time was limited. The land sale act that Travis previously had hailed as "the most important law ever passed by the state gov't.," became amended with ever more generous land offers. Ostensibly the sales were to provide funds for defense against the Indians; in reality the Monclova legislators were trying to enrich themselves while they still could—at the expense of Texas lands. They dumped it for as little as a fifth of its value.

Certainly James Bowie fared well. Utilizing that old charisma, Veramendi influence, and borrowed money, he acquired claim to what his friend Caiaphas Ham described as "thousands of acres of land in Texas." Historian William C. Davis, who concentrated on Bowie's land enterprises, maintained, "Bowie suddenly held in his hand a title to more than half a million acres, some 850 square miles, four times his known Louisiana and Arkansas frauds, and all at a fraction of the trouble. . . . "

Though technically legal, the Monclova land sales reeked of corruption, and the foul odor carried up into Texas to be condemned by most of the colonists.

Even worse, the stench also drifted south. Indignant, Santa Anna promptly nullified the land sales and dispatched his brother-in-law, Martin Perfecto de Cos, the new commandant of the eastern interior provinces, to close down the Monclova legislature.

Santa Anna would have gone to Monclova himself, but he had more pressing matters. The fiercely independent province of Zacatecas—Farias' old domain—was rebelling against his autocracy, specifically against his edict diminishing all local militias. Zacatecas demanded the personal attention of the Napoleon of the West. He planned to make an example of it that would discourage other provincial revolts.

Martin Perfecto de Cos

General Cos' army approached Monclova in early April 1835, only to be met outside the city by a militia force. Riding at the head of the militia was Big Jim Bowie. He had a fortune at stake, and unlike most of the other speculators, he was willing to fight for it. He taunted the Mexican *soldados*, apparently trying to provoke a battle. If it was another bluff, it worked. Uncertain as to whether he should commit his troops, Cos withdrew.

His retreat bought Governor Agustin Viesca a little time. With Saltillo supporting Santa Anna, Viesca sent a rider galloping up to Texas with a plea for a hundred volunteers.

The Texian colonists in the Brazos and Nacogdoches departments again ignored the appeal. There was still concern for Austin's safety. They were still prosperously complacent. And more than that, the Texian colonists felt little incentive to go to the aid of the morally corrupt Monclova legislature.

Only Juan Seguin and some of the Bexarenos seemed to appreciate the ironic ambiguity—this attack on a corrupt legislature actually simultaneously constituted an assault on a democratic government by a dictatorship. Seguin rallied twenty-five of his fellow *Tejanos* and galloped south.

Travis played no role in the Monclova episode. Not because he had become complacently prosperous—although he now certainly qualified as prosperous. He had invested in several business ventures, expanded his land holdings, and acquired a few slaves—including a tall, black skinned twenty-year-old man named Joe.

The reason Travis avoided the Monclova incident was that he had personal matters to deal with at that moment.

His wife, Rosanna, had come to Texas. She was in Brazoria, and she had both of the children with her.

In mid-April Travis rode down to Brazoria to meet her. It must have been a bittersweet reunion. He had not seen his son, Charles Edward, for four years. Travis had to be impressed at how much Charles had grown. At the same time, Travis felt both remorse and pain that the boy, now only six or seven years old, had virtually no memory of his father.

Then there was the daughter, Susan Isabella, born after his hasty departure from Alabama. Travis may have questioned her paternity, but now he held her for the first time.

Most important, there was Rosanna, the woman he had once loved. Anger had characterized her correspondence to him in recent years, and perhaps she had played hateful games with his son. But there was no time or place for anger now.

Travis was in love with Rebecca Cummings. And whether or not Rosanna had ever been unfaithful to her husband, she now had a man waiting for her back in Alabama. So, without malice, they agreed that she should continue the divorce proceedings.

And she also agreed to let Travis keep young Charles Edward.

That must have been the hardest part. Could she have kept her tears concealed from the boy as she gave him that last hug and then gently prodded him towards Travis? What thoughts flooded young Charles' mind as he gingerly approached the outstretched arms of this stranger who was his father?

Then Travis took Charles to his new home in San Felipe, and Rosanna and Susan Isabella sailed back to Alabama. Travis would never see either of them again. But soon afterwards he prepared a will that divided his estate between both of his children and provided for their education.

Now Travis finally had his son, Charles, and soon he would be free to marry. Certainly he must have dashed young Charles out to Mill Creek and introduced him to the woman who would be his new mother. And certainly Rebecca doted on the confused little boy.

Sadly, fate would leave Travis little time to savor the love of either of them.

In May Antonio Lopez de Santa Anna marched his army of thirty-five hundred *soldados* against the rebellious province of Zacatecas. Unlike

Monclova, Zacatecas boasted the finest militia in Mexico, over ten thousand well-equipped troops funded by the rich silver mines in the region. Such an army had been beneficial to Santa Anna in his wars against the centralists. Now Santa Anna was leading a centralist army, and the Zacatecan militia posed a critical threat.

The Napolean of the West lived up to his self-appointed title that day. He launched a rear assault that utterly routed the federalist militia but cost the Mexican army less than a hundred casualties. A large number of federalist prisoners were executed. Santa Anna favored executions; it saved him from ever having to forgive his enemies.

Then, to set an example for all of Mexico to remember, Santa Anna rewarded his victorious troops by presenting them with the capital city of Zacatecas. For two days the Mexican *soldados* plundered and pillaged and raped and murdered. No accurate statistics survive describing the casualties suffered by the Zacatecan militia and civilians, but estimates as high as twenty-five hundred dead—probably an exaggeration—resounded across Mexico.

By the time Juan Seguin arrived in late May, Monclova had heard of the massacre at Zacatecas. The news created a panic that threatened to empty the city. The legislature hastily enacted a law enabling the capital to be relocated to San Antonio de Bexar. Then, with a bodyguard of one hundred twenty-five militia and Seguin's twenty-five men, Governor Viesca set out for Texas.

Abruptly Viesca changed his mind. He dismissed his bodyguard, apparently assuming he would have a better chance of evading Mexican troops with only a few men.

It was a mistake. General Cos swept through Monclova. Viesca and members of the legislature were apprehended before they reached the Rio Grande. Cos' *soldados* arrested some of the land speculators, including the hard luck filibuster, Ben Milam, who once again would take up residence inside a Mexican prison.

And the Mexicans captured James Bowie.

Seguin and his men escaped back to Bexar where they pledged themselves "to rouse Texas against the tyrannical government of Santa Anna." Seguin dispatched an agent to Brazoria "to sound out the temperament of the [Anglo colonists]." The agent subsequently reported that "there was a great deal of talk about a revolution in public meetings but that the moment for an armed movement was still remote."

Certainly things were changing under Santa Anna. Colonel Domingo Ugartechea, who had surrendered the garrison at Velasco, had returned to Texas to take command of the garrison at Bexar. And a company of *soldados* under Captain Antonio Tenorio had arrived at Anahuac to reestablish a fort and resume collecting duties there. Mexico was deep in debt. Santa Anna needed money, especially to support his army.

The only good news was that Stephen F. Austin had been released from prison in December. Yet he remained a prisoner confined to Mexico City, and his continued captivity still concerned most of the colonists. To William Barret Travis, who knew firsthand about such things, Santa Anna was holding Austin hostage. It frustrated Travis. The Texians could not afford to wait until Austin was safe or until Austin had returned to advise them what to do. Yet if Austin were to be killed by the Mexicans, a "thousand of their contemptible red skins" would be sacrificed, Travis vowed, letting a little prejudice slip. Of course he had found comfort in the arms of a few *señoritas*—and he could genuinely respect such men as Juan Seguin—but like many of the Anglo colonists, he felt more than a little superiority over the common *Tejano vaquero* or Mexican peon.

Captain Tenorio had received an even chillier reception from the colonists than Bradburn before him. A fracas soon occurred between his *soldados* and some of the townspeople. Tenorio arrested two men, Andrew Briscoe and DeWitt Clinton Harris, both friends of Travis. Incredibly history was about to repeat itself, at the same site, but this time it was William Barret Travis to the rescue.

Travis dashed down to the coast. At Lynch's Ferry some twenty assembled men elected him "captain" of the expedition. With a six-pound cannon loaded onto the sloop *Ohio*, on June 29, 1835, they sailed across Galveston Bay to Anahuac.

The cannon boomed, announcing the ship's approach in the late afternoon. It was almost dark by the time the Texians had disembarked with their cannon. Travis sent word to Tenorio demanding his surrender. Then Captain William B. Travis led a torch-lit procession toward the newly constructed barracks.

They were empty. Though outnumbering the Texians nearly two-to-one, the Mexicans had fled into the nearby woods. Travis ordered the cannon to be fired at the trees. Shortly afterwards word came that Tenorio wanted to meet personally with Travis at the water's edge.

It would be a tense encounter, both captains fearing an ambush from the other side. Travis kept Texian riflemen back in the shadows—just in case—as he strode boldly out into the moonlight along the beach. For a moment it was just him, with the coastal breeze rustling tree leaves and the waves washing against the shore. Travis called out, and Tenorio replied from the opposite trees. Now even more brazen, Travis walked away from his marksmen, into the shadowy blackness from which the voice had emerged.

Surrender, he said coldly, or he would order the Mexicans to be "put to the sword."

He was lying, of course. He would never allow or condone such brutality. But it was dark, and the bluff worked. Tenorio surrendered his larger force to William Barret Travis, agreeing never again to take up arms against Texas.

It was just the sort of daring enterprise that James Bowie seemed to pull off with regularity. Such episodes seemed to embellish Bowie's reputation. However the Bowie magic apparently did not apply to Travis. When he conveyed his prisoners to Harrisburg on July 4, it was Tenorio and his garrison who received the reception usually afforded the conquering hero. The townspeople, anxious to mitigate the political impact of the incident, invited the prisoners to partake of the holiday festivities. The *soldados*, who probably had not eaten well since their arrival in Texas, stuffed themselves on barbecue. Captain Tenorio charmed the gentlemen and waltzed with their ladies.

Leaving his prisoners there to be shipped back to Mexico, Travis returned to San Felipe. There he met with even greater antagonism. By now the radicals had become identified as the War Party. In a general sense it was comprised of single men, the adventurers and speculators who had recently arrived in Texas. The majority Peace Party consisted primarily of the earlier colonists, men who had brought their wives and children with them, men who had carved out farms and erected towns, men who had the most at stake if war erupted.

"I have as much to lose by a revolution as most men in the country," Travis once wrote. "Yet I wish to know, for whom I labor—whether for myself or a plundering robbing, autocratical, aristocratical jumbled up gov't which is in fact no gov't at all. . . . "

The Peace Party ignored his explanations and publicly condemned his rash actions at Anahuac. Travis' former political opponent, centralist sympathizer James H. C. Miller, observed with no regret that, "Travis is in a peck of troubles."

As a prisoner of the Mexicans, James Bowie also had been in a peck of troubles. But being Bowie, he somehow managed to escape. Significantly, Bowie had learned that Cos was commandeering ships at Matamoras to bring the Mexican army to the Texas coast. Bowie communicated this intelligence in a letter to San Felipe. Yet some leaders of the Peace Party doubted the veracity of the letter, arguing instead that Bowie and the other land speculators were fomenting a war for independence just to restore title to their corrupt land purchases.

At least the citizens of Nacogdoches believed Bowie's account. They had just learned of the Anahuac incident when James Bowie arrived there. On July 13, fearing retaliation from General Cos, the townsmen formed a militia, and they elected Bowie as their "colonel."

It seems curious that the citizens of Nacogdoches passed over some of their own prominent leaders—men like *jefe* Henry Rueg or their new, distinguished resident, Sam Houston—to pick a man who resided clear across Texas. But just having escaped his Mexican captors, Big Jim Bowie was the man of the moment. He was the hero of the sandbar fight, the San Saba Indian battle, and he had previously led men from Nacogdoches to capture General Piedras.

It was the first time the rank of colonel, however honorary, ever had been bestowed on Bowie. Prior to that time he had just been "Mr." Bowie. There was a saying from that era that seemed especially appropriate for the "gentlemen" who had Gone To Texas. "If a man did not have a title before his name [such as Dr., Judge, or any military rank], he either had no friends—or no imagination." Bowie had plenty of friends and imagination, but he had fared well without the pretensions of a title. Now, however—and from now on—he would be Colonel James Bowie.

Colonel Bowie swung into action. He led his militia against the Mexican armory. They bullied their way in without bloodshed and confiscated all the weapons for the Texians.

Then Bowie intercepted some official Mexican correspondence intended for the Mexican Consul at New Orleans. The letters confirmed General Cos' imminent occupation of Texas. Also there was a demand for the arrest of the Texian leader at Anahuac, William Barret Travis.

In San Felipe, a much-chastened Travis had learned of Bowie's capture of the arsenal. They hardly knew each other, but on July 30 Travis felt compelled to write Bowie. "The truth is, the people are much divided here,"

Travis noted, cautioning that unless the War Party could be united, "had we better not settle down and be quiet for a while?"

Travis continued:

> God knows what we are to do! I am determined, for one, to go with my countrymen; "right or wrong, sink or swim, live or die, survive or perish," I am with them.

No one in San Felipe yet knew that Travis was to be arrested, but some of his countrymen, most notably James H. C. Miller, were advocating just such an action—surrendering Travis to placate the Mexican authorities. Miller asserted that until the leaders of the War Party were dealt with, "Texas will never be at quiet."

On August 4 Colonel Ugartechea at San Antonio de Bexar received orders from General Cos, still in Matamoras. Cos had written:

> As it is impossible that the attack upon the garrison of Anahuac should pass with impunity, I require . . . your honor to proceed immediately and without excuse to the apprehension of the ungrateful and bad citizen, Juliano Barret Travis, who headed the revolutionary party; and to cause him to be conducted to Bexar . . . in order that he may be tried and punished according to Law. [He] is an injury to these inhabitants of Texas, and it is a shame that the public authorities should, in cold blood, be tolerating his excuses, when he ought to have been punished long since.

Others also had been singled out for arrest. Dr. Lorenzo de Zavala's liberal views once had cast him into a Spanish prison. Having strongly denounced Santa Anna's rise to despotism, the first man to sign the Constitution of 1824 had no desire to return to similar confinement under a Mexican banner. He had taken refuge in Texas.

Francis W. Johnson was doubly damned as both a leader of the War Party and a land speculator. He had eluded Cos' troops at Monclova and slipped back into Texas.

The colorful attorney Robert M. Williamson still reigned as one of the most radical leaders in Texas. In early July he had tried to rouse the Peace Party with a published appeal: "Already we can almost hear the bugles of our enemies; already have some of them landed on our coast; and you must prepare to fight. . . . Liberty or death should be our determination, and let us one and all unite to protect our country from all invasion, and not lay down our arms so long as a soldier is seen in our limits."

Word of the impending arrests arrived in San Felipe before any *soldados* did. Rather than disappear into a Mexican prison, Three-Legged Willie and Buck Travis mounted their horses and galloped out of San Felipe into the wilderness to the north. They would stay hidden for several weeks.

They need not have bothered. Their extreme actions might have been condemned by many of the Texians, but those same Texians would be damned before they would let the Mexicans arrest Travis, Williamson, and the others. The very existence of the arrest warrants swung the political pendulum in the favor of the War Party. As early as August 8, Dr. Lorenzo de Zavala called for a new convention to be held October 15. And this time all of Texas was listening

And then, suddenly, Stephen F. Austin was back on Texas soil. Released under a general amnesty law, he had left Mexico City on July 13 and sailed from Vera Cruz to New Orleans. From there on August 21 he wrote to his cousin, Mary Austin Holley:

> General Santa Anna told me he should visit Texas next March
> —as a friend. His visit is uncertain—his friendship more so.
> We must rely on ourselves and prepare for the worst.

He landed in Texas on September 1, gaunt and frail, and spent a week recuperating at his sister's home. On September 8 he addressed a banquet held in his honor at nearby Brazoria. He endorsed the pending convention, or "consultation," as he called it, to be held in mid-October at San Felipe.

Only a week later, General Cos, at the head of five hundred Mexican troops, landed at Copano Bay. He sent word that the Texians must disband their militias, relinquish their weapons, and surrender their radical leaders. Or he would invade the colonies.

Austin responded by issuing a call to arms. "War is our only recourse," he wrote. "There is no other remedy but to defend our rights, our selves, and our country by force of arms."

Stephen F. Austin had joined the War Party, and Texas would follow him.

Chapter 18: *Gonzales*

With the Texians priming their long rifles and shotguns, with General Cos advancing toward La Bahia en route to San Antonio, Colonel Ugartechea frantically sought to disarm the confrontation—or at least the Texians. Someone apprised him of the tiny cannon at Gonzales, the westernmost Anglo settlement, only eighty miles east of Bexar. Ugartechea dispatched Lieutenant Francisco Castaneda to retrieve the cannon but, if possible, to avoid conflict.

A hundred mounted *soldados* from the Alamo Company followed Castaneda across a rain-drenched prairie. On September 29, 1835, the Mexicans arrived at the west bank of the flooded, tree-shaded Guadalupe River.

The town, comprised mostly of simple log structures, extended from the opposite bank above the ferry crossing. The ferry itself was securely moored on that bank, guarded by a mere handful of armed men.

Thirty-five-year-old Almaron Dickinson (who also spelled his name Dickerson) typified that small band. A Pennsylvanian by birth, he may have received artillery training during a stint in the United States Army. Then he had headed west. By 1829 he was in Tennessee where he eloped with Susanna Wilkerson, a young woman only half his age. He brought her to Texas, arriving in Gonzales in February 1831. He worked in the center of town as a blacksmith, and he also entered into a partnership with George Kimble to operate a hat factory. On December 14, 1834, Susanna gave birth to a daughter they named Angelina Elizabeth. As he confronted the Mexican troops, he must have thought of the baby, clutched in the anxious arms of its mother.

Kentuckian Jacob C. Darst, then forty-two years old, arrived in Gonzales with his wife, Margaret, and two children a month before the Dickinsons. Although he farmed on land upriver, he was just the sort of man who would grab a long rifle or shotgun and run to the defense of his town.

Thomas Jackson, a former seaman from Ireland, had been in Gonzales since 1829. About that same time a Missouri couple named Cottle arrived with their two sons, Almond and George Washington, and a daughter named Louisa. Jackson married Louisa that same year, and they now had four children. Louisa's brother Almond stood near Jackson as they stared at the hundred *soldados* across the river.

Forty-year-old Thomas R. Miller, from Tennessee, migrated to Gonzales in 1830 where he opened a general store. He was deemed the richest man in town. In March 1832 he married sixteen-year-old Sidney Gaston. But their only child died in infancy, which may have contributed to the couple's separation in July 1833. Infant deaths were far more common than divorces, which could be scandalous, but Miller's reputation remained untarnished. He subsequently served as clerk for the Gonzales Town Council, which met at his home. His ex-wife married an eighteen-year-old boy from Kentucky named John Benjamin Kellogg, who recently had rambled into town.

Albert Martin from Providence, Rhode Island, seemed an unlikely choice to have been elected leader of this small band. Only twenty-seven years old, he had been in Gonzales less than half a year, operating a general store in competition with Miller's. Yet Martin obviously possessed those natural traits that made men fall in behind him.

There were a baker's dozen more, including Judge Ezekiel Williams, former *alcalde* of Gonzales, whose farm would soon play a key role. Gonzales would later honor them all as the "Old Eighteen." But four of those men—Martin, Miller, Darst, and Jackson—would subsequently join another volunteer group that would be revered as the "Immortal Gonzales Thirty-two."

The Texians guarding the river refused to send the ferry across, and they refused to surrender the cannon. Apprised of Castaneda's approach, Martin had buried the cannon in a peach orchard, and he had sent riders galloping for reinforcements. Now he could only stall for time.

Unwilling to test the flooded river's rapid current under enemy rifle fire—uncertain if he should even engage the Texians—Castaneda camped his troops back on the prairie.

By the next day at least one hundred fifty men, from settlements as far away as San Felipe, had mustered in Gonzales. They elected John Henry Moore as colonel of their combined forces. Moore, a thirty-five-year-old Tennessean, had been one of Austin's Old Three Hundred. A veteran Indian fighter, his blockhouse, Moore's Fort, had expanded into the site of La Grange.

On October 1 they dug up the cannon of contention. It was a tiny "six-pounder," which meant it was bored to accommodate a small, six-pound lead ball. It was just a tube, not even mounted on a carriage. Moreover someone, presumably Arredondo's Spanish *soldados*, had "spiked" the cannon, hammering a metal rod into the touchhole to prevent it from firing. The citizens of Gonzales had been able to discharge the gun only by extending a long fuse from the powder charge out through the muzzle. In that manner the cannon did little more than produce noise and flash and smoke, but that had been enough to scare the Comanches away from the town.

Such a cannon hardly seemed worth all the commotion it had stirred. But the nearly useless weapon now had evolved into a symbol of defiance. Throughout history men have rallied, fought, and died for symbols. Some enterprising Texian, perhaps Colonel Moore himself, painted a crude representation of the cannon barrel onto the center of a white banner. At the top was a five-pointed star. Beneath the cannon barrel the artist printed a brazen challenge: "Come and Take It."

The Texians did their best to transform the symbol back into some semblance of a weapon. They rigged it with wheels borrowed from a cotton wagon. Jacob Darst managed to bore the spike out. The operation enlarged the touchhole to thumb-sized diameter, which weakened the compression of the blast, but at least the cannon could fire a light charge at close range.

Captain James Clinton Neill, a dedicated forty-five-year-old North Carolinian, was placed in command of the Texian artillery, which consisted of that one cannon. Neill had received military experience in the United States Army during the Creek Indian war. Like Houston he had been wounded at Horseshoe Bend.

Almaron Dickinson served on the cannon crew. They loaded it with horseshoes, nails, and other metal scraps from John Sowell's blacksmith shop. Cannon balls were for battering down defenses; grapeshot and cannister proved more effective against masses of men, literally transforming the cannon into an oversized shotgun.

That evening, veiled by darkness, the ferry quietly shuttled back and forth across the Guadalupe, conveying the Texian force to the west bank. But a fog settled in during the predawn hours of the following morning, October 2, 1835. The blinded Texians settled amid trees along the river. As they waited for daylight, they feasted on watermelons from Ezekiel Williams' farm.

The morning sun burned away the fog, and the Texians saw the *soldados* encamped beyond the rows of cornstalks on a rise some three hundred fifty yards away. Riflemen emerged from the trees and sniped at the

Mexicans. Castaneda dispatched his lancers to drive the Texian marksmen back into cover.

Then a barely literate Anglo doctor named Launcelot Smither emerged from the Mexican position. He had been returning from Bexar with mules packed with supplies when he had encountered Castaneda's force. Learning their objective and striving to avoid armed conflict, the busybody doctor had eagerly volunteered his services to negotiate with the Gonzales authorities for the surrender of the cannon. But with an armed force of Texians now on the west bank of the river, Castaneda promptly arrested Smither as a spy and impounded his money, mules, and supplies. Then Castaneda sent the dismayed Smither out to request a parley.

Seeing Smither advancing from the Mexican position, the Texians did not trust him any more than had Castaneda. Colonel Moore also ordered Smither's arrest. At this point the hapless doctor regretted his involvement and desired only the return of his possessions.

Moore agreed to meet with Castaneda midway between the two camps, and he allowed the whining Smither to accompany him.

Castaneda joined them. Appearing dismayed and incredulous, he asked why he had been attacked. He had issued no threats, and he now professed to be a federalist. It may have been the truth. Many of the *soldados* in the Alamo Company still opposed centralist authority.

Moore responded sharply that if Castaneda truly were a federalist, he would join the Texians in the war against Santa Anna and fight to restore the Constitution of 1824.

But Castaneda snapped that a soldier must follow orders. Ignoring Smither's babbling pleas for his property, the Mexican officer turned and marched back to join his forces. The parley had failed.

Moore and a disgruntled Smither returned to the Texian army. Moore gave orders. The Texians formed up outside of the trees. Neill's crew wheeled the small cannon forward of the line. Someone waved the taunting "Come and Take It" flag. But the Texians did not wait to see if the Mexicans would respond to the dare. Moore gave Neill the order to "Fire!" Neill echoed the order to his crew. The cannon roared. Then the riflemen fired a volley. Colonel Moore bellowed "Charge!" and his men surged forward through the cloudy wall of gun smoke their weapons had just spewed—only to catch sight of the Mexicans in flight. Castaneda had ordered a retreat—all the way back to Bexar.

The minor skirmish at Ezekiel Williams' Farm soon became known as the "battle" of Gonzales and later celebrated as the "Lexington of Texas." The Texas Revolution had begun.

The Texians did not suffer any significant casualties. Castaneda left behind one or two dead *soldados*. In the first official battle of the Texas Revolution, the first to die belonged to the Alamo Company.

Ironically, neither of the two men perhaps most responsible for the escalating hostilities had been present. James Bowie had made an impromptu trip back to the United States. William Barret Travis, frustrated as he watched others ride off to the arena of action, had remained in San Felipe, bedridden with the common flu.

Chapter 19: ## *The Cannon and Victory*

T he English word *"disaster"* combines two Latin terms that *roughly translate as "evil star." Since prehistoric times, comets were perceived as harbingers of impending doom. According to legend, as recorded on France's Bayeaux Tapestry, court astrologers warned the Saxon king Harold the Ruthless of one such ominous heavenly omen that appeared early in 1066. Later that year the comet's dire prophecy was fulfilled when knights under William of Normandy invaded England. Harold died at the battle of Hastings where the Normans routed the Saxon army and conquered England.*

In 1682 twenty-six-year-old British astronomer Edmond Halley saw that same comet soaring through the stars. Halley accurately computed that the comet orbited around the sun to reappear in the earth's heavens every seventy-six years. Halley died before the comet's return in 1758. History records that Halley's Comet was especially bright on its next cycle—in the early fall of 1835.

One week after the skirmish at Gonzales, Captain George Collinsworth led over a hundred Texian volunteers against the Mexican garrison at Goliad, still more commonly known as La Bahia. En route the Texians stumbled across a scraggly, unshaven *norteamericano* who had just escaped from a Monterrey prison. It was Ben Milam, and he eagerly fell in with the Anglo force.

Somewhat ambitiously, Collinsworth hoped to capture General Cos and his five hundred troops at Goliad. In the predawn hours of October 10, 1835, the Texians launched a surprise assault on the presidio.

It fell easily. Too easily. Cos had already departed for San Antonio de Bexar, leaving behind a garrison of only fifty *soldados*. The Texians suffered a single casualty in the attack. A Mexican musket ball shattered the shoulder of a freed slave named Samuel McCulloch.

The Texians captured Mexican arms and equipment. More important, they had cut off Cos' vital corridor to the coast. Any aid or supplies for Bexar now would have to march overland from Mexico.

News of the fall of La Bahia added to the rowdy euphoria at Gonzales where volunteers continued to assemble from across Texas. Stephen F. Austin arrived. So did William Barret Travis, still pale from his own illness. The Texian army swelled to some three hundred men. The blending of victory and corn liquor made a powerful intoxicant, and the rambunctious celebration that had begun the evening after the battle continued day after day.

Noah Smithwick, the blacksmith who claimed to have made a replacement knife for Bowie, entered Gonzales the day after the battle. He recalled:

> I can not remember that there was any distinct understanding as to the position we were to assume toward Mexico. Some were for independence; some for the constitution of 1824; and some for anything, just so it was a row. But we were all ready to fight.

"On to Bexar!" became the battle cry that overzealous, would-be soldiers echoed through the town. They elected Stephen F. Austin as their general. He did not want the position. He had returned from his Mexican imprisonment feeling old, exhausted, and feeble. Moreover he had no real military experience. But once again Austin put the needs of Texas before his own welfare. He reluctantly accepted the command. Otherwise the various militias would have bickered over leadership and some might have returned home. Austin was the only man who could unify the motley rabble that pretended to be an army.

On October 12 General Austin led the march west from Gonzales.

On to Bexar.

Smithwick provided a colorful description of the ragtag rebel force to which Austin had attached the impressive label "Federal Army of Texas."

> Words are inadequate to convey an impression of the appearance of the first Texas army as it formed in marching order. It certainly bore little resemblance to the army of my childhood dreams. Buckskin breeches were the nearest approach to uniform, and there was wide diversity even there, some being new and soft and yellow, while others, from long familiarity with rain and grease and dirt, had become hard and shiny. Boots being an unknown quantity; some wore shoes and some moccasins. Here a broad-brimmed sombrero overshadowed the military cap at its side; there a tall "beegum" rode familiarly beside a coonskin cap, with the tail hanging down

behind, as all well regulated tails should do. A fantastic military array to a casual observer, but the one great purpose animating every heart clothed us in a uniform more perfect in our eyes than was ever donned by regulars on dress parade.

Creed Taylor, who served as an orderly under General Austin, also accompanied the march from Gonzales. He remembered, "our cannon flag was proudly borne by a man mounted upon a small, wiry pony that had an inclination to dash off at full speed every time the boys gave vent to their feelings with a ringing cheer, which was quite frequent."

The Texian "artillery" followed. It still consisted of nothing more than the tiny Gonzales cannon, mounted upon a flimsy four-wheeled carriage. The carriage broke down frequently, causing numerous delays. The fate of the cannon remains a subject of debate. According to some sources, General Austin decided to abandon the nearly useless cannon, burying it along the banks of Sandy Creek. Other sources argue that the Texians dragged it all the way to San Antonio.

On October 16 the army stopped at Cibolo Creek, only twenty miles east of Bexar and camped for several days to allow stragglers and new recruits to catch up. Only a handful of reinforcements arrived, but among them, riding into camp on the night of October 19, was James Bowie, just returned from the United States.

Austin had plenty of subordinate officers. His adjutant was Bowie's old comrade Warren D. C. Hall. There were two lieutenant colonels: John H. Moore and a thirty-seven-year-old North Carolinian named Edward Burleson. Burleson had more genuine military experience than most of the soldiers in Austin's army. He had fought in the War of 1812 and later served as captain of a Missouri militia. Migrating to Texas in 1832, he was elected lieutenant colonel of the Austin Municipality militia. Like Moore, Burleson was a seasoned Indian fighter.

Edward Burleson

Captain James Walker Fannin, a thirty-one-year-old Georgia slave trader, enjoyed the prestige of being the only Texian officer with West Point experience. That honor overshadowed the fact that he had dropped out after only two years.

There were plenty of other militia captains, including Ben Milam—and even more lieutenants. Austin had assigned that rank to young William Barret Travis.

But of all these men, Austin probably needed Colonel James Bowie the most. Not only did Bowie always seem to resolve the unresolvable, but being a resident of Bexar and a friend of the *Tejanos* still within the city, he could provide invaluable information. Austin made Colonel Bowie a volunteer aide-de-camp—in essence, a troubleshooter for the army.

The next morning the Texians advanced to Salado Creek, only five miles from Bexar, and again encamped for several days. Austin sent a message to General Cos requesting a parley. The Mexican commander curtly responded, "I shall never treat with the ungrateful Texians save as rebels."

Cos could afford to be curt. Combining the troops he had brought from Matamoras with the garrison at Bexar, he commanded approximately six hundred fifty *soldados*. He had twenty cannons, the largest collection of artillery west of the Mississippi. His troops worked diligently to fortify the entrances to the city and also to strengthen the defenses of the crumbling old mission just across the river. Cos had made his headquarters inside the Alamo.

Texian reinforcements continued to drift into Austin's camp. He now had some four hundred fifty soldiers and two six-pound artillery pieces. Another prominent figure caught up with them at the Salado. Creed Taylor remembered, " . . . a lone horseman—his length of limb sadly out of proportion to that of the horse he rode—came up in our wake and was greeted by Austin as 'General Houston.'"

Houston had just left San Felipe, where the few delegates who had assembled for the Consultation had nominated him as commander-in-chief of the army of Texas. Unfortunately, there had not been enough delegates for a quorum. Most of those elected to the Consultation—including Burleson, Travis, and Austin himself—were instead marching against Bexar. The Consultation had been postponed until November.

Houston surveyed the Texian army and did not like what he saw. Overconfident, undertrained, and undisciplined, the volunteers could not have changed much since the French and Indian War when General James Wolfe had described his Americans as "the worst soldiers in the Universe."

Actually, in that war and subsequent ones, militias often had proven effective utilizing commando tactics learned from the Indians. But militia rarely succeeded against a regular army. The popular song "The Hunters of Kentucky" credited the victory at New Orleans to the rugged backwoodsmen's unerring accuracy with their long rifles. "For every man was half a horse and half an alligator," the chorus proclaimed. In fact the fog that morning had inhibited long-range marksmanship; most of the British were felled by cannister from Jackson's artillery.

Worse, the half-horse, half-alligators that comprised the Texian army were not well equipped. There were not enough rifles, muskets, or shotguns for all of the men and not enough powder and ammunition even for those weapons. Yet these Texians wanted to attack a fortified position defended by a superior number of artillery and trained infantry troops! The so-called Texian cavalry would have little chance against skilled Mexican lancers. Texians on foot would have no chance at all.

The Texians were being led to the slaughter, Houston told the men in a speech, and it would be suicide to attack San Antonio. Instead Houston recommended that all delegates return to the Consultation to provide the army with both a government and an official cause for the war. Houston advised the army to withdraw to Gonzales or Goliad until it had been adequately trained, supplied, and provided with appropriate numbers of men and artillery.

Perhaps only Sam Houston fretted over the portentous star traveling through the night sky as he preached restraint and patience: "It is better to do well late than never!"

Most of the delegates to the Consultation agreed to follow him back to San Felipe. But the Texian soldiers overwhelmingly rejected Houston's advice with resounding cheers of "On to Bexar." The Consultation would have to do without General Austin, who would remain in command of his army.

Houston's ego, as oversized as his massive frame, did not take the rejection well. Enraged, he retired to his tent where he probably found solace in a bottle. Or perhaps several bottles. Moseley Baker, a War Party advocate but no friend of Houston's, later chided him about that evening: " . . . the hour of midnight was disturbed by howlings of your madness, calling for a pistol to kill yourself. . . . " Fortunately James Bowie intervened, preventing Houston from being his own destroyer.

When he sobered, Houston departed with the delegates. But other volunteers continued to arrive, swelling the ranks of the Texian force to over six hundred men. Among these new recruits was that most unsung of all Texas heroes, the incredible Erastus Smith. Commonly called "Deaf" (pronounced Deef) because of a hearing impairment, forty-eight-year-old Smith was one of the most popular figures among the Texas colonists. Born in New York, raised near Natchez, Smith had ventured into Texas in 1821. Like Bowie, Smith had taken a Mexican wife and had settled in San Antonio de Bexar where he became recognized as one of the best hunters and trackers on the frontier. Away on an extended hunt when the war erupted, he had returned to Bexar to find that his wife and children were in a city fortified by Mexican troops.

Initially Smith had tried to remain neutral. Riding up to the Mexican barricades, he explained to an officer his desire to return to his home and family. The guard informed Smith that he could not pass without specific permission from General Cos. Smith would have to return on the following day.

Smith spent that night at the Texian camp, where Austin, Bowie, and other friends urged him to enlist in their cause. Smith politely refused. The next morning he rode back to Bexar. Suddenly the officer at the barricade grabbed the bridle of Smith's horse. Then Smith saw a squad of Mexican cavalry thundering toward him. Smith managed to wheel his horse, duck under a flashing Mexican saber, and outrace the cavalry back into the Texian camp. Then he swung down from his lathered horse, stormed into Austin's tent, and announced, "General Austin, I told you yesterday that I would not take sides in this war but, Sir, I now tender you my services as the Mexicans acted rascally with me!"

Austin added Smith to his company of scouts and spies, and old Deaf soon became recognized as "the eyes of the Texas army." General Cos apparently recognized that Smith posed a threat, for word leaked out of Bexar that Cos had posted a thousand-dollar bounty on the head of "one Smith called El Sordo [the deaf one]." Smith casually responded with an offer of five hundred dollars for the head of Cos, claiming that was all it was worth.

Smith was joined by Hendrick Arnold, a free black man who had married Smith's stepdaughter. Arnold would distinguish himself in battles to come.

On October 23 Austin received other valuable support from Juan Seguin, the *alcalde* of San Antonio de Bexar, who entered the Texian camp at the head of thirty-seven *Tejano* volunteers. Seguin had escaped Bexar before Cos marched in ten days earlier. But Seguin's father, the venerable

Don Erasmo, stubbornly remained in the city, even as he had done years earlier when Arredondo's Spanish troops arrived. Don Erasmo displayed federalist sympathies, like many of the Bexarenos, and he always had been a true friend of the colonists now in rebellion. Worse, his son, Juan, had become a radical enemy of Santa Anna. Cos promptly dismissed Don Erasmo from his longstanding position as postmaster and forcibly evicted him from Bexar. The elder Seguin had trudged the thirty-odd miles back to his Casa Blanca estate near Floresville.

For Juan Seguin, as with old "Deaf" Smith, the war had become personal.

Other *Tejanos* rode in from local haciendas and from as far away as Victoria and Goliad. Austin commissioned Seguin a captain of the army and placed him in command of the *Tejano* company with instructions to "contract with the inhabitants or owners of ranches" for quantities of corn and beans with which to feed the Texian army. This noncombative assignment may have been influenced by the distrust some Anglos felt toward the *Tejanos*. However, feeding the army had become one of Austin's major concerns. Nothing could undermine a soldier's morale faster than hunger. On October 22 Austin had written Captain Philip Dimmitt, a forty-year-old Kentuckian who now commanded the Texian force at the Goliad presidio, to forward food supplies. " . . . I assure you the men here are beginning to suffer greatly for the want of bread etc etc. . . . " Austin stated. He also advised Dimmit of Seguin's appointment to captain, adding, "Inform your men of this that he may be respected as such and as a devoted friend of the Constitution."

Aside from feeding his army, Austin's other primary concern was determining the best approach to San Antonio. With both of these priorities in mind he placed Colonel James Bowie in command of Captain James Walker Fannin's first division of the first battalion with orders to proceed to the missions of San Juan, Espada, and San Jose. Bowie was to gain information regarding "the disposition of the inhabitants" toward the Texian cause, determine "the quantity of corn and other provisions," and "endeavour to procure a number of cartloads of corn and beans" to be sent back to the main body of the army. "It is important to keep possession of one of the missions as it will secure supplies of provisions and also protect the La Bahia road," Austin wrote. "You and Capt. Fannin will however use your discretion as to retaining possession at this time."

Bowie arrived at Mission Espada, about eight miles below the city, around 4:30 the afternoon of October 22. A guard of five Mexicans who had been stationed there fled at the approach of the Texians, and the mission was occupied without incident. From the local citizens, who were "well disposed and quite communicative," Bowie gained considerable insight into the situation within Bexar. That night he and Fannin jointly wrote back to Austin that the city was well fortified, but the Mexican army also suffered from lack of food supplies. Bowie and Fannin suggested that Austin send them fifty additional reinforcements, then remove the main body of the army to a position north of the city. Between the two forces they could starve out the Mexicans.

The next day Bowie and Fannin scouted the San Juan and San Jose missions, but found no stores of food at either place. They fell back to Espada and again sent a dispatch back to Austin asking for reinforcements and food supplies.

The following morning Mexican troops approached Mission Espada and engaged in a skirmish with the Texians. In their official report to Austin, dated "7. oclk A.M 24th octr 1835," Bowie and Fannin wrote:

>   Half an hour since we were attacked by the enimy, who were repulsed, after a few fires being exchanged.
>
>   Only a few men were seen—say about fifty—tho, from the dust etc. it is believed 200 or more, were in the company—Dr Archer says that Col. Ugartichea was the commandant, as he plainly saw him, and recognised him—The place is in a good condition, or can be made so in an hour, for defence. . . .

On the morning of October 27, Austin moved the main body of his army from the Salado to join Bowie and Fannin at Mission Espada. There Austin authorized Lieutenant Travis to raise "from among the existing companies a command of fifty to eighty volunteer cavalrymen, each to be armed with a double-barreled shotgun or carbine, and a brace of pistols."

That same day Austin ordered Bowie to advance and "select the best and most secure position that can be had on the river, as near Bejar as practicable to encamp the army tonight, keeping in view in the selection of this position pasturage and the security of the horses, and the army from night attacks of the enemy."

Bowie was to reconnoiter the approaches to Bexar and to make his report "with as little delay as possible, so as to give time to the army to march and take up its position before night." Then Austin added, "Should you be attacked by a large force, send expresses immediately with the particulars."

Bowie commanded the two companies under captains Fannin and Robert M. Coleman. The young orderly Creed Taylor was there and Noah Smithwick, the blacksmith, and a red-bearded scout named Henry Karnes. There also was Richard "Big Dick" Andrews, a large, jovial fellow, whose unfailing sense of humor made him popular with the men. "Deaf" Smith also may have been among the ninety, perhaps assigned to guide the company.

They left the main camp at Mission Espada about noon. They exchanged volleys "at long range" with a contingent of Mexican *soldados* who promptly fell back into the town. Noah Smithwick remembered:

> We went on up, made our observations, and camped in a bend of the river on the east side, about a quarter of a mile above the old mission of Concepcion and distant some two miles from San Antonio, expecting the main army to follow right on, but for some reason Colonel Austin did not do so.

Bowie's courier did not reach Austin until after nightfall, and the general feared moving his army in the dark. Bowie was on his own until morning. Because of his proximity to the enemy, he took no chances. Strategically, the horseshoe bend of the river proved an ideal location. The steep banks, five or six feet high, afforded excellent cover. A high bluff and thick timber on the west bank prevented the possibility of an assault from the rear. Any attack would have to come from the plain above the east bank. With Fannin and his forty-nine men secured in the south wing of the river bend, and Coleman with forty-one men dug in on the north, an enemy force attacking from the plain would be caught in a lethal cross-fire. To guard against a surprise attack, sentries were hidden in the underbrush away from the river. Another sentinel was stationed in the bell tower of the old mission, where, in the daylight hours, he could command a view of the entire area.

The night was clear and uneventful. But before dawn a heavy fog enveloped the entire region along the river valley.

Within San Antonio de Bexar, General Cos had been advised of the Texian advance, and he planned to isolate and capture this advance party before the main body of the army arrived. The dense morning fog afforded him the opportunity to advance his troops on the enemy position without discovery. Around 6:00 A.M. he dispatched Colonel Ugartechea with a force of about three hundred troops, including cavalry, infantry, and two artillery pieces. The Mexicans moved as quickly and quietly as possible down the west side of the river. Ugartechea left his cavalry behind the Texian position, presumably to cut off any escape, for the dense woods lining the steep riverbank effectively neutralized their offensive potential. The Mexican infantry and artillery under Lieutenant Colonel Don Jose Maria Mendosa continued to a point below the Texians and forded the river. They formed a line on the prairie about three hundred yards from the Texian position with the two cannons in the center and Mission Concepcion at their right flank.

The Texians rose before the sun and breakfasted on jerked beef and corn bread. Suddenly they heard the sound of gunfire. Henry Karnes and the other sentries charged out of the thick fog, Mexican musket balls whizzing past them. Just as Karnes leapt to safety down into the riverbed he exclaimed, "Boys, the scoundrels have shot off my powder horn."

Another Texian, Pen Jarvis, had an even closer call. Struck by a Mexican ball, he toppled back into the riverbed. His comrades thought at first that he was killed, but as they raced to him they discovered that the ball had been deflected by the Bowie knife that Jarvis wore in the front of his waistband. The impact had shattered the knife, causing cuts and bruises, so he had sustained a painful wound though not a mortal one. Thereafter he was known as "Bowie-knife" Jarvis.

The Mexicans began an erratic fire, but the thick fog masked the Texian position, and the bullets passed harmlessly overhead. The Texians secured their horses in the safety of the river bottom and used their knives to cut steps into the steep bank so that "we could ascend, fire, fall back, and reload," Creed Taylor remembered. "Bowie urged the boys to be cool and deliberate and to waste no powder and balls, but to shoot to hit."

In his official report to Austin, Bowie noted that the battle commenced "at about the hour of eight o'clock, A.M. on Wednesday, 28th of October."

> The discharge from the enemy was one continued blaze of fire, whilst that from our lines, was more slowly delivered, but with good aim and deadly effect, each man retiring under cover of the hill and timber, to give place to others, whilst he reloaded. The battle had not lasted more than ten minutes, before a brass double-fortified four-pounder was opened on our line with a heavy discharge of grape and cannister, at the distance of about eighty yards from the right flank of the first division. . . .

The Mexican grapeshot and cannister crashed through the pecan trees along the bank, raining ripened nuts down on the Texians. Noah Smithwick saw men gathering and eating the nuts "with as little apparent concern as if they were being shaken down by a norther." Smithwick praised Bowie "as a born leader, never needlessly spending a bullet or imperiling a life," who "repeatedly admonished us, 'Keep under cover, boys, and reserve your fire; we haven't a man to spare.'"

Under the cover of their artillery fire, the Mexican infantry began an advance on Fannin's position. Perceiving the threat, Bowie ordered some of Coleman's men to reinforce Fannin. Smithwick was among those who raced to Fannin's aid. He and most of the reinforcements followed the curve of the riverbed, but Richard Andrews and a few others took a dangerous shortcut across the prairie, exposed to Mexican fire. For Andrews it was a fatal mistake. Smithwick encountered him on the other side, "lying as he had fallen, great drops of sweat already gathering on his white, drawn face, and the life blood gushing from a hole in his left side, just below the ribs."

"Smith," he said, "I'm killed."

There was no time for sentiment. Smithwick placed something under the dying man's head to make him as comfortable as possible, then grabbed his rifle and scrambled up the riverbank to help repel the attack. Three times the Mexicans charged bravely into the withering fire from the riverbank; three times they were repulsed with heavy losses. The Mexicans manning the cannon fared no better. "It seemed that at one volley every artilleryman hit the dust, and those who took their places shared a like fate," recalled Creed Taylor. Noah Smithwick agreed, "Three times we picked off their gunners, the last one with a lighted match in his hand. . . ."

Then the Texians suddenly took the offensive. In his official report, Bowie described the Texian war cry as "The cannon and victory!" Creed Taylor remembered:

> When they were driven back the third and last time, and while their officers were vainly trying to rally them on their colors, which had been placed on the cannon, Jim Bowie shouted, "The cannon, boys! Come on and let's take the cannon." And with a wild cheer the men rushed forward, seized the color standard, wheeled the gun, which was loaded, and turned it on the enemy who fled in the direction of San Antonio. The fight was over.

At that moment Lieutenant Travis appeared, riding at the head of his newly formed cavalry. Galloping ahead of the Texian army, he arrived barely in time to help chase the retreating *soldados* back into Bexar.

The Mexicans had sustained about seventy casualties in the battle. One Texian was wounded, "Bowie-knife" Jarvis, and one killed, Richard Andrews, who lingered long enough to learn of the Texian victory.

The battle of Concepcion, or the Horseshoe, as it was then called, qualified as the first major engagement of the Texas Revolution. Bowie had done it again. Although outnumbered—as always, it seemed—he had reduced the Mexican army and captured a cannon. But he had not won a decisive victory. Only after the last vestiges of black powder smoke had drifted from the prairie did Austin and the main body of the Texian army march into view. Had Austin arrived earlier, he might have captured the entire Mexican assault force. Then General Cos, his army reduced by nearly half, would have been compelled to surrender San Antonio de Bexar on that very date. Instead, Cos resolved not to risk any more of his troops outside of the fortified city.

Both armies dug in for a long siege.

For the moment, the comet sailing overhead seemed to bode poorly for the Mexicans. Only after the harbinger's return to the black void of space would its true message of doom finally be realized.

Chapter 20: ***Bexar***

"**I** wish a great migration this fall and winter from Kentucky, Tennessee, everywhere; passports or no passports, anyhow," Stephen F. Austin had written his cousin, Mary Austin Holley. "This fall and winter will fix our fate—a great immigration will settle the question."

As he sat in his tent on the plain outside of Bexar, his head buried in his hands, General Austin needed that great immigration now. His own army had become a larger problem than the *soldados* defending the city.

"Whether the army can be kept together long enough to await the arrival of reinforcements, and the necessary supply of heavy battering-cannon and ammunition, I am sorry to say, is somewhat uncertain," he wrote Captain Philip Dimmitt at Goliad.

Within a few days of initiating the siege, perhaps as many as two hundred of his men had left. Since they were volunteers, he had no authority to detain them.

These men had marched to Bexar expecting an immediate battle. Many of the colonists could not endure a protracted siege. They had responsibilities—families and farms—that required their attention.

The adventurers merely found the siege boring, the monotony lifted only by an occasional exchange of cannon fire. They had received no compensation and saw little prospect for it.

Unseasonably cold weather also encouraged the desertions. The northers blew in early that year, bearing icy rains and a grim foreboding of a severe winter. Then diseases set in. "There is no medicine in camp," Austin bewailed, "nor anything else to provide for the sick and wounded."

Even as some men left, others drifted in. Or dashed in, as was the case with twenty-three-year-old Asa Walker, just arrived from Tennessee. Scrambling through Washington-on-the-Brazos on his way to Bexar, he left some clothing and a hastily scribbled note for John Grant, a new acquaintance who had just become an unwitting patron:

> I take the responsibility of taking your overcoat and gun—
> your gun they would have had anyway and I might as well

have it as anyone else. If I live to return, I will satisfy you for all. If I die I leave you my clothes to do the best you can with. You can sell them for something. If you overtake me, you can take your rifle, and I will trust to chance—the hurry of the moment and my want of means to do better are all the excuse I have to plead for fitting out at your expense. Forgive the presumption and remember your friend at heart.

That brief note would be Walker's legacy. He would later join the defenders of the Alamo. Mr. Grant would have to sell his clothes.

Other arrivals at Bexar were not always the kind of men that Austin wanted. In early November the hapless, semiliterate Dr. Launcelot Smither wrote from Gonzales bewailing a company of stragglers en route to Bexar, who "treated the wimon of this place worse than all the comanshee nation could have done and draged me out of the house and nearly beat me to death."

Austin himself lamented the number of men in his army who drank to overcome the tedium. Too often they celebrated by discharging their weapons, risking lives and squandering the limited supplies of powder and ammunition.

And inevitably there were problems with his subordinate officers. Although Austin publicly praised Bowie's performance at Concepcion, privately the general may have blamed Bowie's tardiness in sending for the main army, thus allowing the Mexican force to retreat back into Bexar. And Bowie probably attributed the enemy's escape to Austin's slow advance on the morning of the battle.

Despite whatever friction may have existed between them, Austin still respected Bowie's advice. In a curious double reversal of character, the usually cautious Austin had proposed an immediate assault on Bexar. But the daredevil Bowie had dissuaded him, arguing that the Mexicans were too well entrenched with their artillery. Austin also followed Bowie's suggestion to move the main body of the army north of Bexar, thereby pinning Cos between his force and Bowie's meager command to the south.

On October 31 Austin encamped on the Alamo canal, just a mile northeast of the town. From that proximity he recognized the validity of Bowie's earlier warning—both the Alamo and the entrances into San Antonio de Bexar were more strongly fortified than he had assumed.

Rumors quickly leaked out of Bexar into Austin's new camp. The Mexicans had a large *caballado*, a herd of horses, on the prairie somewhere to the south. Austin gave William Barret Travis a battlefield promotion to captain and dispatched his cavalry to capture the mounts.

Austin also heard a rumor that two companies of Cos' *soldados* were planning to defect to his camp on the following day. To aid in their desertion, Austin advised Bowie to create a diversion on the south end of Bexar.

That same day Bowie brazenly sent a surrender demand to General Cos. "Before further hostilities are resumed," Bowie wrote, "I am induced by the most friendly and humane considerations for my Mexican fellow-citizens to open a communication with you in order to close the war & unnecessary effusion of blood." Despite the polite tone, Bowie resorted to a little intimidation, flaunting his recent victory at Concepcion where he commanded "only a small detachment of ninety-two men."

Cos returned the demand unopened.

Apparently unaware of Bowie's action, Austin submitted his own surrender demand the next day, November 1. It, too, was returned unopened.

Bowie became even more audacious that morning. To create the diversion that Austin had requested, Bowie boldly advanced his ninety men to a position along the river just eight hundred yards below the city. His volunteers dug in there, taunting the enemy. No *soldados* charged out to engage them. Nor, however, did any Mexicans desert to the Texians north of the city.

"They must certain know [the size] of our force," Bowie and Fannin anxiously wrote to Austin, maintaining that they were in a more exposed situation than the general's command. A "more equeal [*sic*] division of force" would be desirable, they added. Their troops would not be satisfied without immediate reinforcements.

About that same time the Mexican cannons within the Alamo discharged four times at the Texians to the north. The rounds had no effect, except perhaps to unnerve Austin. He responded to Bowie and Fannin's request: "The forces are not so unequally divided as appears at first view." His position was "far from being a strong one," and his own command had been reduced by the absence of Travis and his cavalry. "It is known that head quarters are here," Austin added, "and the main attack will be here if any is made." He could not spare any troops for Bowie.

Instead Austin proposed that Bowie and Fannin consider uniting with his force.

The next day Bowie held a council of his officers and had Fannin poll them. The officers voted to "immediately unite with the main army above Bexar." Bowie concurred with the decision, but he was clearly frustrated.

Bowie respected Austin as a man, but not as a military leader, especially now when Austin's infirmity seemed further to cloud his judgement. That afternoon Bowie tendered his resignation to Austin.

Austin simply refused it. He still needed his most experienced warrior. Instead he promoted Bowie to acting adjutant and inspector general, temporarily replacing Warren D. C. Hall, who had just departed for the Consultation.

On November 5 one hundred fifty reinforcements marched into camp dragging three cannons. At last the Texians could initiate a bombardment of the Mexican defenses. The new arrivals were needed perhaps more desperately than the artillery. Simultaneously a large contingent of Texians were preparing to withdraw from San Antonio de Bexar. Some, like Hall, were bound for the Consultation. Some were going home. Some were going anywhere more exciting—and more lucrative—than Bexar.

John H. Moore, whom Austin had promoted to full colonel, was among those leaving. Early on the morning of November 6, Austin had Bowie assemble the men and instruct them to elect a new field colonel to replace Moore.

There was no formal slate. No time for campaigning. The men simply voted on the most qualified officers, men like Lieutenant Colonel Edward Burleson, Captain James Walker Fannin, and Captain Frank Johnson. Burleson won with three hundred sixty-one votes.

Bowie himself received five votes.

Most historians have completely misunderstood this election. Some have taken it out of context, misconstruing the vote as an election to replace Austin for total command of the army. Bowie's modern critics have gloated that the drunken land swindler subsequently resigned in frustration.

Yet it seems incongruous that Big Jim Bowie—the charismatic hero of the sandbar, San Saba, Nacogdoches, and now Concepcion—would garner such little support from the army. To be sure, Bowie had been involved in the despised Monclova land grab, but so had Frank Johnson, and he had received more votes than Bowie.

The most plausible explanation is that Bowie should not have received any votes at all. He already held the rank to which Burleson was elected, a colonel in the volunteer army. Moreover Bowie served as Austin's aide-de-camp, and he had just been promoted to adjutant and inspector general under Austin.

To be sure Bowie, unlike Burleson, had no specific command of his own. However as Austin's troubleshooter he had seen more action, and more glory, than Burleson's predecessor, Moore. And Austin yet could place Bowie at the head of any division in the army.

Therefore Bowie hardly would have been perturbed by the results of the election.

Yet something obviously rankled Bowie. That afternoon he did, again, resign his commissions. At that same moment there were many disgruntled men preparing to abandon the army. But Bowie had no intention of leaving Bexar. He advised Austin, "I will be found in Captn Fannins Company where my duty to my country and the principles of human rights shall be discharged on my part to the extent of my abilities as a private."

Perhaps coincidentally, perhaps not, Travis resigned that same day. He had returned empty handed from his hunt for the *caballado*. It seems unlikely that the even-tempered Austin, or anyone else, would have criticized Travis for failing to locate a rumored horse herd. Perhaps whatever had irked Bowie provoked the same response from Travis. Certainly he mimicked Bowie, accepting the rank of private in his own cavalry company. Austin then named Andrew Briscoe to command the company. Immediately Austin dispatched the unit, guided by the army's most formidable scout, Deaf Smith, on a reconnaissance loop around Bexar.

Neither Bowie nor Travis would remain privates very long.

The very next morning, November 7, Austin again assembled the army and announced that he himself was resigning. Already exhausted and emaciated, he had been further drained by both the bitter north winds and the responsibilities of command. Perhaps he assumed that he could be a greater asset at the Consultation than on the battlefield. He would accompany those men departing for San Felipe.

Austin wanted to keep the Texian army at Bexar so he certainly could not insult his volunteers by placing them under the command of a man whom they had just rejected in a popular election. Instead Austin knew he had to replace himself with a leader the men respected and would readily follow.

He told the assemblage that he passed full command of the army to Colonel James Bowie.

Robert Boyd Irvine, who had arrived at Bexar with a company of volunteers from San Augustine in time to fight with Bowie at Concepcion, conveyed this information in a letter to Houston:

Col. Bowie will remain at the head of such as are actuated under a sperit [*sic*] of patriotism for the purpose of driving off the cattle, hauling off all the corn, and burning the grass, in the vicinity of the town when they will also be compelled to return, unless reinforced.

Then, to further confuse matters, Austin abruptly changed his mind the next day. "My proper judgement is to be at the convention," he explained, but since the army intended to remain at Bexar "at all hazards," he would remain with them. He readily conceded that a man of robust health could do more good for the army than he could.

If the abrupt demotion distressed Bowie, he gave no show of it. Rather, perhaps by mutual agreement, Bowie took Austin's place as escort for the men returning to San Felipe. William Richardson, whom Austin had recently appointed surgeon of the Texas army, accompanied Bowie. So did Captain Archibald Hotchkiss, who recalled that Bowie was dispatched to the Rio Grande to burn the grass on the route to prevent the advance of the Mexican cavalry and lancers, "a duty which he promptly performed."

On November 8, the same day that Bowie's party left for San Felipe, Andrew Briscoe's cavalry detachment reined in their horses along the shady banks of the Medina River south of Bexar. They had circled west around the besieged city, found no evidence of enemy activity, and Briscoe now advocated returning to Austin's camp. Private William Barret Travis objected. He wanted to continue exploring further south. A dozen men, including some *Tejanos* and old Deaf Smith, supported Travis' argument.

Briscoe allowed them to separate from the main cavalry unit. The dozen men quickly elected Travis as their captain.

It did not require Deaf Smith's talents to decipher the tracks they discovered the next day. A large herd of horses, perhaps the rumored *caballado* that previously had eluded Travis, was preceding them southward. The profusion of horse tracks provided no clue as to how many Mexicans might be guarding the herd. Travis did not care. The *caballado* would not escape him again.

In fact only seven Mexicans drove the horses. On the night of November 9 they camped along San Miguel Creek, building fires for cooking and warmth against the cold, damp wind.

The Texians rested only a few miles away. Knowing the quarry was near, Travis gave orders that no fires be lit. He and his men wrapped themselves in blankets and endured the penetrating cold as best they could.

The Mexicans arose with the sun and began preparations for the day's journey. Suddenly thundering hoofbeats shattered the stillness of dawn. Out of the semidarkness galloped William Barret Travis, like a knight from a Sir Walter Scott novel, leading his cavalry directly into the Mexican camp. Caught totally by surprise, the Mexicans gave no resistance. Two managed to escape, the other five surrendered. The Texians also captured their weapons and over three hundred horses.

Travis, like Bowie, was proving himself a capable leader of men.

He returned to the Texian camp to receive praise from General Austin. Thereafter Travis' cavalry continued to patrol the country surrounding Bexar.

The Consultation, originally called for mid-October, had belatedly convened on November 3 when enough delegates finally arrived to comprise a quorum. They elected Branch T. Archer of Virginia to preside over the convention.

Good news had just been conveyed from Bexar—the victory at Concepcion. The delegates quickly passed a resolution commending Bowie, Fannin, and their men.

Then the delegates addressed the primary issue of conflict that divided them. Were the Texians engaged in an internal revolution to overthrow Santa Anna and restore the Constitution of 1824? Or were they fighting for independence from Mexico?

The more radical members of the War Party, notably William H. Wharton, Robert Williamson, Sam Houston, and irascible old Henry Smith, argued for independence. Had he been there, Travis' voice would have echoed their sentiments.

The Peace Party, now finally reconciled to war, supported the notion that Texas should remain part of Mexico. But their rebellion should serve as the powder keg that ignited a new federalist revolution against the centralists. General Stephen F. Austin and many of the colonists in his army besieging Bexar—including Captain Juan Seguin and his *Tejanos*—supported this philosophy. So did the majority of Monclova land speculators, desperately desiring to validate their claims. To further their goal, the Peace Party advocated taking the war down into Mexico, beginning with an invasion of Matamoras.

On November 6 the delegates voted thirty-three to fifteen against declaring independence from Mexico. President Archer himself favored independence, but he strove to reconcile the factions and supplant conflict with compromise. On the next day the delegates issued a carefully worded declaration supporting the "principles" of the 1824 Constitution. Avowing that Texians had the right to take up arms in defense of their rights and liberties, the declaration proclaimed:

> That Texas is no longer morally or civilly bound by the compact of union; yet, stimulated by the generosity and sympathy common to a free people, they offer their support and assistance to such of the members of the Mexican confederacy as will take up arms against military despotism.

The declaration further asserted that the Texians retained the right "during the reign of despotism, to establish an independent government" —a republic.

The delegates then created a provisional revolutionary government. It was headed by a governor. A lieutenant governor presided over a general council composed of one member from each municipality. Compromise again persisted in the election of officers to these positions. For lieutenant governor the delegates selected a forty-five-year-old Indianan named James W. Robinson, a former law partner of William Henry Harrison. Robinson and most of the men chosen for the council ardently represented the Peace Party.

The Consultation passed over the nomination of Stephen F. Austin and elected obstinate, tactless Henry Smith as governor.

Smith's fellow War Party stalwart Sam Houston was chosen commander-in-chief of the army. Of course the only two armies at that time were the volunteer force besieging Bexar and Dimmitt's small volunteer command at Goliad. Since the Consultation denied Houston any authority over volunteers, Houston reigned as a general without an army. However, the Consultation urged the militia soldiers to enlist in the regular army and their officers to appear before the governor and council to receive official commissions.

On November 13, the day before it adjourned, the Consultation adopted a Plan of the Provisional Government, composed of twenty-one articles, with an additional twelve articles devoted to the military. Acting on a recommendation from Houston, Article XVIII of the Plan invalidated all land grants "illegally and fraudulently made by the legislature of Coahuila and Texas . . . within the limits of Texas." Houston did not want this war to be fought for corrupt land acquisitions.

The duties of the governor and council were described in the Plan, but it did not create checks and balances and failed to define the limitations of their powers.

The oversight would prove to be a fatal mistake.

The Plan also called for another convention to be held at Washington-on-the-Brazos on March 1, 1836.

That same day the delegates heard a distressing rumor. Santa Anna was assembling a large invasion army and preparing to march north into Texas. Whether or not the volunteer Texian army could defeat Cos at Bexar, Houston doubted that there were enough men within all of Texas to repulse a large invasion army. Houston already had published a proclamation in the United States promising liberal bounties of land to men who would "Come with a good rifle, and come soon." The Consultation supported the land grants to volunteers. Land was all Texas had to pay its soldiers. Recognizing the need for men, money, and supplies, the delegates designated three men to journey to the United States and procure aid: Branch T. Archer, William H. Wharton, and Texas' most able diplomat, Stephen F. Austin, assuming he could be induced to retire from the army.

After detouring south to burn the grass, which added three days to a two-day journey, James Bowie rode into San Felipe late in the night of November 13 or early on November 14. Acting on stale news, Sam Houston heartily congratulated Bowie on his appointment as commander of the volunteer army, a misconception that Bowie quickly corrected. If Bowie were commander of the volunteers, it would have made Houston's position more tenable, for he and Bowie were forged from the same steel, and they shared a mutual respect. Even upon learning that Houston had instigated the nullification of his fortune in Monclova land grants, Bowie did not reject his friend or align himself with the other frustrated speculators clustered within the Peace Party. It was that loyalty thing again, and maybe even the idealistic notion of fighting for liberty instead of personal gain. After the Consultation had concluded, Bowie and Houston retired to Peyton's inn and raised a glass or two. Or eight. Or ten.

Many years later Anson Jones, the last president of the Republic of Texas—and no friend of Sam Houston—remembered seeing Bowie there "dead drunk." So did George Patrick, who had been assigned to convey the results of the Consultation—including Austin's appointment as emissary to the United States—to Bexar. Certainly Bowie drank that night. However, after his long, cold trip he may have been more exhausted than inebriated.

But apparently Houston had requested that Bowie escort Patrick back to Austin's camp, and the courier waited impatiently.

It took an hour to rouse Bowie enough to hoist him onto his horse. Bowie graciously apologized for the delay, saying, "Patrick you have been kind enough to wait for me and I guarantee to make up the lost time." Then Bowie sank in his spurs and galloped hell bent for leather to the west, a stunned Patrick following behind. "Good as his promise he made things quite lively enough for me," Patrick later recalled.

An incredible performance for a "dead drunk."

They rode into Bexar on November 18 to find the situation had worsened. The Texian army, which had crested with some six hundred men, now numbered only about four hundred. Most of the colonists had withdrawn, and there hardly would have been an army at all except for the arrival of new volunteers from the United States. Austin was getting his "great migration," but a decade earlier he would have denied many of soldiers entry into Texas. To be sure, there were some men of ideals and character, like thirty-year-old William R. Carey of Virginia. He had arrived in Texas just in time to participate, as a private, in the skirmish at Gonzales. He later wrote home:

> . . . Oh! my dear sister and brothers how often have I thought of you when I have been walking the lonely wood or barren field as a sentinel exposed to all the inclemencies of the weather and suffering many privations which you can not have the least idea of, but all was sweet when I reflected on our forefathers in the struggle for liberty.

On October 28 he had been promoted to second lieutenant of artillery and later to first lieutenant.

But too many of Austin's army came only for the plunder. Others were fugitives from justice. And most lacked any semblance of discipline. Truly Austin commanded the worst army in the universe.

The quality of his command had improved slightly on November 9 when a company of seventy men had ridden into camp hauling two cannons. The men all wore matching gray coats and trousers and sealskin caps, making them the only uniformed company in the Texian army. They were volunteers who had been organized in New Orleans on October 13 by United States supporters of Texas independence. Appropriately they were called the New Orleans Greys.

In fact there were two companies of Greys. Captain Robert C. Morris commanded the men who had just arrived at Bexar. They had sailed from New Orleans on the schooner *Columbus*, docking in Velasco on October 22. Then they had taken a boat up the Brazos to Brazoria where they received a "tremendous welcome." Flowers were strewn at their feet by the fair ladies of the city. The citizens prepared a banquet for them. Mrs. Jane Long personally greeted them at her home.

Then they had marched to La Bahia. There, Captain Philip Dimmitt outfitted them with mustangs for the final leg of their journey to Bexar.

Approximately fifty men comprised the other company of Greys commanded by Captain Thomas H. Breece. A German emigrant named Herman Ehrenberg ranked as the youngest; he turned nineteen on the journey. For some reason Breece's company had taken a different route into Texas. They rode the steamboat *Washita* up the Mississippi and Red Rivers to Alexandria.

From Alexandria the company marched overland through Natchitoches. They had to circle wide around Fort Jesup, built to guard the U.S./Mexican border. With the official United States policy of neutrality, the American garrison at Jesup had been instructed to prevent volunteer militia from entering Texas.

Breece's company crossed the Sabine at Gaines Ferry on the Camino Real. As they stepped onto Texas soil, a delegation of settlers met them. Obviously the arrival of the Greys had been anticipated. Ehrenberg remembered:

> The tender hand of a Texas woman gave us in the name of all beauties of the land a splendid blue silk flag on which the following inscription appeared: "To the first company of Texan Volunteers from New Orleans."

They were wined and dined at Nacogdoches, and *alcalde* Adolphus Sterne, one of the original sponsors of the Greys back in New Orleans, provided them with provisions and horses. With their new banner flapping above them in the frigid north wind, the Greys rode westward, finally reuniting with Morris' Company at Austin's camp above Bexar on November 21.

The first of the three flags believed to have waved over the Texian defenders of the Alamo had arrived almost within the shadow of the old mission-fortress.

Flag of the New Orleans Greys

Following Morris' company by a week and a half, Breece's Greys had feared they would miss the battle. Instead they almost initiated it.

Austin was torn between his assignment as emissary to the United States and his fear that the Texian army would disintegrate in his absence. The arrival of the Greys—men who at least looked like soldiers—inspired a desperate solution. As demoralized as were his own soldiers, Austin suspected that the Mexicans within the besieged city had to be suffering even more. With his enthusiastic new reinforcements, Austin felt confident he could launch an immediate assault and capture the city. Then, in triumph, he could leave for the United States.

He proposed the plan to his officers. They polled the men and then returned with depressing news. More than half of the army could not be induced to fight.

It was all over. The siege was doomed. With no spirit to fight and a bitter winter encroaching, the army would have to fall back to La Bahia.

Finally broken, his morale as feeble as his body, Austin agreed to accept his appointment as emissary to the United States. Captain Fannin tendered his resignation. So, for a second time, did Travis.

On November 24, just before Austin left Bexar, the volunteers chose Colonel Burleson as their commander of the volunteer forces at San Antonio. It would be a thankless job, for Burleson was not expected to do more than lead the army in retreat to winter quarters. It was what Houston had originally proposed and what he still advocated after his appointment as commander-in-chief. In fact Houston never recognized any strategic significance to San Antonio de Bexar. Rather, to Houston, La Bahia—Goliad —protected the coast against a naval invasion and also defended the most direct overland route from Mexico into the colonies.

Austin authorized Colonel Bowie, who had resumed his position as adjutant and inspector general at Bexar, to go to Goliad, "have it fortified as strongly as possible" and made ready to receive the army in the event they abandoned the siege of Bexar. Although Bowie received the assignment from Austin, the original directive probably came from Houston. Significantly, with Austin's departure, Bowie now had become Houston's troubleshooter.

Curiously, however, Bowie did not depart Bexar with his usual promptness. His delay afforded him one more daring enterprise. Two days later Deaf Smith galloped excitedly into camp. The old scout had seen a large pack train, guarded by one hundred fifty *soldados*, approaching Bexar. A wild, exhilarating rumor swept through the Texian encampment that the mules carried silver coins with which to pay the besieged Mexican troops. "I immediately ordered out from thirty-five to forty cavalry under command of the Adjutant & Inspector General James Bowie and Col Wm H Jack with about one hundred Infantry," Colonel Burleson wrote in his report of the incident. "I moved on soon after with a few men mounted on horseback & joined the infantry." Deaf Smith, probably after bounding onto a fresh mount, charged ahead with Bowie.

If Burleson had preached caution to Bowie, it had been a waste of breath. Galloping far ahead of the infantry, Bowie came upon the convoy as it crossed a dry creek bed. Though outnumbered, Bowie led his howling men on an attack directly into the midst of the pack train. Braying mules scattered as the guard of dragoons dismounted and found cover in an empty arroyo. Bowie and his Texians swung from their saddles and dove into a parallel streambed.

"The enimy [*sic*] charged him with over three times his number but were immediately repulsed with considerable loss," Burleson wrote.

General Cos, seeing the fight raging a mere mile from town, dispatched reinforcements—even as Burleson's infantry raced to the sound of gunshots. These two forces clashed in a separate "very warm engagement."

Bowie's command repelled two more desperate assaults. The dragoons fell back to join the reinforcements from Bexar.

Burleson reported, "The main force of our army then reinforced by Col Bowie and his party charged the Enimy and drove them back about three hundred yards towards Town."

It was Concepcion all over again.

"During the engagement a heavy [cannonading] was kept up between the Alimo [*sic*] & our encampment," Burleson recalled.

" . . . in relation to the conduct of officers and men, I have but one remark & that is, that none could have fought more bravely," Burleson reported. He commended some of his officers, including "Adjutant Brister of the New Orleans Greys [who] sustained his post during the action with bravery that reflects much credit on himself & the gallent [*sic*] corps with which he marched to our assistance." However his report mentioned Bowie more than any other subordinate.

In his *History of Texas from 1685-1892*, John Henry Brown interviewed, or consulted accounts from, a half dozen participants of the battle. "All agree that Bowie was the hero of the occasion," Brown concluded, "and that General Burleson and his men did all that was possible under the circumstances."

In the last phase of the engagement Cos sent out artillery to cover the escape of his *soldados*. But the big guns proved unnecessary. As the Mexicans fled back into Bexar, Bowie and the Texians directed their attention to the abandoned mule train. But the packs did not yield silver coin. Rather freshly cut grass, fodder for the starving horses within the besieged city, tumbled onto the cold ground.

Creed Taylor remembered, "This ludicrous affair, almost approaching a battle, was then dubbed and is since known in our history as the 'Grass Fight.'"

The Grass Fight cost the Texians only four wounded and one missing. (The frightened deserter later reappeared in the settlements to become the butt of many jokes.) Burleson reported fifteen dead *soldados* and seven wounded were found on the field, but he estimated the Mexican casualties as being much higher.

The ludicrous affair had at least one major significance. It energized a majority of the Texian soldiers. "When Burleson took command the army was divided, one faction arguing that it would be a piece of unwarranted foolishness to undertake to capture Bexar," Taylor continued.

> Those in favor of the assault brought forth the argument that, while the town was well fortified, the Mexicans could not stand up before the Texas riflemen; . . . that General Cos did

not have over six hundred effective men in Bexar; and that his ammunition was short, his men on half rations, unpaid and woefully disspirited, all of which was true as it was eventually shown.

In fact the attack on Bexar almost started spontaneously. The Texians had excavated a cannon emplacement in a cornfield west of the Alamo. Because the entrenchment was a half mile from the cover of woods, anyone approaching or departing the position either waited until nightfall or risked enemy fire as they raced across the open field. Nineteen-year-old Herman Ehrenberg recalled being one of eight Greys who decided to advance to the position in daylight.

> ... the enemy, as if he had directed all the cannon of the fort against us, enveloped us with his grapeshot like heavy rain. We were obliged for a moment to seek shelter under a large pecan tree. After we had taken our place here, we looked at each other and laughed at the fact that we, eight men, stood behind a single tree while the malicious laughter of our comrades, those in the trench as well as those in the camp, accompanied every full load that struck our faithful pecan tree and the rattling down of the dry limbs.

Eventually the eight Greys reached the gun emplacement. Here the Texian artillerymen entertained themselves by transforming their bombardment into a game of chance. "Before firing every man was first required to indicate in advance which part of the Alamo specifically he intended to demolish, and thereby bets were placed accordingly for or against him," Ehrenberg reported. Most of the wagers were merely for rifle balls. However one overconfident artilleryman wagered his pistols, "the best on the ground," that he could hit between the third and fourth windows of the Alamo's old *convento*. A "backwoodsman in a greenish pea jacket" accepted the bet. When the cannon ball missed its mark, the hapless backwoodsman readily tendered his own pistols in exchange for the artilleryman's pair, which "were at least the next best."

Then, offering the artilleryman a chance to win back his fine pistols, the backwoodsman in the greenish jacket stepped behind the cannon. His right hand traced geometrical patterns in the air as he meticulously sighted down the long barrel. Finally he put the torch to the touchhole. Ehrenberg related:

Driven by the mighty load of powder, the destroying ball flew towards its mark. The rattling of the stones indicated to us, before the smoke had cleared away, that he had hit his mark. But after the smoke had disappeared we searched in vain for the third and fourth windows.

Even as the ancient, hard luck mission endured its destruction in stoic silence, Ehrenberg learned that the backwoodsman was old Deaf Smith, "the most gallant Texan that ever chased across the prairie," who "never missed his mark" and always shot his game in the head.

Their diversion was abruptly interrupted by rifle fire from the underbrush just across the river. Some Mexican snipers had ventured from the city in an effort to dislodge the cannon crew.

Approximately thirty Greys sallied into the trees along the opposite bank of the river and trained their rifles on the snipers. The Mexicans fell back into the city. Ehrenberg recalled that, "without consulting anyone," the Greys charged forward toward Bexar's defenses. Some of the Greys in the trench, including Ehrenberg, joined the impromptu attack. The startled *soldados* fell back from the barricades, and the Greys pursued them into the streets. The Texian army, or at least a small part of it, finally had entered San Antonio de Bexar. Ehrenberg reported that they raided the outer houses, looting "much needed cooking utensils." Then they could hear bugles sounding the alarm, and suddenly "Mexican blue coats were swarming out of the streets like bees."

The Greys raced from the town to a grove of trees extending from the river. Here again they were pinned down by grapeshot from the Alamo's cannons. Then the Mexican infantry surged out of the town towards the small number of Greys trapped in the trees. "Conscious of their enormously overwhelming numbers, they would not let themselves be held back, and with a wild mixture of blowing of bugles they pressed forward to surround us," Ehrenberg wrote, " . . . but suddenly, imagine our pleasure! the old strains of Yankee Doodle chimed merrily, and around a projection of the forest came the backwoodsmen and the remaining companies, in order, as they said, to help the Greys out of a pinch."

Deaf Smith led the rescue that drove the Mexicans back behind the barricades of Bexar. Ehrenberg maintained that the incident aroused the Texians "from their lethargy." Burleson, seeing how easily the barricades had been breached, began to reconsider his withdrawal.

If only Big Jim Bowie were still there.

But Bowie had missed the spontaneous attack. After the Grass Fight he had ridden to Goliad. There he met with Captain Philip Dimmitt, the forty-year-old Kentuckian who commanded the old Spanish presidio.

Dimmitt had been one of the earliest and most vocal proponents of uniting with the federalists of northern Mexico to defeat Santa Anna and restore the Constitution of 1824. To that end he had commissioned a Mexican flag made, "the colours, and their arrangements the same as the old one—with the words and figures, 'Constitution of 1824,' displayed on the white, in the centre."

Then Dimmitt had reversed himself. He joined the War Party and declared for independence. On November 11 Agustin Viesca and the Scottish land speculator Dr. James Grant, having escaped from their Mexican captors, stumbled into Goliad. Dimmitt provided hospitable refuge, but he adamantly refused to acknowledge Viesca's office as governor of Coahuila y Texas.

Austin had learned of this conflict before leaving Bexar. From his Peace Party perspective, such an embarrassing slight of the prominent federalist leader could prove disastrous for the Texians. In perhaps his last directive to Colonel Bowie, Austin had asked his former adjutant to try to mitigate the political crisis.

However Bowie would have little time for politics or for strengthening the defenses at Goliad. Shortly after his arrival there, a courier brought word that the Texian army finally had stormed San Antonio de Bexar. The big battle was raging, and Jim Bowie was missing it.

Early in December, John William Smith, a forty-three-year-old Virginian, entered the Texian camp north of Bexar. Like James Bowie and Erastus "Deaf" Smith (with whom there was some obvious confusion), John W. Smith lived in San Antonio and was married to a *Tejano* woman. He had settled there at least eight years earlier, establishing himself as a merchant, engineer, and surveyor. Because of his red hair, the *Tejanos* called him "el Colorado." When the Texian forces advanced on Bexar, General Cos confined Smith and the handful of other Anglos within the besieged city. Smith, Samuel Maverick, and a man named Holmes finally convinced Cos to let them leave for Louisiana. But once beyond the barricades, they circled into the Texian camp.

Their knowledge of the Mexican fortifications proved invaluable to Burleson. He ordered an attack for that night. But then, like Austin, he changed his mind, fearing that the Mexicans had discovered his plans. On

December 4 Burleson assembled the men and announced that he and his adjutant, Colonel Francis Johnson, had decided to withdraw from the siege until spring. Burleson was especially concerned about reports that Colonel Ugartechea had escaped from Bexar, galloped south, and could return with Mexican reinforcements at any time.

The announcement discouraged most of the army, now generally disposed to fight. A number of disgruntled men deserted even as the rest begrudgingly prepared for their removal to Goliad.

Then a Mexican cavalryman defected to the Texians, describing the low morale of the five hundred seventy *soldados* remaining in the town. The morale of the mulling Texians improved dramatically when forty-seven-year-old Benjamin Rush Milam—filibuster, Mexican prisoner, and Monclova land speculator—stepped before them. Creed Taylor recalled:

> He drew a line on the ground with the stock of his rifle. Then waving his old slouch hat above his head, he cried in stentorian voice, "Boys! Who'll go with Ben Milam into Bexar?" The quick commingled responses, "I will," were almost deafening. "Well, if you are going with me, get on this side," shouted Milam. And with a rush, animated cheers, and loud hurrahs, the men formed in a line to the number of about three hundred—every one eager to follow the old hero in any venture and at all hazards.

Before dawn on December 5, Texian artillery under Colonel James Clinton Neill commenced a bombardment on the Alamo. It was a diversion that lured many of the *soldados* to the old mission. Then Milam and Colonel Johnson, acting on recommendations from John W. Smith, led two columns of Texians against the weaker northern defenses of the city. They breached the barricades and poured into the town, entrenching themselves in abandoned houses. A desperate house-to-house battle began that would last for four days.

On the second day Deaf Smith and some of the Texians captured the Veramendi house and established it as a temporary command post. Climbing onto its roof, Smith was wounded by a Mexican ball, probably fired from *soldados* in the bell tower of the San Fernando Church. The Texians cut a hole in the roof and gently lowered him down into the house.

But Bowie's old home was the scene of even greater tragedy on December 7. During a conference of Texian leaders in the Veramendi yard, a

Mexican sniper in the trees along the river leveled his sights on old Ben Milam. The ball struck Milam in the head, killing him instantly.

The Mexican snipers used Baker rifles, but most of the *soldados* had been issued smooth bore Brown Bess muskets, cheap British surplus from the Napoleonic Wars. Quicker to load than a rifled barrel and intended for massed volley fire, they were notoriously inaccurate at their limited range of seventy-five yards. In contrast, many of the Texians carried long hunting rifles that could shoot with accuracy at a target more than two hundred yards. Texian marksmanship took a fierce toll on the enemy.

After Milam's death, command of the attack passed to Colonel Frank Johnson. The Grey's former captain, Robert Morris, assumed leadership of Milam's column. Even the skies seemed to weep for the fallen Texian commander, but the icy drizzle provided additional cover for the battling Texians.

"Of daring and heroic deeds occurring during the assault, a volume could be written," Creed Taylor related, "every man fought for himself and everyone proved himself a hero." He recalled a dramatic incident from that third day when the Mexicans had trained a cannon on a house just captured by Taylor and some other Texians.

> This gun was playing havoc with our shelter. Seeing this, a young man from Nacogdoches, by the name of Sylvester, of Captain Edward's command, made a dash for the gun, shot one of the gunners, knocked another down with his rifle, spiked the cannon, and escaped back to the lines.

William R. Carey wrote that three Texians were wounded and two more killed next to him while discharging a cannon "that was ordered by a fool in the open street immediately before the enemy breastworks within 120 yards of their heavy fires, but he was my superior and I did obey." A Mexican ball ripped through his hat, grazing his skull, but Carey managed to dismount the enemy cannon with a "lucky shot," allowing the Texians to fall back to cover.

Cutting through the walls of houses to avoid Mexican grapeshot, the Texians inched ever closer to the main plaza. Some of Morris' men circled around to the southwest and captured Antonio Navarro's house, almost in the shadow of the San Fernando Church.

The church bell rang furiously on the morning of December 8, welcoming six hundred Mexican reinforcements, commanded by colonels Domingo de Ugartechea and Jose Juan Sanchez Navarro, who had just marched up from the south. However less than a third of the new troops were experienced soldiers. The raw recruits, according to Sanchez Navarro, "did not know even how to load" and only contributed to the confusion of battle. And a Mexican prisoner confided to Creed Taylor that the reinforcements "only helped to consume the meager supply of food yet remaining."

Moreover the reinforcements were offset that night by the desertion of four companies of cavalrymen from the Alamo, who nearly trampled over General Cos in their flight. His forces sorely depleted by the desertion, Cos ordered all his remaining troops to consolidate inside the fortified old mission. He would make his stand within the Alamo.

About that time James Bowie, Captain Philip Dimmitt, and some of his men from Goliad galloped into Bexar. One of Dimmitt's men is noted in Burleson's report of the battle.

Dimmitt, or more likely one of the *Tejanos* in his command, carried the 1824 banner. The second of the alleged Alamo flags had arrived at San Antonio.

The dawn of November 9 illuminated the hopelessness of the Mexican situation. The Texians, at nearly their original strength, commanded the city to the west and the prairie to the east. Thirty-two-year-old Dr. Amos Pollard from New York, whom Austin had appointed surgeon of the regiment on October 23, recorded only two dead Texians and two more with mortal wounds in the official report he and Dr. Samuel Stivers submitted to the governor and council. Thirteen more Texians had sustained severe wounds, and a few of them may have expired.

Cos had suffered at least one hundred fifty casualties. The remnants of his army, entrenched in the Alamo, had been further reduced by desertion to less than two hundred effectives. There was scarcely enough food provisions to maintain even that number. To save the rest of his "brave men," Cos dispatched Sanchez Navarro to obtain the best terms possible. Colonel Nicolas Condelle lamented that his proud Morelos infantry battalion had never before surrendered. But having sustained the most casualties, the battalion had been reduced to less than half strength.

On December 10, for the second time in a quarter century, the saintly statues staring blankly down from the niches in the church's facade witnessed the surrender of the hard luck mission. For the first time ever, the Alamo was in the hands of the Texians.

"All has been lost save honor," the meticulous Colonel Sanchez Navarro scribbled into his diary. "We were surrounded by crude bumpkins, proud and overbearing." Yet those bumpkins extended him extremely favorable terms of surrender. The *soldados* who had not defected to the Texian side were paroled back "into the interior" of Mexico under pledge that they would never again take up arms against the Constitution of 1824. The Mexicans could retain their personal weapon and ten rounds of ammunition—and even take one small cannon—all for personal defense against hostile Indians.

With the departure of General Cos' army, all Mexican troops finally had been expelled from Texas. Despite persistent rumors that Santa Anna was preparing a massive invasion force, many in the army naively believed that the war was over. Even if Santa Anna planned an invasion, he could not possibly mobilize it in the midst of a blustering winter. By spring the Texians would have time to prepare an appropriate reception.

Thus many of the Texians, including virtually all of the few remaining colonists, left San Antonio de Bexar. Burleson departed, turning command over to Colonel Francis Johnson. Only a small garrison, comprised of a few hundred recent arrivals from the United States, remained in the city.

However at least one colonist stayed. Throughout the campaign, Gonzales blacksmith Almaron Dickinson had displayed a knack for artillery. He may have remained because of the twenty captured Mexican cannons, the largest collection of artillery west of the Mississippi.

With the battle over he sent for his wife, Susanna, and their daughter, Angelina, just now turning one year old. Arriving in Bexar, Susanna moved into the home of former *jefe* Ramon Musquiz, where she did laundry for the Texian troops.

Herman Ehrenberg, the youngest of the New Orleans Greys, recalled that after the Mexicans marched out, many of the volunteers moved into the Alamo. "Each one, according to his own pleasure, searched out a favorite retreat for protection against the cold and storm of winter." Nine men found quarters in the enclosed rooms within the old church, though Ehrenberg remembered they did not tarry long when passing beneath the ancient stone arches just inside the door. He added:

> The outer side was provided with several figures of the saints chiseled out of sandstone, in front of which the Mexican women regularly every morning knelt down without being disturbed in the least by the passing in and out of the volunteers. It was being said that the sandstone saints were being visited more now than ever before. . . .

It was the inexhaustible James Bowie, of course, who galloped back to San Felipe with the official report of the victory. There he quickly became embroiled in a different kind of battle. Virtually everything the Texians had gained in the capture of San Antonio would be compromised by the bitter political feud that resulted over the Matamoras expedition.

Chapter 21: **Matamoras**

At first it had seemed like a good idea.

The Nueces formed the southern border of Texas. Matamoras, on the lower bank of the Rio Grande, lay deep within the province of Tamaulipas. It would be an ideal location from which to advance the revolution into northern Mexico. Capturing Matamoras also extended Texian control of the Gulf coast southward more than a hundred miles, deterring any plans Santa Anna might entertain for a naval invasion. Moreover, revenue from the captured port could help finance the revolution.

The idea had been especially popular among the council, many of whom were land speculators. By overthrowing Santa Anna and remaining part of Mexico, they could recover a fortune in land grants.

Though disposed towards Texas independence, Governor Henry Smith, in a rare mood of compromise, initially went along with the Council. On December 17 he authorized his commander-in-chief, Sam Houston, to adopt such measures as he deemed best "for the reduction of Matamoras."

That same day Houston delegated the task to, of course, Colonel James Bowie. Houston wrote:

> Should you not find it within your power to attain an object so desirable as the reduction of Matamoras, you will, by all possible means, conformably to the rules of civilized warfare, annoy the troops of the central army; and reduce and keep possession of the most eligible position on the frontier, using the precaution which characterizes your mode of warfare.

That last phrase seemed a little curious considering Bowie's legendary boldness. "You will conduct the campaign," Houston emphasized. "Much is left to your discretion."

Houston dispatched the letter to Goliad, where he assumed Bowie to be. However Bowie left Bexar about that same time for San Felipe.

On that same date, December 17, Travis tendered his opinion on the subject. "I hope the council will take measures to fit an expedition immediately to take the port and city of Matamoras," he wrote Lieutenant

Governor James Robinson. "I intend to join the expedition if one is gotten up, unless prohibited by superior orders, and I will execute to the best of my ability any command which the council may see fit to confer on me."

But there was one command in particular he craved. Two weeks earlier, in a proposal to the council, he had enthusiastically endorsed the formation of a cavalry battalion, comprised of between one hundred sixty and one hundred eighty soldiers, each man armed with swords, pistols, and double-barreled shotguns. The battalion would be commanded by a lieutenant colonel, the rank and position to which Travis aspired.

Instead he had been unofficially notified of his appointment as major of artillery. In his December 17 letter he advised Robinson " . . . believing that I could not be so useful in the artillery as elsewhere, I beg leave to decline the office or if I have been commissioned to resign same."

He posted the letter from Mill Creek where he and Rebecca enjoyed some time together after his long absence on the Bexar campaign and where they waited for his divorce to be finalized.

Only after he arrived in San Felipe did Bowie learn of his orders to lead the Matamoras expedition. He also would have learned about a dispatch written by Col. Francis W. Johnson at Bexar just after Bowie had left there.

Johnson had received news that General Joaquin Ramirez y Sesma had arrived at Laredo "with 500 cavalry & 1,000 infantry," intending to reinforce Cos. Johnson wrote, "it is to be feared that they have immediate intentions of proceeding to offensive measures, & every prepreation [*sic*] should be made on our part without dealy [*sic*], as I have too much reasons to believe that the information received is as nearly as possible correct. . . . "

Colonel Johnson, entrenched in the Peace Party, warned that Texas would be opposed by both Mexican political parties if "we are fighting for independence instead of Liberty & the Constitution of 1824."

Houston at that moment was only thirty miles upriver at Washington-on-the-Brazos, and Bowie probably rode up to confer with him. Then back to San Felipe. On December 28 he reported to the council and delivered a stirring oration that essentially reiterated Houston's plan. Although tensions were building between the Peace Party council and the War Party governor and his commander-in-chief, many on the council were impressed by Bowie's presentation.

On the following day the council drafted a resolution requesting the governor "to authorize Col. James Bowie, to raise and rendezvous all the troops he possibly can, to be enrolled according to the provisions of the ordinance and decree creating an auxiliary volunteer corps of Texas, and report himself at Goliad, at as early a day as possible."

The council proceedings on January 6, 1836, read: "James Bowie exhibited to the council orders from the commander-in-chief of the army, to proceed against Matamoras...." The council detained him only long enough to secure a copy of his orders and then gave him leave to proceed to raise and lead an army.

Certainly Bowie had just cause to believe he had been authorized to lead the Matamoras expedition.

In fact, ignoring Governor Smith and General Houston, the council had already acknowledged Colonel Francis Johnson's intention to lead the expedition.

Despite the threat of an impending attack on Bexar, Johnson and Dr. James Grant had exhorted the remaining army, including several volunteer companies that had arrived after the battle there, to join a campaign against Matamoras. By promising the spoils of war, they easily won over troops who had received no compensation. Johnson and Grant saw larger spoils for themselves. As partners in the Monclova land grab, both had a significant financial investment in keeping Texas part of Mexico. Grant even more so, for he owned extensive property in Coahuila. While Johnson in San Felipe secured authority from the council to lead the expedition, Dr. Grant proclaimed himself "Acting Commander-in-Chief of the Federal Volunteer Army." On January 3 he looted most of the provisions from the town and marched out of Bexar with nearly two hundred men. All but twenty-three of the New Orleans Greys followed Grant—including young Herman Ehrenberg, who explained, "we did not like at all a military life that was too quiet." Curiously, the few remaining Greys kept their blue flag at the Alamo.

Then, inexplicably, on January 7 the council appointed James Walker Fannin as their "agent" to lead the Matamoras expedition. Oblivious to the council's action, Governor Smith that same day commissioned Fannin a colonel of artillery in the regular army. Fannin did not waver between his two assignments for long. On the next day he issued a proclamation calling for volunteers to rendezvous at San Patricio to join in the "expedition to the west."

Suddenly there were three campaigns to Matamoras, each under a different commander.

That same day, January 7, Sam Houston, still in Washington, scribbled a hasty letter to Governor Smith:

> I will set out in less than an hour for the Army. I will do all that
> I can. I am told that Frank Johnson and Fannin have obtained
> from the Military Committee orders to Proceed and reduce
> Matamoras. It may not be so. There was no Quorum, and the
> council could not give power.

About that same time Smith received a correspondence, dated January
6, from Lieutenant Colonel James Clinton Neill, who had been left in command of the handful of Texians remaining at Bexar. "It will be appalling to
you to learn, and see herewith inclosed our alarming weakness," Neill
opined. He had about twenty-four pieces of artillery but only one hundred
four men and no provisions or clothing since Johnson and Grant left. "If
there has ever been a dollar here I have no knowledge of it," he wrote, bitterly adding that the two hundred men who left with Johnson and Grant
had violated the policy of their enlistment and "should not be entitled to
neither compensation, nor an honorable discharge. . . ."

Neill continued, praising the efforts of a twenty-nine-year-old-Kentucky
lawyer, Major Green B. Jameson, who had assumed the duties of chief engineer. He had been rebuilding the Mexican fortifications damaged during
the siege and mounting the eighteen functional cannon. Jameson's services
"to this army, and to his Country, cannot be too highly appreciated," Neill
wrote, "the present army owes in a great part its existence to his exertions,
and management, and so far as I am concerned in my Command, I assure
you that I cannot get along without him."

After signing the letter, Neill added a hasty postscript. He had just been
informed that one thousand Mexican troops were now on the march from
Laredo to San Antonio.

Governor Henry Smith could endure no more. On January 10 he sent a
lengthy communiqué to the council in which he condemned the members
for the chaos resulting from the Matamoras expedition. "You have acted in
bad faith, and seem determined by your acts to destroy the very institutions
which you are pledged and sworn to support," Smith asserted. Brazenly he
adjourned the council until the March 1 convention.

Two days later the council responded by impeaching the governor for
violating both the Constitution of 1824 and the declaration of the Consultation, and also for perjury and slander.

It would have been better for Texas if the government had simply
ceased to exist. Instead the council promoted James Robinson to acting
governor and dispatched Marshall J. H. Money to obtain possession "of all

all the papers, records, public correspondence and public documents of every kind belonging to the Executive Department of Texas." Smith adamantly refused to surrender the archives and threatened to shoot "any son of a bitch" who tried to claim them. The two branches of government continued to operate independently of each other, simultaneously feuding with a vengeance that would have been better reserved for Santa Anna. Both Smith and Robinson issued public proclamations justifying their actions. Robinson and the council continued their support of the Matamoras expedition while Smith and Houston now opposed the offensive campaign and prepared for the defense of Texas.

In another strike at the governor and his general, the council issued a proclamation on January 11 charging that the governor, "without the advice, consent, or knowledge of the Council . . . had just given to James Bowie, not known to the government as an officer of any rank whatever, orders, through the Commander-in-Chief, to raise an army and proceed against Matamoras."

At least part of it was a blatant lie. The council had sanctioned Bowie's mission. The rest of the decree, denying official rank to the most experienced and successful leader in Texas because he was a Houston man, displayed petty stupidity. But it did not matter. Despite every effort to transform the Texian army into a regular military force, it would remain dominated by volunteers. And volunteers elected their own leaders.

Virginia artilleryman William R. Carey knew nothing of the disintegration of the government when, on December 12, he wrote from Bexar to his brother and sister. He described his role in the long siege and proudly noted that afterwards he had been elected captain of the artillery company. He called his men the "invincibles," because they would "wade through h-ll" if he gave the order. He continued, "The forces here is commanded by Lieut. Colo J. C. Neill who has his quarters in the Town which is called the left wing of the forces and your brother William has command of the Alamo which is called the right wing."

Before the war erupted he had been courting a lady from Natchitoches. "My selection is nothing to boast of," he conceded, "she is tolerably ugly and tolerably poor and tolerably illiterate." But she was "virtuous and a good housekeeper." However since his arrival in Bexar he had been "conversing with a Mexican lady." She had told him that "in time of peace the ladies would gladly embrace the offer or accept the hand of an officer, but in these war times they would too soon become a widow."

"She may be right but I don't think it," he added. "I must close by saying that if I live, as soon as the war is over I will endeavor to see you all."

General Sam Houston raced to Goliad to try to dissuade the volunteers from participating in the Matamoras expedition. Arriving on January 14, he found James Bowie waiting there. Grant's force had already passed through, plundering that garrison as it had depleted Bexar. Captain Philip Dimmitt had resigned in disgust. Houston planned to pursue Grant to Refugio, but before he left Goliad he received another desperate appeal from Colonel Neill at Bexar. Neill wrote:

> The men in my command have been in the field for four months. They are almost naked . . . and almost everyone of them speaks of going home, and not less than twenty will leave tomorrow, and leave here only about 80 efficient men under my command.

The Bexarenos had been supportive, supplying groceries and beeves, and since Grant had taken the garrison horses, several *Tejanos* had agreed to serve as scouts.

"I hope we will be reinforced in 8 days or we shall be overrun by the enemy," Neill predicted, "but if I have only one Hundred men, I will fight one thousand as long as I can; and then not surrender. . . . "

Neill asked for one hundred reinforcements. Houston could not spare that many men. But he could send thirty men under James Bowie. "Colonel Bowie will leave here in a few hours for Bexar," Houston wrote Governor Smith on December 17. "I have ordered the fortifications in the town of Bexar to be demolished, and if you think well of it, I will remove all the cannon and other munitions of war to Gonzales and Copano, blow up the Alamo, and abandon the place, as it will be impossible to keep up the Station with volunteers."

Contrary to popular misconception, Houston did not order Bowie to blow up the Alamo. Rather Bowie was to demolish the defenses in Bexar. Clearly there were not enough Texians to defend the entire city of San Antonio—Cos could not hold it with an army many times larger. As to whether the Texians entrenched themselves across the river in the Alamo —or destroyed it and retreated with the artillery—was a decision Houston had left to Smith's discretion.

Colonel Bowie "met the request [to go to the relief of 'Lieutenant Colonel Neill'] with his usual promptitude and manliness," Houston reported to

Smith. " . . . and to this I freely add that there is no man on whose forecast, prudence, and valor I place a higher estimate than Colonel Bowie."

Arriving at Refugio on January 21, Houston addressed the men under Johnson and Grant. Houston commended their bravery but warned the followers of the Matamoras expedition that they would not have the anticipated support from Mexican federalist rebels. And "a city containing twelve thousand souls will not be taken by a handful of men who have marched twenty-two days without . . . necessary supplies for an army." It would be far wiser to defend Texas and engage the Mexican troops after "long marches and other hardships had exhausted and demoralized them."

Herman Ehrenberg, the youngest of the New Orleans Greys, recalled that "cheers of joy greeted [Houston's] eloquent appeal." Approximately two hundred men consented to withdraw to Goliad with Colonel Fannin. Frustrated but undaunted, Johnson and Grant continued toward Matamoras with only about sixty men.

Back in Washington-on-the-Brazos on January 30, Houston submitted a long, fuming report to Smith. With his own authority compromised by the council's appointments, Houston had not been able to abort the Matamoras campaign, but he had succeeded in persuading the majority of men to reinforce Goliad. "Should Bexar remain a military post, Goliad must be maintained, or the former will be cut off from all supplies arriving by sea at the port of Copano."

Houston condemned the "*extraordinary* conduct of the council," which had acted repeatedly without proper authority. They had sanctioned Dr. James Grant's self-appointment as acting commander-in-chief, which Houston wryly observed was "a title and designation unknown to the world." And the council had provided Grant with a draft for seven hundred and fifty dollars.

Houston continued:

> While every facility has been afforded [by the council] to the mediated campaign against Matamoras, no aid has been rendered for raising a regular force for the defence of the country, nor one cent advanced to an officer or soldier of the regular army, but every hindrance thrown in the way.

Houston also attacked Colonel James Walker Fannin, the council's "agent" of the provisional government. The council, Houston maintained, had anointed Fannin with authority surpassing the governor and the commander-in-chief of the army, "nor is he responsible to the council or the people of Texas. . . . His powers are as unlimited and absolute as Cromwell's ever were."

Houston quoted from a letter in which Fannin advised the council that his "troops should be paid out of the first spoils taken from the enemy."

Houston retorted, "This, in my opinion . . . divests the campaign of any character save that of a piratical or predatory war."

"I do not consider the council as a constitutional body, nor their acts lawful," Houston concluded, " . . . and therefore I am compelled to regard all their acts as void."

On December 18, after covering ninety miles in one day, James Bowie led thirty men into San Antonio de Bexar. Notable among his company was Second Lieutenant James Butler Bonham, Travis' neighbor from his youthful days at Red Bank Church, South Carolina.

Bonham was a rebel. Had he been born a quarter century later into a Confederate gray uniform, he might have rivalled J. E. B. Stuart and Nathan Bedford Forrest. But even in 1836 the tall young man with curly black hair would carve out his own legend.

He had always been a rebel. South Carolina College had expelled him for leading a student protest. He opened a law office in Pendleton, but during South Carolina's nullification crisis he eagerly traded in his legal books for a dashing uniform with silver epaulets and a red sash. Gallantly bedecked, he stood ready to fight for John C. Calhoun and secession. But all the excitement wound down without any action, and he dutifully returned to his law practice.

Once, in court, he even rebelled against a judge's ruling. An opposing attorney had insulted Bonham's female client. Bonham responded as any chivalrous gentleman would—he caned the offensive lawyer right in front of the judge's bench. When the judge called for order and demanded an apology, Bonham offered to elongate the magistrate's nose. During his three-month confinement for contempt, he became the darling of the town's ladies. They kept his cell decorated with flowers and his stomach filled with pastries.

On October 17, 1835, Bonham was in Mobile, Alabama, when the Shakespeare Theater hosted a rally to gain support for the Texians. Suddenly Bonham was helping to organize the Mobile Grays. The rebel had found his rebellion.

The Grays arrived at Bexar on December 13, three days after the surrender of Cos, but Bonham had preceded them into Texas. From San Felipe on December 1, he wrote to Sam Houston, volunteering his services and declining all compensation. Houston was impressed. Bonham received his commission as second lieutenant of cavalry on December 20. Still, Bonham remembered the nullification crisis. This rebellion, too, would pass, and then he would need employment. The January 2, 1836 issue of the *Telegraph and Texas Register* carried an advertisement for the opening of his law office in Brazoria.

The Mobile Grays marched out of Bexar behind Dr. James Grant. However as the rift in the provisional government widened, Bonham's loyalty remained firmly behind Governor Smith and General Houston. Houston reciprocated. On January 11, during their last hours of civility, he recommended to Lieutenant Governor Robinson that Bonham receive a promotion to major. "His influence in the army is great," Houston stated, "more so than some who '*would be generals*.'" The council ignored the recommendation, of course, because Bonham was a Houston man.

Arriving at San Antonio, Bonham and Bowie were instrumental in organizing a citizens' and soldiers' meeting held on January 26. Colonel James C. Neill presided over the assembly. He assigned Bonham to chair a committee to draft resolutions from the Bexar garrison to be published in the Texas newspapers. James Bowie, Green B. Jameson, Doctor Amos Pollard, Juan Seguin, Jesse Badgett, and Don Gasper Flores also served on the committee.

The resolutions declared the garrison's unqualified support for Henry Smith and Sam Houston. They condemned the council for land speculation, misappropriation of funds, and, especially, "the illegal appointments of agents and officers . . . in relation to the Matamoras Expedition." The resolutions declared that "all officers under the commander-in-chief are elected by the volunteers themselves. . . . "

As for the garrison, the resolutions proclaimed, "we cannot be driven from the Post of Honor and the sacred cause of freedom."

Houston had little time to appreciate the resolution from Bexar. Two days later Henry Smith granted him a furlough from the army until the March 1 convention. "Your absence is permitted in part by the illegal acts of the council in superseding you," Smith wrote. In fact, Houston had an important matter to address. The Mexicans had agents inciting the Cherokees and other east Texas tribes to rise up against the colonists. Texas was ill-prepared for Santa Anna's invasion from the south; it could not sustain a war on two fronts. And who was better qualified to negotiate a treaty of neutrality with the Cherokee than Sam Houston?

Houston had sent his troubleshooter, his agent, his best officer, "Colonel Bowie," to the relief of "Lieutenant Colonel Neill." But Bowie was no mere courier. The juxtaposition of titles Houston used suggests he intended Bowie to assume a supervisory capacity over the garrison in the same manner Austin had placed Bowie over Fannin's command during the siege of Bexar.

Neill's official commission from the council did not matter to anyone in San Antonio; his real authority came from his election by the volunteers. He was a responsible and competent officer, although he lacked Bowie's assertiveness. When Bowie arrived, Neill essentially gave him free rein, and no conflict developed between the two. "I cannot eulogize the conduct and character of Col Neill too highly," Bowie later wrote, "no other man in the army could have kept men at this post, under the neglect they have experienced."

James Bowie
Painting by Michael Schreck

Bowie also formed a close attachment with engineer Green B. Jameson. They might have met in San Felipe before the war and certainly encountered each other when they were besieging Bexar and the Alamo.

Before Bowie's arrival on January 18, Jameson had written to Houston stating what the commander-in-chief already knew: "We have too few to garrison both places [the Alamo and Bexar], and will bring all our forces to the Alamo tomorrow as well as the cannons."

While awaiting word from Governor Smith about the fate of the Alamo, Jameson probably gave Bowie a tour of the defenses. General Cos' Mexican engineers had initiated the transformation from crumbling mission into fortress. They had pulled down the arches from the roofless church and used the stone to construct a platform where cannon could fire over the rear walls of the church toward the east. A wooden ramp that started just inside the church door gradually sloped up to the cannon platform. The two small rooms, the baptistry and confessional, that flanked the entrance to the church, served as the powder magazines. The front windows of the church, which opened into these rooms, had been filled with stone to protect the powder from both moisture and enemy musket and cannon fire.

The Mexicans also had erected a lunette to protect the main gate in the south wall and a palisade to enclose the gap between the east end of the south wall and the southwest corner of the church. Both were constructed of vertical posts with earth sloped against the exterior wall to absorb cannon fire. The earth had been excavated from a ditch that extended along the exterior length of the palisade and lunette and effectively added to the height of the wall.

An artillery emplacement inside the compound further protected the entrance. The two cannon mounted there waited to spew death at any *soldados* who penetrated the lunette and main gate.

Jameson might have been wiser to reverse that emplacement. The most vulnerable part of the Alamo was the north wall, in part because of its remoteness from the rest of the fort, and in part because of severe deterioration. Virtually the whole wall needed repair, but at one point a gap existed where the long neglected adobe bricks had simply crumbled away. Jameson filled the breach with timber and earth.

For the moment Jameson busied himself moving the artillery from Bexar into the mission/fortress. He had already mounted the largest of the

The Alamo compound
Original painting by Joseph Musso

Alamo cannon, the eighteen-pounder, on the southwest corner of the Alamo "so as to command the Town and the country around." The cannon platform had necessitated the destruction of the rooms in that corner of the wall—the same rooms in which Toribio Losoya had always lived. The former private in the Alamo de Parras Company had enlisted with Juan Seguin's *Tejanos* and fought against Cos in the battle of Bexar. Now as a member of the Alamo garrison, he may have helped build the ramp and platform that destroyed his family home.

Jameson had sent a drawing of the Alamo defenses to Houston. "You can plainly see by the plat that the Alamo was not built by a military people for a fortress," he wrote, "tho' it is strong, there is not a redoubt that will command the whole line of the fort." Jameson intended to construct half moon batteries to resolve that problem. And he would dig defensive trenches within the walls, even inside the rooms.

He praised the assistance of Seguin and the citizens of Bexar but complained that the poorly clothed and hungry garrison had been reluctant to work. "Since we heard of 1000 to 1500 men of the enemy being on the march to this place duty is being done well and punctually," he added, "in case of an attack we will move all into the Alamo and whip 10 to 1 with our artillery."

When Jameson wrote that letter on January 18, he counted one hundred fourteen defenders including the sick and wounded from Bexar, "which leaves us about 80 efficient men." The arrival of Bowie's men brought the number only to one hundred ten effectives. Despite Jameson's optimism, as Bowie surveyed the Alamo he realized that the vast size of the three-acre compound was the fort's greatest weakness. There scarcely were enough men to adequately staff all the artillery. That left long stretches of walls completely unprotected. Bowie had to know right then that without a large reinforcement the Alamo could not hold.

But he had not received orders from Governor Smith to abandon the place. And anyway there were no draft teams in Bexar to remove the cannon.

In the meantime rumors kept drifting in about the advance of the enemy. On January 23 Colonel Neill wrote to Smith about intelligence that "Santa Anna has arrived at Saltillo with three thousand troops, also that at the Town of Rio Grande there are sixteen hundred more."

By February 2 Bowie had heard that the Mexican force on the Rio Grande numbered two thousand and that "five thousand are a little back and marching on."

Grimly Bowie wrote, " . . . they intend to make a descent on this place in particular, and there is no doubt of it."

In his most dramatic mode Bowie wrote:

> The salvation of Texas depends in great measure on keeping Bejar out of the hands of the enemy. It serves as the frontier picquet guard and if it were in the possession of Santa Anna there is no strong hold from which to repell him in his march towards the Sabine. . . . Colonel Neill and myself have come to the solemn resolution that we will rather die in these ditches than give up this post to the enemy. These citizens deserve our protection and the public safety demands our lives rather than to evacuate this post to the enemy.

With that letter James Bowie had set the historical stage for the siege of the Alamo. But then, in a more subdued postscript to the letter, he added, "Our force is very small . . . only one hundred and twenty officers & men. It would be a waste of men to put our brave little band against thousands."

Reinforcements would arrive the following day.

It came as an early Christmas present. William Barret Travis received his long-desired commission as lieutenant colonel of cavalry on December 24. There was only one problem. He had to recruit the cavalry himself.

And there was a belated Christmas present. On January 9 the state of Alabama finally granted his divorce from Rosanna. But Travis may never have learned that he was finally free to marry Rebecca. The news might not have arrived by January 21 when Governor Henry Smith ordered him to raise one hundred volunteers and ride immediately to the relief of Bexar.

Suddenly everything depressed Travis. There may not have been time for another trip to Mill Creek, but he did take the opportunity to say farewell to six-year-old Charles Edward, whom he had entrusted to the care of his friend David Ayers. The uniform he had ordered had not yet arrived, however he purchased a flag for five dollars. Worst of all he could only raise a force of about thirty men.

Accompanied by his twenty-one-year-old slave, Joe, Travis led them out of San Felipe on January 24. Had he pressed hard he might have reached Bexar in two or three days. Instead, by January 28 he had only reached Burnham's Ferry on the Colorado River. From there he wrote Governor Smith, "Our affairs are gloomy indeed." He found the Texian people indifferent, exhausted with war, "and in consequence of dissensions between contending and rival chieftains they have lost all confidence in their government and officers."

"The patriotism of a few has done much," Travis asserted, "but that is becoming worn down."

He was describing himself. He had enjoyed little sleep, and he had strained his own credit to purchase supplies for the cavalry company.

The next day he still lingered at Burnham's and grew even more depressed. Again he wrote Smith:

> . . . I beg that your Excellency will recall the order for me to go to Bexar in command of so few men. I am willing, nay anxious, to go to the defense of Bexar, and I have done everything in my power to equip the enlisted men and get them off. But sir, I am unwilling to risk my reputation (which is ever dear to a soldier) by going off into the enemies country with such little means and so few men, & them so badly equipped.

Travis even threatened to resign his commission. Perhaps wisely, Smith never responded. Dutifully Travis pressed on. During the first week of February he finally arrived in San Antonio with his five-dollar flag, the last known of the Alamo banners. Unfortunately, no description of it remains.

At the same time other volunteers advanced toward Bexar. Some were enthusiastically idealistic men like twenty-four-year-old Daniel W. Cloud, who, like Bowie, had been born in Logan County, Kentucky. (His middle name usually is given as William, but some family descendants claim it to be Washington.) An attorney and farmer, he journeyed through the states with a party of other Kentucky lawyers, including B. Archer Thomas, Peter Bailey, William Fontleroy, and Joseph Washington. On Christmas Day, 1835, Cloud wrote from Natchitoches, Louisana, to a friend that "next week, heaven willing, we shall breathe the air of Texas." But he and his party were not going as mere spectators, he asserted, "no, we go with arms in our hands, determined to conquer or die. . . . "

Cloud had admired the soil when they passed through Illinois, but Yankee lawyers were numerous. There was "less litigation in [Missouri] than in any other state in the union." Dockets and fees were large in Arkansas, and Cloud knew they would have made money rapidly there. But they pushed on west. "Ever since Texas has unfurled the banner of freedom, and commenced a warfare for liberty or death, our hearts have been enlisted in her behalf," Cloud explained in a December 26 letter to his brother.

The cause of Philanthropy, of Humanity, of Liberty & human happiness throughout the world call loudly on every man to come to aid Texas.

If we succeed, the Country is ours. It is immense in extent, and fertile in its soil and will amply reward all our toil. If we fail, death in the cause of liberty and humanity is not cause for shuddering.

Forty-two-year-old Micajah Autry from North Carolina possessed the quiet soul of a poet. And, typically for artistic types, no sense for making money. His law practice at home foundered, so he moved wife, Martha, and the children west into Jackson, Tennessee. There he tried storekeeping. That enterprise also failed. He left his family there and joined the migration that had "Gone to Texas."

He arrived at Natchitoches on December 13 "after considerable peril." He promptly wrote to his wife that the war was going favorably for the Texans. " . . . it is thought that Santa Anna will make a descent with his whole force in the Spring," he related, "but there will be soldiers enough of the real grit in Texas by that time to overrun all of Mexico."

A month later, "after many hardships and privations" he had walked the one hundred fifteen miles to Nacogdoches. There he fell in with "a small company of select men, 4 of them lawyers." It was the Kentucky lawyers. Autry considered them perfect gentlemen and found himself sharing Cloud's enthusiasm. "I go whole hog in the cause of Texas," he wrote.

He vowed to provide her "a sweet home." He would receive 640 acres for his service in the army, and an additional 4,444 acres for settling his family in Texas.

In a postscript he described standing guard one night and savoring the "splendor and majesty" of the rising moon:

> With what pleasure did I contemplate that lovely orb chiefly because I recollected how often you and I have taken pleasure in standing in the door and contemplating her together. Indeed I imagined that you might be looking at her at the same time. Farewell Dear Martha.

Then, in a second postscript, he cited a name that needed no introduction.

"P. S. Col. Crockett has joined our company."

Chapter 22: ## *The Lion of the West*

Of the Alamo defenders, the most famous played the least significant role in its history. Yet the mere belated presence of David Crockett elevated the prominence of the 1836 battle. Simultaneously it resurrected his own foundering popularity.

Yet by the advent of the twentieth century, Crockett had faded back into general obscurity, just another backwoods pioneer, probably not as well known as Daniel Boone. All that changed on December 15, 1954, when the new television series, Disneyland, presented, "Davy Crockett, Indian Fighter," the first episode in a trilogy about Crockett. By the time the third episode, "Davy Crockett at the Alamo," aired two months later—appropriately on February 23—the entire country had succumbed to a coonskin cap craze that compelled Disney to compile the episodes into a theatrical feature, Davy Crockett, King of the Wild Frontier, which was released that summer. For an entire generation Walt Disney and a previously unknown actor named Fess Parker had revitalized and remanufactured the image of Crockett and the story of the Alamo.

> Born on a mountain top in Tennessee,
> Greenest state in the land of the free,
> Raised in the woods so he knew ev'ry tree,
> Kilt him a b'ar when he was only three.
> Davy, Davy Crockett, king of the wild frontier!

Actually David Crockett was born August 17, 1786, a decade before Tennessee joined the union. His birthplace, near the Nolichucky River in what would become Greene County, was not on a mountain peak but in the shade of the Appalachian Mountains. Yet it was the wild frontier. His grandparents had been massacred by Creek Indians in 1777.

Crockett knew little about his origins except that his father, John Crockett, was "either born in Ireland or on the passage from that country to America." His mother, the former Rebecca Hawkins, hailed from Maryland. "It is likely I may have heard where they were married, but if so, I have forgotten," Crockett admitted in his autobiography.

He had a similarly vague knowledge of his father's experiences in the American Revolution—"it happened to be a little before my day"—but he recalled that John Crockett fought at King's Mountain. It seems curious that oral history played such a minor role in his development, for one of Crockett's greatest talents would be storytelling. His autobiography, A *Narrative of the Life of David Crockett, by Himself*, published in 1834, was a colorful and generally accurate account of his career.

> My father and mother had six sons and three daughters. I was the fifth son. What a pity I hadn't been the seventh! For then I might have been, by *common consent*, called *doctor*, as a heap of people get to be great men. But like many of them, I stood no chance to become great in any other way than by accident. As my father was very poor, and living as he did *far back in the back woods*, he had neither the means nor the opportunity to give me, or any of the rest of his children, any learning.

On the frontier, the traditional escape from poverty was to move west. In 1794 John Crockett moved his family to Cove Creek. There he entered into a partnership to build a mill "when there came the second epistle to Noah's fresh, and away went their mill, shot, lock, and barrel."

John Crockett moved again, this time to Jefferson County, where he opened a tavern on the Abbingdon-Knoxville road. It did not prosper, in part because he imbibed too often in his own product. To help survive, he virtually rented out ten-year-old David to a passing stranger driving a herd of cattle to Rockbridge County, Virginia—the birthplace of Sam Houston. At the end of the journey, more than a hundred miles later, the man refused to release young David. But the boy escaped into a blizzardy night, trekked seven miles through knee-deep

David Crockett
Painting by Michael Schreck

drifts in the snowy woods, joined some wagoners heading back west, and eventually found his way home.

When David was thirteen his father enrolled him in a small country school. Only a week later he engaged in a fight with another student, "a boy much larger and older than myself." Crockett triumphed in the altercation, but then he began to fear retribution from the schoolmaster. The next morning, instead of going to the school, Crockett hid out in the woods and then returned home at the usual time in the evening. "Things went on in this way for several days," he wrote.

> At last, however, the master wrote a note to my father, inquir-
> ing why I was not sent to school. When he read this note, he
> called me up, and I knew very well that I was in a devil of a
> hobble, for my father had been taking a few *horns*, and was in
> a good condition to make the fur fly.

David explained that he would be "cooked up to a cracklin" by the schoolmaster. His father promised similar punishment if David did not leave immediately for school. "Finding me rather too slow about starting, he gathered about a two year old hickory, and broke after me," Crockett remembered. "We had a tolerable tough race for about a mile; but mind me, not on the school-house road, for i was trying to get as far t'other way as possible."

Crockett escaped into the forest. Now fearful of his father's wrath, he made a "strategic withdrawal," hired out to wagoners, and remained gone for approximately two years. When he finally returned to his home at the age of fifteen, he had "been gone so long, and had grown so much" that his family did not recognize him immediately, "for they had all long given me up for finally lost." He was just one more traveler invited to share the hospitality of a meal. It was his oldest sister who suddenly sprang from her chair, threw her arms around his neck, and exclaimed, "Here is my lost brother!"

Crockett wrote:

> The joy of my sisters and my mother, and, indeed, of all the
> family, was such that it humbled me, and made me sorry that I
> hadn't submitted to a hundred whippings, sooner than cause
> so much affliction as they had suffered on my account.

For the next year Crockett worked off debts owed by his father. One of his employers was a Quaker named John Kennedy. At the age of sixteen Crockett collided with love for the first time in his life. When Kennedy's niece visited from North Carolina, Crockett remembered, "I soon found myself head over heels in love with this girl, whose name the public could make no use of." Unfortunately the young lady already was engaged.

> This news was worse to me than war, pestilence, or famine.
> ... I saw quick enough my cake was dough, and I tried to cool
> off as fast as possible; but I had hardly safety pipes enough, as
> my love was so hot as mighty nigh to burst my boilers. But I
> didn't press my claims any more....

The incident inspired Crockett to attend a nearby school, thinking he might be a more desirable paramour if he had some education. In a six-month period he learned to read a primer, scrawl his name, and work simple math problems. It was the only formal schooling he ever would receive.

At the age of eighteen he became enamored of a young lady named Margaret Elder. "I got to love her as bad as I had the Quaker's niece," Crockett wrote, "and I would have agreed to fight a whole regiment of wild cats if she would only have said she would have me." He pressed his claim on her, gave her very little peace, and at last she accepted his proposal.

"I had by this time got to be mighty fond of the rifle, and had bought a capital one," he recalled. "I most generally carried her with me wherever I went...." However he soon found that he was more successful at shooting game and winning target matches than he was at love. Margaret broke off their engagement.

> My appetite failed me, and I grew daily worse and worse.
> They all thought I was sick; and so I was. And it was the worst
> kind of sickness—a sickness of the heart, and all the tender
> parts, produced by disappointed love.

But Crockett rebounded. At nineteen he began courting Mary (Polly) Finley. During that time, while on a wolf hunt, he did indeed become "lost in the woods," just as the song claimed. "And for the information of young hunters, I will say... that whenever a fellow gets bad lost, the way home is just the way he don't think it is," Crockett recalled. He hiked for six or seven miles. Nothing seemed familiar, and then cold darkness began to envelop the forest. Crockett remembered "at this distressing time I saw a little woman streaking it along through the woods like all wrath, and so I cut on too." He overtook her, and when she turned, he saw it was Polly. While searching for her father's horses, she, too, had become fearfully lost—her panic increasing with the descending gloom. When sunlight no longer filtered through the branches, and a nocturnal chorus emanated from the shadows, the forest became a sinister place.

The coincidence—a damsel in distress rescued by her ardent suitor in that vast woodland—might strain credibility in a work of fiction. Certainly it was a fortuitous encounter—almost as if it were fated. His presence with that trusty long rifle calmed her. Together they found a path that led to a sheltering farmhouse. "I stayed up all night courting," Crockett recalled.

He and Polly married on August 14, 1806. She bore him two sons, John Wesley and William. "I found I was better at increasing my family than my fortune," Crockett conceded. In 1811, faced with mounting debts, he chose the customary solution and moved his family southwest to the Mulberry fork of the Elm River in Lincoln County. "It was here that I began to distinguish myself as a hunter," he recalled. However he forfeited his land when he could not pay his taxes, and in 1813 the family moved further south to Bean's Creek just above the Alabama border. Although he was on the opposite side of Tennessee, he named his new homestead "Kentuck," possibly an homage to those half-horse, half-alligators.

> *He fought single-handed through the Injun War*
> *Till the Creeks was whipped an' peace was in store,*
> *And while he was handlin' this risky chore,*
> *He made hisself a legend for evermore.*

As with Bowie's father and most other trans-Appalachian pioneers, Crockett basically ignored the distant War of 1812 until August 30, 1813, when the Creek Indians massacred the five hundred settlers at Fort Mims, just above Mobile, Alabama. Then, over Polly's protests, Crockett enlisted in the militia. He wrote, "my countrymen had been murdered, and I knew that the next thing would be, that the Indians would be scalping the women and children all about there, if we didn't put a stop to it."

On September 24 Crockett and his trusty long rifle rode south with the Tennessee Volunteer Riflemen. While waiting for Andrew Jackson's army to arrive from Nashville, a Major Gibson asked for "two of his best woodsmen, and such as were best with a rifle," to participate in a scouting party. Crockett volunteered and then asked that a young man named George Russell be his companion. Major Gibson retorted that Russell did not have beard enough—he wanted men, not boys. "I know'd George Russell, and I knowed there was no mistake in him," Crockett wrote, "and I didn't think that courage ought to be measured by the beard, for fear a goat would have preference over a man." Crockett won the argument.

Gibson led twelve scouts across the Tennessee River. On the following day they split up, Crockett leading the second group. Finding evidence that a large war party of Creeks was moving north to engage the army of Andrew Jackson, Crockett galloped back to camp with the information. He wrote:

> When I made my report, it wasn't believed, because I was no officer; I was no great man, but just a poor soldier. But when the same thing was reported by Major Gibson!! why, then, it was all true as preaching, and the colonel believed it evry word.

Although no tragedy had resulted, the elitist attitude burned into Crockett's mind. In later years he would regard himself as a champion of the common man.

Andrew Jackson's regular army rendezvoused with the militia shortly afterward, and the campaign moved south. On November 3, 1813, they attacked the Creek village Tallusahatchee. It was Crockett's first battle, the first time he ever saw a man killed by an arrow. A squaw had fired the fatal shaft into a lieutenant named Moore. Crockett recalled that "his death so enraged us all, that she was fired on, and had at least twenty balls blown through her." The soldiers shot the Indians "like dogs." When forty-six warriors retreated into a house, the soldiers burned it to the ground with its occupants trapped inside.

Four days later the Creeks again suffered defeat at Fort Talladega. Over three hundred Creeks were slain, more than twice as many as Jackson lost, but a large number of Indians managed to break through the militia lines and escape into the woods. The war would continue, but not for David Crockett. With his ninety-day term of enlistment expiring, Crockett chose to go home rather than continue the pursuit. Consequently he missed Horseshoe Bend, the climactic battle that launched young Sam Houston's fame.

Crockett had no greater success at making himself "a legend for evermore" when he reenlisted to fight the redcoats at Pensacola. He wrote, "our arrival was hailed with great applause, though we were a little after the feast; for they had taken the town and fort before we got there." Then Crockett missed an even bigger battle. Jackson marched his army west to greater glory at New Orleans, leaving Crockett's regiment the thankless job of wading through the cold Florida swamps in wintertime tracking renegade Indians. Ultimately hunger became a more relentless enemy than the Indians. Crockett put his talents to use. He and the other backwoodsmen hunted every day. Crockett recalled, "it was a rule with us, that when we stop'd at night, the hunters would throw all they killed in a pile, and then we would make a general division among all the men."

Eventually they depleted the game in the surrounding forests, and starvation drove the army into retreat. They passed by Fort Talladego and Crockett saw a grisly sight. The old battleground, "looked like a great gourd patch; the sculls of the Indians who were killed still lay scattered all about, and many of their frames were still perfect, as the bones had not separated."

Crockett left the army a month early and returned home to find that Polly had given him a daugher named Margaret. Crockett paid a young man to serve out the rest of his enlistment. "This closed my career as a warrior," he noted, adding that he was glad he was through with "war matters."

> But in this time I met with the hardest trial which ever falls to the lot of man. Death, that cruel leveller of all distinctions,—to whom the prayers and tears of husbands, and of even helpless infancy, are addressed in vain,—entered my humble cottage, and tore from my children an affectionate good mother, and from me a tender and loving wife.

Impoverished, with three young children, Crockett came to a simple conclusion—"I must have another wife." After Polly's death in the summer of 1815 he began courting a widow named Elizabeth Patton. Her first husband had been killed by Creeks, leaving her with two young children and a not inconsiderable sum of money. Crockett wrote "we soon bargained, got married, and then went ahead." It was, for both of them, a marriage of convenience.

The next fall Crockett and three neighbors set out on a long hunt into Alabama. Near the later site of Tuscaloosa, their horses wandered away. Crockett trailed after them, covering fifty miles in a single day, but he never caught them. Instead he contracted malaria. Too weak and dizzy to continue, he settled back against a tree in the wilderness and waited for recovery or death. Some passing Indians found him and offered ripe melons, but Crockett could not eat. "They then signed to me, that I would die, and be buried; a thing I was confoundedly afraid of myself." The Indians conveyed him to a nearby farmhouse. Crockett languished near death for weeks. But he finally recovered. "I was so pale, and so much reduced, that my face looked like it had been half soled with brown paper."

When he returned to his home, "it was to the utter astonishment of my wife; for she supposed that I was dead." His fellow hunters had returned to Tennessee some time earlier with the report of his demise.

In 1816 Crockett moved his family to Shoal Creek in what would become Lawrence County. There, using some of Elizabeth's capital and borrowing heavily, they erected a three-thousand-dollar complex that included a grist mill, a gunpowder mill, and a distillery. From Crockett's perspective, he could provide virtually all the

David Crockett

necessities of the backwoods. However, as had happened to his father, Shoal Creek flooded, washing the complex away. Throughout his whole life, Crockett would never escape poverty and debt.

> *He went off to Congress an' served a spell,*
> *Fixin' up the Government and laws as well,*
> *Took over Washington so we hear tell,*
> *An' patched up the crack in the Liberty Bell!*

On May 21, 1815, David Crockett had been elected lieutenant in the Thirty-second Militia regiment of Franklin County, Tennessee. It was the modest beginning of a political career. In 1817, after the move to Lawrence County, he was chosen justice of the peace. "My judgements were never appealed from, and if they had been they would have stuck like wax," he boasted, "as I gave my decisions on the principles of common justice and the honesty between man and man, and relied on natural born sense, and not on law... for I had never read a page in a law book in all my life."

The following year he was elected town commissioner and then colonel of the Fifty-seventh Militia regiment. Now he was Colonel David Crockett.

In 1821 he won a seat in the Tennessee legislature as representative from Lawrence and Hickman Counties. This contest required active campaigning and worst, speechifying. Crockett was an inexperienced and uncomfortable orator, and he was intimidated by the political experience of his opponent. He tried to avoid speaking at a public barbecue following a squirrel hunt, but the opponent goaded him to the stump first. "The truth is he thought my being a candidate was a mere matter of sport; and didn't think, for a moment, that he was in any danger from an ignorant backwoods bear hunter," Crockett reflected.

Standing before the crowd, Crockett related a story about a man seen thumping on a barrel. When asked why, the man answered that there had been cider in the keg a few days earlier, but if any remained now he could not get to it. Crockett explained that he was like that man. There was a speech in him earlier, but now he could not get it out. The crowd laughed, and Crockett entertained them with more anecdotes.

Then, knowing his opponent was waiting his turn at the stump, Crockett shrewdly remarked that he was dry as a powder horn and it was time for everyone to wet their whistles. As his dismayed opponent rose to speak, Crockett led most of the crowd away to the liquor stand. "I was elected, doubling my competitor, and nine votes over," he proclaimed.

Crockett later confided another of his campaign strategies. He had a buckskin hunting shirt made with two large pockets, one to hold a huge twist of tobacco and the other for a bottle of liquor.

Crockett wrote:

> . . . I knowed when I met a man and offered him a dram, he would throw out his quid of tobacco to take one, and after he had taken his horn, I would out with my twist and give him another chaw. And in this way he would not be worse off than when I found him; and I would be sure to leave him in a first-rate good humor.

Such antics characterized all Crockett's subsequent campaigns. His homespun humor and backwoods wit—as keen as his marksmanship—compensated for his lack of political acumen. But at the same time he projected a genuine sense of honesty and humility that more polished politicians could not emulate.

After his election to the legislature, Crockett again moved his family, this time to the sparsely settled Obion River in the northwest corner of Tennessee. During the great New Madrid earthquakes a decade earlier, much of the land had sunk, creating Reelfoot Lake, and wild game flourished along its wooded shores

Crockett lost his first bid for Congress in 1825, and he consoled himself by going on extended hunts. According to his count he killed one hundred five bears in that season.

Two years later the voters sent him to Washington. Though he still capitalized on his backwoods persona, he never wore buckskins in Congress. He generally dressed in a plain frock coat and simple cravat. An acquaintance remembered that Crockett always looked like a German farmer in his Sunday best.

As the champion of the common man he proposed closing West Point because of its inherent elitism. He had never forgotten the slight he had

Lithograph from Samuel S. Osgood portrait of Crockett.
Courtesy the David Zucker Collection.

received early in the Creek Indian War. More significantly he devoted himself to a land reform bill that would help squatters acquire titles to their land. Such a bill was not popular with the monied land speculators, and the bill stagnated. Crockett received a second term in 1829, when his fellow Tennessean, Andrew Jackson, entered the White House. Although he initially endorsed the president, Crockett and Jackson split over the president's Indian Removal Bill, which Crockett foresaw would lead to the tragic Trail of Tears. He wrote:

> Several of my colleagues got around me, and told me how well they loved me, and that I was ruining myself. They said this was a favorite measure of the president, and I ought to go for it. I told them I believed it was a wicked, unjust measure, and that I should go against it, let the cost to myself be what it might.

It was the sort of moral stance on which Crockett would not yield or compromise, the sort of stance that would produce his personal motto:

"I leave this rule for others when I am dead,
Be always sure you are right—then go ahead."

But there were severe costs to him. His Tennessee constituents favored the bill because they coveted the Indian lands and because they faithfully supported their native president. Crockett lost the 1831 election and returned home to the Obion River wilderness.

But he had left his mark and established his reputation.

On April 25, 1831, James Kirke Paulding's new play *The Lion of the West* opened at New York's Park Theater and quickly proved itself to be a commercial success. Its protagonist, Colonel Nimrod Wildfire, clad in fringed buckskins and a ferocious wildcat cap, descended from the fictional writings of James Fenimore Cooper and Washington Irving. But everyone knew that David Crockett provided the flesh and blood prototype. To the general public, Colonel Crockett and Colonel Wildfire were indistinguishable.

Certainly the popularity of the play helped Crockett win reelection in 1833. On a cold December evening that year, the Honorable David Crockett settled into a box seat at the Washington Theater to view a special benefit performance of *The Lion of the West*. Prancing out onto the stage, actor James Hacket as Wildfire saluted his inspiration, and, to the audience's thunderous delight, Crockett stood for a bow.

Perhaps that moment completed David Crockett's transformation into "Davy" Crockett.

The book *Life and Adventures of Colonel David Crockett of West Tennessee*, attributed to Matthew St. Claire Clark, was published in early 1833, sold out, and was reprinted that same year as *Sketches and Eccentricities of Colonel David Crockett of West Tennessee*.

And there were other books, most notably a series of humorous *Davy Crockett Almanacks* that continued in publication for years after his death. And there were songs. The Crockett mania of the 1830s rivaled that of the 1950s. Crockett emerged as the definitive half-horse, half-alligator—with a mite touch of snapping turtle. He could grin a raccoon right out of the tree, outhug a bear in a bear hug contest, and whip his weight in wildcats. He could wade the Mississippi, leap the Ohio, and ride upon a streak of lightning.

Crockett's personal contributions to his image were more realistic. In 1834 he wrote his own autobiography, *A Narrative of the Life of David Crockett, by Himself*, in which he "endeavoured to give the reader a plain, honest, homespun account of my state in life, and some of the few difficulties which have attended me along its journey. . . . " Although he already had posed for several portraits in his frock coat, he commissioned artist John Gadsby Chapman to portray him as if "on a bear hunt in a harricane." Since in Washington Crockett had no appropriate backwoods attire, he had to borrow a hunter's frock and a wide-brimmed slouch hat.

Lithograph from John Gadsby Chapman portrait of Crockett.
Courtesy the Joseph Musso Collection.

The Whig Party, then in opposition to Jackson's Democrats, readily embraced Crockett and tantalized him with the possibility of a run for the White House. They promoted him by sponsoring a speaking tour of the East Coast. In Philadelphia he probably saw the Liberty Bell, and the Whigs there rewarded him as if he had patched it up. They presented him with numerous gifts: an engraved watch, a tomahawk, a butcher knife, and most impressive, a silver mounted rifle. He named it "Pretty Betsy," to distinguish it from his favorite hunting rifle, "Old Betsy." In fact Crockett generally scorned such shiny embellishments. They conflicted with his image as champion of the common man, and, more important to a genuine woodsman, they might reflect a glint of sunlight, alerting his potential prey.

Yet despite all the Whig's promotional efforts, Crockett never made an effective legislator. Detesting the long-winded speeches, he frequently skipped congressional sessions. He never got a bill passed; his oldest son, John, became a congressman and finally pushed through his father's land reform bill. Crockett was, at once, too naive, too honest, and too uncompromising. At the next election he again fell to the Jackson machine and their candidate, peg-legged war hero Adam Huntsman.

The unexpected defeat devastated forty-nine-year-old David Crockett. But he had started over many times before, always moving west. Only now he had run out of space in Tennessee. At the Union Hotel Bar in Memphis he delivered his immortal farewell: "Since you have chosen to elect a man with a timber toe to succeed me, you may all go to hell and I will go to Texas." Then, donning his coonskin cap and accompanied by his nephew, William Patton, and two neighbors, he boarded the ferry and departed Tennessee forever.

They feted him in Little Rock, Arkansas, and again in Clarksville, Texas. Crockett served up his "go to hell" speech generously salted with homespun anecdotes. After leisurely exploring the Red River valley, he arrived in Nacogdoches around January 5, 1836. There he signed the oath of allegiance and enlisted as a six-month volunteer in Captain William B. Harrison's company—the same unit that included Micajah Autry and Daniel W. Cloud. The men quickly adopted the title Crockett's Tennessee Mounted Volunteers, though Crockett held no rank and few of the others had come from Tennessee.

From San Augustine on January 9, Crockett dispatched a last letter back to his family:

> The cannon was fired here on my arrival and I must say as to what I have seen of Texas, it is the garden spot of the world. . . . I have but little doubt of being elected a member to form a Constitution for this province. I am rejoiced at my fate. I had rather be in my present situation than to be elected to a seat in Congress for life. I am in great hope of making a fortune for myself and my family, bad as my prospects has been.

Then he closed the letter: "Do not be uneasy about me, I am among friends . . . . Your affectionate father. Farewell."

Then the Lion of the West rode off for his historical rendezvous with the Napoleon of the West.

> *He heard of Houston and Austin and so*
> *To the Texas plains he jest had to go,*
> *Where freedom was fightin' another foe*
> *And they needed him at the Alamo.*

Chapter 23: *Fannin*

Crockett's Tennessee Mounted Volunteers rode into San Antonio de Bexar just a few days after Travis' arrival. Of course Crockett was called upon to orate. He stepped onto a wooden box in the main plaza of town and again recited the now well rehearsed "go to hell, I'm bound for Texas" speech. The Texians cheered and applauded.

"We are now one hundred and fifty strong," Green B. Jameson wrote Governor Henry Smith on February 11. "Col Crockett & Col Travis both here & Col Bowie in command of the volunteer forces."

The cast had assembled.

The previous night, February 10, San Antonio had held a ball in Crockett's honor. Antonio Menchaca described the event in his memoirs. During the dance, a breathless courier rushed in asking for Juan Seguin. Informed that Seguin was not in attendance, the courier handed Menchaca a dispatch, written in Spanish, containing the latest intelligence about Mexican troop movements. The letter, dated four days earlier, announced that a large concentration of *soldados* was mobilizing at Presidio Rio Grande preparing to march on Bexar.

James Bowie walked up and read the dispatch. He called to Travis, but at that moment Travis could not be interrupted. Not for another rumor. Not while he was dancing with the most beautiful señorita in all of San Antonio. It was typically Travis. Rebecca was a long distance away, even if he still wore the ring she had given him.

Bowie, noting that the correspondence was of grave importance, gathered Travis and Menchaca; Crockett also joined them. Since the Tennessean did not speak Spanish, Travis translated the dispatch into English. Then Travis casually noted that it would take the Mexican force thirteen or fourteen days to march to San Antonio. "This is the fourth day," Travis said. "Let us dance tonight, and tomorrow we will make arrangements for our defense."

He returned to the waiting arms of his beautiful señorita, and the dance continued until seven o'clock the next morning.

Menchaca himself supplied the incident with an appropriate Byronic stanza from *Childe Harold's Pilgrimage: Canto the Third*:

> There was a sound of revelry by night,
> And Belgium's capital had gather'd then
> Her Beauty and her Chivalry, and bright
> The lamps shone o'er fair women and brave men;
> A thousand hearts beat happily; and when
> Music arose with its voluptuous swell,
> Soft eyes look'd love to eyes which spake again,
> And all went merry as a marriage bell;
> But hush! hark! a deep sound strikes like a rising knell!

Colonel James Clinton Neill had not participated in the impromptu officers' conference at the ball. Jameson wrote that Neill had left the garrison "on account of an express from his family informing him of their ill health."

In consequence of their lack of pay, clothes, and provisions, a number of volunteers also were threatening to abandon San Antonio on the following day, Jameson added. No record exists that a large contingent of soldiers did withdraw from Bexar. They may have been induced to remain because Neill promised to return within three weeks bearing money to sustain the garrison. Or the volunteers may have stayed because the famous Davy Crockett now was among them.

Neill's departure displayed that, despite the persistent rumors, no one actually anticipated the enemy for another month. A responsible officer, Neill would not have left his command if he thought a battle was imminent. Ironically, however, his departure generated a small-scale conflict.

Before he rode out, Neill passed temporary command of the garrison to Travis. The appointment energized Travis. At last he had a real command, even if it was over a small and pitiful army defending an artillery position—the very assignment the young cavalryman had previously rejected. Yet no longer did Travis consider resignation. On the following evening, February 12, he retired into the Alamo headquarters, located in one of the old Indian cells along the west wall. He dipped his quill into the inkwell and, by flickering candlelight, penned the first of many letters from the Alamo.

The latest reports placed Santa Anna at Saltillo with twenty-five hundred men, he wrote Governor Henry Smith. General Sesma commanded another two thousand *soldados* already on the Rio Grande. Santa Anna had issued a proclamation threatening to exterminate all the white men within the limits of Texas. "This being the Frontier Post nearest the Rio Grande, will be the first to be attacked," Travis asserted.

He urged Smith to send money, clothing, and provisions, but most of all reinforcements. " . . . with 200 more men I believe this place can be maintained & I hope they will be sent as soon as possible," Travis stated. "Yet should we receive no reinforcements, I am determined to defend this place to the last, and should Bexar fall, your friend will be buried beneath the ruins."

In his role as the new commander, the proud and defiant William Barret Travis had reemerged. But only briefly. Because again, abruptly, everything went wrong.

Aside from the obvious grumblings about lack of provisions, there had been no conflict in the three-way relationship between Neill, Bowie, and the garrison. But now, with Travis inserted in the equation, loud mutterings of discord emerged from the men.

As Travis' faithful adjutant John J. Baugh noted, the men resented Travis because he was a "Regular officer," an authorized agent of the despised council. But Travis may have augmented the dissension by flaunting his new authority. And there was more.

Travis had never possessed a charismatic personality. Outside his small circle of close friends, he was not especially popular. Moreover his experience as a leader only slightly exceeded his very limited combat experience. Why should the volunteers settle for Travis when they had in their midst Big Jim Bowie, the most competent and successful of all Texian commanders.

And of course there also was old Davy Crockett, and he had more military experience than Travis, and years of wisdom to boot. But Crockett must have felt that he had gotten himself between the old bear and the young wolf. He wisely sidestepped the duel of egos. "I have come to aid you all that I can in your noble cause," he had told the men, "and all the honor that I desire is that of defending as a high private, in common with my fellow-citizens, the liberties of our common country."

But even Crockett must have wondered what kind of snake den he had blundered into. He, too, could readily see the futility of one hundred fifty men trying to defend that broken down old mission-fortress against thousands of Mexican *soldados*. But surely other reinforcements would arrive soon, following after him and his Tennessee boys.

Travis could not afford risking an exodus from Bexar of men dissatisfied with an appointed leadership. He allowed the volunteers—virtually everyone except the thirty regulars he brought with him—to hold an election.

Not surprisingly, Bowie won.

On February 13 both Travis and adjutant Baugh wrote nearly identical whining letters to Governor Smith. Bowie never bothered to record his side of the subsequent conflict. Indeed he may never have known of the correspondence from Travis and Baugh.

"Bowie was elected by two small companies," wrote Travis.

" . . . none but the volunteers voted & in fact not all of them," agreed adjutant Baugh. A garrison so long neglected was entitled to a bit of apathy. However Baugh conceded that Bowie enjoyed "popularity among the volunteers" and had been elected "without opposition."

Perhaps unintentionally, Baugh made it sound like the men rejoiced to have Bowie as their leader. Or maybe the garrison just needed an excuse to celebrate. "Bowie immediately sent to the Alamo for troops and they immediately paraded in the square, under Arms, in a tumultously and disorderly manner," Baugh wrote, "Bowie, himself, and many of his men, being drunk which has been the case ever since he has been in command."

Travis concurred, " . . . since his election [Bowie] has been roaring drunk all the time." Their allegations made it sound like Bowie had led his men on a week-long binge. In fact, the election had been just the previous night. The overly enthusiastic victory celebration had only lasted into the next day.

Both Travis and Baugh accused Bowie of "interfering with private property" by stopping carts "laden with the goods of private families removing to the country." And Bowie also had given orders for the release of all civil and military prisoners "for Labor, or otherwise." Even Bowie's old friend Erasmo Seguin, then serving as judge in Bexar, protested the release of a prisoner named Antonio Fuentes.

Actually Bowie had used his authority to declare a state of martial law, just as his previous commander, General Andrew Jackson, had done at New Orleans. Bowie had appropriated provisions and men for the garrison. Upon his release from jail, Antonio Fuentes fell in with Juan Seguin's *Tejano* company—to take up a rifle and share the fate of the other Alamo defenders.

There was at least one point on which Bowie and Travis agreed. Amid his condemnations of Bowie, Travis virtually repeated Bowie's earlier assertion that Bexar was the "key of Texas." Travis wrote, "By the 15th of March I think Texas will be invaded & every preparation should be made to receive them."

As he had done before, Governor Smith simply ignored Travis—effectively sanctioning the election that had placed Bowie in command. However, almost as quickly as it began, the feud ended. "By an understanding of today Col. J. Bowie has the command of the volunteers of the garrison, and Col. W. B. Travis of the regulars and volunteer cavalry," Bowie and Travis together wrote Smith on February 14. "All general orders and correspondence will henceforth be signed by both until Col. Neill's return."

It was a truce, and a strained one at that—and one that obviously favored Bowie, who retained command of more than two-thirds of the garrison. But at least he and Travis were cooperating. It would be easy to credit the more pragmatic Bowie with initiating the peace, but in the absence of historical evidence that is unfair to Travis. However Bowie, with his Bexareno connections, certainly was responsible for the five hundred dollars they managed to borrow from citizens in San Antonio for the benefit of the garrison.

Again they reiterated to Smith that Bexar would be the "first point of attack" by the invading army and the necessity of sending reinforcements, "as speedily as possible."

Dr. Amos Pollard had written the day before. He did not even mention the clash between Bowie and Travis. Instead Pollard advised Smith of the absence of medicine at Bexar, stating, " . . . in the event of a siege I can be of very little use to the sick under such circumstances."

Travis probably called for other letters to be collected from the garrison.

Travis entrusted these letters to Erastus Smith, the "Bravest of the Brave in the cause of Texas." Old Deaf had recovered from the wound he received at the battle of Bexar, but now, like Neill, he faced his own family crisis. He had sent his wife, Guadalupe, and their four children to Columbia for safety. Then he had received distressing news that, destitute, they had been shunned by the Anglo community because they were Hispanic. For Deaf Smith, as with so many other colonists, Texas would have to wait until he had taken care of his family. Nevertheless he agreed to detour to San Felipe with the dispatches from the Alamo.

Governor Henry Smith probably received the letter from the Alamo two days later. But there was nothing he could do in response to Travis' appeals for help. Only two other forces existed in Texas, one under the joint command of Colonel Frank Johnson and Dr. James Grant and the other led by Colonel James Walker Fannin. All three men had thrown their loyalty behind the council.

James Walker Fannin
Courtesy the Dallas Historical Society.

After Houston had persuaded much of their army to remain at Goliad, Johnson and Grant had continued south toward Matamoras with about seventy men. They expected to be reinforced both by Fannin and by a larger federalist force from below the Rio Grande.

"Fear nothing for Bexar or Goliad or any point of Texas if an attack is made on Matamoras," Johnson wrote back to Fannin on February 9. "The enemy will be compelled to change his plan of attack and we will maintain the war in his own territory with his own means with every advantage on our side."

However Fannin, whom the council recognized as the commander-in-chief of the Texian army, had received distressing news at Refugio. General Jose Urrea, commanding six hundred *soldados*, had routed the Texian's federalist allies and had occupied Matamoras on January 31.

Fannin hastily abandoned his strategy to capture Matamoras and instead, on February 12, fell back to Goliad. There he commanded over four hundred men, the largest army in Texas. He also held the old Spanish presidio, the strongest fort in Texas. He christened it Fort Defiance.

But it was not what the council wanted. On February 13, Lieutenant Governor Robinson wrote to Fannin:

> I do not think the Enemy will attack either San Antonio De Bexar or the Fortress of Goliad. But that he will endeavor to throw reinforcements into Matamoras is more probable— Therefore you will always Keep in view the original objects of the campaign against the latter place, and dash upon it as it is prudent to do so in your opinion.

Later that day the council received information finally convincing them that Santa Anna indeed was marching into Texas. Belatedly, Robinson realized the necessity of aborting the Matamoras expedition. Fannin would have to fight a defensive war. Robinson shot off a second, hasty note to Fannin countermanding all previous orders. The new instructions were vague. "You will occupy such points as you may in your opinion deem most advantageous," Robinson wrote.

He was ordering Fannin to make his own decisions. To command. It was the one thing Fannin did not want to do.

His combat experience had been limited to the Bexar campaign when he had served under Bowie. Fannin had received half the credit for the victory at Concepcion. But no one knew better than Captain Fannin that Colonel Bowie had given all the orders.

On February 14 James Walker Fannin, the council's agent and commander in chief of the army, wrote to Robinson:

> I do not desire any command, and particularly that of chief. I feel, I know, if you and the council do not, that I am incompetent. Fortune, and brave soldiers, may favor me and save the State, and establish for me a reputation far beyond my deserts. I do not covet, and I do earnestly ask of you ... to relieve me, and make a selection of one possessing all the requisites of a commander.

Two days later Fannin wrote Robinson, "If Genl Houston does not return to duty on the Expiration of his furlough, and it meets your approbation I shall make headquarters at Bejar. . . . " In other words, if Houston did not appear to resume command, Fannin would march to San Antonio.

Such a strategy definitely did not meet with the council's approbation.

Some modern historians, myopically looking only at rank, have concluded that had Fannin arrived at Bexar, he would have assumed command of the Alamo garrison.

In 1836 Lieutenant Governor Robinson and the council feared otherwise. Command of the largest army in Texas was the only trump the council held in its feud with Governor Smith. Since the volunteers at Bexar had rejected all council appointments and agents—including Travis—Fannin could not automatically assert his authority there. Young Herman Ehrenberg, the New Orleans Grey then serving in Fannin's command, shared that perspective. He wrote, "In Goliad [Fannin] held undisputably the first position, which rank, however, he would have had to resign if he combined with the main Army [at Bexar]."

Moreover, considering Fannin's plunging self-confidence, he might willingly have relinquished his command to his former superior—the devoted Smith and Houston man—Colonel James Bowie.

But Fannin did not march to Bexar. On February 21 Fannin wrote that he was fortifying Goliad. Yet he still pleaded for the council to release him from the army, "at least as an officer." And on the following day he added, "I am a better judge of my military abilities than others, and if I am qualified to command an Army, I have not found it out."

It must have been disconcerting for the council. In their duel with Governor Smith, they had usurped the authority of the most competent commanders in Texas, Houston and Bowie, instead awarding absolute power to the one man who had absolutely no idea what to do with it.

At Bexar the garrison continued their preparations for the invasion. Writing Governor Smith on February 16, engineer Green B. Jameson described ambitious plans for the Alamo. He would square the compound and construct large redoubts jutting from each corner so that Texian artillery could spray deadly grapeshot and cannister down the outside of the walls. Jameson also planned to surround the mission/fortress with a moat.

Jameson had the vision and the manpower. All he needed was time.

To Jameson's letter Travis attached another plea for men, money, and provisions. Travis gave the correspondence to his old acquaintance James Butler Bonham. Travis surely gave Bonham verbal instructions as well. Bring reinforcements. From Goliad, Gonzales, San Felipe, anywhere. The enemy were not expected for several weeks—perhaps even a month—but it might take that long to gather new volunteers within the Alamo's walls.

Bonham rode out of Bexar understanding full well the importance of his mission. Without immediate reinforcements, the Alamo was doomed.

All Travis and Bowie could do was wait.

A precious week passed. The garrison grew ever more depressed. Moreover they were exhausted from digging ditches and strengthening redoubts. February 21, the eve of George Washington's birthday, provided an excuse for a sorely needed diversion—another fandango.

No doubt Travis danced with the prettiest señoritas in Bexar. David Crockett found an old fiddle, an instrument he played passably well, and contributed to the festivities. And if Crockett was not noisy enough, twenty-eight-year-old John McGregor, a sergeant in Captain William

Carey's artillery company, the Invincibles, had brought bagpipes from his native Scotland.

McGregor was not the only Britisher celebrating the birth of the man who had led the thirteen colonies to independence from King George. There were perhaps a half dozen in the garrison from Scotland, one from Wales, thirteen from Ireland, and fifteen from England.

France and Germany had each contributed a few volunteers. A twenty-eight-year-old painter named Charles Zanco came all the way from Denmark with his widower father. Enlisting with the "First Volunteers at Lynchburg," he had fabricated the company flag bearing a single star and the slogan, "Independence." It may have been the first "Lone Star" flag, and perhaps it, too, had found its way to the Alamo.

During the siege of Bexar, Zanco had been assigned to the artillery, and so he, like McGregor, now served in Carey's company. So did Anthony Wolf, a fifty-four-year-old Indian scout said to have been "born and raised a Spanish subject." Wolf may have attended the party, but he probably entrusted his two sons, only eleven and twelve years old, to the care of friendly Bexarenos.

James Bowie may have made an appearance at the fandango, but if so he probably retired early. He was not well. It had descended upon him with the bitter winds and icy rains that swept down from the north. Weakness. Dizziness. Headaches. His lungs on fire. The violent coughing spasms.

He had talked to Dr. Pollard and Dr. John Sutherland. Sutherland, a forty-three-year-old Virginian had arrived in Bexar around the end of December and immediately began assisting Dr. Pollard. Sutherland described Bowie's disease as "being of a peculiar nature . . . not to be cured by an ordinary course of treatment." It hardly mattered. Virtually no medical supplies existed in Bexar.

It rained again that night of the Washington birthday celebration. With the droplets cascading from the brim of his hat and his coat held tight at his throat, Bowie trudged up muddy Soledad Street to the Veramendi house.

He had been staying there since his return to Bexar a month earlier. However he was not the only occupant.

Twenty-four-year-old Juana Navarro was the niece of the noted federalist Jose Antonio Navarro. She had been one of twelve children. When her mother had died, her father reluctantly entrusted his younger children to the care of various family and friends. Juana had been adopted by her aunt and godmother, Josefa Navarro Veramendi. Juana's cousin, Ursula Veramendi, became her sister.

A marriage in 1832 left Juana a son, Alejo. Her husband died in 1834, possibly of the cholera that had brought so much sadness to her family.

When the Texians besieged Bexar in late 1835, Juana lived in the Veramendi house with her son and her teenaged sister, Gertrudis. During the storming of the city the Texians had captured and fortified the house. Deaf Smith had been wounded on its roof; Ben Milam had died in its yard.

Perhaps Horace Alsbury had found refuge inside the house during the battle. One of Austin's "Old Three Hundred," Alsbury termed himself a doctor, although he had been much more active in political matters.

Alsbury was attracted to the young widow, and she accepted his proposal. The war discouraged the traditional courtship, and anyway there was not much of her family left. They were married in January.

It was better for Bowie that the house was not empty. The loneliness would have been too haunting, the silence utterly deafening. And yet Juana brought back so many bittersweet memories of Ursula.

Even his own illness reminded Bowie of his wife; he had been sick when he had learned of Ursula's death.

Did he have the malaria again? Or was it something else?

The coughing always seemed to worsen in the evening. He stretched out on his bed and piled blankets on top of his shivering body.

"I, as chief executive of the government, zealous in the fulfillment of my duties to my country, declared that I would maintain the territorial integrity whatever the cost," declared Antonio Lopez de Santa Anna. "This would make it necessary to initiate a tedious campaign under a capable leader immediately."

And whom did Santa Anna have in mind as a capable leader? He wrote:

> With the fires of patriotism in my heart and dominated by a noble ambition to save my country, I took pride in being the first to strike in defense of the independence, honor, and rights of my nation. Stimulated by these courageous feelings, I took command of the campaign myself, preferring the uncertainties of war to the easy and much-coveted life of the palace.

Because of Santa Anna's leadership, both Texas and Mexico would pay a heavy price.

But to *El Presidente's* credit, it had not been an easy task. On December 5, 1835—even as the battle of Bexar had raged four hundred miles to the north—Santa Anna arrived in San Luis Potosi. Already he had dispatched General Joaquin Ramirez y Sesma with more than fifteen hundred forty *soldados* and eight artillery pieces to march to the relief of General Cos. Santa Anna had instructed Sesma:

> The foreigners who wage war against the Mexican Nation have violated all laws and do not deserve any consideration, and for that reason, no quarter will be given them as the troops are to be notified at the proper time. They have audaciously declared a war of extermination to the Mexicans and should be treated in the same manner.

On December 30 the Mexican Congress, acting on Santa Anna's request, decreed that all foreigners in armed opposition against Mexico would be regarded as pirates—and executed.

At San Luis Potosi, Santa Anna began preparation for his Army of Operations that would complete the extermination of the foreigners occupying Texas. "His Excellency himself attends to all matters whether important or most trivial," recalled a Mexican officer. The first obstacle was financing. Years of revolution had depleted the Mexican treasury and left the country mired in debt. Santa Anna needed money for his army, and he needed it immediately. He secured a personal loan for ten thousand pesos. Enough to get started. He reminded the Catholic Church of the favors it owed him and received money from that source. Still not enough. He resorted to money-lenders and acquired another four hundred thousand pesos—though as his personal secretary, Ramon Caro, noted, "the terms of the contract proved very disadvantageous to the nation." The interest rate amounted to nearly fifty percent a year.

Secretary Caro also accused Colonel Ricardo Dromundo, the commissary general of the army, of corruption. Caro noted that Dromundo "had been given the necessary funds for two months provisions and supplies for 6,000 men," yet the *soldados* were only issued half rations of hardtack. It helped Dromundo's scam that he was a brother-in-law of His Excellency.

Santa Anna awarded the almost meaningless title of second commander-in-chief to Vicente Filisola. Though an Italian by birth, Filisola's career in the Mexican army dated back to 1811. He had served under Iturbide, fighting on both sides during the revolution from Spain. In 1831 he acquired an *empresario* grant in east Texas but could not fulfill his contract for six hundred families. In 1833 he was appointed commander of the eastern interior provinces, the same position held by General Arredondo when he invaded Texas. Filisola had the proper credentials, if not the proper ruthlessness, for the Texas campaign.

Finding officers was not a problem. There were so many ways they could profit in the corrupt army bureaucracy. General Antonio Gaona, commander of the First Infantry Brigade, bought up all the supplies in sight and sold them back to the army at double the cost. General Manuel Fernandez Castrillon, Santa Anna's aide-de-camp, loaned money to the army at a modest interest rate of only four per cent, but Ramon Caro suspected him of pocketing a one-thousand-peso donation from the cathedral at Monterrey.

Recruiting men had been harder. There were not enough trained *soldados* in the army and very little inducement to enlist. Santa Anna remembered that half of his army were "raw recruits . . . hastily enlisted to fill the ragged companies." Among these "raw recruits" were Mayan Indians forcibly drafted from the Yucatan. They spoke an Indian dialect rather than Spanish and never had hefted a musket.

Yet somehow, owing largely to the sheer determination of Santa Anna himself, the Army of Operations grew to over six thousand men, of whom fifteen hundred already were marching north under General Sesma.

Then word arrived of General Cos' defeat at Bexar. Santa Anna determined that such news would unnecessarily distress the government, so he did not forward the information to Mexico City. But he himself was enraged. Almost immediately he began ordering his brigades north to Saltillo. He arrived there on January 7 and began a month of organizing, training, and drilling. New recruits were given their uniforms. Although the uniforms varied according to unit, the typical Mexican *soldado* wore a blue tailcoat mounted with epaulets and a tall, black leather shako bearing a tricolor plume and a brass shield identifying the brigade. Despite their British surplus weapons, they at least looked Napoleonic.

And now the Napoleon of the West faced a formidable task reminiscent of his French namesake's invasion of Russia. In the midst of a bitter winter, Santa Anna would march his army north three hundred sixty-five miles across the barren deserts to San Antonio de Bexar.

Lithograph of Mexican uniforms of the period by Richard Knotel.
Courtesy the Joseph Musso Collection.

General Filisola, like Sam Houston, perceived no strategic value to the *Tejano* city standing on the western frontier. Supported by other generals, Filisola recommended a more direct route through Goliad and into the Anglo settlements. But Santa Anna could not be swayed. He dispatched General Jose de Urrea with over six hundred *soldados* to proceed through Matamoras to Goliad. However the main body of the army would march on San Antonio. Strategic or not, the defeat of his brother-in-law had made it personal. "Bexar was held by the enemy and it was necessary to open the door to our future operations by taking it," Santa Anna insisted.

For Santa Anna, like Bowie and Travis, Bexar was the key to Texas.

On January 25, General Martin Perfecto de Cos arrived at Saltillo. Santa Anna simply overruled Cos' pledge never to take up arms against the Texians and promptly ordered his brother-in-law to prepare to march back north.

General Castrillon, Santa Anna's aide-de-camp, asked Colonel Sanchez Navarro, who had returned with Cos, if the colonel believed the Texians would fire even a single shot in resistance. Sanchez Navarro soberly retorted that the Texians would fire a million shots.

Growing increasingly impatient, Santa Anna reviewed his troops that same day and determined that his Army of Operations was ready for the campaign. Secretary Ramon Caro wrote:

> During the first days of February the army set out for Monclova together with His Excellency. He remained there only a few days, for on the 9th he set out with his staff and 50 mounted men for Rio Grande for the purpose of joining the brigade of General Ramirez y Sesma which was there. Before leaving, he issued orders setting the time and the manner of the departure of the second and third brigades and of the cavalry.

The small force accompanying Santa Anna's moved quickly across the northern desert. His scattered brigades lumbered along more slowly, burdened as they were by supply wagons, artillery, and the noncombatant *soldaderas*. The Mexican army reluctantly tolerated *soldados'* families to accompany a long campaign. They further drained supplies, and the children were little more than a burden, but the wives cooked and foraged and supplied other morale-sustaining comforts for the troops.

On that dismal march, the troops needed all the morale that could be mustered. Ramon Caro remembered that only a few medical students with an inadequate supply of drugs accompanied the army. The bitter cold and lack of adequate food supplies took a deadly toll. Since there were no hospital wagons, the *soldados* and *soldaderas* who collapsed along the march had to be crammed into munitions wagons already overloaded with the sick and dying. Caro wrote:

> I remember particularly. . . a poor wretch whom we found, at the point of death, unable to move, loaded down with his gun and pack. We placed him in one of the wagons, but he expired before the day's journey was over. Of course, he, like many others, received no spiritual consolation. Such was the sad spectacle offered by the army on its march. In fact, only the heroic constancy and the unlimited endurance so often displayed by the Mexican soldier succeeded in overcoming the disheartening spectacle presented to their eyes.

Then somehow it got even worse. A devastating blizzard roared in on February 13. Exhausted pack mules, lying on the ground, suffocated under the rising snow. Fifty teams of oxen that had pulled wagons and artillery for the First Infantry Brigade perished. Caught out on the prairie with no shelter, the *soldados* and *soldaderas*, most of them inadequately clothed, huddled together for protection and warmth. No one ever bothered to record how many died, but the mortality rate must have been highest among the pathetic Mayans from the tropical Yucatan, who had never before seen snow.

And among the children.

The blinding snow afforded some *soldados* the opportunity to desert their units, but many were recaptured by the brigades marching behind. The army needed men too badly to resort to executions for punishment. Instead the deserters were sentenced to extended reenlistment without pay.

Yet they may have been the fortunate ones. Even if a deserter eluded the army, he risked a more terrible fate from the bands of hostile Indians that trailed the expedition preying on stragglers.

The Mexican Army of Operations paid a dear price before it ever faced the guns of the Alamo.

The Napoleon of the West himself suffered far less. He rode in the relative comfort of a luxurious coach pulled by six white mules. Or he would dress in his silver trimmed uniform weighted with war medals, buckle on his seven-thousand-dollar sword, don his Napoleonic style bicorne hat, and ride before the troops mounted on his gold-trimmed saddle with a golden eagle head serving as the saddle horn.

On February 19, above the Rio Grande, Santa Anna's party overtook General Sesma's vanguard brigade. He now commanded more than fifteen hundred *soldados*, although the rest of his Army of Operations extended southwest for three hundred miles. Two days later Santa Anna celebrated his forty-second birthday by reaching the tree-lined Medina with its crystal clear waters. It was the site of his first great military victory. And just across the river was the province of Texas. He was only twenty-five miles from Bexar, and his forced march through the midst of winter had caught the Texians unaware.

The war was virtually over, Santa Anna had claimed in a letter he had written from the Rio Grande back to Mexico City. The Anglo Americans would be driven out and the land awarded to his troops and to industrious Mexicans.

It very nearly was over for the Alamo garrison. That day a delegation of friendly Bexarenos arrived at the Mexican camp. There had always been *Tejanos* loyal to the centralist regime. And others merely loyal to the winning side. At that moment Santa Anna appeared to be the winner.

The Bexarenos advised Santa Anna that the Texians were planning a fandango for that very evening. They would be dancing in the streets. Drunk and helpless. They could easily be taken by surprise.

Santa Anna ordered General Sesma to mount up his cavalry. But at that moment the rains began. The untimely downpour transformed the gentle Medina into an impassable flood. The cavalry could not cross.

Once again Santa Anna would have to be patient.

But not for much longer.

The rain did not douse the celebration of Washington's birthday at San Antonio de Bexar. The cantina lights blazed late into the night, illuminating the boisterous fandango.

> *Did you hear it?—No; 'twas but the wind,*
> *Or the car rattling o'er the stony street;*
> *On with the dance! let joy be unconfin'd*
> *No sleep till morn, when Youth and Pleasure meet*
> *To chase the glowing Hours with flying feet—*
> *But hark!—that heavy sound breaks in once more,*
> *As if the clouds its echo would repeat;*
> *And nearer, clearer, deadlier than before!*
> *Arm! Arm! it is—it is—the cannon's opening roar!*

George Gordon, Lord Byron
Childe Harold's Pilgrimage: Canto the Third

Myths, Mysteries, and Misconceptions

Did Bowie Have Any Children?

Here yet is another mystery that has stymied historians. Even the most reliable sources, brother John and friend Caiaphas Ham, disagreed. And they both may have been wrong. John Bowie reported that Ursula had "one child, but both mother and child were followed to the grave" before James Bowie died. Family friend William Sparks also cited one child, whose brief existence was further supported by testimony given in *Veramendi v. Hutchins*, the prolonged legal battle for Bowie's estate.

However Caiaphas Ham wrote, "Two children were born to him, but both died young."

Most subsequent writers perpetuated the notion that Bowie had two infant children, who both died with their mother of the cholera. Unfortunately the chroniclers could not agree whether Bowie had two sons or a son and a daughter. Amelia Williams gave the two children theory historical credibility when the *Southwestern Historical Quarterly* published her dissertation "A Critical Study of the Siege of the Alamo and of the Personnel of its Defenders" in three parts in 1933. In her chapter "A Biographical Sketch of James Bowie," she embellished the tragic letter that Antonio Navarro wrote Samuel Williams by including Bowie's children among the dead. Curiously, this fraudulent fictionalization of fact had not appeared in her original 1931 University of Texas dissertation.

In *James Bowie—Texas Fighting Man* (1994), Clifford Hopewell wrote that Bowie had a daughter born in 1832 and that Ursula gave birth to a son after she arrived in Monclova. That might explain why John Bowie only knew of one child. Hopewell cites the International Geneological Index of the Mormon Church as his source for the children. Unfortunately the Mormon Church subsequently conceded that their information on Bowie's children came from the exceedingly fictional novel *The Iron Mistress*.

Frustratingly, no historical records have surfaced to support the existence of any Bowie children. There are no birth or baptismal records at San Fernando Church, and the parish priest in Monclova did not record the death of any children he attributed to Ursula.

Perhaps Ursula was pregnant when she left for Monclova and Bowie departed for the United States. James might have told John that Ursula was carrying a child, and John may have assumed the baby was born before her death. John did not mention the child's sex, perhaps because he never knew. This theory also would explain why no birth records exist.

Possibly she did give birth to a son before her death. The harried priest in Monclova recorded the death of an adopted son of Veramendi named Santiago. A common enough name, but is it mere coincidence that James Bowie was often called Santiago Bowie by his *Tejano* family and neighbors? Could the overwhelmed priest have made a mistake and attributed Ursula's son to her father?

The obvious drawback to these theories is that if James had known his wife was pregnant, why would he not have made provisions for his own child in his will? After all he did provide for Stephen's orphaned children.

The question of Bowie's children seems destined to remain an enduring Alamo riddle.

Why Did Travis Go to Texas?

Unlike James Bowie, William Barret Travis' early career was largely devoid of mystery or controversy. The notable exception concerned why Travis left Alabama to set out on the journey that would finally lead to the Alamo.

As historian Archie MacDonald noted in his 1976 volume *Travis*, a diversity of possible explanations had surfaced in the form of popular legends. According to one theory Travis became disgruntled after losing a political dispute to determine the seat of Clarke County. Another account relates that a prankster cut the tail off Travis' horse, and the irate Travis vowed that he could never live in a state where such atrocities were perpetuated.

Whether either of these incidents occurred, neither provided sufficient justification for his departure from Louisiana. To Texans, their Alamo hero required something more dramatic to compel him to abandon his wife, infant son, and unborn daughter.

The most prevalent legend appeared in several variations. A man had been murdered and another man, often portrayed as a hapless slave, had been charged with the crime. Judge James Dellet appointed Travis to defend the alleged killer. But despite Travis' oratorical abilities, he saw that the case was lost. At a private late night meeting with his mentor, Travis explained that he knew the slave to be innocent because he himself had perpetrated the crime. The victim had been engaged in an affair with Travis' wife, Rosanna. Judge Dellet offered three options. Travis could remain silent, and the slave would hang. Or Travis could confess and mount the gallows himself. Or Travis could leave a written confession—and escape prosecution by fleeing to Texas.

This latter story is the one that has been taught to countless students of Texas history. Unfortunately not one shred of historical evidence exists that Travis ever killed anybody. Travis family tradition suggests that Travis at least believed that Rosanna had been unfaithful—which certainly could have influenced his decision to leave Alabama.

However in his book *Three Roads to the Alamo* (1998), William C. Davis unearthed the James Dellet Papers at the Alabama Department of Archives and History in Montgomery and the Benjamin F. Porter Collection in the Auburn University Archives. Here, finally and conclusively, was the reason Travis fled to Texas. Dellet prosecuted Travis for excessive indebtedness, and Dellet's partner, Porter, witnessed the proceedings. If Travis had remained in Alabama, he would have been sentenced to debtor's prison. He chose Texas—and immortality—instead.

Was Bowie an Alcoholic?

John Bowie wrote that his more famous younger brother "would take a glass, in merry mood, to 'drive dull care away'; but seldom allowed it to 'steal away his brains,' or transform him into a beast."

Translation: James Bowie imbibed, but rarely to excess. Of course John rarely saw James in the later years, after the death of Ursula when tradition states that Bowie turned to drink.

In his 1996 PBS documentary production *The West*, Ken Burns perpetuated the more popular notion when he dismissed Bowie as an "alcoholic adventurer."

However the historical record provides very few accounts of Bowie being inebriated.

Both Anson Jones and George M. Patrick claimed to have seen him drunk at the Consultation. Both accounts were written many years after the event. Moreover Jones hated Houston, and therefore his malice extended to Bowie. Patrick's account was written more than forty years later and garbled a few facts. Nonetheless there is no reason to doubt the essence of their contention. But having just come off an exhausting five-day ride, it would not have taken much alcohol to make Bowie appear more intoxicated than he was. Even Patrick marveled at how quickly Bowie recovered and set out on a "lively" ride back to Bexar. There, according to Patrick—after another draining trip—Bowie promptly got drunk again.

The only other recorded instance of Bowie's drinking to excess occurred on the day after his election as commander of the Bexar garrison. And, curiously, the only two references to this incident were the poor losers, Travis and his loyal adjutant Baugh. As John Myers Myers noted in his book *The Alamo* (1948), "a man with only a reasonable amount of liquor under his belt can seem mightily drunk to anyone not so enjoying himself." Neither Green B. Jameson nor Dr. Amos Pollard, both of whom wrote to Governor Smith about that same time, made any mention of the dispute or Bowie's drunkenness.

Dismissing the personal biases and faulty memories that might taint the credibility of these accounts still provides only three recorded instances when Bowie was drunk. Probably there were other unrecorded instances. Significantly, however, virtually no one else who knew Bowie ever referred to his drinking. Moreover, it seems extremely unlikely that Stephen F. Austin and Sam Houston would have trusted their most critical assignments to a man whose brains frequently were stolen away by alcohol.

Bowie certainly drank, perhaps sometimes to excess—as did many of his contemporaries. But there hardly is enough historical evidence to conclude that he drank more than most others. Rather his drinking, like his knife fighting, was an exaggeration that evolved into his legend.

Did Crockett Wear a Coonskin Cap?

The absurd notion that Crockett never wore a coonskin cap found its way into the media during 1986, the year Texas celebrated its Sesquicentennial—including the one hundred fiftieth anniversary of the fall of the Alamo. Armed with that misinformation, CBS began production of a television miniseries, *Thirteen Days to Glory*, in which Brian Keith portrayed Crockett in a modern cowboy hat.

All of this ignores historical evidence. Crockett's daughter Matilda described his departure for Texas, the last time she ever saw him: "He was dressed in his hunting suit, wearing a coon skin cap, and carried a fine rifle presented to him by friends in Philadelphia." In fact Matilda was mistaken about the rifle; Crockett left "Pretty Betsy" at home. A young girl might be confused about the similarity in guns. But would she have been mistaken about his headwear?

In his *History of the City of Memphis* (1873), journalist James D. Davis recalled witnessing Crockett's departure from that city. "He wore that same veritable coon-skin cap and hunting shirt," Davis wrote, "bearing upon his shoulder his ever faithful rifle."

Certainly the historical evidence suggests that Crockett wore a coonskin cap on his way to Texas.

Faced with these accounts, revisionist historians again revised their story and proclaimed that Crockett never wore a coonskin cap until after Nimrod Wildfire had pranced across the stage in a fur hat. True, the original illustration promoting the *Lion of the West* subsequently was used to depict Crockett in the series of Almanacks that bore his name. But Crockett had nothing to do with either project. And, yes, when Crockett posed for the Amos Chapman painting, he was waving a slouch hat. However Crockett had not brought his hunting clothes to Washington. He had to borrow the wardrobe for the painting. In Washington a coonskin cap may have been hard to find.

But not in the snow-draped backwoods of Tennessee and Kentucky. Fur caps made from raccoon, fox, skunk, and other animal hides were extremely common during the cold winter months. In the summertime, however, they would have been uncomfortably hot.

David Crockett may never have regarded the coonskin cap as a personal trademark until after Nimrod Wildfire popularized it. But it is ridiculous to argue that he had never worn a common and practical style of backwoods winter headgear until he saw one adorning an actor in a play. Crockett may have been catering to his image when he wore the cap in Memphis. But by the time he got to Texas, winter had set in, and during the bitter cold siege of the Alamo, Crockett almost certainly kept his scalp warm under his coonskin cap.

What Was Bowie's Illness?

Dr. John Sutherland described it as "being of a peculiar nature." Malaria frequently recurs in those who have been afflicted by it, but Sutherland and Dr. Pollard would have been expected to recognize its symptoms.

Juana Alsbury believed that Bowie had contracted typhoid fever, another likely candidate. But if Bowie had either malaria or typhoid fever, it obviously degenerated into pneumonia.

Yet other sources, including Mrs. Dickinson, suggested that the hard living, hard drinking Bowie suffered from tuberculosis.

The one consistency in all the theories is that Bowie had an infection of the lungs. On a Mississippi sandbar ten years earlier, Major Norris Wright plunged a cane sword into Bowie's lungs. Bowie survived that attack, but the lungs never heal completely. Ironically, whatever Bowie had contracted, Major Wright's blade may have contributed to it.

Only one thing can be said for certain. Bowie's illness did not result from complications due to injuries he sustained in a fall from a cannon emplacement. Reuben M. Potter, perhaps the first serious Alamo historian, introduced the story in an 1860 essay. Potter later concluded that the story was unfounded. His source had proved unreliable and no other witness or account verified Bowie's fall. Thus Potter deleted the story from his 1878 version of *The Fall of the Alamo*.

Yet once published, the story refused to die. Monte Barrett featured it in his novel *Tempered Blade* (1946). Raymond Thorp told it in *Bowie Knife* (1948), and Paul Wellman embellished it in *The Iron Mistress* (1951).

Perhaps works of fiction can be forgiven for opting for the more dramatic scenario. But Clifford Hopewell kept the myth alive in his 1994 biography *James Bowie: Texas Fighting Man*. And William R. Williamson gave it even more credibility when he included it in his James Bowie entry for the first printing of the *New Handbook of Texas* (1996). That error and others in Williamson's Bowie entry were corrected for the second printing.

Part Four: *Thirteen Days*

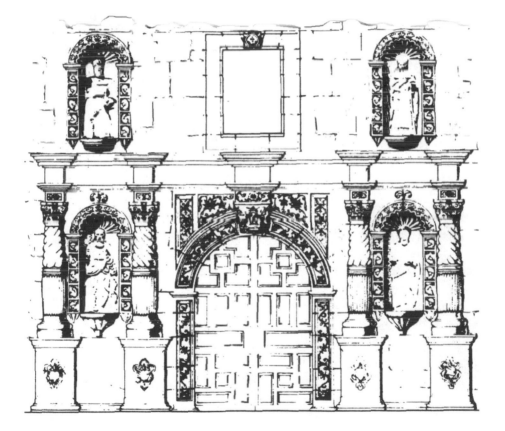

Tuesday, February 23, 1836: *The First Day*

San Antonio de Bexar

The discordant screech of wooden wheels churning through the boggy streets aroused William Barret Travis. He peered through the window of his quarters. The rain had finally stopped. Squinting into the glaring sunlight, Travis observed a procession of anxious Bexarenos wending through the streets. Some carried their belongings, others had crammed their possessions into the ox carts whose solid wood wheels produced the offensive squeal.

Dressing hastily, Travis raced outside into the midst of the frantic parade. The Bexarenos seemed reluctant to answer his questions. They were going into the country to prepare their crops, someone told him. Travis knew otherwise. Finally, around 11:00, someone admitted that the Bexarenos had received a report that the Mexican army was camped on Leon Creek only eight miles west of San Antonio.

One young Bexareno recalled that a *Tejano* had arrived at his house early that morning announcing that he had seen Santa Anna himself, in disguise, watching the preceding night's fandango.

An absurd rumor, of course. But could the Mexicans have arrived in the vicinity of Bexar without the Texians being aware? The Texians were not ready! Reinforcements had not come. There was no food in the mission.

Travis began issuing commands. He ordered a sentry into the bell tower of the San Fernando Church. Then he borrowed one of the two horses Dr. Sutherland kept in the city and sent a rider to round up the Texian horse herd, then grazing out on the Salado. Travis planned to scout the prairie to the west.

But before the rider had returned with the horses, Travis heard the church bell ringing frantically. As he raced across the plaza to the church, he heard the sentry calling out, "the enemy are in view." Other Texians anxiously congregated at the church. A few scrambled up into the bell tower, their gaze following the sentry's outstretched arm pointing to the west.

The prairie was empty.

"False alarm," someone called down. But Travis could hear the sentry's loud curse, insisting that he had seen the Mexican army.

Most of the assembled Texians began to mill away, grumbling that the sentry had only imagined the enemy. However Travis could not afford to share their sense of relief. If this was a false alarm, it had awakened him to all the things that had to be done before Santa Anna did arrive.

And if it was not a false alarm—!

Dr. Sutherland still had a horse in Bexar, but he was a relative newcomer to the region. He remembered, "I then proposed to Colonel Travis that if any one who knew the country would accompany me, I would go out and ascertain to a certainty the truth or falsity of the whole."

Red-haired John W. Smith volunteered. El Colorado had lived in Bexar about nine years, and he had a horse in town. As Dr. Sutherland climbed into his saddle he remarked to Travis that if the two riders were seen "returning in any other gait than a slow pace, he might be sure we had seen the enemy."

Sutherland and Smith rode west at a moderate pace, for the rains had left the road slick with mud. A half mile. A mile. No sign of the enemy. But another half mile brought them to a gentle rise. Suddenly they could only gape at what they saw. Sutherland wrote that they were "within one hundred and fifty yards of fifteen hundred men, well mounted and equipped; their polished armor glistening in the rays of the sun...."

Fearful that they had been spotted, the two scouts spun their horses around and sank in spurs. Sutherland's horse slipped and somersaulted, tossing its rider over its head and then rolling on top of Sutherland's legs. Sutherland's rifle snapped at the breech when it struck the ground. Smith galloped back to help the injured doctor remount. Fortunately the Mexican cavalry was not in pursuit. Together Smith and Sutherland raced back toward Bexar, the church bell ringing frantically as they galloped into the main plaza. There they encountered David Crockett astride his own horse. The Tennessean advised them that Travis had already removed his headquarters into the Alamo. He had ordered all the Texian force to assemble there.

Nat Lewis, an Anglo merchant in Bexar, packed whatever he could carry and prepared to flee the town. Lewis had little confidence in the Texian army. They cursed worse than an "army in Flanders," and some had even sold their rifles for money to buy liquor. Those men were now scrambling desperately to acquire new weapons.

Few Texians had a worse reputation for drunkenness than thirty-year-old Irish artilleryman William B. Ward. Yet as Lewis fled briefly to the Alamo, he noticed that Ward was sober and calm as he manned the guns over the gate.

Juan Seguin and some of his *Tejanos* were among those who grabbed whatever they could carry and rushed toward the Alamo. Seguin recalled El Colorado riding into town yelling, "there comes the Mexican army composed of cavalry, infantry, and artillery." Seguin added, "As we marched 'Potero Street,' now called 'Commerce,' the ladies exclaimed 'poor fellows, you will all be killed, what shall we do?'"

His mission completed, Smith hurried away to tend to his own affairs. Eight-year-old Enrique Esparza recalled that Smith galloped up to the Esparza house to warn of the approach of the Mexicans. Smith was the godfather to Enrique's younger brother Francisco. Enrique also had two more younger brothers and an older sister. Their father, twenty-seven-year-old Gregorio Esparza, served in Seguin's company, even though his own brother, Francisco, remained a centralist. Gregorio promised his wife, Ana, that he would send a wagon for her and the children. Then he rushed off to drive his own cattle into the mission/fortress.

According to Enrique, James Bowie also was herding cattle into the Alamo. Then he and others scrounged for whatever food they could find, locating some ninety bushels of corn in the hastily abandoned *jacales* of La Villita just south of the Alamo.

Then Bowie had another urgent mission. He raced back to the Veramendi house to help Dr. Horace Alsbury with Juana, little Alejo, and Juana's sister Gertrudis move into the Alamo.

Since Crockett and Sutherland were mounted, they avoided the frantic mob of Texians shoving across the footbridge. Instead Crockett and Sutherland crossed the river at a shallow ford below the bridge and rode into the Alamo.

Assisted by his slave, Joe, Travis had established his headquarters in a room built into the north end of the west wall. There he hastily scribbled a note to Andrew Ponton, the *alcalde* of Gonzales:

> 3 o'clock P.M. The enemy in large force are in sight. We want men and provisions. Send them to us. We have 150 men and are determined to defend the Alamo to the last. Give us assistance.

Travis handed the message to Dr. Launcelot Smither, who scurried out the door. The man was no fighter, but he knew the road between Bexar and Gonzales, and he would make a convenient courier. Smither must have galloped through the gate only moments before Crockett and Dr. Sutherland rode in. As Sutherland dismounted outside Travis' headquarters, his injured knee gave way. Crockett helped him to his feet and into the room.

Sutherland made a quick report to Travis. The co-commander told Sutherland to ride to Gonzales and rally the settlers to the relief of the Alamo. Perhaps Travis intended for Sutherland to accompany Dr. Smither. Before he left the room, Sutherland heard Crockett say, "Colonel, here am I. Assign me to a position, and I and my twelve boys will try to defend it." Travis entrusted the Tennessee Mounted Volunteers with the defense of the palisade that joined the church to the south wall.

Outside, Sutherland saw the frantic last minute preparations for a defense. Jameson had men mounting cannons, building parapets, and strengthening the walls. The cattle were herded into the enclosed area on the northeast side of the fort where once the mission artisans had labored. Sutherland reported that the bushels of corn were stored in "the small rooms of the barracks." He probably meant the long barracks, as the old *convento* was generally known. Its upstairs still served as a hospital, sheltering the sick members of the garrison as well as those still recuperating from the wounds they received in the battle of Bexar.

Having secured Dr. Alsbury, Juana, Gertrudis, and young Alejo in a room on the west wall near the headquarters, Bowie joined Travis in time to cosign a desperate appeal to Colonel Fannin at Goliad.

> We have removed all the men to the Alamo where we make
> such resistance as is due our honor, and that of the country,
> until we can get assistance from you, which we expect you to
> forward immediately. In this extremity, we hope you will send
> us all the men you can spare promptly. We have one hundred
> and forty six men, who are determined never to retreat. We
> have but little provisions, but enough to serve us till you and
> your men arrive.

It was classic Travis, a model for more dramatic letters to follow. Travis closed the letter with a direct shot at Fannin. "We deem it unnecessary to repeat to a brave officer, who knows his duty, that we call on him for assistance," Travis repeated to the one officer in Texas who already had admitted that he did not know his duty.

Sutherland remembered that Travis entrusted this correspondence to a courier named Johnson.

In fact Travis had been lucky. Considering how totally unprepared the Texians had been, they had managed to get enough beef and corn inside the Alamo to last several weeks, perhaps even a month. They had plenty of captured Mexican muskets to augment their own weapons and over nineteen thousand paper cartridges for the muskets. But the supply of powder for the artillery was limited and of dubious quality.

The one great critical scarcity was men. There were not enough men to defend the walls.

At that moment not every Texian was inside the Alamo. Even as the Mexican troops advanced on the outskirts of Bexar, a handful of defiant Texians raised a flag in the center of Military Plaza. The flag was a variation of the Mexican tricolor with two stars, representing the separated states of Texas and Coahuila, gleaming from the white center bar. Tradition assigns this flag to Seguin, for of the Alamo garrison only his *Tejanos* retained their loyalty to the Constitution of 1824. The Anglos, having declared their support for independence, would not have flown a Mexican tricolor.

As the vanguard of the Mexican army marched into the city, the Texians hastily lowered the flag and withdrew into the Alamo. There, also, a flag would have been hoisted. Perhaps several—one on the church, another over the long barracks. No historical record survives to describe which flags might have flown where.

Captain Almaron Dickinson, the Gonzales blacksmith attached to the artillery, may have been among the men retreating from Military Plaza. About that time he galloped up to the Musquiz house where his twenty-two-year-old wife, Susanna, had been staying with their fifteen-month-old baby, Angelina. "The Mexicans are upon us," Dickinson called out to Susanna, "give me the babe and jump up behind me."

"I did so," Susanna remembered, "and as the Mexicans already occupied Commerce Street, we galloped across the river at the ford south of it, and entered the fort. . . ."

The Dickinsons could not have missed Dr. John Sutherland by much. Departing the Alamo too late to overtake Dr. Smither, Sutherland encountered John W. Smith near the river ford. As a civilian, Smith was under no orders to assemble in the Alamo, but he also was anxious to procure aid for the Texians. Sutherland recalled, "We halted and were paralyzed for a moment when we saw the enemy march into Military Plaza in regular order." They were joined by Bexar merchant Nat Lewis. "He, too, was

View from rear of the Alamo church, looking toward San Fernando.

bound for Gonzales with as much of his valuables as he could carry in his saddle bag," Sutherland wrote, "leaving the remainder in his storehouse, a contribution to the enemy."

As the Mexican troops marched into the center of the city, Juan Diaz, the son of the custodian of the San Fernando Church, scrambled up into the bell tower for a better view. "I will never forget how that army looked as it swept into town," he later wrote. "At the head of the soldiers came the regimental band, playing the liveliest airs, and with the band came a squad of men bearing the flags and banners of Mexico. . . . "

The Mexican army also made a lasting impression on young Enrique Esparza. Crossing the Main Plaza, he witnessed the arrival of the enemy:

> Pennants were flying and swords sparkling in the bright winter sun. Riding in front was Santa Anna, el Presidente! This man was every inch a leader. All the officers dismounted, but only the general tossed his reins to an aide with a flourish.
>
> No one had expected a forced march to cross the cold, arid plains of south Texas in winter. Santa Anna had done just that at the cost of the lives of a great many men and livestock. He intended to avenge the insult to his pride without a thought of the price.

Watching from the Alamo's walls, the Texians' view of the activity on the plaza was blocked by the buildings on the east end of San Antonio. But then they observed something that was not obstructed. Something they were meant to see.

From the top of the San Fernando Church's bell tower, a crimson banner flapped in the brisk wind.

If the Texians were unaware of the December 30, 1835 decree condemning them as pirates, they certainly knew the meaning of that blood red flag.

No quarter.

In Indian fighting, familiar to many of the garrison, it was generally understood that mercy was neither requested nor granted. But the concept of "no quarter" rarely applied to civilized warfare. Perhaps Santa Anna was bluffing, as Travis had done when he intimidated the Mexican garrison at Anahuac into surrender. On the other hand, who had not heard rumors of the slaughter at Zacatecas?

Squinting at the red flag of death, Travis barked an order. The eighteen-pounder roared its defiance.

Santa Anna later claimed that the cannonball killed two of his men and wounded eight more. If it had struck a formation of soldiers it could have accounted for that many injuries. However Santa Anna often was quite imaginative when numbering casualties. No other Mexican officer reported any fatalities on that first day, and they probably would have.

But if nothing else, the cannon shot infuriated Santa Anna. The audacity of those Texians! He already knew, from cooperative Bexarenos, that the garrison only numbered about one hundred fifty. And they were entrenched within "an irregular fortification hardly worthy of the name."

On that point his secretary, Ramon Caro, agreed. He described the Alamo as a "mere corral and nothing more." Though not a military man himself, Caro also noted that most of the Alamo's walls were made of adobe. Adobe bricks might deflect Indian arrows, even musket balls, but they could not long endure a bombardment from twelve-pound cannonballs.

The problem was that both of the Army of Operation's twelve-pound siege guns were traveling with General Gaona's First Brigade, roughly a two-week march away. Sesma had brought only two four-pounders, two six-pounders, two eight-pounders, and two howitzers, the latter capable of lobbing fused bombs over the Alamo's walls. Santa Anna ordered the howitzers to reply to those insolent Texians.

Two shells whistled over the walls and exploded within the compound. Dirt and stones erupted from the impact craters. The men at the cannon emplacements ducked behind ramparts, those on the ground scattered for cover. Then two more shells exploded within the walls.

No one sustained injuries.

But the siege of the Alamo had begun.

James Bowie, coughing more than ever, retreated from the walls back into the Alamo headquarters. It was better for him, out of that cold wind. And he needed to rest. And to think.

Perhaps Travis' cannon shot had been a bit hasty. If only he and Travis had taken more seriously the rumors of the Mexican advance. But no one had anticipated the enemy for at least another week. With only the vanguard of the Army of Operations at Bexar, the Mexicans already had enough men to storm the Alamo. The only reason they might not launch an immediate assault was out of respect for the Texian artillery. Bowie could only hope that the Mexicans did not know how limited the Alamo's powder was. And how inexperienced most of the Texian gun crews were.

There had not been enough teams to evacuate the artillery to the east. But the Texians could have shuttled the cannon down to Mission Concepcion. Not only were Concepcion's outer walls in better repair, but the mission compound was smaller than the Alamo, more easily defended by a tiny garrison.

Even Santa Anna had recognized the validity of such a strategy. Upon his arrival at Bexar, he had diverted a portion of his army to investigate the site. And he probably was grateful that the Texians had not entrenched themselves within the smaller mission. If they had, James Bowie might have won a second battle of Concepcion.

There was one obvious reason the Texians had chosen to defend the Alamo. They expected reinforcements, and they would need the larger area to accommodate the relief forces.

But now the prospect of reinforcements had dwindled dramatically. And it would further diminish as more Mexican troops arrived at Bexar. A Texian relief force would have to sneak past the enemy or fight their way through the Mexican lines. Even the four hundred men under Fannin, the largest army in Texas, could be attacked on the open prairie and annihilated.

It may have been Green B. Jameson or Juan Seguin who advised Bowie that the Mexican bugles had called for a parley. Motioning for Jameson to wait, Bowie quickly found some paper and a quill and dictated a letter to

Seguin, who transcribed it in Spanish. As he had done during the siege of Bexar, Bowie took it upon himself to communicate with the enemy general. Only this time Bowie held legitimate command over most of the garrison.

Seguin scribbled down Bowie's words:

> Because a shot was fired from a cannon of this fort at the time that a red flag was raised over the tower, and a little after they told me that a part of your army had sounded a parley, which, however was not heard before the firing of the said shot. I wish, Sir, to ascertain if it be true that a parley was called, for which reason I send my second aide, Benito Jameson, under guarantee of a white flag which I believe will be respected by you and your forces.

Three weeks earlier James Bowie had proclaimed that he would "rather die in these ditches than surrender." His letter now did not ask for surrender. Perhaps he was stalling, buying precious minutes at a crucial time. Perhaps he was trying to ascertain information. Or perhaps he was investigating the possibility of capitulation. He had initiated this battle, but it was not only his life at stake. If the Mexican commander offered terms as generous as the Texians had given Cos—a parole for all men and officers—Bowie might have considered it rather than waste his "brave little band against thousands."

It all depended on that blood-red flag.

Seguin closed the letter, "God and Mexico," and handed the document to Bowie for inspection. Bowie crossed out the last phrase and replaced it with "God and Texas!" Big Jim Bowie was not going to be conciliatory, not even if contemplating the possibility of surrender.

Then, his hand trembling from the fever that racked his body, he signed his name, identifying himself as the "Commander of the volunteers of Bexar."

But to whom was he writing? Was General Sesma in command? Or had Santa Anna himself arrived? Bowie resolved the question by addressing the letter to "the Commander of the invading forces below Bejar."

Moments later, bearing the letter and a white flag, Jameson rode out of the Alamo's gate. At the narrow bridge he was met by Colonel Juan Nepomuceno Almonte, the United States educated diplomat whose 1834 tour of Texas had temporarily eased tensions. Almonte claimed that Jameson inquired if honorable terms would be offered for surrender.

Almonte agreed to convey the letter to Santa Anna. Jameson rode back to the Alamo.

Perhaps it was the "God and Texas" that enraged Santa Anna. Or perhaps it was the address. "Commander" to "Commander!" As if this Bowie considered himself an equal of the president of Mexico! There would be no parole. With General Cos and his *soldados* back in Texas, Santa Anna knew how worthless a parole was. He relegated the response to his aide Jose Batres.

Bowie's letter also infuriated Travis. Bowie had violated his agreement that they would co-sign all correspondence. Curiously, Travis retaliated by sending out his own emissary.

Albert Martin, the Rhode Islander who had led the "Gonzales Eighteen," also met Almonte on the bridge. Martin said that if Almonte wished to confer, Travis would receive him with much pleasure. Almonte replied that "it did not become the Mexican Government to make any propositions" through him. He only had permission "to hear such as might be made on the part of the rebels." He handed Martin the written response to Bowie's letter, and Martin trudged back to the Alamo.

Travis read the reply. So did Bowie.

> . . . the Mexican army cannot come to terms under any conditions with rebellious foreigners to whom there is no other recourse left, if they wish to save their lives, than to place themselves immediately at the disposal of the Supreme Government from whom alone they may expect clemency after some considerations are taken up.

Unconditional surrender—at the "disposal" of Santa Anna. Or fight to the death. Now Bowie and Travis agreed. Again the San Antonio valley reverberated from the eighteen-pounder's thunder.

And every man in the Alamo prayed for reinforcements.

The Alamo did receive one more soldier that evening. Around sundown Gregorio Esparza ushered his wife and children toward the gate. Esparza had hoped to send his family away from Bexar, but he announced that he himself was going into the fort. His wife, Ana, insisted, "Well, if you go, I'm going along and the whole family, too."

They found the lunette empty. All the sentinels had withdrawn inside and secured the gates. "Furious, Mama pounded on the gate and demanded that it be opened," remembered young Enrique. "When the sentries recognized Papa as being one of their best Mexican soldiers, they called him to a side window."

The family circled around behind the church to a high window on the east wall that opened into the sacristy. A long-armed Texian reached out as Esparza lifted up his wife and each of the children. Young Enrique remembered climbing "through the window and over a cannon that was placed inside the church immediately behind the window."

The musty sacristy with its domed ceiling had become the refuge for most of the noncombatants. Enrique recalled seeing one *Tejano* woman nervously tracing circles in the dirt with the tip of her umbrella. Enrique remembered it because he had seen "very few umbrellas." He later learned that her name was Juana and that she had married an American, thirty-eight-year-old Eliel Melton from Georgia, who served as quartermaster.

Juana Melton's sister, Concepcion, the wife of Toribio Losoya, had taken her three young children into the sacristy after their home in the southwest corner of the mission had been demolished to accommodate the eighteen-pounder. Enrique recalled another *señora*, Victoriana de Salina, had three daughters. Dona Petra Gonzales was an elderly woman, and twenty-seven-year-old Trinidad Saucedo once had been a servant of the Veramendi family.

And there were the *norteamericanos*—Anthony Wolf's two young sons and Mrs. Dickinson with her baby, Angelina.

Ana Esparza ground some corn and boiled it into a mush for her children. Enrique remembered that Mrs. Dickinson was scared and seemed not to know what to do. "I heard mother say *pobrecita* and take the lady some food."

Gregorio Esparza joined a party of Texians who took advantage of the nightfall to foray outside the walls. They returned with six pack mules and some prisoners. One of the captives was a *soldado*; the others apparently were Bexarenos sympathetic to Santa Anna. They would have been incarcerated in the fort's *calabozo*, located at the south end of the old granary building, now used primarily for barracks. Throughout the siege, Enrique remembered, the prisoner would interpret the various Mexican bugle calls.

As the Alamo settled into a tense silence, across the river Santa Anna remained busy, still overseeing everything himself. He located his headquarters in the one-story Yturri house on the northwest corner of the main plaza. Almonte would stay with him there. His Excellency enjoyed the food prepared by that Negro cook, Ben, whom Almonte had brought back from the United States.

Santa Anna authorized his *soldados* to pillage the town for food supplies and other provisions. He ordered an artillery battery to be established on the river behind the Veramendi house. Always better to construct the protective earthworks under cover of the night. And finally Santa Anna dispatched General Ventura Mora's cavalry to circle around to the north and east of the Alamo. They were to prevent any Texian reinforcements from entering the fortress.

And prevent anyone in the Alamo from escaping.

Wednesday, February 24, 1836: *The Second Day*

San Antonio de Bexar

Despite his late night, Antonio Lopez de Santa Anna arose early. The Mexicans had discovered the abandoned stores belonging to Nat Lewis and John W. Smith. Santa Anna ordered an inventory. Of greatest value were a large supply of captured shoes. Many of the *soldados* had worn out their footwear in the long march north. Santa Anna personally supervised the distribution of the shoes to his "preferred companies."

Then he joined General Mora's cavalry and rode completely around the Alamo to familiarize himself with both the Texian defenses and the terrain. Colonel Almonte remembered that Santa Anna brazenly passed "within musket shot of the fort." If so, it was a missed opportunity for the Alamo defenders. But perhaps their attention had been diverted by a crisis within the compound.

James Bowie had not risen early that morning. He did not get up at all. The one adversary his big knife could not intimidate finally had overpowered him. Wracked with fever and too weak to rise from his cot, he surrendered full command of the garrison to Travis. Bowie may have feared that his disease was contagious. If so, it could have defeated the Texian garrison before the Mexicans ever launched their assault. As Mrs. Alsbury recalled, Bowie thought it "prudent" that he be relocated to a small room in the low barracks of the south wall near the gate. As a couple of Texians carried him out, he told Juana: "Sister, do not be afraid. I leave you with Col. Travis, Col. Crockett, and other friends. They are gentlemen and will treat you kindly."

James Bowie, whose "die in these ditches" letter had committed Texian forces to the defense of the Alamo, would no longer be a factor in that defense. The man Henry Clay once termed the "greatest fighter in the Southwest" could barely defend himself.

The Esparza family also had moved into the low barracks, adding credence to young Enrique Esparza's claim that he "saw Señor Bowie while he was ill."

"Travis was a brave leader," Enrique remembered. However he probably expressed the sentiments of most of the Texian garrison when he added, "Father would rather follow Bowie, because they were friends."

William Barret Travis
Painting by Michael Schreck.

William Barret Travis had never enjoyed such popularity. But now, for the first time he bore the sole responsibility of command over the Alamo.

There could be no more whining letters. No more romantic dalliances. Though he had not been elected by the volunteers, Travis somehow would have to keep them there. In the Alamo. Facing overwhelming odds. Until reinforcements arrived.

About that time, the Mexican bombardment resumed, and again all of the Texians scrambled for cover to escape the flying rocks and shrapnel. The Mexican battery on the river near the Veramendi house had been completed. It consisted of two howitzers and two cannons well entrenched behind earthworks. Having returned from his reconnaissance, Santa Anna had ordered it to commence fire. Colonel Almonte recalled that the battery kept up "a brisk fire" until the feared eighteen-pounder and another Texian cannon had been dismounted.

Perhaps because of the translation from Spanish, Almonte's account is frequently misunderstood. The Mexican artillerymen were more experienced than their Texian counterparts, but it is unlikely that any Texian cannons were incapacitated during the barrage. Travis simply did not have enough powder to engage in an artillery duel. By "dismounted" Almonte probably meant that the Texians had pulled their cannons down the ramp out of danger.

In the evening, with darkness descending, Travis retired to his quarters. Sitting at his desk he drew some paper to him and dipped his quill in the inkwell. He addressed the letter "To the People of Texas . . . " But then, was it his arrogance?—or a sense of posterity?—that compelled him to add, "& all Americans in the world."

He continued:

> Fellow citizens & compatriots—I am besieged, by a thousand
> or more of the Mexicans under Santa Anna—I have sustained
> a continual Bombardment & cannonade for 24 hours & have
> not lost a man—

There had been no bombardment during the previous night, but Travis
was not exactly lying. Just sort of exaggerating for effect. He used the word
"continual," which meant sporadically recurring, rather than "continuous."

> The enemy has demanded a surrender at discretion, other-
> wise, the garrison are to be put to the sword, if the fort is
> taken—I have answered the demand with a cannon shot, &
> our flag still waves proudly from the walls—I shall never sur-
> render or retreat.

He paused to underline that last sentence. Somehow he had to rouse
the colonists from their lethargy, make them recognize that his situation
was dire.

> Then, I call on you in the name of Liberty, of patriotism &
> everything dear to the American character, to come to our aid,
> with all dispatch—The enemy is receiving reinforcements
> daily & will no doubt increase to three or four thousand in
> four or five days.

In fact Santa Anna had not yet received any reinforcements. But Travis
may have observed the arrival of the Mexican troops that had been diverted
to Concepcion. And certainly additional brigades were even then marching
toward Bexar.

> If this call is neglected, I am determined to sustain myself
> as long as possible & die like a soldier who never forgets what
> is due to his own honor & that of his country—Victory or
> Death.

He underlined that last phrase three times. But it was more than a dramatic statement. That blood-red flag afforded the Alamo no other options.

He signed his name in full:

> William Barret Travis
> Lt. Col. comdt

Then a postscript occured to him. It would not hurt to include a little divine intervention, even at the risk of exposing his own unpreparedness.

> The Lord is on our side—When the enemy appeared in sight
> we had not three bushels of corn—We have since found in
> deserted houses 80 or 90 bushels & got into the walls 20 or 30
> head of Beeves—

It was a short letter. But for now that was all he had time for.

He could not know that he had just written one of the most dramatic—and sacred—documents in all Texas history.

He entrusted the letter to Albert Martin. There was hardly any moon that night. The *soldados* remained quartered in the town across the river to the west. Mexican cavalry patrols would pose the greatest threat. But if Martin were lucky. . . .

The Alamo gates swung open and Martin galloped out into the darkness. His luck held. He encountered no mounted lancers. He rode up the hill, past the watchtower and powder house and ancient Spanish earthworks, spurring his horse on to Gonzales, eighty-five miles to the east.

He may have been luckier than he knew. Santa Anna also was taking advantage of the darkness. He had sent his engineers across the river. But they might not have noticed the lone rider as they excavated a new gun emplacement in La Villita, just south of the Alamo. During his tour around the Alamo, Santa Anna had observed several weaknesses in the Texian defenses. And he planned to take advantage of them.

But for now he resorted to a form of psychological warfare. Sporadically the Mexican artillery shattered the night. Enrique Esparza heard, perhaps even felt, the solid cannonballs striking the church and long barracks. The bombardment would be accompanied by musketry and shouts, "intended to make the impression that a night assault had been planned," wrote a Mexican cavalry officer, "and also to make it appear to the beleaguered that their expected reinforcements, while trying to make their way into the Alamo, had become engaged with the enemy and were being destroyed."

Santa Anna wanted the Texians awake and alert all night. So that they would be exhausted by morning.

When the real attack would come.

Thursday, February 25, 1836: *The Third Day*

San Antonio de Bexar

Just after daylight the Mexican artillery opened fire, both from the battery across the river and from the new position at La Villita. The Alamo cannons boomed in response. It was the first time that Enrique Esparza had heard so many of the Texian cannons discharging at once. "The noise they made was terrible to me," he recalled.

Santa Anna appeared at the river battery around 9:30 that morning. According to General Filisola, "The commander in chief, with the companies of *cazadores* [light infantry] from Jimenez and Matamoras [battalions] crossed the river and took up a position in the houses and huts to the south of the Alamo about half a rifle shot's distance from the enemy parapets."

Here was the first weakness that Santa Anna had discovered. The houses and huts extended from La Villita almost to the Alamo's southwest corner. They impeded the Texian field of fire and provided excellent cover for the advancing Mexican forces.

The Texians had committed a strategic blunder leaving those *jacales* standing, only adding to Santa Anna's scorn for his enemy. But he would gain some respect for them before that two-hour skirmish had ended.

"Today at 10 o'clock A.M. some two or three hundred Mexicans crossed the river below and came up under cover of the houses until they arrived within virtual point blank shot," reported Travis, "when we opened a heavy discharge of grape and cannister on them, together with a well directed fire from small arms which forced them to halt and take shelter in the houses. . . . "

During the engagement some of the Texians sallied from the fort and manned the five-foot-deep trenches that extended in front of the palisade and lunette. "During the action the enemy kept up a constant bombardment and discharge of balls, grape, and cannister," Travis wrote.

The Mexicans attempted a second advance against the fort, only to be hastily aborted by the fierce fire from the Texians. Then, according to Travis, "the enemy retreated in confusion, dragging many of their dead and wounded."

As the Mexicans retreated, two Texians armed with torches charged from the Alamo and set fire to the nearest *jacales*, which had afforded the enemy cover. One of the arsonists was Robert Brown, not yet out of his teens. The other was Charles Despallier. His father had died at the battle of the Medina.

Jacal

Travis praised their action "in the face of enemy fire," and he also commended his artillery captains, William Carey, Almaron Dickinson, and twenty-nine-year-old Samuel Blair from Tennessee. "Indeed, the whole of the men who were brought into action conducted themselves with such heroism that it would be injustice to discriminate," asserted Travis. Perhaps he, too, felt some degree of vindication.

"We know from actual observation that many of the enemy were wounded—while we, on our part, have not lost a man," Travis reported. "Two or three of our men have been slightly scratched by pieces of rock, but have not been disabled."

Most Mexican accounts only list two slain *soldados* and four more wounded. However considering the poor quality of medical treatment and the high risk of infection, a wound too often proved mortal. Santa Anna could not indefinitely squander his men without inflicting casualties on the enemy.

The Napoleon of the West had made a mistake that morning. He had underestimated his enemy. He had learned a lesson about the superiority of Texian marksmanship.

Contrary to the popular image, most Alamo defenders were not crack shot hunters wearing buckskins and coonskin caps. Many of the doctors and lawyers, storekeepers and schoolteachers, and other professions that comprised the garrison would have felt more secure wielding a double-barreled shotgun. But at least some of the Texians had lived on the frontier long enough to develop a deadly accuracy with their long rifles that the Mexican *soldados* could not match.

And, of course, the most famous American frontiersman of all defended the Alamo. "The Hon. David Crockett was seen at all points, animating the men to do their duty," wrote Travis.

"Crockett seemed to be the leading spirit," Enrique Esparza agreed. "He was everywhere. He went to every exposed point and personally directed the fighting."

Since Captain William B. Harrison officially commanded the Mounted Tennessee Volunteers defending the palisade, Crockett technically was free to lend his long rifle—and sense of humor—to any part of the Alamo. "He could shoot from the wall or through the portholes," remembered Esparza. "Then he would run back and say something funny." The morale-sustaining laughter generated by Crockett's humor may have been as important to the Alamo as his marksmanship. But Crockett shared the frustrations of most of the garrison. He once confided to Mrs. Dickinson. "I think we had better march out and die in the open air; I don't like to be hemmed up."

At least some of the Mexicans came to know him. Captain Rafael Soldana of the Tampico Battalion recalled.

> A tall man, with flowing hair, was seen firing from the same place on the parapet during the entire siege. He wore a buckskin suit and a cap all of a pattern entirely different from those worn by his comrades. This man would kneel or lie down behind the low parapet, rest his long gun and fire, and we all learned to keep at a good distance when he was seen to make ready to shoot. He rarely missed his mark, and when he

fired he always rose to his feet and calmly reloaded his gun seemingly indifferent to the shots fired at him by our men. He had a strong, resonant voice and often railed at us, but as we did not understand English we could not comprehend the import of his words further than they were defiant. This man I later learned was known as "Kwockey."

When his morning assault failed, Santa Anna realized that he could not risk another daylight attack against the Alamo. He also realized that the conquest would take longer than he originally anticipated.

Fortuitously, he engaged in another type of conquest that would help him endure the tedium of the long siege.

During the attack General Castrillon had ducked into a *jacale* that had remained occupied. Its inhabitants were a Señora Barrera and her seventeen-year-old daughter, Melchora. With the battle raging all around, the astonished Castrillon asked why they had not fled. Señora Barrera replied simply that the *jacale* was her home and she had no other place to go. Besides, as the widow of a Mexican officer, she was not afraid.

Castrillon later related the incident to Santa Anna, adding that the daughter had been quite beautiful. That was all the recommendation Santa Anna needed. He asked Castrillon to bring the girl to him.

General Castrillon snorted and brazenly replied that he was no man's procurer. Santa Anna's eyes flashed with anger. But then General Minon, ever eager to garner the *presidente's* favor, volunteered for the mission.

It was not as simple as Minon had anticipated. Señora Barrera proved to be a strong-willed, even defiant, woman. She told him she was respectable, from a good family. Her daughter was not destined to be a common mistress. But, her eyebrows arching, Señora Barrera announced that Melchora might consent to be a wife—of the *presidente* of Mexico.

General Minon hurried back to Santa Anna and gave his report. Both men recognized the one problem. Santa Anna already was married.

But Minon could be resourceful. He had a sergeant, a bit of a rogue with natural acting talents, who knew Latin. He could dress up like a priest and perform the ceremony.

The mock wedding took place, and while his army besieged the Alamo, Santa Anna enjoyed his honeymoon.

However he did not let his dalliance interfere with his obsession to destroy the rebel traitors within the Alamo. That night he ordered the Matamoras Battalion to guard the Alameda. Working through the night, the engineers excavated an entrenchment that would protect the *soldados* of the battalion.

Colonel Almonte recalled that "the cavalry was posted on the hills to the east of the enemy, and in the road from Gonzales. . . . "

It was becoming more perilous to deliver mail from the Alamo. And Travis had another letter to send out.

He wrote it to Sam Houston, who would be arriving at Washington-on-the-Brazos to attend the convention beginning March 1. Travis related the previous events of the siege, enthusiastically describing the defeat of the Mexicans that morning. But then his tone turned more somber.

> Our numbers are few and the enemy still continues to approximate his works to ours. I have every reason to apprehend an attack from his whole force very soon; but I shall hold out to the last extremity; hoping to secure reinforcements in a day or two. Do hasten on aid to me as rapidly as possible, as from the superior number of the enemy, it will be impossible for us to keep them out much longer. If they overpower us, we fall a sacrifice at the shrine of our country, and we hope posterity and our country will do our memory justice.

Then Travis shifted from his dramatic rhetoric to an impassioned personal plea.

"Give me help, oh my country!"

Again he closed the letter, "Victory or Death!"

But who should attempt to carry the letter to Houston? In true federalist manner, Travis let his officers vote. They chose Juan Seguin. Seguin himself remembered, "Colonel Travis opposed my taking this commission, stating that . . . my presence in the Alamo might become necessary in case of having to treat with Santa Anna."

Travis may have had another, more valid reason to keep Seguin in the compound. Travis liked Seguin. Respected him. But Travis may have felt uncomfortable with the handful of *Tejanos* who had followed Seguin into the Alamo. Travis did not trust them. He doubted they would honor his authority after Seguin left. They were different—ethnically, culturally, and politically—from the rest of the garrison. Of the men of the Alamo, only the *Tejanos* still clung to the notion of restoring the Constitution of 1824. They may have been fighting beside the Texians, but they were fighting for a different cause.

But Seguin's election held, and he chose to take his orderly, Antonio Cruz y Arocha, with him. Seguin wrote, "we left at eight o'clock at night after having bid good-bye to all my comrades, expecting certain death."

Enrique Esparza believed that Seguin rode out on James Bowie's horse. Certainly Bowie would have offered his mount to his friend if Seguin had needed it. But other accounts suggest that Seguin and Cruz y Arrocha stole from the mission on foot and acquired horses from Bexareno friends on the outside.

Either way, they still ran into a detachment of Mexican cavalry patrolling the eastern horizon. Seguin portrayed himself and Antonio as local ranchers returning to their hacienda. The lancers bought the story and allowed them to pass.

Darkness brought on a cold north wind, but no end to the hostilities. Travis took advantage of the night to send some men out to burn down more of the *jacales* that stood in close proximity to the fort. The north winds fanned the roaring flames, quickly incinerating the huts.

The Mexicans also utilized the blackness. Travis reported that "on the night of the 25th they made another attempt to charge us in the rear of the fort, but we received them gallantly by a discharge of grape shot and musketry. . . . " Perhaps Santa Anna was probing the foundering north wall, another weakness he must have detected during his morning tour of the enemy defenses. If so, it cost him a few more casualties.

The Texians had driven back two attacks. Minor attacks, to be sure. But for the moment the skirmishes had boosted the morale of the Alamo garrison. Yet standing on the walls facing the onslaught of the descending norther, Travis had to wonder. How long before the entire Mexican army arrived in Bexar? How long before Santa Anna launched a massive assault? How long could the Alamo hold out if reinforcements did not arrive?

Travis could not know that already Texas was responding to his appeals.

Gonzales

In his mind Albert Martin could still hear the cannon fire that rumbled across the prairie as he had galloped away from the Alamo on the previous day. Finally splashing across the Guadalupe River into Gonzales on February 25, he furiously scribbled his own note onto the letter, not even pausing for punctuation.

> Since the above was written I heard a very heavy Canonade
> during the whole day think there must have been an attack

made upon the alamo We were short of ammunition when I left Hurry on all the men you can in haste When I left there was but 150 determined to do or die tomorrow I leave for Bejar with what men I can raise. . . .

Martin passed the letter to Dr. Launcelot Smither, who had just ridden in from Bexar the day before. The barely literate doctor added his own comment in the margin. "I hope that Every One will Rendcvu at gonzales as soon poseble as the Brave Solders are suffering," he scrawled. "do not neglect this powder is very scarce and should not be delad one moment."

Then, as Martin mustered reinforcements at Gonzales, Smither swung back into his saddle and rode east toward San Felipe.

Goliad

About that same time Colonel James Walker Fannin was organizing an even larger relief. From his headquarters within the old presidio he had converted into Fort Defiance, Fannin scripted an almost apologetic letter to the council. "The appeal of cols Travis & Bowie cannot . . . pass unnoticed," Fannin declared. "Much must be risked to relieve the besieged."

He would leave from eighty to one hundred men at Goliad. The rest of the army, under his command, would start for Bexar the next morning.

Friday, February 26, 1836: **The Fourth Day**

San Antonio de Bexar

"The northern wind continued very strong; the thermometer fell to 39 degrees, and during the rest of the day remained at 60 degrees," wrote Colonel Juan Almonte in the journal he kept daily. "At daybreak there was a slight skirmish between the enemy and a small party of the division of the east, under command of General Sesma."

The Texians probably had darted from the Alamo to gather firewood for warmth against the near freezing wind. At the same time others were spotted drawing water from the eastern fork of the *acequia* that flowed behind the mission.

According to Sergeant Francisco Becerra, the Texians were engaged by two Mexican companies on a reconnaissance. Becerra claimed that the Mexicans charged within range of the Texians' deadly rifles, and "thirty were killed within a few minutes." But Becerra was known to exaggerate. Almonte would not have dismissed the death of thirty *soldados* as "a slight skirmish."

The Alamo had a well. Enrique Esparza placed it "a little south of the center" of the convent yard, which now served as the horse corral. But the old well could not supply enough water even for the small garrison. Most of the Texians relied on the *acequia* that flowed from the northeast. It branched into three channels. The east and west forks flowed in southerly directions just outside the Alamo's east and west walls. The center fork, which supplied the Alamo water, slipped under the north wall and flowed south along the inside of the west wall. Then it emerged from the south wall just west of the lunette to reunite with the west fork for the final journey into the river.

Enrique Esparza recalled that during the bombardments those on the east side of the mission found it safer to dart out to the stream behind the church rather than to risk the exploding shells landing all around the *acequia* within the compound.

"During the day firing from our cannon was continued," Almonte reported. "The enemy did not reply, except now and then."

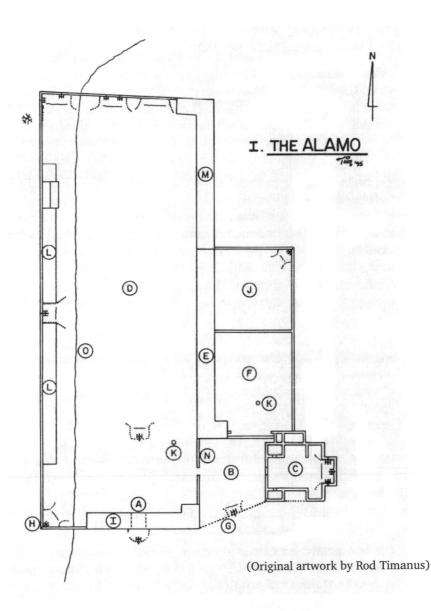

I. THE ALAMO

(Original artwork by Rod Timanus)

A. Main entrance of the Alamo fortress

B. Inner courtyard

C. Alamo chapel (sometimes referred to as the church)

D. Main plaza

E. Hospital and barracks

F. Horse quartel

G. Wooden palisade

H. Southwest artillery position

I. Low barracks

J. Cattle pen

K. Conjectural position of wells

L. West wall with series of small rooms

M. Long barracks

N. Low wall

O. Irrigation ditch

The Texians continued to conserve powder. They would need all of it, at the end, if reinforcements did not come.

Goliad

But reinforcements were on the way. Colonel James Walker Fannin, commanding three hundred twenty men, four cannon, and several supply wagons, had left Fort Defiance and begun the ninety-mile march "to the relief of those brave men now shut up in the Alamo," Fannin proclaimed. Herman Ehrenberg and the New Orleans Greys had eagerly volunteered for the mission to rescue their brother Greys.

Frustratingly, only two hundred yards from Goliad, a wagon broke down. The whole expedition halted for repairs. Then they had to ford the San Antonio River. Fannin wrote, "it was necessary to double teams in order to draw the Artillery across the river, each piece having but one yoke of oxen." But by nightfall the relief expedition was encamped on the opposite bank, huddling around campfires.

San Felipe

By then Austin's capital had learned that the Alamo was under siege. Travis' close friend Robert M. Williamson announced that he would leave for Gonzales in the morning, "and rest assured that no exertions on my part will be wanting to give the earliest aid practical to our fellow soldiers in the Alamo."

Acting Governor James Robinson immediately addressed a letter to General Sam Houston: "Wherever he may be. Send this by express night and day."

To the general whose authority he had previously undermined, Robinson urgently wrote:

> Come quickly and organize our countrymen for battle. Call the militia out en masse. . . . Say it is done by the order of the Gov. & Council & by your own order, and by the unanimous call of Texas.

San Antonio de Bexar

For the moment, the Alamo could only hold out. Throughout the day, as the Mexican cannonade continued, the Texians sallied outside for firewood and water. But now they were continually under fire from Mexican marksmen armed with accurate Baker rifles rather than muskets.

During the night Travis again dispatched a raid to burn even more of the *jacales*, further restricting Mexican cover while simultaneously expanding the Alamo's field of fire. By this time the Texians were racing a considerable distance away from the Alamo's protective walls and ditches.

Witnessing the raid from across the river, Santa Anna ordered Colonel Juan Bringas to engage the Texians. Their movement must have been illuminated by the blazing huts. "... the enemy opened fire upon this group and killed one man," recalled secretary Ramon Caro. "In trying to cross the bridge, the colonel fell into the water and saved himself only by a stroke of good luck."

Colonel Bringas may not have felt so lucky as he emerged from the frigid waters to see the Texians scurrying back into the safety of the Alamo.

San Patricio

"The night was very raw and excessively cold," remembered General Jose Urrea, leading his troops on a forced march up from Matamoras. It began to rain, and for a moment Urrea thought it might be turning into snow. He wrote:

> The rain continued and the dragoons, who were barely able to dismount, were so numbed by the cold that they could hardly speak. Nevertheless, being as brave as they were faithful, they showed no discouragement and we continued our march.

After leaving Refugio, Johnson and Grant's Matamoras expedition had continued only forty miles further south to San Patricio on the Nueces River border between Texas and the province of Tamaulipas. The town had been established in 1829 as a community for Irish-Catholic settlers from New York.

Although a handful of *Tejanos* served under Johnson and Grant, as well as with Fannin back at Goliad, the majority of the local Hispanic population generally resented all three commanders of the Matamoras expedition. The Texians had foraged among the ranches, rudely appropriating whatever supplies they needed. Some of the Irish-Catholic citizens at San Patricio also displayed a preference for the centralist regime.

Consequently, General Urrea had received excellent intelligence concerning the movements of Johnson and Grant. Urrea knew that Dr. James Grant had taken twenty-six men south toward Agua Dulce Creek to capture mustangs for the campaign. That left Colonel Frank Johnson with only forty Texians at San Patricio.

The Texians, on the other hand, had received no information about General Urrea's column. As he worked late at his desk, Colonel Johnson was oblivious to the fact that Urrea was marching all night through that blustery weather.

Planning to descend on San Patricio before sunrise.

Saturday, February 27, 1836:   *The Fifth Day*

San Patricio

General Jose Urrea did not want to alienate the *Tejano* population of Texas or any other settlers and colonists who could be induced to support the Mexican cause. A popular legend, that just might be true, relates that he had sent spies galloping ahead of his column to alert the loyalists at San Patricio to leave a lantern burning in a window. The Mexican *soldados* would not molest any house so identified.

The forty men in Colonel Frank Johnson's command were scattered about the town. Eight of the Texians weathered the bitterly cold night encamped on the public square. Johnson and the more fortunate ones had found refuge in three different houses.

Shortly after three in the morning, Urrea's dragoons charged into San Patricio, catching the small Texian force completely by surprise. The Texians camped in the square must have been overwhelmed quickly, but Urrea reported that the enemy "defended himself with firmness in the houses." Yet it did not last long. The Mexicans killed ten Texians and captured eighteen more. The first branch of the Matamoras expedition had been demolished.

Somehow Frank Johnson and four men escaped from the battle, perhaps because Johnson had worked late the previous night, the candle on his desk flickering in the window.

Urrea wrote, "I am now in search of doctor Grant." To that end he led his victorious force south, for the moment away from Goliad.

San Antonio de Bexar

The fearful blue norther continued its assault on Texian and Mexican alike. Colonel Almonte recorded that the wind was strong at daybreak, and the thermometer would crest at thirty-nine degrees.

Goliad

Colonel James Walker Fannin, still encamped on the lower San Antonio River, had problems other than the bitter cold. As his shivering men awoke that morning and hastily built up their campfires, someone noticed that the oxen teams had wandered off during the night. Fannin sent men looking for them. An hour passed. Then another.

In the meantime there had been no food for breakfast. " . . . not a particle of breadstuff, with the exception of half a tierce of rice, with us," Fannin conceded, "no beef, with the exception of a small portion which had been dried—and not a head of cattle, except for those used to draw the Artillery, the ammunition, &c."

Worse, the nearest source of food supplies would be the Seguin ranch, seventy miles to the north. One of Fannin's officers proposed a council of war, and Fannin readily agreed. All of his commissioned officers attended. They discussed the lack of provisions, their inability to transport their artillery, and, perhaps most important, "by leaving Fort Defiance without a proper garrison, it might fall into the hands of the enemy."

The officers "unanimously determined" to return to Fort Defiance and "complete the fortifications," Fannin wrote. It must have been a relief for the reluctant commander not to have made the decision himself.

Herman Ehrenberg and the New Orleans Greys were preparing to break camp and march to San Antonio when they heard an officer shouting, "Back to Goliad! The larger part of the troops prefer to defend the fort."

"From where Fannin derived his conclusion that the Volunteers were not inclined to rescue the lives of their brothers in the Alamo was not explained to us," Ehrenberg fumed, "and without taking the vote of the army, everybody went back to Goliad."

Yet the decision to return to Fort Defiance would be vindicated when riders galloped in to report the Texian defeat at San Patricio. Mexican troops were only fifty miles from Goliad!

After recrossing the river, Fannin's journey back did not take long. He had only marched two miles from Fort Defiance.

San Antonio de Bexar

It was just as well that Fannin did not continue to the Seguin ranch. He would have arrived too late to find much in the way of food supplies. The Mexican army at Bexar also had depleted their provisions. Santa Anna knew that the Seguins opposed him. He selected their ranch, and that of another rebel *Tejano*, and dispatched troops to appropriate all cattle, hogs, and corn.

Santa Anna also wrote an impatient letter to his second-in-command, General Vicente Filisola, with the rear guard of the Army of Operations, somewhere near the Rio Grande. Santa Anna instructed Filisola to order the brigades to march "with all haste, since up to this time they are moving very slowly."

Filisola also was to forward: provisions, since the troops at Bexar were "very short on supplies"; payroll, as "there is an urgent need for money"; and salt, "since there is not a single grain here, and it is greatly needed."

Santa Anna kept his engineers busy that day. He had them pushing the La Villita cannon emplacement closer to the Alamo's south wall. And he sent others to construct the earthworks for a new cannon position along the *acequia* northeast of the fort. And while they were there, he had another chore for them.

Enrique Esparza recalled overhearing another defender ask *Tejano* Antonio Fuentes: "Did you know they had cut the water off?"

Santa Anna may have learned from General Cos of the inadequacy of the old Alamo well. And during his reconnaissance around the fortress he must have noticed the vulnerability of the *acequia*. He ordered his engineers to dam the stream above the forks and divert it away from the Alamo.

Anxiously observing the Mexican engineers at work on the dam, Jameson assigned some of the Texians to excavate a new well in the main courtyard. They soon struck water, but their efforts ultimately proved unnecessary. To the frustration of the Mexican engineers, the small Texas stream proved to be as stubborn as the Alamo defenders. It refused to be blocked, and water continued to flow down the *acequia*.

It was another minor victory. But whatever satisfaction Travis garnered would have been obliterated if he had seen the letter Santa Anna dispatched to General Filisola that afternoon.

> From the moment of my arrival I have been busy hostilizing the enemy in its position, so much so that they are not even allowed to raise their heads over the walls, preparing everything for the assault which will take place when at least the first brigade arrives, which is now sixty leagues away. Up to now they still act stubborn, counting on the strong position which they hold, and hoping for much aid from their colonies and from the United States, but they will soon find out their mistake. After taking Fort Alamo, I shall continue my operations against Goliad and the other fortified places, so that before the rains set in, the campaign shall be absolutely terminated up the Sabine River. . . .

Santa Anna ended the correspondence with a traditional closing: "God and Liberty." As the defender of the Church, Santa Anna certainly could invoke God; but as a self-proclaimed dictator, his casual use of the word "liberty" seemed bitterly ironic.

Sunday, February 28, 1836:   **The Sixth Day**

San Antonio de Bexar

"The weather abated somewhat. Thermometer at 40 degrees at A.M.," Colonel Juan Almonte recorded in his journal. "The cannonading was continued."

The battery to the north of the Alamo had joined the bombardment. Here Santa Anna had placed two cannons. From this vantage the artillery slammed solid balls against the Alamo's decayed north wall. However, for the moment, the cannon emplacement was too far away to do any damage that Jameson's shovels could not repair.

By now the Texians almost had become inured to the continual cannonade. David Crockett had seen the tension in every man's face, the shivering of the women and children, even when huddled close to a warm fire in the sacristy. He had found a fiddle somewhere. Mrs. Dickinson recalled, "Colonel Crockett was a performer on the violin, and often during the siege took it up and played his favorite tunes."

With the weather warming to a comfortable fifty-five degrees that night, a popular Alamo legend may have been enacted. Those Texians who could be detached from the walls clustered with the noncombatants inside the church. The four-foot-thick stone walls provided protection from the enemy cannonballs but could not muffle the sinister serenade that still occasionally emanated from the Mexican band.

The artillery ramp inside the church provided an adequate makeshift stage. There, according to legend, the Scotsman John McGregor pitted his bagpipes against Crockett's fiddle to see who could render the most noise. And, perhaps for a little while, they overpowered the Mexican band—and also the fears of that tiny, besieged garrison.

Travis, too, would have appreciated the impromptu concert and its beneficial effect on the Texians. But the young commander could never stop worrying. Perhaps he wandered up the ramp, relieving Captain Dickinson to join his family. Standing on the artillery emplacement at the rear of the church, Travis would have stared out into the eastern night. He could hear, if not see, the Mexican cavalry patrols milling around Powder House Hill.

But Travis could only visualize the empty prairie that extended beyond the crest of the hill.

Six days—and no sign of reinforcements. Had Texas forsaken them? Where were the volunteers from Gonzales and the colonies? Where was Fannin?

At that moment Santa Anna was wondering the same thing. He had just received intelligence that two hundred Texians from Goliad were advancing to the relief of the Alamo. Effective spying, even if there had been over three hundred Texians. But now, unknown to Santa Anna, they were entrenched back at Fort Defiance.

Goliad

Fannin's thoughts ran similar to those of Travis at the Alamo. Seated in his headquarters in the old presidio, he wrote to acting Governor Robinson.

> It is now obvious that the enemy have entered Texas at two points, for the purpose of attacking Bexar and this place—the first has been attacked and we may expect the enemy here momentarily—Both places are important—

He paused, his frustration mounting. "What must be the feelings of the volunteers now shut in Bexar—& what will be those of this command if a sufficient force of the enemy should appear to besiege us here...." he asked rhetorically. "Will not curses be heaped on the heads of the sluggards who remained at home with knowledge of our situation."

Washington-on-the-Brazos

"Some are going, but the vile rabble here cannot be moved," William Fairfax Gray scribbled in the diary he meticulously kept. The forty-seven-year-old Virginian, known as Colonel Gray because of his rank in the War of 1812, had arrived in Washington-on-the-Brazos on the previous night to attend the convention. Travis' letter of the twenty-fourth had generated considerable consternation among the early arriving delegates.

James Robinson already was there, and Gray noted that the acting governor was "treated coldly and really seems of little consequence." Instead Gray considered Lorenzo de Zavala, who arrived that evening, to be the "most interesting man in Texas." Gray made a memo to himself to acquire Zavala's volume describing his travels in the United States.

Goliad

Fannin had time to draft one more letter. "The enemy have the town of Bejar, with a large force," he wrote Joseph Mimms, "and I fear will soon have our brave countrymen in the Alamo."

He reported the defeat of Johnson at San Patricio and the advance of the Mexicans towards Fort Defiance. "I have about 420 men here, and if I can get provisions in tomorrow or next day, can maintain myself against any force," Fannin proclaimed. "I will never give up the ship, while there is a pea in the ditch. If I am whipped it will be well done—and you may never expect to see me."

Fort Defiance, the presidio at Goliad.

Monday, February 29, 1836: *The Seventh Day*

Washington-on-the-Brazos

"A warm day, threatening rain from the south," William Fairfax Gray noted in his journal. Sam Houston had ridden into Washington-on-the-Brazos, creating "more sensation than that of any other man." Houston retained his political wiles. Gray reported that the general was a "people's man" who took pains to ingratiate himself with everybody. "He is much broken in appearance, but has still a fine person and courtly manners," Gray added.

San Antonio de Bexar

An energetic westerly wind whirled the dust around within the Alamo compound. To the east, the Texians could see an unusual amount of Mexican troop movement.

Santa Anna faced a problem. He could not ignore the reported advance of the Texian relief expedition from Goliad. Yet his own dawdling reinforcements—General Antonio Gaona's First Brigade with over fifteen hundred *soldados*, and further back the eighteen hundred troops in Brigidier General Eugenio Tolsa's Second Brigade—had failed to arrive. That left him with only the fifteen hundred men in General Joaquin Ramirez y Sesma's Vanguard Brigade to keep the Alamo under siege. Ten-to-one odds, to be sure, but not a comfortable margin considering that he would now have to divide his command.

His written orders to General Sesma were uncharacteristically polite: "It is a very good idea for you to go out in search of the enemy since they are so close by." Sesma would take the Jimenez Battalion and the Dolores cavalry regiment, a total of nearly six hundred troops. "Try to fall on them at dawn in order that you may take them by surprise," Santa Anna advised. He had not yet learned of Urrea's success at San Patricio. But the dawn attack was one of Santa Anna's pet strategies.

Then a stern reminder: "In this war you know that there are no prisoners."

Santa Anna concluded his murderous orders by resuming his congenial manner, "Your most affectionate friend, who sends you greetings."

With Sesma's departure—on what would prove to be a wild goose chase—Santa Anna was left with less than a thousand *soldados* to guard the Alamo. Only about ninety cavalry. Suppose the Texians attempted to break out? Could he overtake them in a race to the east?

Santa Anna could never understand that William Barret Travis, a gentleman of honor, would never abandon his sick and wounded.

"Before undertaking the assault," Santa Anna later maintained, "I still wanted to try a generous measure, characteristic of Mexican kindness, and I offered life to the defendants who would surrender their arms and retire under oath not to take them up again against Mexico."

It seems incredible that Santa Anna, who that same day had reminded Sesma to take no prisoners, would suddenly display such beneficence toward the stubbornly troublesome defenders of the Alamo.

Unless he wanted to minimize the conflict while his own force was reduced.

Unless he was counting on their obstinacy to remain within the Alamo. And if a few chose to leave, well, that would only weaken the garrison.

Santa Anna wrote, "Colonel Don Juan Nepomuceno Almonte, through whom this generous offer was made, transmitted to me their reply which stated that they would renew fire at a given hour." Almonte would have been the logical choice to tender the "generous offer." But curiously he made no mention of it. Neither did Santa Anna's secretary, Ramon Caro. Nor any other Mexican officer.

Nor did Travis refer to the "generous offer" in any of his subsequent surviving communications. In fact, the only support for Santa Anna's claim came from eight-year-old Enrique Esparza, whose own accounts, written late in his life, could be confusing and contradictory.

But the story just might be true.

Enrique remembered a three-day armistice that occurred "after about seven days fighting." If Santa Anna did tender such an offer, Travis certainly would have accepted. It benefitted the Texians as much as the Mexicans. Surely, in three days, reinforcements would arrive.

Enrique maintained that he heard about the truce from James Bowie. According to Enrique, Bowie called the Texians around his sickbed and announced:

> All of you who desire to leave here may go in safety. Santa
> Anna has just sent a message to Travis saying there will be an

> armistice of three days to give us time to deliberate on surrendering. During these three days all of you who desire to do so may go out of here. Travis has sent me the message and told me to tell those near me.

Significantly—if the story was true—Travis was adhering to the tradition that volunteers should decide for themselves.

And perhaps the brief break in the weather had benefited Bowie's condition. His cot might have been brought out from his musty room, where Bowie could suck in fresh air and help boost the morale of the garrison. And, with Seguin gone, Travis probably would have asked Bowie to communicate the news to the Bexarenos.

In one account Enrique claimed that only Trinidad Saucedo, the attractive former servant of the Veramendi family, took advantage of the offer to leave. But in a later version, Enrique listed six *Tejanos* who departed. This, too, seems to support the credibility of the armistice. Only three days later Travis would bitterly observe that only three *Tejanos* remained in the Alamo. Yet he was being unfair. The *Tejanos* had lost their leader, Juan Seguin. They were a minority in a garrison largely composed of newly arrived *norteamericanos*. Most of the Anglos could not speak Spanish, nurturing distrust and tension. And though Santa Anna was their common enemy, the *Tejanos* and Texians were fighting for very different causes.

Finally, the Bexarenos may not have been as optimistic as the Texians. Enrique remembered:

> During the armistice my father told my mother she had better take the children and go, while she could, to safety... But my mother said: "No, if you're going to stay, so am I. If they kill one, they can kill us all."

Some *Tejanos*, like Toribio Losoya, may have retained childhood memories of the panic and terror when Arredondo descended on Bexar. Yet Losoya and his wife and children also remained within the Alamo. It had always been their home.

Those Bexarenos who left the Alamo did not present themselves to the besieging Mexicans. Even Enrique Esparza heard that Santa Anna, like Arredondo before him, "had offered to let the Americans go with their lives, but the [*Tejanos*] would be treated as rebels." Instead the departing Bexarenos escaped into the night. That would not have been difficult.

Sesma's departure with most of the cavalry had greatly reduced the number of Mexicans patrolling the escape routes to the east.

At least one Anglo accompanied the *Tejanos*. Enrique recalled that Dr. Horace Alsbury was "sent for succor then." Susanna Dickinson only recalled that Alsbury left at some time during the siege. Presumably he did ride for help, because his wife and stepson remained back in the Alamo.

There is not enough evidence to conclude with certainty that Santa Anna and Travis actually agreed on an armistice. At the very least hostilities seem to have diminished for a brief period. But the fighting did not stop altogether. A Mexican officer recalled that a *soldado*, Secudino Alvarez, was killed by a Texian rifleman.

If the armistice occurred, Travis had bought some precious time. But though he had sent out several couriers, Travis had received no response. Were reinforcements on the march? Did anyone care?

He could not know that Henry Smith, before leaving San Felipe to attend the convention at Washington-on-the-Brazos, had published a stirring public notice. "The enemy are upon us!" Smith proclaimed. "Citizens of Texas, descendants of Washington, awake! Arouse yourself!!"

Still maintaining his embattled position as governor, Smith called upon the Texians to "turn out."

> He who longer slumbers on the volcano, must be a madman.
> He who refuses to aid his country in this, her hour of peril and
> danger, is a traitor. *Our rights and liberties must be protected;*
> to the battlefield march and save the country.

News of the besieged Alamo already extended beyond the Sabine. It was announced in a New Orleans broadside—under the banner "Texas Forever!!"—that promised free passage and eight hundred acres of land to anyone who would emigrate to the "Garden of America." In the tradition of all propaganda, the broadside asserted, "The wives and daughters of Texas will be saved from the brutality of Mexican soldiers."

Even if Travis had been aware of the efforts in the United States to aid him, he must have known that he could not hold out long enough for them to reach him. The Alamo's only hope rested with the men of Texas.

General Sesma also was concerned with Texian reinforcements. As he marched south, he still did not know Fannin had retreated back to Goliad.

Ironically, Sesma's departure had weakened the Mexican position east of the Alamo. That made it convenient for the Texian relief force even then slipping closer to the mission-fortress.

Tuesday, March 1, 1836: *The Eighth Day*

Washington-on-the-Brazos

When Colonel Gray had retired the night before, the mild temperature had compelled him to shed some of his clothing. "In the night the wind sprung up from the north and blew a gale, accompanied by lightning, thunder, rain and hail, and it became very cold," he wrote in his diary. He noted that the temperature dropped to thirty-three degrees.

San Antonio de Bexar

During that blustery night thirty-two men leaned low over their horses, as much for warmth as for concealment. It was after 1 A.M., and through the darkness and the howling storm, they were approaching the Alamo.

History would remember them as the "Immortal Thirty-Two." At their core was the Gonzales Ranging Company of Mounted Volunteers, which had been organized on February 23, before Gonzales had received news of the siege. But Smither's arrival the next day with Travis' first appeal had prompted others to join. According to the muster role, the company placed itself under the command of Travis. The volunteers elected thirty-three-year-old George Kimble of Pennsylvania as their lieutenant. A huge man, standing taller than six feet and weighing over two hundred pounds, Kimble had arrived in Gonzales as a bachelor and entered into a partnership with blacksmith Almaron Dickinson to operate a hat factory. In June 1832 he had married Prudence Nash, a widow with three children. Their son, Charles, was born two years later. And now, in February 1836, Prudence was pregnant with twin daughters.

Determined to join his business partner, Dickinson, and place his company under its designated commander, Travis, Kimble had scrambled to make the preparations. On February 27 he secured fifty-two pounds of coffee "for the use of the men that has volunteered to go to Bexar to the Releaf of our boys." That afternoon he led the mounted company out of Gonzales.

Albert Martin rode with Kimble, anxious to deliver the reinforcements Travis needed so desperately. And there were three members of the "Gonzales Eighteen" who had served under Martin during the cannon fracas that had triggered the revolution: Kentuckian Jacob Darst; Irishman Thomas Jackson; and Thomas Miller, the richest man in Gonzales.

Jackson was accompanied by his brother-in-law, twenty-five-year-old George Washington Cottle, who also left behind a pregnant wife, Nancy. She later would give birth to twin sons.

James George, thirty-four, rode alongside his brother-in-law, William Dearduff. After the skirmish at Gonzales, the Texian army had appropriated a team of George's oxen to haul the little cannon to Bexar.

Thomas Miller's wealth had never purchased happiness. After the death of their baby, his young wife, Sidney, had divorced him and married John Benjamin Kellogg II. Now eighteen, Johnny Kellogg also rode to Bexar, leaving Sidney pregnant with his son.

Sidney's brother, seventeen-year-old John Gaston, also had enlisted in the company. Gaston remained fond of Miller and may have ridden to Bexar to be with his ex-brother-in-law.

Two members of the relief expedition were even younger. In 1830 Galba Fuqua, now sixteen years old, had come from Alabama with his father, Silas, and uncle, Benjamin. Silas died and Benjamin married Nancy King, whose family took in young Galba.

Nancy's younger brother, William Phillip King, was only fifteen years old. Their father, John Gladden King, had enlisted in the mounted company on February 23. However a popular tradition maintains that young William volunteered to assume his father's place in the ranks so that the elder King could remain with the family, then stricken with illness.

At the other extreme, forty-four-year-old Andrew Kent held the distinction of being the senior member of the relief expedition. Born in Virginia, he was only nine when his family moved west into Spanish territory. In April 1816 Kent married Elizabeth Zumwalt in St. Charles County, Missouri. Later, according to family tradition, he lost his savings in one of Moses Austin's failed banks. Destitute, he, Elizabeth, and their nine children joined the migration that carved "G. T. T." onto their cabin doors. They had settled in De Witt's colony in June 1831.

Isaac Millsaps, forty-one, also ranked among the oldest Gonzales volunteers. Born in Mississippi, Millsaps served in the War of 1812 before relocating his family to Texas in March 1835. He left behind a blind wife named Mary and seven young children.

Although a tentative list exists of the "thirty-two men from Gonzales," the actual roster remains a subject of conjecture. Due to the incomplete muster roll, drawn up on February 23 before all the men had enlisted, some of the volunteers credited to the Gonzales mounted company may already have been at Bexar. And men assumed to have been in the Alamo garrison since the siege began actually may have arrived with the Gonzales relief expedition. Charles Despallier is generally included with the Gonzales thirty-two, something that only would have been possible if, after burning the *jacales* on February 25, he had left the Alamo—presumably, like Albert Martin, carrying a dispatch from Travis.

Moreover, not all of the thirty-two hailed from Gonzales. John W. Smith of Bexar accompanied the men back to the Alamo. In fact there were only thirty-one volunteers until they arrived on Cibolo Creek. There twenty-seven-year-old David P. Cummings, a surveyor from Pennsylvania, joined the company. His cousin, Dr. John Purdy Reynolds, twenty-nine, already was in the Alamo, having enlisted in Captain Harrison's company at Nacogdoches and journeyed to San Antonio with David Crockett.

Cautiously approaching Bexar shortly after midnight on the bitter cold morning of March 1, the Gonzales Ranging Company of Mounted Volunteers encountered yet another rider. He asked, in English, "Do you wish to go into the fort, gentlemen?" When they assented, the stranger said, "Then follow me." He reined his horse into the lead, offering to guide them past the Mexican encampments.

Something about the stranger aroused John W. Smith's suspicions. "Boys," Smith stated, "it's time to be after shooting that fellow." The stranger overheard the remark, sank in his spurs, and bolted into the cold, wet night.

Fearful that their presence had been discovered by the enemy, the Gonzales volunteers spurred their own mounts into a gallop and raced toward the distant black walls of the Alamo. Their sudden emergence from the darkness startled the Texian sentries at the gate. A volley of rifle fire rudely greeted the long awaited relief expedition. One of the Gonzales rangers may have been wounded before the shouting, cursing reinforcements convinced the Alamo defenders to open the gates.

"When Señor Smith came from Gonzales with the band of men he had gathered, there was great shouting," remembered young Enrique Esparza. "The Texians beat drums and played on a flute."

Although heartily welcoming the new arrivals, William Barret Travis knew that thirty-two men were not enough. The Alamo needed ten times that number. However, staring at the blossoming light just starting to illuminate the eastern prairie, he thought surely these volunteers were only the vanguard of more reinforcements. The Alamo yet would be saved.

Colonel Juan Almonte recorded thirty-six degrees that morning. The storm subsided, leaving a clear, frigid day.

Washington-on-the-Brazos

Colonel William Fairfax Gray reported that everyone was "shivering and exclaiming against the cold," a mere one hundred sixty miles to the east at Washington-on-the-Brazos. Settlers had occupied that region since 1821, but the town had not been laid out until December 1833. Perched on bluffs above the Brazos and more commonly known merely as Washington, it had prospered as a supply depot for emigrants traveling further west, and by 1836 boasted a booming permanent population of one hundred citizens.

Local businessmen had lured the convention to Washington-on-the-Brazos by offering a free assembly hall. The delegates might have reconsidered had they known in advance about their facilities. " . . . the members of the Convention . . . met today in an unfinished house, without doors or windows," Gray wrote. "In lieu of glass, cotton cloth was stretched across the windows, which partially excluded the cold wind."

San Antonio de Bexar

The cold wind did not hinder the ongoing celebration within the Alamo. Perhaps Crockett pitted his fiddle against McGregor's bagpipes for another noisy contest. That afternoon Travis, who had been conserving his powder, ordered his artillery to fire two cannonballs into the town across the river. Travis had a specific target in mind. Perhaps he had received intelligence from friendly Bexarenos, or perhaps he simply had noticed an unusual amount of activity around the building. One cannonball missed its mark, but the second crashed into the Yturri house—Santa Anna's headquarters.

If there ever had been an armistice, that cannon shot ended it. If Santa Anna had offered a chance for surrender, he would not extend that generous offer again.

Unfortunately for the Texians, Santa Anna was not at the house when the cannonball impacted. The Napoleon of the West had reconnoitered to the north of the Alamo, planning his strategy. Staring at the old mission's crumbling north wall, Santa Anna ordered more trenches excavated.

General Sesma's column returned that afternoon, the infantry marching back into Bexar and the cavalry resuming their position guarding the eastern hills. The Texian festivities within the Alamo might have been stifled had they realized that Sesma had found no trace of Fannin's relief column.

Goliad

Colonel Fannin had little to do but write letters. In one dispatch to Robinson and the Council at Washington-on-the-Brazos, Fannin reasserted that he no longer could be considered acting commander-in-chief and that he was "desirous to be erased from the list of officers."

He maintained:

> . . . unless the people of Texas, forthwith, turn out in mass . . .
> those now in the field will be sacrificed, and the battles that
> should be fought here, will be fought East of the Brassos [*sic*],
> and probably the Trinity.

Fannin added that he was resolved to await orders from the council and not make any movements.

Yet in a second correspondence that same day, the eternally indecisive Fannin speculated that he might leave two hundred men to guard Fort Defiance and take two hundred more men to cooperate with the efforts to relieve the besieged garrison at Bexar. He wrote, "I would risk life and all for our brave men in the Alamo."

Gonzales

James Butler Bonham knew nothing of Fannin's waverings. Two weeks earlier, before the siege of the Alamo had begun, Bonham had ridden to Goliad to deliver a dispatch from Travis. Then he probably traveled to San Felipe and Washington-on-the-Brazos—Houston remembered seeing him during the siege—and Bonham picked up a dispatch from the provisional government.

On March 1, Bonham rode his lathered horse into Gonzales. Robert Williamson was there, hobbling around on his peg leg, rallying men to march to Bexar. Learning that Bonham was continuing on to the Alamo, Three-Legged Willie gave the courier a letter to Travis.

"You cannot conceive my anxiety," Williamson wrote his friend. "Today it has been four whole days that we have not the slightest news relative to your situation and we are therefore given over to a thousand conjectures regarding you." Williamson continued:

> Sixty men have left this municipality, who in all probability
> are with you by this date. Colonel Fannin with 300 men and

four pieces of artillery has been on the march toward Bexar three days now.

Tonight we await some 300 reinforcements from Washington, Bastrop, Brazoria, and S. Felipe and no time will be lost providing you assistance.

"For God's sake hold out until we can assist you," Williamson added in a postscript. "Best wishes to all your people and tell them to hold on firmly by their 'wills' until I go there."

Preparing for his journey back to the Alamo, Bonham encountered eighteen-year-old Benjamin Franklin Highsmith, a Missourian who had settled in Bastrop. Six months earlier he had raced to Gonzales to help defend the cannon. Then he had joined the march to Bexar, participating in the siege and battle that defeated General Cos. Afterwards Highsmith remained with the small force in Bexar. He, like Bonham, had been sent by Travis with a dispatch calling for reinforcements.

Then he had tried to return to Bexar.

Highsmith made it as far as Powder House Hill. He could see the besieged Alamo below him. But Mexican lancers spotted him. He spun his tired horse back to the east and sank in spurs. The Mexican cavalry thundered after him for six miles before they finally fell back.

Describing this incident to Bonham, Highsmith tried to encourage Bonham to wait for a large relief force. It would be almost suicidal to ride back to the Alamo alone.

Bonham responded, "I will report the result of my mission to Travis—or die in the attempt."

Wednesday, March 2, 1836: *The Ninth Day*

San Antonio de Bexar

"Commenced clear and pleasant," Almonte noted in his journal, "thermometer 34 degrees—no wind."

Santa Anna kept busy. Learning that there was still corn hidden on the rebel Seguin's farm, His Excellency sent riders to secure it. Then Santa Anna dispatched Colonel Bringas to ride back to General Gaona with instructions for Gaona to send his best companies on ahead at a forced march.

Almonte reported the discovery of a "covered road within pistol shot of the Alamo." No doubt it had facilitated the departure of couriers from the fort. Santa Anna ordered the Jimenez Battalion to be posted there.

There was no reported activity from the Alamo. The excitement generated by the arrival of the Gonzales mounted volunteers had faded. Now Travis and the Texians could only huddle around campfires and wait for more reinforcements.

But even if no Texian marksmen fired from the walls—and no Texian cannonballs smashed into the city—the Mexicans suffered another casualty. A *cazador* (light infantryman) named Trinidad Delgado slipped into the icy San Antonio River and drowned.

While the Texians within the Alamo saw no action that day, the twenty-six men under Dr. James Grant encountered more than they wanted. Unaware of the fate of Johnson's command, that morning they drove a herd of captured mustangs back to San Patricio. Some twenty-five miles below the town, on the prairie near Agua Dulce Creek, they were ambushed by more than sixty dragoons under the command of General Jose Urrea. Even though mounted, the Texians were no match for the skilled Mexican cavalrymen. Fourteen of the Texians were killed, including Grant, whose body had been pierced by lances and swords. Six Texians managed to escape the field to later join Fannin's command at Goliad. Six others were captured. Urrea added them to the prisoners he had taken at San Patricio.

Although Santa Anna specifically had ordered the execution of all captured Texians, Urrea sent his prisoners to the dungeons in Matamoras. It saved their lives. In chains, they would be the only members of the Matamoras campaign to reach their destination.

While Santa Anna had inflicted no casualties on the one hundred eighty-odd defenders of the Alamo, Urrea's smaller command had destroyed the force under Johnson and Grant. The only surviving contingent of the Matamoras expedition was Colonel Fannin at Goliad.

Washington-on-the-Brazos

At Washington-on-the-Brazos the delegates wasted no time resolving the longstanding dispute between the Peace and War parties. That morning, according to Colonel Gray, George Campbell Childress "reported a Declaration of Independence, which he read in his place."

Childress, a thirty-four-year-old Tennessean, was a widower lawyer who had arrived in Texas in December 1835. There he joined his uncle, Sterling Robertson, and both men were elected to represent Milam municipality at the convention. Generally acknowledged as the author of the Texas Declaration of Independence, Childress may have drafted it before he arrived at Washington-on-the-Brazos.

In format it borrowed extensively from the United States Declaration of Independence. Childress listed the grievances against Mexico and then concluded that the delegates "do hereby resolve and declare, that our political connection with the Mexican nation has forever ended, and that the people of Texas do now constitute a free, Sovereign, and independent republic. . . ."

Gray reported that the document was "received by the house, committed to a committee of the whole, reported without amendment, and unanimously adopted, in less than one hour from its first and only reading."

Officially, at least, Texas had become a republic. On Sam Houston's birthday. It was certainly the best present that Houston could have wanted.

That evening, as the delegates drafted a copy of the declaration to be signed the following day, a courier arrived with Travis' February 25 dispatch detailing the attack on the south wall.

Houston quickly prepared the text for a public broadside, announcing the declaration of independence and urging the citizens of Texas to maintain it by marching to combat. In a postscript he noted:

> The fate of Bejar is unknown. The country must and shall be defended. The patriots of Texas are appealed to, in behalf of their bleeding country.

But perhaps his concern for the Alamo had been premature. The delegates also had received a dated correspondence from Fannin stating that he was leading three hundred fifty men to the relief of Travis. "This, with the other forces known to be on the way, will make the number in the fort some six or seven hundred," Gray wrote in his diary. "It is believed the Alamo is safe."

Goliad

In fact Colonel Fannin still entertained the notion of marching to Bexar. Fannin's aide, Captain John S. Brooks, wrote to his mother that Fort Defiance had just received intelligence from Bexar. The Texians had repulsed two Mexican attacks. "Probably Davy Crockett 'grinned' them off," Brooks quipped.

He added, "We will probably march tomorrow or the next day, if we can procure fresh oxen enough to transport our baggage and two six-pounders." Then he, like Travis, like Fannin, called for the Texians to "awake now if they wish to preserve their freedom. . . . "

"Now or never," Brooks concluded.

Thursday, March 3, 1836: *The Tenth Day*

Washington-on-the-Brazos

The day dawned clear and cold and still. The delegates to the convention assembled at 9:00 A.M. Again they heard a reading of the declaration of independence. Then all of the members began affixing their signatures to it. The fourth man to sign it was fifty-three-year-old Francisco Ruiz—Bexar's first schoolmaster, lieutenant in the Bexar Provincial Militia, defector to the Republican Army of the North, veteran of the battle of the Medina, exile for almost a decade, commander of the Alamo de Parras Company, and Indian peace commissioner.

Perhaps it would have been more appropriate if his signature had led the others. No one else within that cold room was more qualified. Ruiz had lived in Texas longer, had been the first to fight for Texas independence, and had sacrificed more for the land he loved.

Did he know that his son, Francisco Antonio Ruiz, the *alcalde* of Bexar, had been placed under house arrest by order of Santa Anna, because of suspected loyalty to the Texian cause?

Signing immediately after Ruiz, his nephew, Jose Antonio Navarro—longtime friend of Austin and the colonists—was the only other native *Tejano* to place his name on the declaration of independence. Did Navarro know that his niece, Juana Alsbury, even then was cloistered in a small room in the west wall within the besieged Alamo?

Goliad

Colonel James Walker Fannin finally decided to remain at Fort Defiance. His decision was not popular with most of the garrison, especially the New Orleans Greys. According to Herman Ehrenberg, Fannin believed that the Alamo defenders, "if they wanted to, could surely withdraw."

"This is the only thing that I can say in his justification," wrote Ehrenberg. "I cannot believe that he feared to face the miserable and partly conscripted hordes of Santa Anna. . . . "

In a sense, Ehrenberg was correct. To Fannin's credit, he was not forsaking the Alamo out of cowardice. Perhaps his decision had been triggered by news of Grant's defeat at Agua Dulce Creek. With Urrea's forces advancing, Fannin once again concluded that he must not abandon Goliad.

It would be certain defeat to be caught out on the open prairie.

San Antonio de Bexar

As he approached the Alamo late that morning, James Butler Bonham veered wide to the north to avoid the Mexican entrenchments on Powder House Hill that guarded the Gonzales road. By 11:00 A.M. he was resting his horse on the eastern rise overlooking San Antonio de Bexar. He could see the Alamo below—a thousand yards away—a perilously long gallop through exposed country. And he could see the surrounding earthworks that protected the Mexican infantry encampments and artillery positions. To the west in the city. To the south along the Alameda. And most disturbingly, to the northeast along the *acequia*. Bonham could see the Mexican engineers and *soldados* still working to push the entrenchment ever closer to the north wall. Now it was within musket shot of the Alamo, and therefore he, too, would be in musket range when he made his final dash. He would have to run a gauntlet between the Dolores cavalry position on Powder House Hill and the *soldados* at the earthworks along the *acequia*.

But there was no sense in waiting for a Mexican patrol to stumble upon him. He tied a white bandana around the crown of his hat, a signal to any trigger-happy Alamo sentry that he was on their side. Then he dug his heels into his horse's flank and bolted forward through the mesquite and cactus. The surprised Mexicans never got off a shot. Bonham galloped into the Alamo to report the result of his mission.

The garrison erupted in fresh enthusiasm upon Bonham's arrival. The contents of Williamson's letter spread through the fort. Fannin was still coming. There were sixty more men due from Gonzales, and then an army of three hundred would follow them. They would be saved.

Travis did nothing to douse his men's hope—he even allowed them to fire a few cannon rounds at the city—but secretly he did not share their optimism. Not yet. Fannin had had plenty of time to get to Bexar if he was really coming. And where were the sixty men who should have preceded Bonham? Was it all false dreams?

Santa Anna had more to celebrate than did the men of the Alamo. Later that afternoon he received news of the defeat of Johnson's men at San Patricio. A minor victory, to be sure. But the Mexican army had not experienced victory in Texas. Now the tide was reversing. Now Santa Anna himself could understand the significance of that comet, which only two weeks earlier had finally drifted off into oblivion. Now he could recall the exhilaration of that wonderful day on the Medina, so many years ago, when he had relished the sight of the rebel army crumbling before him.

He gave instructions. The bells of San Fernando would celebrate the victory.

Suddenly the tolling bells in town were joined by excited cheers, by martial music, and by the thundering of cannon. Enrique Esparza overheard the sulking *soldado* prisoner in the Alamo remark that Mexican reinforcements had arrived. The Texians on the walls could see the smartly dressed column marching from the west. It was the advance battalions, the picked troops, of General Gaona's First Brigade under acting commander Colonel Francisco Duque.

They had camped the previous evening on the Medina River. That morning they donned their dress uniforms and began the final march into Bexar, arriving before 5.00 P.M. that evening. Santa Anna's martial bands and booming artillery welcomed the reinforcements—the Aldama, Toluca, and Zapadores Battalions—nearly one thousand men counting officers and wagon drivers.

Ironically, many of the Alamo defenders mistakenly believed that General Sesma had been commanding the Mexican forces until that moment, and that the festivities in Bexar signaled the belated arrival of *El Presidente* himself. The Texians might have been more outraged to learn that Santa Anna's brother-in-law, General Martin Perfecto de Cos, and his aide, Colonel Sanchez Navarro, had accompanied the reinforcements. After their defeat at Bexar, both men had been paroled back to Mexico under the promise that they would never again raise arms against Texas.

The arrival of the Mexican troops abruptly ended the jubilation within the fort. The Texians shouted jeers and curses from the Alamo walls, but they hardly could be heard over the commotion in Bexar.

Santa Anna's own disposition soured slightly when he learned that the fool, Gaona, had not sent the large twelve-pound siege guns. His Excellency was advised that he had not specifically requested the big cannon, and therefore Gaona had assumed that Santa Anna did not need them. The siege artillery would not arrive for another four days.

No matter. Santa Anna now had nearly twenty-four hundred *soldados* in Bexar. It would be enough.

Still, as always, there was much to personally oversee. He mounted his horse and galloped around the compound for yet another reconnaissance, perhaps venturing too often into the Alamo's range of fire. Santa Anna "presents himself to needless danger," observed Sanchez Navarro, but "General Sesma takes to withdraw from places where there is no danger."

Returning to Bexar, Santa Anna decided to consolidate all his artillery to the entrenchments south and north of the Alamo. He especially wanted to concentrate his cannon fire on that decaying north wall.

A somber mood settled over the Alamo as darkness descended. With the arrival of Mexican reinforcements, an attack could be imminent. Would the Texian relief arrive in time?

Travis retreated into his headquarters. Williamson had written that he had not heard anything from the Alamo in four days. Well, now Travis would remind them he was still there.

He addressed his first letter to the president of the convention, supplementing the information already written to Houston on the twenty-fifth. Since that time the enemy had encircled the Alamo with entrenchments and kept up its bombardment.

> I have so fortified this place that the walls are generally proof against cannon-balls; and I shall continue to entrench on the inside, and strengthen the walls by throwing up dirt. At least two hundred shells have fallen inside our works without having injured a single man; indeed we have been so fortunate as not to lose a man from any cause, and we have killed many of the enemy. The spirits of my men are still high, although they have had much to depress them.

Travis pleaded for supplies—powder, cannonballs, and lead—and for reinforcements. He no longer believed the rumors that Fannin was coming to his relief. "I look to the colonies alone for aid; unless it arrives soon, I shall have to fight the enemy on his own terms," he wrote. " . . . I feel confident that the determined valour and desperate courage, heretofore evinced by my men, will not fail them in the last struggle, and although they may be sacrificed to the vengeance of a Gothic enemy, the victory will cost the enemy so dear, that it will be worse for him than a defeat."

It was Travis at his most dramatic. He continued, explaining his strategy for defending the Alamo, striving to make it the "great and decisive battle ground:"

> The power of Santa Anna is to be met here or in the colonies. We had better meet him here, than to suffer a war of desolation to rage in our settlements. A blood red banner waves from the church of Bexar, and in the camp above us, in token

that the war is one of vengeance against rebels; they have declared us as such, and demanded that we surrender at discretion or this garrison should be put to the sword. Their threats have had no influence on me or my men, but to make all fight with desperation, and that high souled courage which characterizes the patriot, who is willing to die in defense of his country's liberty and his own honour.

Then bitterness slipped in. The Bexarenos had proven to be his enemies, Travis wrote, except for three *Tejanos* who, with their families, remained within the Alamo. It was an unjust charge, displaying Travis' tinge of racism. He could not understand the legacy of terror left by Arredondo, and now perpetuated by Santa Anna. Those sympathetic Bexarenos within the occupied town could only watch and pray silently.

"God and Texas!" Travis concluded the letter.

"Victory or Death!!"

He paused, then reached for a second piece of paper. This time he wrote a private message, one the world has never seen. Presumably it was to Rebecca Cummins. What might he have told her in that last communication? As he scrawled it, did he notice the cat's eye ring on his finger glistening in the candlelight?

"Do me the favor to send the enclosed to its proper destination instantly," he implored his friend Jesse Grimes, in the third letter Travis wrote that evening. Again he summarized the events of the siege, this time venturing into the politics of the convention, of which he had received no communication.

> Let the Convention go and make a declaration of independence, and we will then understand, and the world will understand, what we are fighting for. If independence is not declared, I shall lay down my arms, and so will the men under my command. But under a flag of independence, we are ready to peril our lives a hundred times a day, and to drive away the monster who is fighting us under a blood-red flag, threatening to murder all prisoners and make Texas a waste desert.

With five hundred more men, Travis vowed that he could drive the invaders beyond the Rio Grande. But he could not defend the Alamo with the few he had. He declared, "if my countrymen do not rally to my relief, I am determined to perish in the defense of this place, and my bones shall reproach my country for her neglect."

It was getting late. Just time for one more quick note. This one to David Ayers, who was caring for young Charles Edward.

> Take care of my little boy. If the country should be saved, I may make for him a splendid fortune; but if the country be lost and I should perish, he will have nothing but the proud recollection that he is the son of a man who died for his country.

John W. Smith had volunteered to carry the expresses from the Alamo. No doubt other Texians also gave him messages to forward to their families, but sadly these all have been lost to history.

Colonel Almonte recalled that the Texians "attempted a sally in the night" to a sugar mill on the river north of the fort, but they "were repulsed by our advance."

Earlier raids from the Alamo had been for water or firewood. Whatever strategic importance the sugar mill may have held is not known. Perhaps the raid was just a diversion to allow John W. Smith to escape into the darkness.

However historian Thomas Lindley presents a convincing argument that what the Mexicans mistook as a sally from the Alamo was actually the arrival of more reinforcements, presumably the sixty men from Gonzales mentioned by Williamson. If so, that gave Travis two hundred fifty men.

Ironically some of the *Tejanos* Travis had disparaged in his letters that day may have returned with that reinforcement.

But it was still not enough. Not to adequately man the long, crumbling walls that enclosed the three-acre Alamo compound. And how much longer would Santa Anna wait before he attacked with ten-to-one odds?

Friday, March 4, 1836:   ## *The Eleventh Day*

San Antonio de Bexar

"The day commenced windy, but not cold—thermometer 42 degrees," recorded Colonel Almonte. "Commenced firing very early, which the enemy did not return."

Now, more than ever before, Travis felt the necessity of conserving powder.

Washington-on-the-Brazos

That afternoon the Convention passed a resolution that "General Sam Houston be appointed major general, to be commander in chief of the land forces of the Texian army both Regulars, Volunteers, and Militia ... and that he forthwith proceed to take command, establish headquarters and organize the army accordingly."

William Fairfax Gray remembered that the meeting adjourned early that day to allow various committees to confer "on the Constitution, on finance, on the army, on the organization of the militia, etc."

San Antonio de Bexar

That afternoon, Santa Anna called his commanders to a council of war. The moment for the assault was near. Santa Anna proposed an attack as early as Sunday, March 6. General Sesma and Colonel Almonte supported His Excellency's notion.

However General Castrillon argued that the large, twelve-pound siege guns should arrive by Monday, March 7. They could certainly open a breach in the Alamo's north wall, and the Mexicans would lose fewer *soldados* gaining entrance into the fort. General Cos and several other officers sided with Castrillon. "In this state things remained—the General not making any definite resolution," Almonte recalled.

Then another point of contention arose on which Santa Anna was definite. There would be no prisoners. He cited Arredondo's ruthlessness after the battle of the Medina. Castrillon may have pointed out that Arredondo did in fact spare some prisoners. Certainly Castrillon argued for more humane treatment of any Texians taken alive. Almonte and some other officers also balked at the decree. But Santa Anna would not be swayed.

Though Santa Anna had not committed himself as to when the assault would take place, he ordered the engineers to advance the northern battery even closer to the Alamo's north wall. They worked into the night, pushing the entrenchments to within two hundred yards of the wall.

Reenactment of Mexican *soldados*

To the Texians within the fort, that day must have seemed the longest of all. Their only hope of survival lay in the promised reinforcements from Gonzales. Throughout the day, as the Mexican cannons continued pounding the walls and the howitzer shells exploded within the compound, the Texians had watched to the east. Waiting. Hoping.

Travis knew the attack would come soon. When the Mexicans charged the walls, the Texians would not be able to keep them out. But what were their options? Retreat was an impossibility, although some men might be able to scramble over the walls and escape into the night. That left surrender—or death. Had he been alone, Travis unhesitatingly would have chosen the latter. But for all his fiery rhetoric, realistically he had to consider the welfare of his garrison—these storekeepers and schoolteachers and blacksmiths and lawyers and doctors—these fathers and husbands and brothers and sons—who called themselves soldiers. Few had any real military training. Yet they had honor. They had not left their post to join in the plunder promised by the Matamoras expedition. And they had not abandoned their post when the enemy appeared in overwhelming numbers. But none of them was suicidal. They might risk their lives in battle, but none of them wanted certain death.

Perhaps Travis seriously considered the option of surrender. General Filisola later heard a report that:

> Travis Barret, commander of the enemy garrison, through the intermediary of a woman, proposed to the general in chief that they would surrender their arms and fort with everybody in it with the only condition of saving his life and that of his comrades in arms.

According to Filisola, Santa Anna informed the woman that any surrender must be unconditional, "without guarantees, not even of life itself, since there should be no guarantee for traitors."

However Mrs. Dickinson had a different perspective on the events of that night. She believed that Juana Alsbury had deserted to the enemy and advised Santa Anna of the Texians' inferior numbers, thus convincing the Napoleon of the West to launch an immediate attack. In fact Santa Anna already knew the weaknesses of the Alamo garrison. And if Juana Alsbury did leave the Alamo, she then returned to it. Hardly the act of a betrayer.

But possibly the act of an emissary.

Colonel Jose Enrique de la Peña, recently arrived with the reinforcements, interpreted the matter even differently. No fan of Santa Anna, de la Peña argued that Travis' offer to surrender actually "precipitated the assault, because [Santa Anna] wanted to cause a sensation and would have regretted taking the Alamo without clamor and without bloodshed, for some believed that without these there is no glory."

If Juana—or another Mexican woman—represented Travis in a meeting with Santa Anna, the Alamo commander had his answer. His final answer. As Filisola noted, "With [Santa Anna's] reply it is clear that all were determined to lose their existence, selling it as dearly as possible."

Saturday, March 5, 1836: *The Twelfth Day*

San Antonio de Bexar

Colonel Almonte reported that the day commenced clear, at a moderate fifty degrees, and the thermometer climbed to sixty-eight by midday.

Shortly after noon, as Santa Anna listened to the percussion symphony of his artillery, he announced his decision to storm the Alamo on the following day, Sunday, March 6.

General Castrillon again protested, lamenting the Mexican *soldados* that would be needlessly lost by not waiting for the heavy artillery— expected on March 7—to pound a hole in the north wall. Other officers advocated starving the Texians into surrender, thereby eliminating any further Mexican casualties. However Fernando Urissa, an aide to His Excellency, recalled that Santa Anna flourished a leg of chicken upon which he was nibbling and exclaimed:

> What are the lives of soldiers than so many chickens? I tell you, the Alamo must fall, and my orders must be obeyed at all hazards. If our soldiers are driven back, the next line in their rear must force those before them forward, and compel them to scale the walls, cost what it may.

Santa Anna resorted to his favorite battle plan. The Mexicans would attack in the predawn hours. Not only would the Texians be in their deepest slumber, but the darkness would negate the advantage of the Alamo's artillery and the superior range of the Texian long rifles.

Santa Anna proved himself the Napoleon of the West, attending to every detail in his specific orders of attack. At a signal from a bugle at the north battery, the Mexicans would attack in four columns against all four sides of the Alamo.

General Martin Perfecto de Cos would have the opportunity to redeem his tarnished honor by commanding the first column, comprised of the six *fusilier* (line infantry) companies and one *cazador* (light infantry) company of the Aldama Battalion and three *fusilier* companies of the Battalion of San Luis, approximately three hundred fifty men, equipped with ten ladders, two crowbars, and two axes.

The second column, composed of the six *fusilier* companies and one *cazador* company of the Toluca Battalion and the three remaining *fusilier* companies of the San Luis Battalion, about four hundred *soldados*, would be commanded by Colonel Francisco Duque. They would carry ten ladders.

Colonel Jose Maria Romero would lead the third column consisting of the twelve *fusilier* companies of the Matamoras and Jimenez Battalions, over four hundred men equipped with six ladders.

Colonel Juan Morales would command the fourth column consisting of the light infantry, *cazadores*, one hundred twenty-five *soldados* supplied with only two ladders.

All of these troops were to retire at dark so as to be prepared to move into attack position at midnight.

All of the cavalry units, nearly three hundred seventy men under the command of General Sesma, would be stationed at the Alameda, where they would saddle up at 3:00 A.M. "to prevent the possibility of escape."

Santa Anna himself would command the reserves, the recently arrived Zapadores Battalion, and the *grenadaro* (elite) companies from the various battalions, some four hundred men.

And there were other details His Excellency personally had to address. The attacking *soldados* would be supplied with two packages of prefabricated paper cartridges, but the grenadiers with Santa Anna would receive six packages each. Every man must have shoes or sandals, but they could not wear overcoats, blankets, "or anything that may impede the rapidity of their motions."

"The arms, principally the bayonets, should be in perfect order." In Napoleonic warfare, when there was no time to reload, the bayonet often finished the battle.

Santa Anna concluded his written orders, asserting:

> The honor of the nation being interested in this engagement against the bold and lawless foreignors ... His excellency expects that every man will do his duty, and exert himself to give a day of glory to the country and of the Supreme Government, who will know how to reward the distinguished deeds of the brave soldiers of the army of Operations.

In fact Santa Anna hardly needed the big siege guns. The relentless beating from the new Mexican battery was crumbling the north wall as fast as the Texians could shovel dirt into the gap. That was not Travis' only concern. Watching from the ramparts he observed the energy that now characterized the Mexican army as the *soldados* received their equipment and prepared for battle. Perhaps Travis saw the feared siege ladders.

There could be little doubt that time had run out.

Then, curiously, by dark everything outside the fort seemed to get quiet. No more of the continual bombardment. No more of the sudden, sporadic serenades from Santa Anna's bands that had kept the Texians awake and alert night after night.

On Santa Anna's orders, the *soldados* had retired to rest up for the final assault. Few of the Mexicans could sleep, however, knowing that in mere hours they would be charging into the Alamo's deadly guns.

But there was another reason for the unnatural silence. Again the Napoleon of the West was utilizing psychological warfare. For twelve days Santa Anna's artillery and bands had pushed the Texians to the brink of exhaustion. Now he wanted them to lull his enemy into a deep, deadly slumber.

The respite afforded Green B. Jameson and his engineers time to make hasty repairs to the horizontal timbers that braced the improvised earthworks comprising too much of the north wall.

Travis also may have taken advantage of the silence—if there is any truth to the most beloved of all Alamo legends. The historical evidence remains sparse—but what may have happened next would have been very much in character with the dramatic flair of William Barret Travis.

That evening he ordered the men to assemble within the compound. The garrison formed up before him. By now Travis knew many of them. They all had stories. There was thirty-eight-year-old Dr. John Forsyth from New York. His wife had died on Christmas Day, 1828. The loss, the pain, had been too much for him. He came west to establish himself as a farmer. Travis must have identified closely with Dr. Forsyth, who had left his son behind with the boy's grandfather.

More than a few of the garrison were men of some prominence. James M. Rose, thirty-one, from Ohio, was the nephew of President James Madison. John C. Goodrich, twenty-seven, might have been a purser in the United States Navy—the recommendation had been made by then United States Congressman from Tennessee Sam Houston. Instead Goodrich later followed his brother to Texas. While Goodrich defended the Alamo, brother Benjamin Briggs Goodrich attended the Convention at Washington-on-the-Brazos and attached his name to the Texas Declaration of Independence.

A number of men in the Alamo were related by blood or marriage, especially the contingent from Gonzales. George Nelson, thirty-one, from South

Carolina, came to Texas with the New Orleans Greys. His younger brother, Edward, twenty, had arrived in Bexar in time to help capture the city from General Cos. Now, together, they stood before Travis.

In his haste to join the siege of Bexar, Tennessean Asa Walker, twenty-three, had liberated a gun and overcoat from John Grant of Washington-on-the-Brazos. His thirty-seven-year-old cousin, Jacob, already was there. During the siege, Mrs. Dickinson recalled that Jacob Walker often talked to her "with anxious tenderness" about his wife and four children. How he longed to see them again!

John Flanders, thirty-six, left Massachusetts after a bitter dispute with his father, Levi. They had been business partners. John had wanted to foreclose on a widow's property; Levi adamantly refused. So John had migrated to Texas, bitterly vowing never to communicate with his father again. Now, in the Alamo, did he think of his father?

Eighteen-year-old William T. Malone had fled from his stern father back in Alabama. He always had been considered a wild lad—had his recklessness caused the loss of that finger missing from his left hand? One night he got roaring drunk. Rather than face his father's wrath William fled west. His father trailed him as far as New Orleans, but William escaped to Texas—and the Alamo. He had written one letter back to his family. His mother kept it nestled in her bosom until it finally deteriorated.

Gordon C. Jennings, a fifty-six-year-old farmer from Pennsylvania probably was the oldest member of the garrison. His brother, Charles, was with Fannin's command at Goliad. William P. King, fifteen, who may have taken his father's place among the Gonzales volunteers, probably qualified as the youngest.

There were two hundred men, give or take, from twenty states and a half dozen foreign countries. Exactly who was there, and how many, will always remain in dispute. Some of their names may forever elude history.

Standing before them, gazing into their haggard faces, Travis hardly needed to state the obvious. A Mexican assault was imminent. The promised reinforcements probably would not arrive in time. That blood-red flag left them few options.

To surrender at discretion virtually insured their execution.

As an army they could attempt to retreat—fight their way out. That entailed abandoning those in the hospital on the upper level of the long barracks, and also most, if not all, of their artillery to the enemy. Then, almost certainly, they would be surrounded on the prairie, with even less cover than the Alamo's decrepit walls provided—and easily slaughtered.

Travis proposed instead that they stay and pray for a miracle. And if no help arrived, well, they had their artillery. And they had muskets captured from Cos' army, distributed so that each man had several loaded weapons stacked at his side. Perhaps reprising the phrase from his letter of March 3, Travis may have told them that they could make the Mexican victory worse than any defeat.

But every man knew—and Travis knew they knew—that despite Santa Anna's best efforts to surround the Alamo, couriers had galloped in and out. Reinforcements had slipped through the enemy lines. Now, in the dark, with the enemy silent, it seemed an opportune time for any individuals, or small groups of men, to attempt an escape if they so desired.

The garrison was mostly volunteers. Travis left the decision to them.

According to legend Travis drew his sword from its sheath and etched a line in the sand, challenging those who would stay to cross over and join him.

And every man soberly trudged over that immortal line. Save two. James Bowie, too weak to rise from his cot, asked to be carried over.

Only Louis Rose, a fifty-five-year-old Frenchman who had served in the Napoleonic wars, chose to leave the Alamo.

At least that is the way the legend tells it, and there is some flimsy historical evidence to support it. Let the historians endlessly debate the truth. It hardly matters if Travis actually drew a line. Or even made a speech. Every man in the Alamo knew the situation. The options.

And most elected to stay.

There would be one last courier. Twenty-one-year old James Allen volunteered that he was a good rider. He was sure he could make it to Goliad. Travis and others hastily scribbled messages. The Alamo gates swung open, and Allen, riding bareback, galloped out and disappeared into the darkness. To Travis' relief, no shots shattered the dead still night.

After that it would have been an evening of quiet, somber reflection. Of remembering what had been. What might have been. What yet might be, if only, somehow, help would arrive.

In a sense, Gregorio Esparza was more fortunate than most. Enrique remembered that his father left the gun he manned in the church—apparently the same one Enrique had crawled over when he entered the Alamo twelve days earlier—and spent that night in his wife's embrace within their quarters in the south wall.

Followed by his slave, Joe, Travis made one last round of the fort, trying to boost the morale of his exhausted garrison. He wandered into the church and saw Mrs. Dickinson tenderly cradling her infant daughter. Travis removed his cat's-eye ring, pulled a string through it, and gently placed the makeshift necklace around little Angelina's neck.

Crossing the compound, Travis observed that most in the garrison were drifting off to sleep. However Dolphin Ward Floyd probably was still awake. He had sauntered away from his North Carolina farm boasting he was off to marry "some rich old widow." In Gonzales he had found a good wife, if not a rich one. But he had left her to join the relief expedition for the Alamo. Now Floyd gazed at his pocket watch—counting down the hours, the minutes—to March 6. His thirty-second birthday.

Micajah Autry also may have lingered awake to watch the moon rise into the sky. Sadly, he could barely discern it beneath a heavy cloud cover. Was it more visible back in Tennessee? Could his beloved wife, Martha, see it from her cabin door? Was she thinking of him, even now, as he thought of her and the children?

Travis, too, felt drowsy. The long siege had taken its toll on them all. Returning to the headquarters in the west wall, he and Joe retired to their cots.

Travis must have considered that Santa Anna might launch an assault before daybreak. After all, in that one glorious cavalry charge he had led, Travis had attacked at dawn. He had sentries posted outside to raise the alarm. Like every other man in the Alamo, Travis thought of his loved ones, of Charles Edward and Rebecca, as he, too, finally succumbed to sleep.

In the trenches outside the Alamo walls, the sentries battled to stay awake. But the stillness and the silence, after that long siege, descended over them. One by one, their eyelids drooped, their heads nodded, and they finally dozed.

Santa Anna did not sleep at all that night. He ordered Almonte's black cook, Ben, to keep the coffee brewing. They left the Yturri house about midnight and did not return until around 2:00 A.M. Santa Anna impatiently ordered more coffee and threatened to run Ben through if it was not delivered immediately. As he served them, Ben overheard Almonte remark that the attack would "cost them much." Santa Anna snapped that the cost was of no importance, "it must be done."

Then they left the house to launch the final assault on the Alamo.

Sunday, March 6, 1836: *The Last Day*

San Antonio de Bexar

It very nearly worked, just as Santa Anna had planned it.

Just after midnight the four columns had silently taken their positions around the Alamo. There, lying flat on their stomachs in the moist grass, the *soldados* had waited and, deprived of their overcoats, shivered in the cold night air.

Then, around 5:00 A.M., Santa Anna himself had been seen, riding toward the reserves stationed at the northern battery. The Mexican artillery would be mute that morning. Santa Anna knew that his cannon would do more damage to his own attacking troops than to the enemy. Therefore the guns had been pulled back from the embrasures to afford the commander a view of the assault.

The sight of His Excellency arriving at his position was too much for some of the cold, anxious *soldados*. Someone shouted "Viva Santa Anna! Viva the Republic!" and the cry quickly spread along the columns.

Santa Anna motioned to the Zapadore bugler, Jose Maria Gonzales. The bugler sounded the call to "Attention." Then the "Charge." Then, again at Santa Anna's directive, Gonzales blew another shrill bugle call. The *soldado* prisoner within the Alamo would have recognized it as the Deguello, from a verb meaning "to slit the throat." The Spanish had adopted it from the Moors, and Santa Anna used it to remind his troops that no quarter would be shown the Texian garrison. Colonel de la Peña recalled, "we soon heard that terrible bugle call of death, which stirred our hearts, altered our expressions, and aroused us all suddenly from our painful meditation."

A rocket shot into the sky, augmenting the pale moonlight, as the screaming Mexican *soldados* surged forward against all four sides of the Alamo.

Moments earlier, as Travis' adjutant, John J. Baugh, made his morning rounds, he might have suspected that he was the only man awake in all of San Antonio de Bexar. Then suddenly the enemy army was charging from out of the darkness. "Colonel Travis," Baugh shouted into the Alamo headquarters, "the Mexicans are coming!"

Suddenly awake, Travis sprang from his cot. He grabbed his shotgun and sword and bolted from the room. Joe reached for a rifle and followed. "The Mexicans are upon us and we'll give them Hell!" Travis shouted as he raced toward the north wall.

Aroused by the commotion, other Texians scrambled to the battlements, their adrenaline flooding away their drowsiness. They grabbed for their rifles, muskets, shotguns—all waiting, loaded and ready—and fired into the advancing columns. Artillerymen placed their torches on the touchholes of their already charged cannon. The big guns boomed and recoiled, sending their deadly grapeshot into the massed columns.

William Ward appeared at the artillery emplacement above the gate. Below him, Gregorio Esparza dashed from the low barracks to join the cannon crews in the church. His wife and children followed, taking refuge in the musty sacristy. There, Susanna Dickinson held her daughter close as the cannons thundered from the artillery emplacement at the rear of the church. Anthony Wolf's two young sons sat nearby. The blankets in which they were wrapped could not keep them from trembling.

Then suddenly Susanna saw David Crockett enter. In that room, which once had served as a chapel, he "fell upon his knees [and] committed himself to his God," she reported. Then he charged back outside, presumably joining Micajah Autry, Daniel Cloud, and the other Tennessee Mounted Volunteers at the palisade.

In fact the one hundred twenty-five *soldados* in Colonel Morales fourth column, sniping at the south wall from behind the *jacales* that still stood, were little more than a diversion. Santa Anna was throwing his first three columns, nearly twelve hundred men, at the north wall. Colonel Duque's second column advanced toward the center of the wall. General Cos' first column, surging toward the northwest corner, and Colonel Romero's third column, striking at the low walled corrals on the east side, were attempts to outflank the Texian position on the north.

A Mexican soldier, rushing toward the Alamo's west wall with Cos' first column, reported:

> Although the distance was short, the fire from the enemy's cannon was fearful. We fell back; more than forty men fell around me in a few moments. One can but admire the stubborn resistance of our enemy, and the constant bravery of all of our troops. It seemed every cannon or ball or pistol shot of the enemy imbedded itself in the breast of our men.

De la Peña, advancing with Duque's second column against Travis' artillery position on the north wall, observed that "a single cannon volley did away with half the company of *cazadores* from Toluca."

Two of the Toluca captains fell, mortally wounded. A ball struck Colonel Duque in the thigh. He fell and almost was trampled by his charging men. Command of his column passed to General Castrillon.

The terrible noise of battle awakened the citizens of Bexar, some of whom watched from their windows or from the flat roofs of their houses. *Alcalde* Francisco Antonio Ruiz reported that the Texian artillery fire "resembled a constant thunder." Almonte's cook, Ben, saw the whole interior of the Alamo "perfectly illuminated" by the firing of the Americans within. Santa Anna, observing from the northern gun emplacement, also noted that the Texian artillery and musket fire "illuminated the interior of the Fortress and its walls and ditches."

Once the first and second columns had crowded under the Alamo's west and north walls, they were at least safe from the Texian artillery. However the third column, attacking the low walls on the east side, were still exposed to raking cannon fire from the apse of the church and from the guns in the corrals. In desperation, Romero's *soldados* shifted around to the north, mingling with the second column.

Cos' first column stalled under the rifle and musket fire from the west wall. They, too, veered north. De la Peña wrote, "All united at one point, mixing and forming a confused mass."

Only a few of the ladders had made it to the wall. However the *soldados* discovered that they could climb the uneven timbers that braced the crumbling wall. But they were climbing into a withering fire, and those few who made it to the top of the wall were beaten back by pistol fire, Texian rifle butts, and even Mexican bayonets captured from Cos after the battle of Bexar. De la Peña wrote:

> . . . the courage of our soldiers was not diminished as they saw their comrades falling dead or wounded, and they hurried to occupy their places and to avenge them, climbing over their bleeding bodies. The sharp reports of the rifles, the whistling of bullets, the groans of the wounded, the cursing of the men, the sighs and anguished cries of the dying, the arrogant harangues of the officers, the noise of the instruments of war, and the inordinate shouts of the attackers, who climbed vigorously, bewildered all and made of this moment a tremendous and critical one.

Defense of the Alamo

The terrible chaos beneath the north wall endured for perhaps fifteen minutes. Watching—enraged at the stalemate—Santa Anna ordered his reserves into the battle. The advancing four hundred *soldados* gave the Alamo artillery one more target, and the Texians took advantage of it. Four officers and twenty-one Zapadores fell as they charged into the disorderly mass below the north wall.

With their arrival, the tide inevitably turned against the defenders. Many of the Texians on the west and east walls had shifted to reinforce the defenders at the north batteries. Only a few Texians had fallen. But considering the uneven ratio and the sparse number of defenders on the wall, any loss became critical. Worse, the Texians had discharged almost all of their loaded rifles and muskets. The once continual fire from the walls dwindled to sporadic shots. It was impossible to reload while trying to beat back the attackers scrambling up the walls. There were just too many Mexicans. Too few Texians.

Standing atop the north wall, Colonel William Barret Travis perceived the situation becoming desperate. Fighting beside him, ironically enough, were some of the *Tejanos* that Travis had previously maligned in his correspondence to the Convention. Now, over the din of battle, he yelled to them, "*¡No rendirse, muchachos!*" ("Don't surrender, boys!")

Travis fired his shotgun into the melee below him. Joe fired his rifle. Then the newly arrived reserve column discharged a volley. Struck in the forehead, Travis spun and rolled down the ramp, ending in a sitting position against the sloping earth that braced the wall.

The Mexicans scrambling over the north wall literally entered the Alamo over Travis' dead body.

Witnessing his master's death was all Joe could take. He bolted back to the Alamo headquarters, from where he continued to snipe at the Mexicans through loopholes in the wall. Other Texians followed his retreat.

About that same time Cos detached his column from the north and swept back down the sparsely defended west wall. There were no timbers to facilitate climbing, but there were cannon embrasures cut into the adobe that some of the Mexicans could squeeze through, even as others were boosted over the top of the eleven-foot wall.

The perimeter had collapsed. Overrun and outflanked, the defenders abandoned the north wall and the northern end of the west wall. Many, like Joe, took refuge in the Alamo's rooms: the artillerymen's barracks, granary, and long barracks on the east, and the quarters on the west. However a few Texians made their last stand in the open, including a handsome, blond-haired man that de la Peña mistook for Travis. "He would take a few steps and stop, turning his proud face toward us to discharge his shots; he fought like a true soldier," de la Peña wrote. "Finally he died, but he died after trading his life very dearly."

Following Cos' example, Col. Romero veered his command back to its original objective—the eastern corrals—and this time swept over the low walls into the cattle pen.

It had all happened so fast. From his vantage point with the artillery at the back of the church, Almaron Dickinson saw the Mexicans flooding into the fort. He rushed down the ramp into the sacristy. "Great God, Sue, the Mexicans are inside our walls!" he cried to his wife. "All is lost! If they spare you, save my child!" What more could he say? There was no time for sentiment, for lingering farewells. He gave her a quick kiss and returned to his post.

At this point the battle was indeed lost. Any Texian remaining within the fort faced almost certain death from musket ball or bayonet. However a contingency of defenders in the horse corral, reinforced by men retreating from the cattle pen, opted for another alternative—a chance to live and fight another day. All of the Mexicans were to the north and south. In the darkness, at least, the eastern prairie appeared wide open. Those Texians still carrying loaded weapons fired into Romero's column. Then the Texians scrambled over the wall, circled behind the church, and raced through the underbrush for the Gonzales road.

Manuel Loranca, a sergeant in the Dolores cavalry, claimed that sixty-two Texians "sallied from the east side of the fort," but his estimate must have been high.

The flight was exactly what the Mexican cavalry, stationed at the Alameda, had been waiting for. "As soon as I saw this, I sent a company of the Dolores regiment . . . ," Sesma recalled.

The skilled cavalrymen with their eight-foot lances swooped down on the fleeing men. In an effort to aid the refugees, Dickinson hastily spun around a church cannon and fired at the charging horsemen, perhaps wounding or killing a few. The rest galloped over the escaping Texians.

Texians on foot, without loaded firearms, had no chance at all against mounted lancers. "Only one of these made resistance; a very active man, armed with a double barrel gun and a single barrel pistol, with which he killed a corporal of the lancers named Eugenio," reported Sergeant Loranca. He added that all the escaping Texians were killed by the lance, "except one, who ensconced himself under a bush and it was necessary to shoot him."

Dense clouds of pungent gun smoke drifting in the predawn darkness added to the terrible confusion as the Mexicans poured into the compound from the north, the west, and the east. But they found themselves in a deadly crossfire. Supported by riflemen from the south end of the compound, the Texian artillerymen on the emplacement inside the gate whirled their guns around and discharged deadly cannister at the enemy advancing from the north. The defenders entrenched in the rooms along the east and west walls fired through windows and loopholes at both flanks of the Mexicans in the fort. De la Peña remembered:

> The tumult was great, the disorder frightful; it seemed as if the furies had descended upon us; different groups of soldiers were firing in all directions, on their comrades and on their officers, so that one was as likely to die by a friendly hand as by an enemy's.

Sixteen-year-old Galba Fuqua staggered into the sacristy. Susanna Dickinson saw, in horror, that his jaw had been shattered by a musket ball. The pale, frightened boy stood before her, supporting his bloody, disjointed jaw with his hand, trying to tell her something. But, sadly, she could not understand him. The boy gave up—and returned to the battle.

General Morales' column, sniping from the *jacales*, had not attempted a direct assault on the palisade or the lunette that guarded the gate. However their mere presence posed a threat that required Texians to oppose them rather than reinforce the northern defenses. But with the Texians on the south wall suddenly distracted by the Mexicans descending from the north, Morales led a quick charge against the southwest corner. A musket volley dropped some of the Texians. *Soldados* scurried up their two ladders, and their plunging bayonets finished off the few remaining defenders on the gun emplacement. The Texians' formidable eighteen-pounder had been captured.

The Texian artillerymen on the emplacement inside the gate were quickly overwhelmed. The Mexicans now raced to the low barracks. They threw open the gates, admitting the rest of Morales' men. Some of the *soldados* surged up onto the artillery position over the gate. William Ward and his gunners fell under their bayonets.

Other Mexicans charged into the rooms below. Here they found James Bowie. Since the siege had begun, it seemed, he had become an unwilling witness to a contest as to whether his fever or the Mexican bayonets would claim his life. But if he was now still alive, if he was conscious, if there remained any strength in his body, Big Jim Bowie would have tried—one last time—to prove that he was a hard man to kill.

The Texians manning a lunette midway down the west wall found themselves trapped between Mexicans to their north and south. They also attempted a retreat from the Alamo, this time charging west for the river.

Sesma reported fifty in this group, but, again, the estimate certainly was high. Again he dispatched a company of cavalry. This time the Texians took cover in a ditch "and made a vigorous defense of it." Sesma sent in reinforcements, and the Texians "that were protected in that position and who were ready to sell their lives at a very high price were overwhelmed in a few minutes and were killed."

David Crockett and the handful of Tennessee volunteers at the palisade essentially were the only defenders who remained in the open. They shifted, attempting a defense of the low wall in front of the church. Enrique Esparza, who could hardly have seen anything from the sacristy, later maintained that the Texians "clubbed with their rifles and stabbed with their Bowie knives." Unfortunately those weapons had little effect against Mexican volley fire followed by an advancing wall of bayonets attached to the end of five-foot-long muskets. Of the few surviving Texians, some scrambled over the palisade and the rest fell back toward the church. Not all of them made it. Several witnesses later reported seeing Crockett's body in the area in front of the church.

CROCKETT'S FIGHT WITH THE MEXICANS.

The Mexicans had captured all of the outer walls. Only small pockets of Texian resistance remained in the rooms along the east and west walls and in the old church itself.

The Mexicans moved from room to room along the west wall. Juana Alsbury, with little Alejo clutched to her breast, heard the Mexicans outside her door. She persuaded her teenaged sister, Gertrudis, to call out, alerting the Mexicans that only women occupied the room. When Gertrudis opened the door, a burly *soldado* cursed at her and yanked the shawl from her shoulders. Other Mexicans pushed into the room, demanding money. A gallant Texian named Mitchell shoved past the *soldados* and tried to protect Juana and her son. The Mexicans quickly bayoneted him.

Then a panicked young *Tejano* raced into the room, grabbed Juana's arm, and attempted to hide behind her. The *soldados* jerked him free and plunged their bayonets into him, also. Several Mexicans fired into his lifeless body. Then they began rifling through Juana's trunk, plundering her money, jewels, and even her clothes. But the two women and the baby would survive the battle.

Nearby, the Mexicans found Joe hiding in Travis' headquarters. A Captain Barragan, presuming the slave to be a noncombatant—which was not exactly true—prevented two of the *soldados* from killing the young black man. Joe also survived. Travis' headquarters were quickly looted, one *soldado* walking off with a pair of deerskin saddlebags marked "W. B. Travis."

To the east, the doors to the granary and long barracks were protected by semicircular barricades of earth crammed between two animal hides stretched on wooden frames. Texians in these rooms fired determinedly over the barricades and through windows and loopholes punched in the walls.

The Mexicans resorted to the captured artillery on the west wall and used the same strategy to take each room. First a cannon blast to clear the barricade. Then a volley of musket fire into the dark doorway. Then the shrieking *soldados* charged into the blackness. Only random flashes of gunfire illuminated the desperate and bloody hand-to-hand fighting that ensued within each room.

Most of the rooms had no other exit except out into the courtyard. The Texians entrenched in each room could hear the battle progressing relentlessly toward them, but they could only prime their weapons and wait for their turn to die in that hellish darkness.

The granary fell. Then the long barracks.

De la Peña claimed to have seen more than one white flag poking out through a hole or doorway. He wrote:

> Our trusting soldiers, seeing these demonstrations, would confidently enter their quarters, but those among the enemy who had not pleaded for mercy, who had no thought of surrendering, and who relied on no other recourse than selling their lives dearly, would meet them with pistol shots and bayonets. Thus betrayed, our men rekindled their anger and at every moment fresh skirmishes broke out with renewed fury.

Here de la Peña's account rings false. Not the part about some of the Texians trying to surrender. However futile the effort might be, there was no shame in surrender—not for these valiant, exhausted men who already had displayed their courage by staying, who already had endured so much during that long, bitter siege.

Rather the improbability of de la Peña's account lies in his implication that the *soldados*, under orders to take no prisoners, might have considered honoring a flag of truce. Especially in their killing frenzy, after seeing so many of their comrades and officers fall.

When the *soldados* reached the Alamo's *calabozo* at the southern end of the granary they discovered the captured Mexican who had been interpreting the bugle calls. Enrique Esparza later heard that "this poor fellow was afterwards killed because Santa Anna thought he was a deserter."

Lieutenant Jose Maria Torres of the reserve Zapadores, followed by Lieutenant Damasco Martinez, scrambled onto the roof of the old convent building and jerked down the defenders' flag that fluttered above it.

In the expanding glow from the eastern horizon, several Texian artillerymen at the back of the church spotted the two Mexican officers. The Texians grabbed their rifles. Martinez fell. Then Torres. But not before he had hoisted the Mexican tricolor over the Alamo.

That was appropriate, for only the defenders in the church remained. Its entrance was protected by a tall barricade, probably constructed of sandbags and set back inside the entrance to allow access at either side. The Texians firing over the barricade stalled the Mexicans massing outside.

Colonel Morales ordered the captured eighteen-pounder aimed at the barricade. The big gun boomed; the barricade collapsed. The Mexicans fired a volley and then shoved inside.

Dickinson was ready. The old church trembled as a cannon in the apse fired downward into the Mexicans charging through the door.

But there was no time to reload. More Mexicans emerged through the thick, choking cloud of smoke left in the wake of that blast. They trampled over their fallen comrades, up the artillery ramp. Dickinson, Gregorio Esparza, and the others discharged their rifles into the throng—and then died beneath the bayonets.

Bleeding from his wounds, Major Robert Evans crawled painfully toward one of the powder magazines, a torch in his fist. The thirty-six-year-old Irishman served as master of ordnance, and it was his job to keep the powder from falling into enemy hands. A Mexican musket ball ended his effort.

Tejano Brigido Guerrero had had enough of this fight. He darted through the smoke into the dark sacristy where the women and children huddled in sheer terror. Jacob Walker, blood streaming from a wound, also sought refuge there. Mrs. Dickinson, seated on her cot in one corner, held little Angelina close. Ana Esparza crouched in another corner, Enrique and her other children clinging to her dress. Walker retreated to another dark corner, and thought again of his wife and four children.

Deafening flashes preceded the entry of the Mexican *soldados*. One of Anthony Wolf's young boys, seated against the wall near the door, rose to his feet and pulled his blanket across his shoulders. The *soldados* saw only a shape in that dim light. They bayoneted him before the screams of women alerted them that noncombatants occupied the room.

From somewhere Anthony Wolf appeared. He grabbed his remaining son, ducked under the Mexican bayonets, and ran up the cannon ramp to the rear of the church where they were silhouetted in the dawning light. *Soldados* fired after them. Father and son toppled over the edge—dead before they hit the ground below.

The *soldados* in the dark sacristy probed more carefully among the women and children. They discovered Jacob Walker in the corner. Again the deafening muskets roared. Then Susanna Dickinson saw four Mexicans hoist Walker's body on their bayonets "like a farmer does a bundle of fodder on his pitchfork."

Brigido Guerrero also was found. The *Tejano* pled for mercy. "He told them that he was a prisoner in the Alamo and had been brought there against his will," Enrique Esparza recalled. "He said he had tried to escape and join Santa Anna's men." Incredibly, the *soldados* believed him.

Another Mexican threatened Ana Esparza with his bayonet and demanded, "Where is the Texians' money?"

"If they had money, find it," she retorted. The *soldado* slapped her. Enrique screamed. An officer appeared, chased the *soldado* from the room, and placed the women and children under his protection.

Now, almost suddenly, it seemed strangely quiet. *Soldados* escorted the women and children out of the Alamo. They walked through pools of blood. Stepped over grotesque, smoldering bodies. Inhaled the stench of death. Mrs. Dickinson recalled spotting Crockett's mutilated body between the church and the long barrack, "his peculiar cap lying by his side." Across the river in the town, all the survivors were placed in the Musquiz home, the same house the Dickinsons had resided in before the battle.

As the sun broke free of the horizon, a sickly sweet blue haze of powder smoke still drifted over the crimson stained grounds of the Alamo. More blood would yet soak into that hallowed earth. The *soldados* sifted through the enemy corpses, looting what they could find, plunging a bayonet into any Texian form that moaned or moved.

A Bexareno girl also searched through the compound. Then she stopped. Tears streaming from her eyes, she bent down over a fallen Texian, folded his hands across his body, and gently wiped the black grime from his face. Then she placed a small cross over his blood-dampened breast.

The Mexicans saw her and ran her off. One of them spied a stray cat darting amid the dead bodies. The *soldado* raised his musket and fired. After all, it was a Texian cat.

Only then did Santa Anna himself ride down from the northern battery, skirting past the bodies that littered the ground outside the Alamo, and through the south gate. Already he was planning a speech for his victorious troops.

But first, as de la Peña described it, an "unpleasant episode" took place. General Castrillon suddenly appeared leading a haggard group of Texian prisoners. De la Peña said there were seven. Ramon Caro counted only five.

Perhaps they were among the garrison's sick and wounded, discovered in an upper room of the long barracks after the bloodlust of battle had passed. Since they had offered no resistance during the fight, Castrillon had spared them from the "no quarter" rule. But Ramon Caro remembered that when Castrillon presented the prisoners, "he was severely reprimanded for not having killed them on the spot, after which [Santa Anna] turned his back upon Castrillon while the soldiers stepped out of their ranks and set upon the prisoners until they were all killed."

The de la Peña account provided a more vivid description of the executions:

> The commanders and officers were outraged at this action and did not support the order [of execution], hoping that once the fury of the moment had blown over these men would be spared; but several officers who were around the president and who, perhaps, had not been present during the moment of danger, became noteworthy by an infamous deed, surpassing the soldiers in cruelty. They thrust themselves forward, in order to flatter their commander, and with swords in hand, fell upon these unfortunate, defenseless men just as a tiger leaps upon his prey. Though tortured before they were killed, these unfortunates died without complaining and without humiliating themselves before their torturers.

More controversial, de la Peña also identified one of the executed prisoners as "the naturalist David Crockett."

If so, Santa Anna did not seem aware of it. He ordered *alcalde* Francisco Antonio Ruiz to be brought over from Bexar to identify the bodies of Travis, Bowie, and Crockett.

Apparently Santa Anna wanted to be certain. He also had Joe point out Travis' body. And Ben, the Negro cook, claimed that he, too, was ordered to indicate the bodies of the Alamo's leaders, "whom I had before known."

Again His Excellency personally busied himself with details. The Texian bodies were to be stacked and burned, but the brave Mexican *soldados* would receive a Christian burial in the Campo Santo. However, *alcalde* Ruiz, who was assigned to dispose of the bodies, later conceded there was not enough room in the graveyard for all the Mexican fatalities, so he had some of their corpses thrown into the river.

Only one Alamo defender would be spared the flames. Francisco Esparza secured permission from General Cos to have his brother, Gregorio, buried at the Campo Santo.

Around 8:00 A.M. Santa Anna dictated a report back to Mexico City describing his "complete and glorious triumph that will render its memory imperishable."

On that last phrase, alone, he was more accurate than he knew.

Certainly he exaggerated when he claimed to have killed more than six hundred foreigners. He reported his own casualties as seventy *soldados* killed and three hundred more wounded. If he also was diminishing his losses, most of his officers followed his example in their subsequent accounts.

Santa Anna neglected to mention that his failure to provide a medical staff would result in the deaths of many of his wounded. Or that his corrupt brother-in-law, Colonel Ricardo Dromundo, would only release the supplies he had to those who could afford to pay for them.

Several flags had been taken from the Alamo. Santa Anna enclosed the blue silk banner of the New Orleans Greys with his report. Perhaps it was the same flag that Lieutenant Jose Maria Torres had lost his life removing from the roof of the long barracks. Santa Anna asserted that the flag "will show plainly the true intentions of the treacherous colonists, and of their abettors, who came from parts of the United States of the North."

Aide-de-camp Fernando Urissa spotted Santa Anna about that time. As Urissa bowed, Santa Anna commented, "Much blood has been shed, but the battle is over; it was but a small affair."

However, when Santa Anna and his staff returned to the Yturri house, Ben heard Colonel Almonte remark that "another such victory would ruin them."

Colonel Sanchez Navarro repeated those sentiments in his diary. He wrote, "It is well said: 'With another such victory we will be carried away to the devil.'"

De la Peña observed that "the taking of the Alamo was not considered a happy event, but rather a defeat that saddened us all."

Washington-on-the-Brazos

That morning, while William Fairfax Gray breakfasted, a courier arrived with Travis' dispatch dated March 3. The delegates crowded into the convention hall to hear his words read.

> ...I shall have to fight the enemy on his own terms. I will, however, do the best I can under the circumstances; and I feel confident that the determined valour and desperate courage, heretofore evinced by my men, will not fail them in the last struggle, and although they may be sacrificed to the vengeance of a Gothic enemy, the victory will cost the enemy so dear, that it will be worse for him than a defeat.

Robert Potter called for the Convention to adjourn and march to the relief of the Alamo. Houston opposed the motion. The delegates could better serve the new republic as Founding Fathers rather than as cannon fodder. But he himself would go to take command of the volunteers mustering under Neill and Williamson at Gonzales.

That afternoon, about the time *alcalde* Ruiz finally lit the three funeral pyres, Sam Houston, dressed more like an Indian than a general, left Washington-on-the-Brazos with three aides to ride to the rescue of the Alamo.

San Antonio de Bexar

The last defender of the Alamo had already died. Somehow in the dark and confusion, he had eluded the Mexican lancers and found a hiding place under a bridge. But in the daylight that followed the battle, a Mexican woman spotted him. She reported him to the *soldados*. He was immediately executed.

The identity of this last Alamo defender remains unknown.

Perhaps he was an idealistic young Kentucky lawyer who had declared, "death in the cause of liberty and humanity is not cause for shuddering."

Perhaps it was a gentle North Carolinian who longed—one more time —to share the moonlight with his wife and children.

The Aftermath: *Remember the Alamo!*

It took Sam Houston five days to make the easy two-day ride to Gonzales. Like Travis, he had lingered at Burnham's Crossing. In retrospect, Texas would never have forgiven his tardiness if the Alamo had not already fallen before his departure from Washington-on-the-Brazos. Why his lack of urgency? Perhaps he believed the reports that Fannin had relieved the Alamo. But other evidence suggests that he doubted the reports that the Mexicans had invaded Texas. He distrusted Fannin and apparently Travis as well. They might be pawns of the council engaged in a political ploy to remove him from the convention.

If only he had heard from the one man he trusted—James Bowie.

When Houston finally rode into Gonzales around 4:00 P.M. on March 11, some four hundred men had already assembled there. News of the fall of the Alamo had not yet reached the colonies. At Goliad the day before, a soldier named E. Thomas wrote his father, "Davy Crockett and James Bowie are fighting like Tigers."

But shortly after Houston reached Gonzales, two Bexarenos—Anselmo and Andres Barcena—arrived with a disturbing report that the Alamo had been taken and all its defenders killed. The rumor devastated tiny Gonzales, which had contributed more men to the Alamo than any other place. To quell the panic, Houston promptly ordered the Bexarenos arrested as enemy spies.

But he had to know for sure. He sent out his two best scouts, old "Deaf" Smith and Captain Henry Karnes, to ascertain the truth. Only twenty miles to the west, they came across Susanna Dickinson with her infant daughter, Angelina, escorted by Almonte's cook, Ben, and Travis' slave, Joe.

In the days after the battle, Santa Anna himself had interviewed the female survivors clustered in the Musquiz house. Ana Esparza had been defiant. Enrique recalled his mother's interrogation by the Mexican commander.

"I suppose if I let you go you will raise your children to fight Mexico."

"Yes," my mother said. Her sorrow over the death of my father had made her not afraid to die, I think.

"You ought to have your ears cut off," he replied.

This made me and the other children scream.

"Get the mob out!" Santa Anna said. "Give each woman two dollars and a blanket."

But Santa Anna had showed a special interest in Mrs. Dickinson. He wanted to take her and Angelina back to Mexico. He would take good care of the child—and the mother, too.

Susanna broke down, sobbing. Colonel Almonte interceded in her behalf.

Santa Anna shrugged. Well, they could still be useful. They could tell the Texians the fate of all who opposed the Napoleon of the West.

Susanna got her two dollars and blanket, and Santa Anna also provided her a horse and an escort—Almonte's cook, Ben.

Travis' slave, Joe, would make another convenient messenger of defeat. But first His Exellency wanted to impress Joe with a grand review of the Mexican army. General Antonio Gaona's First Brigade had arrived in Bexar on March 8, and General Eugenio Tolsa's Second Brigade finally dragged in on March 11. The review was impressive, but Joe shrewdly doubted Santa Anna's claim that he now had eight thousand men under arms.

Santa Anna also interviewed Joe, inquiring how many soldiers from the United States had joined the Texian army. Were more expected? When Joe nodded, Santa Anna boasted that he had enough men to march all the way to Washington, D.C.

On the evening of March 13 the scouts delivered the survivors of the Alamo—and the confirmation of the garrison's fate—to Houston. As Mrs. Dickinson related what had happened, Houston sobbed with her. The whole town of Gonzales joined in the mourning. Its orphans and widows, some of them pregnant, wailed late into the night.

Houston realized that if a slow moving party of survivors could reach Gonzales from Bexar, so could the Mexican army. And he did not have enough men to fight. On March 14 he gave his first real command to his new army. Retreat. He would fall back to the Colorado River. Order Fannin's four hundred to join him there.

The already suffering citizens of Gonzales now had to endure a flight across the prairie. Houston provided them with three of the army's four wagons. Texians carefully helped young Sydney Kellogg into one of them. Her husband and brother had both fallen in the Alamo, and her baby was due at any time.

The citizens of Gonzales would have to endure even more. Houston ordered their town burned; he wanted nothing left that might benefit the Mexicans.

On the second day of the retreat someone noticed that Alamo defender Isaac Millsap's blind wife, Mary, and her seven young children were not among the refugees. Houston sent a detachment of men back for them.

The bitter cold winter had transformed into a wet spring, and the heavens joined in the weeping. The army trudged through quagmires that once had been roads. They reached the flooded Colorado River on March 17. The army helped the civilians cross first. Houston's men finally forded the river on March 20.

Just in time. General Sesma, with eight hundred troops and two cannon, arrived on the west bank the next day.

Having achieved his crushing victory at Bexar—as General Arredondo had done before him—Santa Anna had assumed that all further resistance would crumble. All that remained of the Texas campaign would be to drive the perfidious foreigners to the Sabine. That could be done with a three-pronged operation.

He had dispatched General Gaona with eight hundred troops to sweep around the north to Nacogdoches.

He sent Colonel Juan Morales, so competent in his attack on the Alamo's southern defenses, with a thousand *soldados* to reinforce General Urrea's five hundred moving against Goliad. Then that column would advance eastward along the coast.

General Sesma would march straight through the center of Texas, trampling over Gonzales, San Felipe, Washington-on-the-Brazos.

General Pedro Andrade's force would remain at Bexar. And so, for the moment would Santa Anna. The war now bored him. He planned to return to Mexico City with his new "bride" and leave his second commander in chief General Filisola to oversee the mopping up.

Most of Houston's men wanted to fight Sesma's column encamped across the river. Avenge the Alamo. That defeat had finally aroused Texas from its apathy. Reinforcements rushed to join Houston. His little army swelled to eight hundred, a thousand, perhaps even twelve hundred men.

But Houston held them back with a tight rein. He had numerical superiority, but no artillery. To attempt to cross the river under Sesma's cannon fire could be devastating. Moreover, even if they won the battle, it would hardly be conclusive, and the Texian force would be weakened, vulnerable to a flank attack.

Better to wait for Fannin.

But once again, Fannin never came.

Despite his orders from Houston to withdraw, Fannin procrastinated. He had sent a contingency of troops under Captain Amon B. King to evacuate the citizens of Refugio, which stood in the path of Urrea's advance. Fannin could not abandon those men. Not until March 17 did he learn that King's men had suffered the same fate as Johnson and Grant.

Even then Fannin wasted another precious day preparing for his retreat. He ignored Houston's directive to sink his cannon in the river. He would pull them with him.

Fannin did not withdraw from Goliad until late in the morning of March 19. Dragging the artillery through the mud made the retreat eastward excruciatingly slow. By early afternoon he was within a mile of Coleto Creek. Suddenly Mexican cavalry was spotted to the rear. Some of Fannin's officers proposed a dash to the tree-lined creek. Instead Fannin halted on the prairie and formed his men into a square.

The Mexican cavalry galloped in a wide circle around the Texians, blocking access to the creek. Then Cos' Mexican infantry appeared from the west, surrounded the Texians, and the battle began.

Throughout the day Fannin held off the Mexicans. The Texians suffered nine killed and another fifty wounded—Fannin among them—but they had inflicted more severe casualties on the Mexicans—fifty dead and one hundred forty wounded.

But by nightfall Fannin had run out of water. He could not ease the suffering of his wounded. He could not cool down his cannon. He was surrounded on the prairie. Outnumbered.

The next morning he surrendered his command.

Fannin naively expected they would be expelled from Texas. Santa Anna had other plans.

The Texians were marched back to Goliad and ignominiously imprisoned within their own Fort Defiance. On Palm Sunday, March 27, three columns of Texian prisoners were marched out under armed escort. The Texians assumed they were being taken to Matamoras. But a short distance from the fort the columns halted. They had hardly marched far enough to justify a rest stop. The Mexicans formed up to the side. They leveled their muskets at the prisoners. And fired.

Somehow twenty-eight Texians, including the young New Orleans Grey Herman Ehrenberg, scrambled into the underbrush, made it to the river, and escaped. Behind them, more than three hundred Texians lay dead.

The wounded Texians who had remained at Goliad, including Fannin himself, were executed in the fort. Only the Texian doctors were spared. Some of them would be sent to Bexar to treat the Mexicans wounded in the assault on the Alamo.

Santa Anna's war was going well. But he abandoned his plans to return to Mexico when he learned that Sesma faced a Texian force of around a thousand men on the Colorado. On March 31 Santa Anna left Bexar in his splendid carriage. General Andrade remained at Bexar with a thousand *soldados*. Accompanied by nearly seven hundred Mexicans troops, the Napoleon of the West rode to join Sesma's force. It was time to end this tedious war.

By then Sam Houston had learned of Fannin's capitulation at Coleto Creek. Houston's force now comprised the last hope for Texas. Again he bellowed the unpopular order to retreat.

Some two or three hundred Texians promptly abandoned the army, racing home to get their families out of harm's way. It seemed the whole population of Texas had joined in a desperate flight to the Sabine that would become known as the "Runaway Scrape."

Those who remained in the Texian army threatened mutiny. They wanted to fight Santa Anna, not withdraw before him. Sam Houston had become the most despised man in Texas. But somehow he herded them through the mud and rain back to the Brazos. They arrived at San Felipe, Stephen F. Austin's capital, on March 28. Surely Houston would make a stand here.

But the next day Houston ordered the army north, up the Brazos River. By then desertions had further reduced his force. Only about five hundred men sloshed through the mud behind him.

The Texians camped in the bottomlands at Jared Groce's plantation. There in the dense woods Houston finally found time to drill his troops in an effort to transform the undisciplined rabble into some semblance of an army.

Reinforcements drifted in. The army began to grow again.

On April 7 Thomas Jefferson Rusk rode into the Texian camp. He had been elected secretary of war by the convention. Dr. Lorenzo de Zavala was the republic's vice-president, and David G. Burnet, a man whom Houston derisively referred to as a "hog thief," was president. Burnet held Houston in similar contempt and had sent him a dispatch through Rusk.

> The enemy are laughing you to scorn. You must fight them.
> You must retreat no further. The country expects you to fight.
> The salvation of the country depends on your doing so.

Rusk added that he had been authorized to assume command of the army if Houston did not take the offensive.

Houston inquired as to the whereabouts of the new government. Rusk replied that they had abandoned Washington-on-the-Brazos and moved south to Harrisburg. Houston snorted that President Burnet and his cabinet, all able-bodied men, had retreated a good deal faster than the army.

David G. Burnet

That same day Santa Anna, whose own bodyguard had increased Sesma's column to fifteen hundred troops, arrived at San Felipe. The town, like Gonzales, had been burned to the ground.

Mexican intelligence had informed Santa Anna that Houston was camped to the north. More important, however, Santa Anna had learned that Burnet and his cabinet were at Harrisburg, only thirty miles to the southeast. The Napoleon of the West formed a new strategy. He would capture the Texian government and quickly end the war.

Detaching companies of grenadiers and mounted dragoons, some seven hundred men, from Sesma's slow moving column, Santa Anna headed for Harrisburg.

On April 11 the Texians, still encamped at Groce's, received a generous and timely gift donated to their cause by the citizens of Cincinnati, Ohio —two small cannon that the Texians christened the "Twin Sisters."

The next day Houston broke camp. Using the steamboat *Yellowstone*, it took two days to cross his army, now over eight hundred strong, to the east bank of the flooded Brazos.

Delayed by the mud, Santa Anna entered Harrisburg on the evening of April 15, only to learn that President Burnet had left that morning for New Washington, nestled on the coast twenty miles to the east. His Excellency ordered Colonel Almonte to take the fifty dragoons and gallop in pursuit.

It almost worked. Only moments before Almonte's cavalry thundered into New Washington on April 16, someone gave a warning. Burnet, his wife, Zavala, and the other members of the cabinet raced to a boat and frantically began rowing against the crashing surf.

Almonte's dragoons galloped up to the water's edge. The boat containing the Texian government was only scant yards away, its occupants engaged in a furious, but seemingly futile, struggle for life. The Mexicans easily could have shot them all.

But the gallant Almonte would not let his men fire. He had spotted Mrs. Burnet in the boat.

The Texas government escaped to a ship in the harbor.

That same day Houston's marching army approached a crossroads. In the midst of the fork stood a huge oak, later to be known as the "Whichway Tree."

Many in Houston's army expected the most despised man in Texas to take the northeast fork and continue all the way to the safety of the Sabine. Some historians today maintain that Houston still intended to retreat.

However as the army reached the fork, Houston fell back. The army itself made the decision. It took the south fork. Toward Harrisburg.

Arriving at New Washington, Santa Anna was disappointed to learn that the Texian government had escaped. He sent dispatches. General Filisola was to pursue Houston, who undoubtedly was retreating toward Nacogdoches. And Santa Anna ordered General Cos to detach five hundred fifty troops and rendezvous with Santa Anna's column.

On April 18 Deaf Smith intercepted a Mexican courier, whose dispatches were carried in a pair of buckskin saddlebags marked "W. B. Travis." The captured communications revealed critical information to Houston. Santa Anna himself was in the Mexican column at the coast.

Houston made a brief address to his men:

> Victory is certain. Trust in God and fear not! The victims of the Alamo and the names of those who were murdered at Goliad cry out for cool, deliberate vengeance. Remember the Alamo! Remember Goliad!

Following Santa Anna's trail, the Texian army forded the eastwardly flowing Buffalo Bayou then turned east and marched along its southern banks. They clomped across the tiny wooden bridge that spanned swollen Vince's Bayou. Another eight miles brought them to the great bend formed by the confluence of Buffalo Bayou with the southerly flowing river named for Saint Hyacinth.

San Jacinto

There, on April 20, amid the moss-draped trees along Buffalo Bayou, Houston established his camp. To the south extended a mile-wide prairie of tall, waving grass.

Apprised of Houston's proximity, Santa Anna hurriedly marched up to the lower end of the plain and also encamped in the trees. A subtle rise in the prairie, about two thirds the distance toward the Mexican camp, prevented the antagonists from seeing each other. But both sides knew the location of the enemy.

From Santa Anna's perspective, he had Houston trapped. To be sure, there was a ferry near the Texian camp that crossed to the east bank of the San Jacinto River. But it would take a full day, perhaps two, to make the crossing. For the moment, at least, Houston did not seem interested in retreat. That would change, of course, after Cos arrived with his five hundred fifty reinforcements. And the other Mexican columns were only a few days behind. The war was over.

In fact Santa Anna's location was hardly better than Houston's. He was backed up against boggy lagoons that could impede his own retreat. More over the Texians held a slight advantage—nine hundred men to Santa Anna's seven hundred.

At that moment neither side was considering retreat. Santa Anna initiated an artillery duel, pitting his twelve-pound Golden Standard against the Texians' Twin Sisters. A cavalry skirmish erupted on the west edge of the prairie. It seemed the battle might be joined that day.

But again to the frustration of his men, Houston curtly called back the cavalry.

Not yet.

Night descended. The Texians spread their bedrolls in the marshy grass, listened to the croaking bullfrogs, and only fought the mosquitoes.

Across the prairie the Mexicans worked furiously, erecting barricades of timber and boxes. It had occurred to Santa Anna that Houston's only real chance would be a night attack. Or he would strike at dawn, as Santa Anna had done at the Alamo. Throughout the night Santa Anna kept his troops awake and alert. Where were Cos and the reinforcements?

Sam Houston was still sleeping when General Cos, after a forced march through the night, arrived at the Mexican camp the next morning. The numerical advantage had shifted to the Mexicans. Now Santa Anna could relax. So could his exhausted army.

It may have been the eagle soaring overhead when Houston awoke that convinced him to attack that day. Or maybe it was just that he was staring up into a cloudless sky. No rain to dampen his men's gunpowder.

But first he needed that bridge over Vince's Bayou destroyed. Its absence would impede the arrival of more Mexican reinforcements. And it would cut off the main avenue of escape from the plain of San Jacinto.

It would be a risky job, because of Mexican lancer patrols. Houston assigned it to the one man in his army he trusted most. Private Deaf Smith.

Smith recruited six volunteers and set off at a gallop. He wanted to be back in time for the party.

At 3:30 P.M. Houston began arranging his troops in the shadows of the trees. Two horizontal lines of infantry. The Twin Sisters in the middle of the column. Cavalry on the right flank.

The Texian army was about to defy the rules of combat. They would march across an open prairie—in broad daylight—to attack a fortified position defended by superior numbers. All the odds were against them.

Riding before his ragged, unshaven army, Houston noted Captain Juan Seguin and his company of approximately twenty *Tejanos*. The general had proposed that they stay back and guard the baggage. The request dismayed Seguin. The *Tejanos*, too, had lost friends at the Alamo. They would fight.

It was nearly 4:00 P.M. Houston drew his sword, slashed the air in front of him, and called out, "Trail arms! Forward!"

The Texian army began its advance across the plain of San Jacinto. The men, their mud-stained faces taut with determination, moved almost silently through the tall grass. The only sound came from the Texian band.

It was not much of a band—a handful of drummers and fifers. They played "Come to the Bower," a jaunty, bawdy love song of the era. The unsung lyrics asked:

> Will you come to the bower I have shaded for you,
> Your bed will be roses all spangled with dew.
> There beneath this glad bower on roses you'll lie,
> With a blush on your cheek—but a smile in your eye.

No army ever marched into battle to a more curious anthem. It was, at least, a song of conquest.

As the Texians marched over the rise into view of the Mexican camp, Deaf Smith galloped in front of them. Flourishing an axe, he yelled, "Vince's bridge is down! Fight for your lives!"

The Twin Sisters boomed. The Texians fired a rifle volley. Someone shouted, "Remember the Alamo! Remember Goliad!" Others echoed the cry until it reverberated across the prairie, as the men broke ranks and surged forward.

Perhaps only then, when a mere handful of musket shots met them, did the Texians recognize their advantage. The Mexican army was in siesta. Santa Anna had been so overconfident he had not even posted advance sentries to alert of the Texian advance.

Yet a few of those Mexican musket shots brought down Houston's horse. Someone gave him another. He continued leading the charge, until a second musket ball shattered his ankle and killed that mount. The screaming Texians charged past him toward the barricades. The Texian cavalry thundered into the enemy's left flank, creating more panic and disorganization in the Mexican camp.

Illustration from Houston's 1855 memoirs depicting Houston's horse shot out from under him at the battle of San Jacinto.

Houston found a third horse, climbed into the saddle, and galloped after his army.

General Manuel Castrillon, the officer who had vainly tried to save some of the Alamo defenders, raced to the Golden Standard and attempted to organize a resistance. Somehow the Mexican cannoneers got off three hasty charges. But as the Texians poured over the barricades, the panicked *soldados* broke and ran. They encouraged Castrillon to flee with them. Standing erect on an ammunition box, he calmly folded his arms. "I've been in forty battles and never shown my back," he stated. "I'm too old to do it now."

A moment later he was dead. With all resistance gone, the battle was over. It had lasted twenty minutes.

But the subsequent slaughter would endure more than an hour. The enraged Texians had learned from Santa Anna the meaning of "no quarter." As they pursued the fleeing *soldados* through the tents, the Texians shot and clubbed and slashed every Mexican they overtook. The *soldados* who dropped to their knees, pleading, were more easily dispatched.

Houston, Rusk, and some of the other officers galloped through their midst, trying to restore order and end the massacre. "Gentlemen!" Houston bellowed with obvious irony. "I applaud your bravery. But damn your manners!"

In their flight, a large number of Mexicans splashed into the lagoons behind their camp, only to become bogged down in thigh deep mud. They made easy targets for the Texians standing on the bank. Following Houston's example, Colonel John Wharton rode up and demanded that the men stop firing at the defenseless *soldados*. One Texian drawled, "Colonel Wharton, if Jesus Christ were to come down from Heaven and order me to quit shooting Santanistas I wouldn't do it, sir!"

The bloodlust finally faded with the sunlight, and the Texians began collecting prisoners.

That evening, back at the Texian camp where doctors removed bone fragments from his ankle, Houston heard a casualty report. Incredibly the Texians had lost only two men killed and some twenty-five wounded, seven of whom would later die.

But they had killed nearly six hundred fifty of the Mexicans, wounded more than two hundred more, and captured most of the rest.

Houston was most concerned about Santa Anna. His body had not been found among the dead. Nor was he among the prisoners. Houston knew that if Santa Anna could escape to his other columns, the war would continue, with the Texians still outnumbered.

Houston need not have worried. Santa Anna was captured the following day, meandering in the tall grass near the site of the destroyed bridge over Vince's Bayou. Ironically, the destruction of that small bridge had secured the independence of Texas.

Santa Anna was brought before Houston, who was sitting propped against a tree, his wounded leg stretched out before him. Most of the clustering Texians called for the Mexican general's immediate execution, but Houston recognized that Santa Anna was more valuable as a living hostage. With cries for his death ringing in Santa Anna's ears, Houston did not find it difficult to persuade His Excellency to order the rest of his troops to withdraw from Texas.

The Napoleon of the West had met his Waterloo. On a marshy plain called San Jacinto.

According to Houston's memoirs, he displayed to Santa Anna a partially eaten ear of dry corn. Houston asked, "Sir, do you ever expect to conquer men fighting for freedom whose general can march for four days with one ear of corn for his rations?"

Houston gives an ear of corn to his army for planting.
From Houston's 1855 memoirs, Drawing by Jacob Dallas, the cousin of
Houston's friend George Mifflin Dallas, vice president of the U.S.

Then he gave the ear to his men, instructing them each to take a kernal home and plant it. "Call it San Jacinto corn," Houston said, "for then it will remind you of your own bravery."

Santa Anna remained a prisoner in Texas for seven months. Later sent to the United States, he was finally released back to Mexico.

Sam Houston, once the most despised man in Texas, become the republic's first president.

Sam Houston

Myths, Mysteries, and Misconceptions

Was the Alamo a Strategic Blunder?

Many modern historians, utilizing the advantage of hindsight, regard the battle of the Alamo as a strategic mistake for both sides. Although the largest city in Texas, San Antonio de Bexar had no particular military significance, aside from the large number of artillery pieces that General Cos had abandoned there.

These modern armchair strategists note that the Texians were foolish to fortify and defend the Alamo. Not having enough oxen teams to remove the artillery, the Texians should have spiked the cannons and consolidated their forces eastward. Instead they entrenched themselves in the Alamo. From that defensive position they did not jeopardize the Mexican supply routes; in fact Santa Anna had none. Nor could the Texians actually hold Santa Anna at Bexar. He easily could have bypassed their fortified position.

But would that have been wise?

Santa Anna, these historians state, would have fared better had he followed the advice of some of his officers, ignored Bexar, and marched through Goliad on the most direct route into the colonies. Whether Santa Anna was trying to mimic General Arredondo's earlier success, or whether the prideful Napoleon of the West was foolishly avenging the tarnished honor of his brother-in-law, Cos, Santa Anna was absolutely determined to recapture Bexar.

Bowie knew that. He wrote, "[the enemy] intend to make a descent on this place in particular, and there is no doubt of it."

Equipped with that knowledge, Travis observed, "The power of Santa Anna is to be met here or in the colonies; we had better meet them here than to suffer a war of desolation to rage in our settlements."

Travis and Bowie never expected to trap themselves inside the Alamo. They anticipated reinforcements, hundreds of men. Supported by the superior Alamo artillery, this Texian army would not have needed to defend the old mission. Rather it could have maneuvered in the open prairie and conceivably defeated the Mexican invasion at San Antonio.

Santa Anna probably expected the Texians to follow Travis' strategy and rally at Bexar. He anticipated winning the war there. Thus he must have been disappointed to find so few Texians in defense of that place. Still he concluded that a decisive victory at the Alamo would set an example that would undermine the determination of the rest of the colonies to defend themselves.

In a sense Santa Anna also trapped himself at Bexar. With only fifteen hundred men the vanguard of his army, he could not easily detach a portion of his command to keep the Texians pinned down at the Alamo while the rest of his army marched east. Based on the earlier successes of the Texians at Gonzales, Concepcion, and the battle of Bexar, five hundred *soldados* might not be enough to contain the Alamo defenders, especially considering the formidable Texian artillery. If they broke out, Santa Anna would have a dangerous army at his rear. Yet if he consigned more men to the siege of the Alamo, it would seriously weaken the main body of his invasion force.

So in a sense the Texians did hold the Mexican army at Bexar. For a precious ten days it was a race to see who would receive reinforcements first. Santa Anna won that contest. The arrival of one thousand *soldados* on March 3 provided him with new options. Now he could proceed into the colonies. Or he could wait for the rest of his Army of Operations to march into Bexar. Then his big siege guns could have pounded the north wall into dust. If that did not compel the Texians to surrender, it at least would have facilitated the capture of the fort. Or Santa Anna simply could have waited for the Texians to exhaust their food supplies. Another two weeks and they would have been starved into submission. Either way his army would have remained intact. Instead Santa Anna resorted to the worst possible recourse. He fulfilled Travis' prophecy to inflict upon the Mexicans a victory that was worse than a defeat. At least it was demoralizing to the Mexicans, even as it gave the Texians a rallying point and a triumphant battle cry.

Certainly both sides made mistakes. However the Alamo was hardly the first battle in history to be fought and decided because "someone had blundered."

The Problem with Sources

History is not an exact science. The historian, like the detective, tries to arrive at conclusions by assembling the testimony from eyewitnesses to an incident. In Bill Groneman's *Eyewitness to the Alamo* and Alan Huffines *The Blood of Noble Men*, the accounts of more than forty alleged participants and witnesses to the siege and battle of the Alamo are conveniently juxtaposed. Immediately the reader becomes startled by the dramatic contradictions in their accounts—often in two or more accounts attributed to the same individual.

There are numerous explanations for these discrepancies that perpetually frustrate historians. The perspective of the witnesses should be considered. What did they personally experience? The women and children huddling in fear during the battle actually saw very little. Even if they had bravely peered out of a door, the darkness, the smoke, and the confusion would have compounded their own fears to such an extent that they could not have seen much. They only personally witnessed the aftermath, when the *soldados* entered their rooms.

Of the Texian survivors only Travis' slave, Joe, actually participated in the battle. And after the death of his master he fled to a room from which he may have fired a few shots, but again the darkness and smoke and fear would have obscured most of his view of the fighting within the walls.

Thus, in reality, the handful of Texian survivors provide only limited insights into the battle.

Hundreds of Mexican *soldados* survived the assault, but only a very few of them, mostly officers, ever recorded any details of the battle of the Alamo. Although their physical perspectives would have been broader than those of the Texian survivors hidden in rooms, the Mexicans still would have contended with the blinding smoke and darkness. Moreover men in the heat of combat generally lose all peripheral vision; the adrenaline flooding through their systems leaves them hopelessly myopic.

The historian must assemble the story of the Alamo from a smattering of severely restricted eyewitness accounts, which hardly could be expected to encompass the whole battle. Moreover, the stories told by the survivors tend to reflect personal biases as much as physical perspectives. People are prone to embellish their own importance and glorify their side while simultaneously denigrating the enemy. Did Joe really see a dying Travis thrust his sword into a Mexican officer? Did Joe really continue fighting after he retreated inside a room? We have only his published word. Not surprisingly most Texian accounts list much higher casualties for the Mexicans than do the Mexican sources.

The historical problem is compounded because some witnesses were interviewed many years after the event, when their memory had faltered. Susanna Dickinson apparently provided interviews, often conflicting with her earlier accounts, almost until her death, at the age of sixty-nine, in 1883. The first of several accounts attributed to Enrique Esparza did not appear until 1901, sixty-five years after the battle, when Esparza was in his seventies. How clearly could they recall events at that time?

Other difficulties can be found with the transcribers—the reporters who wrote down what they thought they were told by witnesses—or what they wanted the witnesses to say. Again psychological and physical perspectives must be considered. By 1880, for instance, the outer walls of the Alamo had been destroyed. Many people mistakenly assumed the battle took place entirely within the church. For instance if a reporter were told that Travis died at the north end of the fort, the listener would naturally assume that Travis fell in one of the rooms along the north wall of the church.

This problem is further compounded by the translators who attempted to convert Spanish accounts into English, with varying success. Two translators of the same Spanish account can provide two different English versions, with more than subtle distinctions.

Moreover both Texian and Mexican witnesses tended to include in their own accounts stories they heard rather than what they personally saw—generally without distinguishing between the two. Thus they emerge as omnipotent observers, but their information becomes more questionable.

Then there is the problem of fraudulent accounts. As an example, Andrea Castanon de Villaneuva, better known as Madame Candelaria, left several detailed—and sometimes contradictory—descriptions of the Alamo siege. She maintained that Houston had written her asking her to go into the Alamo to nurse the sick Bowie. But Houston had no way of knowing that Bowie was ill, and by the time he found out it would have been too late to send any letters to San Antonio. Yet Madame Candelaria managed to convince the proper authorities and received a pension from the state—a good reason to profess her presence at the Alamo. Most historians do not believe she was even there.

Isaac Millsaps of Gonzales certainly was at the Alamo. However a poignant letter allegedly written by him from the besieged Alamo to his blind wife and children in Gonzales is now generally recognized as a modern forgery. Texas history has been rampant with forgeries. Fraudulent copies of the Declaration of Independence or Travis' letter of February 24 do little damage other than to deplete the pocketbook of the gullible buyer. However fraudulent writings attributed to known participants or eyewitnesses at the Alamo can completely distort history. Every conceivable effort should be made to expose such fakes.

Because of these kinds of problems, the true story of the Alamo can never be known in its entirety. Even now, we know less than we think we do.

How Many Times Did Bonham Ride Out of the Alamo?

James Butler Bonham reigns as the most famous Alamo courier. The traditional story goes as follows: On February 16, 1836—before the siege of the Alamo began—Travis sent Bonham with a message for Fannin at Goliad. Bonham returned on February 23, the day the Mexicans descended on Bexar. Then, around February 27, Travis sent Bonham through the enemy lines with yet another appeal to Fannin. Bonham returned to the Alamo on March 3, with the news that Fannin could not reinforce the Alamo garrison.

But there is a historical problem with this story. In his letter of March 3, Travis identifies Bonham as his "special messenger" and cites Bonham's departure (on or around February 16) and his return on March 3—but Travis makes no mention of Bonham returning and leaving in the middle of that period.

Moreover Sam Houston claimed to have seen Bonham during the Alamo siege. That could only have been in Washington-on-the-Brazos. If Houston was correct, it would have taken Bonham two days to reach Goliad and another three to get to Washington-on-the-Brazos. Then he made another two-day ride back to Gonzales where Williamson gave him a letter for Travis. Then another day or two back to the Alamo. Bonham could not possibly have made such a trip in the five days between February 27 and March 3, but he could have visited all those places—and others—if he left on February 16 and did not return until March 3.

That Bonham apparently made only one trip from the Alamo instead of two does not diminish his heroism. Either way he returned to die there. However it is somewhat unfair that Bonham's fame so completely eclipses the other Alamo couriers, especially Albert Martin and John W. Smith, who also left the Alamo and later returned through enemy lines.

Did Travis Draw a Line?

The scene has been portrayed in paintings, poems, songs, and motion pictures. William Barret Travis draws his sword from its scabbard and traces a line in the dirt, challenging those in the garrison who would remain—and fight to the death—to cross over.

There are problems with this most endearing and enduring Alamo legend. It first appeared in the 1873 *Texas Almanac*, thirty-seven years after the Alamo fell. The story was written by William P. Zuber, always a fertile source for lurid tales, who claimed to have heard it from his parents. They, in turn, got it directly from Louis "Moses" Rose, a French veteran of the Napoleonic Wars, who claimed the dubious honor of being the only Alamo defender who had refused to cross the line. After escaping from the Alamo, Rose had recuperated at the Zuber home for several weeks.

William Zuber, then only sixteen, was with Sam Houston's army at the time and did not hear the Rose account firsthand. Yet thirty-seven years later, when he wrote his account for the *Texas Almanac*, he provided Travis with a lengthy speech that ran for several pages and included such stirring passages as:

> And when, at last, they shall storm our fortress, let us kill them as they come! kill them as they scale our walls! kill them as they leap within! kill them as they raise their weapons, and as they use them! kill them as they kill our companions! and continue to kill them so long as one of us shall remain alive!

Zuber acknowledged that Travis' speech was not "reported literally, but the ideas are precisely those he advanced, and most of the language is also nearly the same."

Moreover, Zuber's mother provided a written endorsement of Zuber's account. She wrote that she had examined it and "The part which purports to be Rose's statement of what he saw and heard in the Alamo, of his escape, and of what befell him afterwards is precisely the substance of what Rose stated to my husband and myself."

But a few years after the publication of the account, Zuber made another concession.

> I found a deficiency in the material of the speech, which from my knowledge of the man [Travis], I thought I could supply. I accordingly threw in one paragraph which I firmly believe to be characteristic of Travis, and without which the

speech would have been incomplete. I distinguished said paragraph, by inserting it between brackets: & it was excepted in my mother's certificate. But, both the distinction & the exception, were omitted by the printer. That one paragraph contains every word of fiction in my article in the *Almanac.*

Despite Mary Ann Zuber's endorsement, the critics had ample reason to be skeptical. Here was a third-hand account, related by an admitted embellisher. They could find no concrete evidence that Rose ever really was in the Alamo—or like Madame Candelaria simply made that claim in order to receive land from the state. The Land Commission at least believed him.

And whether Travis confronted his men on March 3, as Zuber reported, or on March 5, as author Walter Lord suggested in *A Time To Stand,* there was still the problem with that paragraph. Even if Travis had made a speech to his men, most historians concluded that Zuber undoubtedly had invented the line in the sand.

Not necessarily. As Wallace O. Chariton pointed out in *Exploring the Alamo Legends,* Zuber's description of the line entails three paragraphs. Chariton found another single paragraph in the speech that he proposed was the one Zuber invented.

Indeed, Travis would hardly have been the first to draw a line. Francisco Pizarro allegedly did it when he landed his *conquistadores* in Peru. According to Creed Taylor, Ben Milam drew a line with his rifle butt prior to the battle of Bexar. And historian Thomas Lindley has found an account stating that Sam Houston challenged his officers with a line.

Moreover, in an undated account probably—but not definitely— written after Zuber's account was published, Susanna Dickinson recalled Travis drawing that line and a man named "Ross" leaving the Alamo. Later Enrique Esparza recalled the line. And so did Madame Candelaria, who probably was not even there.

In his book *Blood of Noble Men,* Alan C. Huffines concedes that "Historians generally do not want to believe that something this melodramatic happened." However, after quoting from the alleged eyewitnesses at the Alamo, Huffines concludes:

> There are three choices here:
> 1) All are experiencing mass-hallucination;
> 2) They are lying;
> 3) They are telling the truth.

There is a fourth option. Like the Mexican accounts of the battle, the Texian survivors merely were including a story they had heard and assumed to be factual.

The debate goes on. Some historians still challenge Rose's presence in the Alamo. Others note that, contrary to the traditional story, Bonham did not bring the dire news that Fannin was not coming. Rather Bonham delivered the optimistic report that troops were gathering at Gonzales. However that alteration hardly affects or diminishes the story of the line. By March 5, the prospect of reinforcements arriving in time to save the garrison had sorely faded.

Ultimately Travis' line must remain a legend. It can neither be proven nor disproved.

But some seem overly eager to deny it.

The Alamo's Holy Trinity: How Did They Die?

Accounts of the deaths of Travis, Bowie, and Crockett range all the way from glorified heroism to craven cowardice, with the weight of evidence usually somewhere in between. Two Bexarenos who arrived in Gonzales on March 11 provided the first known accounts of Travis' and Bowie's fate. Anselma Borgera and Andres Barcena, who admitted that they had heard the story from another *Tejano*, reported that both Travis and Bowie had committed suicide to avoid capture.

Travis:
The suicide story lingered with Travis, because of that mortal wound to his forehead. In a sense Travis did commit suicide, but only by his determination to defend the Alamo to the last.

With Travis, alone among the Alamo's popular triumverate, there is a reliable eyewitness. Travis' slave, Joe, saw his master hit by musket fire and fall within the fort. But in several accounts Joe maintained that the mortally wounded Travis managed to thrust his sword into a Mexican officer coming over the wall. In two of the accounts, Joe identified the Mexican as General Mora.

Some historians quickly dismissed this story as fabricated melodrama, one critic pointing out that General Ventura Mora commanded the Dolores cavalry and did not participate in the storming. However Ramon Caro identified a Colonel Esteban Mora who did attck the north wall. So perhaps Travis did have a Hollywood-style death.

There were other, less reliable, accounts of Travis' death. Sergeant Francisco Becerra provided the most entertaining version. He claimed that after the battle he discovered Travis and Crockett hiding in a room of the Alamo. With a large roll of bank bills, Travis bought some time until General Cos entered the room. Cos warmly embraced Travis as an old friend, and in Becerra's version it is Cos who attempts to intercede, unsuccessfully, with Santa Anna to spare the Texians' lives. On Santa Anna's orders, overly enthusiastic *soldados* on all sides open fire on Travis and Crockett, and although the two Texians died—"undaunted, like heroes"—eight Mexicans were killed and wounded in the incident.

Bowie:

That same, imaginative Sergeant Becerra also encountered a sick man lying on a bed. Becerra wrote that he intended to spare the invalid, despite Santa Anna's orders to give no quarter. Then the sergeant witnessed two other Mexicans enter the room, both intent on fulfilling Santa Anna's orders—only to fall before the bedridden man's pistols. So Becerra changed his mind, shot the sick man, and claimed the dead man's two discharged pistols as a war trophy.

Although he did not identify James Bowie as the sick man, Becerra had provided an oft repeated version of Bowie's death.

"Colonel Bowie was sick in bed and not expected to live," Susanna Dickinson stated in one of her many accounts, "but as the victorious Mexicans entered his room, he killed two of them with his pistols before they pierced him through with their sabres."

Even Enrique Esparza provided Bowie with a Hollywood death scene. "[Bowie] loaded and fired his pistols until his foes closed in on him," Esparza stated in 1907. "When they made their final rush upon him, he rose up in his bed and received them. He buried his sharp knife into the breast of one of them as another fired the shot that killed him."

Madame Candelaria maintained that she was with Bowie when he died. "A dozen or more of the Mexicans sprang into the room occupied by Colonel Bowie," she asserted in an 1899 account. "He emptied his pistols in their faces and killed two of them."

All of these accounts place Bowie in the church, where, conveniently, his death could have been witnessed by the survivors. In the years after the outer walls were destroyed, the church became the Alamo in the public perception. Numerous later accounts focused all the action of the battle there.

But Bowie probably was not in the church. When *alcalde* Ruiz located the bodies of the Alamo commanders for Santa Anna, he found Bowie "dead in his bed, in one of the rooms of the south side." As an officer, Bowie was entitled to a private room. As a sick man, suffering from a disease of a peculiar nature, he would not have wanted to risk infecting the garrison. And, contrary to the accounts of Madame Candelaria and others who professed to nurse him, Bowie probably died alone in that room.

Most accounts have Bowie fighting to the death, at least armed with two pistols, and sometimes with his knife. But if he was bedridden, and he apparently was, the knife would have been of little value. *Soldados* armed with five-foot muskets could have pierced him with their bayonets, and even with a twelve-inch blade extended from a long arm, Bowie's knife could not have reached his attackers.

Unless, of course, the Mexicans were shoving into his room, even as they shoved against the north wall, pushing those in front into range of that deadly blade.

But other accounts exist in which Bowie does not offer resistance. In one of her earlier accounts, Madame Candelaria related that Colonel Bowie died in her arms "only a few minutes before the entrance to the Alamo by the soldiers."

Sergeant Felix Nunez reported a sick man killed in the big room on the left of the main entrance. The transcriber or translator assumed Nunez meant the entrance to the church, but if Nunez meant the gate as the entrance, he would have put this unidentified man in the south wall. "He was bayoneted in his bed," Nunez related. "He died apparently without shedding a drop of blood."

" . . . the pervert and braggart Santiago Bowie, died like a woman, almost hidden under a mattress," an unidentified Mexican soldier wrote to a Mexican newspaper in 1836.

"Buy [*sic*], the braggart son-in-law of Beramendi, [died] as a coward," claimed Sanchez-Navarro in his diary.

Historian William C. Davis (*Three Roads to the Alamo*) interpreted these accounts to suggest that Bowie was too ill to offer any resistance, perhaps only semiconscious, but because he was not in the hospital, the Mexicans assumed he was attempting to hide. Davis wrote, "In a cruel irony at the end of a remarkable life, one of the most fearless men of his generation died at the contemptuous hands of soldiers who mistook him for the worst sort of coward."

But perhaps Bowie did live up to his reputation. An unidentified Mexican captain told Creed Taylor "he did not hear of a sick man being bayoneted while helpless on his bed but there was a sick man who got out of his bed when the Mexicans entered the fortress and died fighting with the rest."

The most outlandish story of Bowie's death came, again, from William P. Zuber, who allegedly heard it from a Mexican fifer named Apolinario Saldigna. In this lurid tale, Bowie was too weak to fight, but he so vehemently lambasted the Mexicans that they cut out his tongue and "pitched him alive upon the funeral pyre."

Ultimately there is no absolutely reliable source as to James Bowie's death. Almost certainly he did not pile up around his cot the numerous Mexican corpses recounted in more fanciful tales. But there was, at least, a historical precedent. The man from the sandbar, who kept fighting after he had been shot, kept fighting after he had been clubbed, kept fighting after he had been stabbed, would not have given up in the Alamo.

If he had had the strength to raise his arms, his hands would have held weapons.

Crockett:

Although it is now in vogue to assume that David Crockett was executed, the evidence is hardly conclusive. In fact more accounts exist supporting his death in combat. But which accounts are the most valid?

Of course the ubiquitous Madame Candelaria saw him die fighting. Enrique Esparza and Travis' slave, Joe, both reported that Crockett fell surrounded by Mexican dead.

As she was led from the church, Susanna Dickinson "recognized Colonel Crockett lying dead and mutilated between the church and the two-story barrack building." She even remembered seeing his "peculiar cap lying by his side." But was she escorted from the Alamo before or after the executions?

Even several Mexican accounts graphically describe "Kwockey's" heroic last stand, clubbing with his long rifle, slashing with his knife, until finally overwhelmed.

Most modern historians dismiss these melodramatic versions and attach more credibility to the sources describing the execution.

Unquestionably some Alamo defenders were executed. Santa Anna's secretary, Ramon Caro, writing the year after the battle, reported that General Castrillon discovered five survivors. In an "outrage which

Death of Crockett

humanity condemns," Santa Anna "severely reprimanded" Castrillon, and Mexican soldiers "set upon the prisoners until they were all dead."

Significantly, Caro made no mention of Crockett. Neither did cavalry sergeant Manuel Loranca, who recalled that Santa Anna ordered an undetermined number of survivors found in the barracks to be shot, "which was accordingly done."

After the battle of San Jacinto, Santa Anna's aide-de-camp, Fernando Urissa, related that Castrillon approached His Excellency with a single prisoner, a "venerable-looking old man." Santa Anna immediately had the prisoner shot. Urissa later heard that the man's name was "Coket."

An account attributed to Colonel Almonte, dated September 7, 1836, identifies Crockett as one of six men that Santa Anna ordered to be shot.

De la Peña, in the most often cited account of Crockett's execution, counted seven prisoners who were tortured to death by swords.

None of these Mexican sources agree on any of the details. Perhaps Crockett was executed, but it is absurd to so conclude based on the conflicting evidence. The case simply would not stand up in any court of law.

Moreover one must ask why did Almonte not mention the execution of Crockett until September 7. Why did Almonte not include the story in his March 6 diary notation?

Why did de la Peña not include the story in the first draft of his memoirs?

Probably because they, like Urissa, "later heard" that Crockett was among those executed. And the Mexicans may not have heard it until after San Jacinto. From the Texians.

Ultimately it was almost too good a story. The defiant Crockett being brought face to face with Santa Anna—then meeting his death heroically. Almost like Custer being the last cavalryman standing at Little Big Horn.

The story was guaranteed to generate hatred toward Santa Anna, and after San Jacinto it proved to be convenient propaganda for the Texians who wished to keep His Excellency a prisoner. And it was equally convenient for Santa Anna's political enemies in Mexico.

But it probably did not happen. And it is equally doubtful that Davy Crockett dispatched a dozen or more Mexicans before they finally killed him. At forty-nine years of age, he was deemed an old man. He had been a backwoodsman, and briefly a soldier, but he had never been recognized as a great warrior.

The odds are that Crockett died a nondescript death in the battle, possibly shot down while retreating toward the church, then bayoneted.

Of course history does not always adhere to the odds.

The de la Peña Dilemma

With the Alamo, Goliad, and San Jacinto all occurring in the same year, Texas placed more emphasis on its establishment as a republic than on its annexation into the United States. Thus in 1936 the whole state engaged in a boisterous centennial celebration. By that time death had silenced all of the survivors, Texian and Mexican, of the Alamo battle. Yet that year one more Mexican eyewitness delivered his testimony.

It appeared in the form of a diary allegedly kept by Colonel Jose Juan Sanchez Navarro during the Texas Revolution. The spew of forgeries that would later haunt Texas document collectors had not yet been discovered, so the Sanchez Navarro account was readily accepted as authentic by a historical community always eager for a new window to the past. And at that time there were no forensic tests that could have proved otherwise.

Still there were some curious aspects to the diary. First, it had no provenance, no real history. Rather it just sort of appeared at a convenient time when excited Texans were commemorating the Alamo. Second, it had been crudely scribbled onto the blank pages of two massive ledger books that indexed the records that Sanchez Navarro had kept while serving as adjutant inspector of the Mexican Departments of

Nuevo Leon and Tamaulipas. The ledger book certainly belonged to Sanchez Navarro, so it was easy to conclude that the diary also originated with him. Yet why would Sanchez Navarro lug around massive ledger books? Reputedly from one of the wealthiest families in Mexico, he certainly could have afforded to purchase a small journal.

Moreover there were striking similarities between the Sanchez Navarro diary and the March 7, 1836 letter by an unidentified Mexican soldier that was published in the April 5, 1836 edition of the Mexican newspaper *El Mosquito Mexicano*. For instance the unidentified *soldado* wrote, "The four columns and the reserves as if by a charm at the same time climbed the enemy's walls and threw themselves inside his enclosure . . . "

The Sanchez Navarro diary stated, "Our chiefs, officers and troops as if by magic topped the walls at one and the same time and threw themselves inside . . . . "

Another striking similarity occurs in the comparison of the deaths of the Alamo's co-commanders. The unidentified Mexican soldier maintained, "The chief they called Travis died like a brave man with his gun in his hand, in back of a cannon; but the perverse and braggart Santiago Bowie, died like a woman, almost hidden under a mattress."

"Travis, the Commander of the Alamo, died as a brave man," reported the Sanchez Navarro diary. "Buy, the braggart son-in-law of Beramendi, as a coward."

However the diary also included an apparent reference to Crockett not found in the newspaper account. The diary recorded, "Some cruelties horrified me, among others the death of an old man they called 'Cocran . . . '" Significantly, the diary does not mention how "Cocran" died, but the allusion to his unusually cruel death in relation to a savage hand-to-hand conflict suggests something more than being slain in battle.

The similarities between the two accounts convinced Walter Lord (*A Time to Stand*) that Sanchez Navarro was the unidentified Mexican contributor to *El Mosquito Mexicano*. But another obvious possibility exists. It would have been relatively easy for a forger to have acquired the authentic Sanchez Navarro ledger and added fraudulent diary entries based on the earlier newspaper account. Indeed if the Sanchez Navarro account is authentic, it would be the only Mexican source written on March 6, 1836, to mention Crockett at all! That fact alone detracts from the diary's credibility.

Despite its controversial reference to Bowie's cowardice and possible suggestion of Crockett's execution, in 1936 the Sanchez Navarro diary did not create a public stir. At that time Texans and Texan historians could accept the authenticity of a Mexican document without blindly believing its contents.

But that changed when the so-called de la Peña diary surfaced. Again it had no provenance; its origins are completely unknown before 1955. Again it made a fortuitous arrival—right in the midst of the Walt Disney/ Davy Crockett craze sweeping the United States. Again it contained striking similarities to earlier known sources. Historian Alan Huffines personally supports the authenticity of the de la Peña diary, but in his book *Blood of Noble Men*, in which he juxtaposes specific excerpts from the various accounts of witnesses to the Alamo, the many similarities of de la Peña to these earlier accounts are striking. Curiously Huffines omitted one of the most remarkable parallels. It appeared in a 1907 letter from the prolific William Zuber and it contains an alleged interview with General Cos after his capture at San Jacinto. In this account, as with Sergeant Becerra's cited above, it is Cos rather than the well-documented Castrillon, who, after the battle of the Alamo, discovers a well-dressed David Crockett in a locked barracks room. Crockett told Cos:

> I have come to Texas on a visit of exploration; purposing, if permitted, to become a loyal citizen of the Republic of Mexico. I extended my visit to San Antonio, and called in the Alamo to become acquainted with the officers, and learn of them what I could of the condition of affairs. Soon after my arrival, the fort was invested by government troop, whereby I have been prevented from leaving it. And here I am yet. a non-combatant and foreigner, having taken no part in the fighting.

In his own letter containing this account Zuber acknowledged that the story was "a gross falsehood" told by Cos "to mitigate his condition as a captive." Yet it sounds suspiciously familiar to de la Peña's description of "the naturalist David Crockett . . . who had undertaken to explore the country and who, finding himself in Bexar at the very moment of surprise, had taken refuge in the Alamo, fearing that his status as a foreigner might not be respected."

Significantly these are the only two known accounts that describe Crockett as a noncombatant trapped in the Alamo. Do they both emanate from a forgotten common source? Does the 1907 Zuber letter, with all its inaccuracies, corroborate the de la Peña diary, which had not yet been published? Or does the Zuber account provide fodder for a later forger using de la Peña's name?

The de la Peña diary also contained historical errors. That alone does not diminish its authenticity—most eyewitness accounts contain some flaws. But the de la Peña account completely misidentifies Travis. Where was de la Peña when the Alamo commander's body was shown to Santa Anna? The de la Peña account also cites "an elderly woman and a negro slave" as the only Texian survivors of the battle. Susanna Dickinson was hardly elderly, and there were more than fifteen other noncombatants who survived, something that a Mexican officer at the Alamo should have known.

And then there was the problem of the diary itself. It is not, in fact, a diary at all. The de la Peña papers include two documents. The first, one hundred nine pages, professes to be a rewrite of de la Peña's daily journal. Historical evidence supports the fact that de la Peña kept a journal, but the original has never been found. Why is it not among the other papers that have been preserved?

This draft contains only a brief description of the battle of the Alamo—a typed transcript extends only for a page and a half. Significantly there is no mention of executions or of David Crockett.

The second manuscript is the account that has been published. More than four times longer than the earlier draft, it obviously contains supplementary information culled from other sources. When published, the Alamo account ran twenty-seven pages. But the original is not bound. Rather it exists in loose stacks comprised of as many as twenty different types of paper. That also raises eyebrows. Forgers scrounge old paper from whatever sources they can find, often ripping out the blank flyleafs from old books. Thus forged manuscripts generally utilize a wide variety of types of paper.

Enter Charles Hamilton. Heralded by the *New York Times* as "the nation's pre-eminent detector of forged manuscripts," Hamilton revealed the well-publicized Hitler diaries to be a fraud. Hamilton also exposed a prolific forger named John Laflin who specialized in fabricating false Jean Lafitte documents. Laflin may also have been the author of the spurious Isaac Millsaps letter from the Alamo. And, according to Hamilton, Laflin also forged the de la Peña papers.

Incredibly, despite these and some other problems, many Texas historians continue to embrace the so-called de la Peña diary as the most reliable of all Alamo accounts—a veritable Mexican gospel. Perhaps it really is authentic. But the weight of evidence definitely leaves room for legitimate doubt.

Certainly the de la Peña account provides the most exciting, vivid, and detailed of all alleged eyewitness descriptions of the battle of the Alamo. But it does not read like a first person account describing just what de la Peña did and what he saw. The pronoun "I" is rarely used. Rather the account takes an almost omnipotent perspective of the battle, jumping from the assault on the north wall to Santa Anna watching from the northern battlements to the Mexican cavalry galloping over the Texians who fled the fort. It is so good, so compelling an account that one almost wishes its authenticity had been verified. The only real controversy concerns Crockett's death, and in fact that should not be a controversy at all.

If the de la Peña account were proved to be genuine, it would not prove that Crockett was executed. De la Peña's expanded memoirs include information that he garnered after the battle, perhaps including the Crockett execution story. To be sure de la Peña claimed to have witnessed the executions, but he would not be the first author to place himself in a story he had only heard. Or perhaps he really did see the executions and later heard that Crockett was among the slain.

On the other hand, if the de la Peña papers should prove to be a forgery, it would not disprove the Crockett execution story. Accounts of Crockett's execution can be traced back to early 1836, well before the appearance of the de la Peña memoirs.

What becomes important, then, is not how Crockett died, but the other information included in the de la Peña diary. Is it just a forger's creative rewriting of other sources? Or is it authentic? Today science possesses the technology to test disputed documents such as the de la Peña and Sanchez Navarro diaries and finally establish or disprove their authenticity. They deserve to be tested.

Did Some of the Texians Really Attempt to Escape During the Battle?

Almost certainly. The usually reliable Colonel Almonte recorded that "the enemy attempted in vain to fly." De la Peña also briefly referred to "those of the enemy who tried to escape."

Sergeant Manuel Loranca and General Joaquin Ramirez y Sesma provided more detailed accounts. Clearly there were several groups of men who attempted to retreat from the fort, although it is difficult to pinpoint, from the accounts, exactly where they went over the walls.

Loranca saw one group sally "from the east side of the fort." He had to be referring to the corral areas north of the church. It seems obvious that these men would not have fled until the walls were breached, at which point every man knew the battle was lost. But they had to leave before Colonel Romero's third column swept in over that area. The logical conclusion is that as Romero stormed the cattle pen to the north, the Texians consolidated in the horse corral and fired a final volley at the approaching Mexicans. Then, not having time to reload, they had only two choices—die or run. The fact that they had fired can be ascertained because only one of them was able to defend himself from the Dolores cavalry.

Sesma described the "center fortin" as a second point of exit. Considering his vantage point to the south, it would seem that he meant either the palisade or the lunette that guarded the gate. However the palisade, with its deep outer trench filled with an abattis of tree branches, would have been difficult to scramble through. And Colonel Morales' fourth column, attacking the southwest corner, would have been in dangerously close proximity to men running from the lunette, especially since the lunette opened to the southwest.

But perhaps Sesma meant the fortin or cannon emplacement that some accounts locate midway down the west wall. That makes more sense. The Texians there were wedged between Morales to the south and the columns descending from the north. And the tree-lined river in front of them offered cover and a possible avenue of escape.

These accounts have long been known, but largely ignored. The legend of the Alamo had overpowered the reality. Only at the Alamo was shame attached to retreat or surrender. At the Alamo, according to the legend, every man had made a pact to fight to the death.

Despite Travis' dramatic rhetoric, that legendary pact is nonsense. Even if the defenders crossed a line, it was only a commitment to stay longer, hoping for reinforcements.

The men of the Alamo were true heroes because they put themselves in harm's way—and ultimately paid with their lives—for a cause they believed in. But no Texian entered the Alamo intending to die. And when the battle was lost, every one of them had the moral right to try to survive. They were heroes, but they were not demigods. They were real men, with real hopes and real fears. Some may have tried to surrender, some were executed, and some tried to escape.

Rather than diminishing their heroism, such actions merely display their humanity and render their sacrifice more poignant.

Were There Any Texian Survivors?

Most of the noncombatants survived. Mrs. Dickinson, her daughter, Angelina, and Joe, are the most famous. But numerous *Tejano* women and children also survived: Juana Alsbury with her son, Alejo—the youngest Alamo survivor—and her sister Gertrudis Navarro; Ana Esparza and her four children; Victoriana de Salina and her three daughters; and Concepcion Losoya and her son, Juan, and her sister, Juana Melton, the wife of Alamo quartermaster, Eliel Melton. As with all things Alamo, this list is only an approximation. There may have been others, and some of the *Tejanos* named here may have slipped out of the Alamo before the final battle.

Joe also remembered other blacks in the Alamo. He recalled a Negro woman "who was found dead lying between two guns."

Bettie, a Negro cook, and a husky slave named Charlie may also have been in the Alamo. John Salmon "Rip" Ford recorded Bettie's story that when the Mexican *soldados* entered the fort's kitchen, Charlie grabbed a small officer leading them and held him up as a shield until the Mexicans agreed to spare the slave's life.

And there is the remote possibility that some of the Texian defenders escaped. Some historians maintain that Henry Warnell, a twenty-four-year-old jockey from Arkansas, survived the battle, only to die of his wounds three month later. Typically, the story is disputed. Other researchers argue that Warnell received his wounds when he left the Alamo as a courier. And yet others argue that he was never there.

The weekly *Arkansas Gazette* did not report the fall of the Alamo until April 5, 1836. However a previous edition, dated March 29, carried an account that is as intriguing now as it was disturbing then. Two men, one of them badly wounded, had arrived in Nacogdoches, claiming that "San Antonio had been retaken by the Mexicans, the garrison put to the sword—that if any others escaped the general massacre besides themselves, they were not aware of it."

Were those two unidentified men survivors of the Alamo? Possibly. At the Goliad massacre, in broad daylight, about thirty Texians escaped the Mexicans. The men fleeing the Alamo had the advantage of darkness. At least one anonymous Texian eluded the lancers that morning. Later that day he was spotted hiding under a bridge, captured, and executed. Perhaps a couple others made it to safety.

How Many Texian Casualties?

It is impossible to follow what Wallace Chariton described as the Alamo numbers game. In their letter of February 23, Travis and Bowie wrote that they had one hundred and forty-six men. Two days later Albert Martin recorded "150 determined to do or die." Some couriers left—so, perhaps, did some *Tejanos*—and the thirty-two men from Gonzales arrived. But on March 3, Travis claimed "145 men." Perhaps he was not counting the sick and wounded among his effectives. Or perhaps he was just estimating.

After the battle, *alcalde* Ruiz, who should have known, reported one hundred eighty-two Texians burned. Santa Anna's secretary, Ramon Caro, listed one hundred eighty-three Texian casualties, "the sum total of their force." By adding the thirty-two men from Gonzales to Martin's earlier estimate of one hundred fifty, the math seems to work out, give or take a dead Texian or two.

However Almonte reported two hundred fifty Texian casualties; the anonymous *soldado* who wrote to the Mexican newspaper *El Mosqito Mexicano*, reported two hundred fifty-seven burned Texian bodies. Sanchez-Navarro also recorded two hundred fifty-seven Texians, "whose bodies I have seen and counted." And de la Peña listed two hundred fifty-three.

Santa Anna's absurd report of "600 corpses of foreigners" should not even be considered. But were there one hundred eighty-odd Texians or two hundred fifty-odd Texians? One possible, but not completely satisfying solution to this contradiction would be the second reinforcement from Gonzales of sixty or more men that historical researcher Thomas Lindley proposes. The arrival of these men late in the night of March 3 or in the early hours of March 4 should have raised the number of Alamo defenders to around two hundred fifty.

Perhaps during the battle, by an uncomfortable coincidence, about the same number of Texians went over the walls and were killed on the surrounding prairie. Then one could argue that Almonte et al were counting total Texian casualties while Caro and Ruiz numbered only those found dead in the Alamo.

But that is not what Caro and Ruiz said.

How Many Mexican Casualties?

In later years, as the legend of the Alamo grew, so did the number of Mexicans assaulting it—to five thousand, seven thousand, even ten thousand troops. And the number of Mexican casualties increased accordingly. In 1906 a Bexareno named Pablo Diaz remembered "Nearly 6,000 of Santa Anna's 10,000 had fallen before they annihilated their adversaries."

Sergeant Francisco Becerra, whose recollection was dismissed by historian Walter Lord (*A Time to Stand*) as "probably the least reliable of all Mexican accounts," described the Mexican losses as "two thousand killed and more than three hundred wounded."

That was almost the total number of Mexican troops in San Antonio at that time. Even counting the reserves and cavalry—which should be considered, since they took part in the engagement—Santa Anna's assault force against the Alamo only numbered about two thousand men. Therefore *alcalde* Ruíz's estimate of sixteen hundred Mexican casualties also seems unreasonably high.

Considering that Santa Anna, in his March 6 report, exaggerated the Texians losses at six hundred, his statement that "We lost 70 men killed and 300 wounded" also would seem suspect. Yet Colonel Almonte listed even fewer Mexican losses: sixty-five killed and two hundred twenty-three wounded. Colonel de la Peña, Colonel Sanchez-Navarro, General Filisola, and General Andrade all followed Santa Anna's example and placed the total of Mexican killed and wounded between three hundred and four hundred. Perhaps some of the officers did not want to contradict their commander. Of course Mexican soldiers could be as guilty of minimizing their own casualties as Texians were of exaggerating Mexican losses.

Ramon Caro, perhaps the most reliable of Mexican sources, deplored "the costly sacrifice of the 400 men who fell in the attack." Caro specified, "Three hundred were left dead on the field and more than a hundred of the wounded died afterwards." Clearly that implies that there were more casualties, and since the wounded usually outnumber the dead, it is not difficult to project more than six hundred Mexican casualties. The account of Dr. Joseph Barnard, a doctor captured at Goliad and sent to Bexar to tend to the Mexican wounded, basically agreed. Barnard heard that some three hundred to four hundred *soldados* had already died, and there were still two hundred to three hundred wounded.

In his 1874 autobiography, Santa Anna wrote, "We suffered more than a thousand dead or wounded, but when the battle was over, not a single man in the Alamo was left alive." Was this tantamount to a death-bed confession? Or just the faulty memory of an old man?

" . . . defenders of better forts than the Alamo seldom slay many times more than their own number," observed Reuben M. Potter, perhaps the first man to attempt an objective history of the Alamo. Potter had the advantage of interviewing a number of the actual participants and witnesses, and he concluded that there were about five hundred Mexican casualties. He wrote, "Neither Mexican troops nor any others are apt to take forts with a loss of more than two-fifths of their number."

But on that dreadful dawn, in the darkness and the smoke and the chaos of dead and dying men, was anybody calculating percentages?

Epilogue: **The Battles Continue**

The Alamo fell on March 6, 1836, with the massacre of its most famous garrison. In a more literal sense, however, the hard luck mission would continue to fall.

General Pedro Andrade had been left in command of the Mexican forces at Bexar, a thousand *soldados*, many of them wounded. There was no medicine to relieve their suffering. His effective troops fared little better. Most had no shoes. Their tattered uniforms rotted off their bodies. They had been reduced to one paltry meal a day.

The horses, also, were starving. More than two hundred already had died.

Only after Andrade received news of the battle of San Jacinto did he realize how fortunate his own troops were.

He had kept them busy rebuilding the old mission's defenses, which had been severely damaged in the assault. Then, on May 22, 1836, he received orders to withdraw from Bexar and join the main body of the Mexican army in its retreat from Texas. The orders also specified that Andrade should spike the cannons and throw them and the ammunition into the river. Destroy all small arms that could not be carried. Tear down the Alamo's fortifications.

It took only two days. The *soldados* attacked the Alamo again, ripping down the palisade, demolishing the outer adobe walls, and filling in the trenches. When the Mexican troops marched out on May 24, the Bexarenos saw smoke rising from the old church. The wooden ramp and cannon emplacement were in flames.

The stone walls of the church survived the conflagration. So did the other stone structures—the long barracks that occupied the ruins of the old *convento* and the low barracks that surrounded the south wall gate. Little else stood.

On June 4 Colonel Juan Seguin took possession of Bexar for the Texian army. According to one story, Seguin personally gathered the charred bones of the Alamo defenders and interred them within the San Fernando Church.

Another account credits *alcalde* Ruiz with collecting and burying the Texian remains.

Ironically only a handful of the men in Houston's army that won Texian independence on the plain of San Jacinto had been in Texas long enough to own land. The weeks and months that followed that battle witnessed a huge influx of new emigrants from the United States. These Anglos knew nothing of the heroic sacrifices of *Tejanos* like Zavala, Navarro, Ruiz, Veramendi, and Seguin. Sadly, older Texians were quick to forget. Mexicans were Mexicans, and they had been defeated.

The Mexican government fueled the ethnic strife by not honoring Santa Anna's gunpoint treaty recognizing the independence of Texas. In early 1837 Seguin received orders to destroy Bexar and the Alamo to prevent them from falling into the hands of a Mexican invasion force. Suspecting it was a ruse by Texas speculators to acquire all that land for themselves, Seguin appealed to President Sam Houston. Houston supported Seguin.

The Alamo, or what was left of it, was saved. Once again Texian troops garrisoned in its ruined barracks.

Ultimately, however, Houston had no more success stemming the rapid tide of racial conflict between Anglos and *Tejanos* than he did trying to get the republic's government to honor his treaties with the native Indian tribes. The term "Texians" gradually evolved into the more anglicized "Texans," a further example of the diminishment of Spanish prestige and influence.

In March 1841 many embittered *Tejanos* joined a Mexican invasion of San Antonio led by General Rafael Vasquez. The Texan forces hastily abandoned the Alamo to the *soldados*. But it proved to be only a token action—a show of Mexican strength. After three days Vasquez withdrew back below the Rio Grande.

A year and a half later, General Adrian Woll, a French-born veteran of Santa Anna's 1836 campaign, launched a more determined invasion of Texas. Or at least of San Antonio. Strategically significant or not, the town attracted every invader from Arredondo to Santa Anna to Vasquez to Woll. General Woll's September 1841 invasion force of fifteen hundred troops also was abetted by a company of *Tejanos*, this time led by the disenfranchised former mayor of Bexar, Juan Seguin.

Again Mexican troops occupied the Alamo. Again Texians mustered to drive the Mexicans away. Two hundred volunteers assembled on Salado Creek, but they were too few to attack the enemy. Instead thirty-eight mounted Texians led by the archetype of Texas Rangers, Captain John

Coffee Hays, brazenly rode up to the Alamo's walls and lured the Mexican force back to the Salado. Woll was defeated and withdrew from Texas.

Back in the hands of the Texians, the Alamo suffered further indignities at the hands of vandals. They etched their names in the limestone walls and chiseled out musket balls and stone fragments for souvenirs. One Texan maliciously decapitated the statues of "angels" set in the niches on either side of the church door. Saint Francis and Saint Dominic, who had witnessed so much history, so much tragedy, would see no more.

Other bored Texians used the female saints in the upper niches for target practice. Eventually the statues of Saint Clare and Saint Margaret of Cortona either crumbled or were stolen.

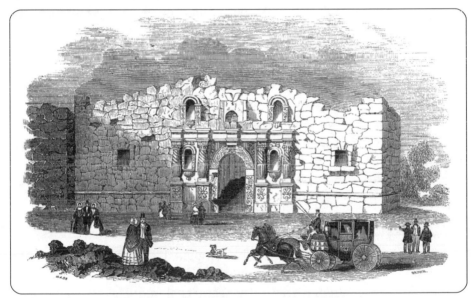

Ruins of the Church El Alamo, published in
Gleason's Pictoral Drawing-Room Companion in 1854.

"The final act of this great drama is now performed," declared Anson Jones on February 19, 1846, "the Republic of Texas is no more." Jones, the fourth and last president of the republic, had just presided over the ceremony finalizing the annexation of Texas into the United States. Officially Texas had joined the union as the twenty-eighth state on December 29, 1845, claiming territory all the way to the Rio Grande.

Since Mexico had never acknowledged the independence of Texas—and only recognized the lower boundary of Texas as the Nueces River—conflict between the two nations was inevitable. The Mexican War began in the spring of 1846.

The ever-resourceful and resilient Santa Anna, then in exile in Cuba, saw new opportunity. He persuaded President James Polk that he could negotiate a peaceful settlement to the conflict. The Americans ferried him through their own naval blockade into Mexico. However, as soon as Santa Anna again held the reins of the Mexican army, he escalated the war. Again he would be defeated. The Treaty of Guadalupe Hidalgo, signed on February 2, 1848, recognized the Rio Grande as the southern border of Texas. It also ceded, for fifteen million dollars, the territories of New Mexico (including present-day Arizona) and California to the United States. Through his military blunderings, the Napoleon of the West had forfeited roughly one half of the lands once claimed by Mexico.

During the war United States troops had occupied San Antonio. Pragmatically, if not reverently, the army transformed the Alamo into a military warehouse. While clearing away rubble in the church, soldiers discovered several skeletons believed to have dated from the siege.

The engineers covered the old convent with a wooden roof—"rebuilt and adapted to our purposes without remorse," conceded Edward Everett, an artist who helped with the initial designs, "but the church we respected as an historical relic." Not exactly. In fact the army subsequently made significant modifications to the church. They raised the walls to a uniform height and constructed a wooden second floor. To provide light for this addition they cut out two upper windows. The one on the right was not quite aligned with the window immediately below it, but it was good enough for army standards.

The U.S. Army engineers finally completed a project that Spanish priests and Indians had begun a century earlier. For the first time in its history, the ancient building was finished and enclosed. The army engineers concealed their peaked wooden roof behind a bell-shaped false front constructed of matching limestone. Everett regretted this hump-shaped parapet, referring to it as a "ridiculous scroll, giving the building the appearance of the headboard of a bedstead."

Meanwhile the city of San Antonio expanded across the river. New buildings rose over the foundations of the west wall and north walls. The great semirectangular compound of the fort became known as Alamo Plaza. A second, larger area below the south wall was named the Plaza de Valero.

The United States Army occupied the Alamo for less than fifteen years. Ironically, the army, too, met a defeat of sorts at the hard luck mission. On February 16, 1861, two months before the guns of Fort Sumter signaled the onset of the War Between the States, a white supremacy group called the Knights of the Golden Circle, secretly aided by David E. Twiggs, a sympathetic Southern general in the Union army, compelled the United States forces to surrender the Alamo and its military supplies.

Southern sympathizers capture the Alamo from Federalist troops, 1861.

Sam Houston, then serving as governor of Texas, denounced secession and subsequently refused to take an oath of loyalty to the Confederacy. Removed from office, he retired to Huntsville and died in 1863, before the terrible war had ended.

During the reconstruction years the U.S. Army returned to San Antonio. After briefly reoccupying the Alamo, the army constructed a new post to the northwest named Fort Sam Houston.

In 1871 the city purchased the south wall from the Catholic Church. The galera, as it was known, which had housed the Alamo's gate and the room where James Bowie probably died, was demolished to unite the Alamo and Valero plazas into one large area.

Six years later the Catholic Church sold the long barracks building to a Frenchman named Honore Grenet. Adding a surrounding two-story porch and capping the structure with three imposing towers armed with wooden cannons, Grenet used the building as a grocery store and museum.

With the south wall demolished and the convent building privately owned, the state of Texas finally took steps to preserve the old church. In 1883 the state purchased the building from the Catholic Church for $20,000.

Three years later Grenet sold his store to the Hugo & Smeltzer Company. However the city condemned the building in 1889.

As early as 1893 an organization called the Alamo Monument Association proposed utilizing unemployed labor to reconstruct the Alamo to its 1836 appearance. However their plans never developed. Instead the physical Alamo suffered further destruction, ironically at the hands of the very group that would later preserve it.

The Daughters of the Lone Star State, a patriotic organization of women who could trace their lineage to Texan settlers prior to annexation, came into existence in 1891. The members quickly voted to rename themselves the Daughters of the Republic of Texas.

In 1892 Adina Emilia De Zavala, a San Antonio schoolteacher with an intense passion for historical preservation, secured from the Hugo & Smeltzer firm a promise for first option on the old convent. The next year Miss Zavala joined the DRT. As the granddaughter of Lorenzo de Zavala, she certainly had the right blood lines.

In 1903 Hugo & Schmeltzer advised Miss Zavala that an Eastern syndicate had expressed interest in purchasing the property on which the convent building stood. Unable to raise the funds necessary to save the site, Miss Zavala approached Clara Driscoll, a wealthy San Antonio socialite who had joined the DRT that year. Miss Driscoll advanced enough of her own money to purchase the property.

In 1905 the state reimbursed Miss Driscoll and presented custody of the Alamo to the Daughters of the Republic of Texas. Then began the most bizarre battle of the Alamo. Although her money had saved the long barracks building, Miss Driscoll advocated the removal of its second story so as not to obscure the view of the church, which the DRT had established as the Alamo shrine. In fact Miss Driscoll may have mistakenly believed that the Hugo & Schmeltzer building had been constructed after the battle and was not part of the original mission complex. It was, in fact, the oldest of the two remaining buildings.

Miss Zavala argued the historical significance of the old convent. More Texians had died within its walls than in the church. In 1908 she even barricaded herself inside the building for a three-day siege to prevent its destruction. Ultimately she lost her battle of the Alamo—the upper floor of the convent was removed—to provide a better view of the post-1836 parapet that crowned the shrine.

Moreover Miss De Zavala and her supporters were legally barred from any further association with the Alamo. Miss De Zavala continued her work in the field of historic preservation while Miss Driscoll basked in the public limelight as the "Savior of the Alamo." When Miss Driscoll died in 1945, her body lay in state within the Alamo shrine. When Miss De Zavala died a decade later, her funeral procession could only pass in front of the Alamo—and the long barracks building she had at least partially saved.

The early twentieth century witnessed a revitalization of the Alamo, prodded by the looming Texas centennial celebration. During the 1920s the second floor in the church/shrine was removed and the wooden roof replaced by a vaulted concrete roof that blended more harmoniously with the limestone—if not with historical authenticity.

The pending centennial was a time to remember the Alamo. And San Jacinto. New monuments were planned.

In fact the first Alamo monument dated from 1841. At the suggestion of early Alamo historian Reuben Potter, Britisher William B. Nangle fabricated it from limestone taken from the Alamo ruins. The ten-foot-tall monument, a obelisk set upon an ornamented pedestal, toured Texas cities—and even made an appearance in New Orleans—before it found a permanent resting place in the vestibule of the state capitol building in Austin.

It was destroyed when the capitol burned in 1881. Ten years later the James S. Clark Company of Louisville, Kentucky, constructed a new granite monument, over thirty-five feet tall, that presently stands on the capitol grounds.

Already an Alamo Monument Association, organized in 1879, had proposed another monument to stand in Alamo Plaza in San Antonio. Accordingly architect Alfred Giles designed a one-hundred-sixty-five-foot-tall monument. When nothing came of the project, Giles became even more ambitious. In 1912 he advocated a massive eight-hundred-two-foot obelisk to tower over the plaza.

Such an undertaking would have required federal funding, and Congress was squeamish about subsidizing any project that would diminish its own five-hundred-fifty-five-foot Washington monument.

The San Jacinto Memorial Association encountered that same congressional reluctance in 1935. Their representatives in Washington, Houston banker Jesse Jones and architect Albert C. Finn, lobbied for funding for a commemorative structure that would appear as if the Washington monument had been set on top of the Lincoln memorial. However they tactfully advised the legislators that the proposed San Jacinto monument would stand five feet shorter than the Washington monument. Somehow the Texans forgot to mention the star. Once they secured the funding they crowned their obelisk with a huge lone star that surpassed the Washington monument by fifteen feet.

Formal groundbreaking for the San Jacinto monument occurred during the centennial year, but the project was not completed until 1939. At that time the monument that rose above the prairie at San Jacinto was the tallest masonry structure in the world, giving the Texans one more thing to brag about.

That same year Alamo plaza finally got its own monument. The Alamo Cenotaph, a sixty-foot marble shaft rising from a granite base, was erected by the Texas Centennial Commission. Renowned Italian sculptor Pompeo Coppini rendered the figures that adorn its sides, including likenesses of Travis, Bowie, Crockett, and Bonham.

During that decade, primarily as a result of New Deal funding, new Alamo walls were constructed, enclosing the roughly four acres extending to the east of the church and long barracks. Only the horse pens and a portion of the cattle pens from the 1836 site were included within the new compound. A limestone structure housing a combination museum and gift shop was built just north of the church.

Alamo Hall, built at the south end of the compound, became the home of the Daughters of the Republic of Texas Library in 1945. Five years later the library moved into a new limestone structure built on the west side of Alamo Hall. The two were joined in 1964.

Two years earlier public restrooms were introduced into the modern Alamo. The restrooms were built into a structure on the northeast corner of the compound that also housed the curator's office.

Already popular culture—paintings, books, articles, and poems—had simplified the Alamo story, generally vilifying the Mexican attackers and glorifying the Texian defenders. The most influential of these media emerged in the early twentieth century. Beginning with a 1911 ten-minute silent epic entitled *The Immortal Alamo*, more than a dozen films and television productions have chronicled the famous battle. All have claimed to be authentic. Most have perpetuated old legends and occasionally introduced some new ones. A scant few have captured the spirit, if not the facts.

Among the most influential of these cinematic endeavors were Disney's *Davy Crockett, King of the Wild Frontier* (1955), a theatrical feature culled from three television episodes, and John Wayne's epic *The Alamo* (1960).

As producer, director, and star of *The Alamo*, Wayne engaged in his own battles. He had intended to film on a cheap location in Latin America, but Texan pressure compelled him to find a new location on Happy Shahan's ranch near Brackettville. Wayne mortgaged almost everything he had gambling on the success of his costly epic. Initially it lost money, in part because of an uneven and dismally inaccurate script by James Edward Grant, and in part because of an overly patriotic publicity campaign by Russell Birdwell

The political climate in America was changing.

Wayne's movie barely preceded the political assassinations of John F. Kennedy, Robert Kennedy, and Martin Luther King, the Watergate scandal, and the onslaught of the Vietnam War, events that would shatter America's rose colored glasses. Afterwards the Alamo and its defenders would be viewed in accordance with the new cynicism.

Perhaps the first cinematic assault on the Alamo came from a cheaply made science fiction television series called *The Time Tunnel*. An episode that originally aired on December 9, 1966, presented—perhaps for the first time—an unflattering perspective on the Battle of the Alamo. Gone from the script—along with any historical accuracy—was any semblance of a heroic last stand against tyranny. Instead, according to the program, the futile battle resulted solely from the fanatical arrogance of Colonel William Barret Travis.

On January 26, 1982, Public Television first broadcast a docudrama entitled *Seguin*, profiling the heroic *Tejano* leader who carried one of Travis' letters from the Alamo. Filmmaker Jesus Trevino relished what he perceived as the irony of filming at Happy Shahan's Alamo Village, the set built for Wayne's movie. Trevino accused Wayne of portraying the Mexicans as "either bandidos, dancing señoritas, sleeping drunks or fiery temptresses."

As in so many things Alamo, perceptions overruled accuracy. Trevino's charges might have applied to numerous Hollywood motion pictures—including some earlier Alamo productions—but not to Wayne's *Alamo*. Wayne had imbued his Hispanics—from the *Tejanos* to the *soldados* to Santa Anna himself—with bravery and dignity. The only true villain in Wayne's film was a renegade Anglo.

Intriguingly both *The Alamo* and *Seguin* challenged traditional beliefs. In Wayne's movie, Travis makes a speech to his command, but he does not draw a line in the sand for them to cross. *Seguin* ranks as the first cinematic treatment of the battle to depict the execution of Texians after the battle—including one wearing a coonskin cap.

The pedestal that had long supported the Alamo defenders was crumbling.

Though countless towns, counties, and schools in Texas had been named for Alamo heroes, in 1989 the Bryan school district put an abrupt halt to that tradition. It refused to name a school after William Barret Travis "on the grounds his character was too flawed." The board reached that decision after hearing Texas A&M professor Walter Buenger characterize Travis as a champion of slavery who deserted his pregnant wife and son to come to Texas.

And at a 1992 fundraiser, Texas Public Radio conducted a mock trial in which Travis was charged as a deadbeat dad.

Similarly, in the spring of 1988, Gary Bledsoe, president of the Austin, Texas chapter of the NAACP, campaigned against naming a new Austin high school after James Bowie because he "smuggled slaves."

And as recently as September 1999 there were discussions about renaming the Bowie Elementary School in Dallas because of Bowie's slave trading activities.

But of the Alamo's holy trinity, perhaps David Crockett came under the largest barrage of fire. With the 1975 publication of the de la Peña account *With Santa Anna in Texas*, translated by former Alamo librarian Carmen Perry, the media immediately pounced on the single paragraph describing Crockett's execution. Historians and other writers seemed eager to accept Crockett surrendering. Although de la Peña had reported that the Tennessean died bravely, Jeff Long, in his book *Duel of Eagles* (1990), and other writers sneeringly branded Crockett a coward.

Yet there were other reasons why de la Peña's account was so readily accepted. In that cynical new age, publishers encouraged controversy, and writers wanted to be published.

And there were psychological factors. In an article for *Texas Monthly* magazine, historian Paul Hutton candidly admitted that he sought to "dismantle" Crockett to free himself "from the shackles of childhood hero worship and prove once and for all my maturity and credibility as a scholar." Other writers probably shared Hutton's coming of age philosophy, if not his honesty in admitting it.

There was no tooth fairy, there was no Santa Claus, and poor old Davy did not go down fighting. But in their hurry to grow up, these same historians could not see that the de la Peña diary might prove to be just as much of a fantasy as the tooth fairy.

On the other hand there were the Crockett loyalists, who would have refused to believe that Crockett was executed even if Mrs. Dickinson and Joe had both seen and reported it in every one of their accounts. Many of these fanatics wrote abusive, even threatening letters to the proponents of the Crockett execution story.

The issue had a polarizing effect. Everyone who weighed in on it became characterized as either a cynical publicity-seeking revisionist debunker or a naive, racist, right-wing Texan. It seemed the name-calling antagonists would allow no middle ground.

In fact, unlike Jeff Long, many of the ardent de la Peña supporters, including Paul Hutton and Stephen Hardin, argued that there was no cowardice in Crockett's execution. But Bill Groneman still found their attitude smug and patronizing. He took it upon himself to champion Crockett's interests in two books, *Defense of a Legend* (1994) and *Death of a Legend* (1999).

In the former volume he wrote:

> It is important to remember that Crockett, a man who gave his life in the defense of his adopted country, went from a hero to a coward in the public's mind, based primarily on the translation and publication of the de la Peña "diary," a document that is very likely a forgery, a fake, a lie. There is something undeniably wrong with that.

Though Groneman personally doubted the validity of the de la Peña manuscript, he conceded the possibility of Crockett's execution. As Crockett's "defense attorney" all he had to do was establish reasonable doubt about the document's authenticity to establish that no one really knows how the Lion of the West died. He succeeded in that effort; de la Peña's manuscript provided him with plenty of historical problems to herald. But he could not absolutely disprove de la Peña or dissuade the document's adherents.

Researcher Thomas Ricks Lindley was another of the few rational voices that publicly disputed the authenticity of de la Peña, though his conclusions differed somewhat from Groneman's. Lindley engaged in a series of debates with de la Peña supporter James Crisp that spanned several issues of *The Alamo Journal*, the official publication of the Alamo Society.

William C. Davis (*Three Roads to the Alamo*) accepted de la Peña as authentic—but not accurate. He concluded that no single account—Texian or Mexican—of Crockett's death was reliable. "We simply do not know," Davis wrote, "and—unsatisfactory as it is for those impelled to have a definite answer—we probably never will."

The furor over de la Peña had hardly died away before it was resurrected again in 1998 when the owners of the manuscript had it auctioned by the firm of Butterfield and Butterfield in San Francisco. It was another Alamo battle.

Gregory Shaw of Butterfield and Butterfield publicly refuted the charge by the late handwriting expert, Charles Hamilton, that the papers were a forgery, even though Shaw's firm used Hamilton's certification to authenticate documents from Bowie and Travis that sold in the same auction.

Historian James Crisp facetiously quipped that his "greatest fear" was that "some right-wing nut case" would buy the manuscript and toss it into the fire.

The University of Texas dispatched Don Carleton in a desperate bid to buy the manuscript. Carleton bid up to $300,000. He was $50,000 short. Two anonymous buyers acquired the de la Peña account in a phone bid.

Carleton need not have feared that the document would be burned. The buyers later turned out to be two wealthy Texans—Thomas Hicks, owner of the Texas Rangers baseball team, and Charles Tate—who promptly donated the diary to the University of Texas. They had only heard about the auction that day and did not want to see the diary leave Texas.

Since the document has been returned to Texas, Groneman proposes that it can finally be tested. De la Peña advocate Stephen Hardin also has called for testing. But who now would want to possibly undermine the generosity of the two benefactors by testing the authenticity of the manuscript? Most likely the battle over de la Peña will continue.

So will other Alamo battles. On February 19, 1982, rock singer Ozzy Ozburne made the evening news reports when he urinated on the Alamo cenotaph. His action exemplified the degree to which the Alamo often had been reduced to scorn—the butt of jokes.

Later that same year the Daughters of the Republic of Texas came under siege when Gary Foreman, a historic preservation consultant relocated from Illinois to San Antonio, brazenly approached them with an unsolicited twenty-page plan for renovating the Alamo site. Foreman was concerned that the Alamo did not provide enough educational information. Moreover visitors there had no sense of the original compound. He proposed rebuilding the south wall/low barracks with the Alamo gate, the palisade that connected it to the church, and the second story of the long barracks/*convento*. "I want to enhance the Alamo so people go there and consider it more than a wayside, a place to buy a Coke and go to the bathroom," Foreman stated.

"Mr. Foreman does not understand that this is a sacred shrine," responded Peggy Dibrell, then serving as the DRT's chairman of the Alamo Committee. "He wants to turn the Alamo into a tourist trap."

When the Daughters rejected his proposal, Foreman found an ally in the media. Writing for *People* Magazine, Lianne Hart described the DRT as "a band of doughty matrons." Foreman told reporters that the Daughters already had transformed the Alamo into a tourist trap. The so-called museum basically had degenerated into a gift shop that sold cheap, imported coonskin caps and rubber Bowie knives.

It was primarily through the sale of such merchandise, of course, that the DRT had managed to support the Alamo—without state funds—for eighty years.

But Foreman had initiated the new siege of the Alamo, this time with the Daughters of the Republic of Texas entrenched behind their WPA walls. In 1988 the League of United Latin American Citizens advocated that it should receive custodianship of the Alamo. LULAC representatives charged that the DRT "suppressed" the contributions of the *Tejanos*, depicted the Mexican *soldados* as "evil oppressors," and inaccurately portrayed Clara Driscoll as the Alamo's savior, a title that correctly should have gone to Adina De Zavala.

The following year state legislator Ron Wilson introduced a bill to transfer the Alamo to the Texas Parks and Wildlife Department. "It seems to me such an important historical landmark should be in the hands of the state of Texas, rather than a private group," Wilson stated.

In August 1992 David Richelieu, a columnist for the San Antonio *Express-News*, described the DRT as "less-than-careful keepers of history." Simultaneously others followed Gary Foreman's example, calling for major renovations of the Alamo. Native American groups argued for the protection of an Indian burial site on the Alamo grounds. Felix Almaraz Jr. advocated that the site should reflect more of the Alamo's role as a mission instead of just a battleground.

In 1993 Legislator Wilson renewed his efforts to wrest control of the Shrine of Texas History from the DRT. "From time to time, the Daughters have been accused of providing a Hollywood version of history," Debbie Graves reported in the March 2 issue of the Austin *American-Statesman*. "Wilson wants a panel of historians, not the DRT, to provide the story of the Alamo for future visitors."

Yet even as they contended with their critics and attackers, the Daughters faced an even more serious challenge. No longer is the Alamo under a continual bombardment from enemy cannon, but acid rain corrodes its elaborate facade and seeping moisture from the ground crumbles the ancient limestone. Resorting to the latest scientific techniques, the DRT battled to preserve the existing structures.

And they continued with their efforts at education. In 1968 in conjunction with the Hemisfair celebration, the remains of the old convent building were restored and opened to the public as the Long Barracks Museum. The displays within depicted the history of the Alamo from its founding to the present.

In 1994 the Daughters initiated the first of a series of "Texas History Forums" in which historians were invited to address a wide variety of relevant issues. That same year members of the DRT participated in the Alamo Plaza Study Committee which considered how best to depict Alamo Plaza. One proposal harked back to the Alamo Monument Association of a century earlier by advocating the reconstruction of the compound as it appeared in 1836. That notion was rejected because it would entail the destruction of other historic buildings erected over the foundations of the Alamo's west and north walls. Another suggestion followed Gary Foreman's plan just to rebuild the south wall and the palisade. Ultimately the committee merely advocated the establishment of a visitors center to provide a better orientation of the original Alamo grounds.

In 1997 the Daughters erected a Wall of History that traced the mission's entire history in conjunction with a time line. The outdoor panels were erected just west of the museum within the original courtyard of the convent. Within that same area—in the shadow of the convent/long barracks building—the DRT also placed a monument honoring Adina De Zavala. The forgotten savior of the Alamo had finally returned.

Only a small portion of the original Mission San Antonio de Valero still stands. But the legends and the history remain—often in conflict.

And the battles for the Alamo will continue.

Bibliography

Books:

Ahlborn, Richard Eighme. *The San Antonio Missions: Edward Everett and the American Occupation, 1847.* Fort Worth: Amon Carter Museum of Western Art, 1985.

Barr, Alwyn. *Texans in Revolt—The Battle for San Antonio, 1835.* Austin: University of Texas Press, 1990.

Barrett, Monte. *Tempered Blade.* (Novel) Indianapolis: The Bobbs-Merrill Company, 1946.

Batson, James L. *James Bowie and the Sandbar Fight.* Madison: Batson Engineering and Metalworks, 1992.

Baugh, Virgil E. *Rendezvous at the Alamo.* Lincoln: University of New Mexico Press, 1960.

Becerra, Francisco. *A Mexican Sergeant's Recollections of the Alamo & San Jacinto.* Austin: Jenkins Publishing Company, 1980.

Binkley, William C. *The Texas Revolution.* Baton Rouge: Louisana State University Press, 1952.

Bolton, Herbert Eugene. *Texas in the Middle Eighteenth Century.* Austin: University of Texas Press, 1970.

Brack, Gene M. *Mexico Views Manifest Destiny 1821-1846.* Albuquerque: University of New Mexico Press, 1975.

Brear, Holly Beachley. *Inherit the Alamo.* Austin: University of Texas Press, 1995.

Brown, Gary. *Volunteers in the Texas Revolution: The New Orleans Greys.* Plano: Republic of Texas Press, 1999.

Brown, John Henry. *Life of Henry Smith.* Dallas: A.D. Aldridge & Co., 1887.

Burke, James Wakefield. *A Forgotten Glory—The Missions of Old Texas.* Waco: Texian Press, 1979.

Castaneda, C.E., Editor. *The Mexican Side of the Texas Revolution.* Austin: Graphic Ideas Incorporated, 1970.

Chabot, Frederick C. *With the Makers of San Antonio.* San Antonio, 1937.

Chariton, Wallace O. *Exploring the Alamo Legends.* Plano: Wordware Publishing, Inc., 1990.

_____. *100 Days in Texas—The Alamo Letters.* Plano: Wordware Publishing, Inc., 1990.

Chemerka, William R. *Alamo Almanac & Book of Lists*. Austin: Eakin Press, 1997.

Clay, John V. *Spain, Mexico and the Lower Trinity—An Early History of the Texas Gulf Coast*. Baltimore: Gateway Press, 1987.

Courtney, Jovita. *After the Alamo—San Jacinto (From the Notes of Doctor Nicholas Decomps Labadie)*. New York: Vantage Press, 1964.

Crockett, David. *A Narrative of the Life of David Crockett of the State of Tennessee Written by Himself.* 1834. Reprint, Lincoln: University of Nebraska, 1987.

Curtis, Albert. *Remember the Alamo*. San Antonio: The Clegg Company, 1961.

_____. *Remember the Alamo Heroes*. San Antonio: The Clegg Company, 1961.

Davis, William C. *Three Roads to the Alamo*. New York: Harper Collins Publishers, 1998.

de la Peña, Jose Enrique. *With Santa Anna in Texas*. Translated and edited by Carmen Perry. College Station: Texas A&M University Press, 1975.

de la Teja, Jesus F. *A Revolution Remembered—The Memoirs and Selected Correspondence of Juan N. Seguin*. Austin: State House Press, 1991.

_____. *San Antonio de Bexar*. Albuquerque: University of New Mexico Press, 1995.

De Zavala, Adina. *History and Legends of the Alamo and Other Missions in and around San Antonio*. 1917. Reprint, Houston: Arte Publico Press, 1997.

Derr, Mark. *The Frontiersman—The Real Life and the Many Legends of Davy Crockett*. New York: William Morrow and Company, Inc., 1993.

DeShields, James T. *Tall Men with Long Rifles*. 1935. Reprint, San Antonio: The Naylor Company, 1971.

Durham, Ken. *Santa Anna—Prisoner of War in Texas*. Paris: Wright Press, 1986.

Eckhardt, C.F. *The Lost San Saba Mines*. Austin: Texas Monthly Press, 1982.

Edmondson, J.R. *Mr. Bowie with a Knife*. Arlington: Write Press, 1998.

Eickhoff, Randy Lee and Leonard C. Lewis. *Bowie*. (Novel) New York: A Tom Doherty Associates Book, 1998.

Fehrenbach, T.R. *Lone Star: A History of Texas and the Texan*. New York: The Macmillan Company, 1968.

Filisola, Don Vicente. *Memoirs For the History Of the War in Texas*. (2 volumes). 1849. English translation, Austin: Eakin Press, 1987.

Fisher, Lewis F. *The Spanish Missions of San Antonio*. San Antonio: Maverick Publishing Company, 1988.

Friend, Llerena B. *Sam Houston—The Great Designer*. Austin: University of Texas Press, 1969.

Foreman, Gary L. *Crockett—The Gentleman from the Cane*. Dallas: Taylor Publishing Co., 1986.

Gaddy, Jerry J. *Texas in Revolt*. Fort Collins: The Old Army Press, 1973.

Gaillardet, Frederic. *Sketches of Early Texas and Louisiana*. Austin: University of Texas Press, 1966.

Gray, William Fairfax. *From Virginia to Texas, 1835—Diary of Col. Wm. F. Gray*. 1909. Reprint, Houston: The Fletcher Young Publishing Co., 1965.

Groneman, Bill. *Alamo Defenders*. Austin: Eakin Press, 1990.

_____. *Death of a Legend*. Plano: Republic of Texas Press, 1999.

_____. *Defense of a Legend*. Plano: Republic of Texas Press, 1994.

_____. *Eyewitness to the Alamo*. Plano: Republic of Texas Press, 1996.

Guerra, Mary Noonan. *The Missions of San Antonio*. San Antonio: The Alamo Press, 1982.

Hardin, Stephen L. *Texian Iliad*. Austin: University of Texas Press, 1994.

Hauck, Richard Boyd. *Davy Crockett—A Handbook*. Lincoln: University of New Mexico Press, 1982.

Haythornthwaite, Philip. *The Alamo and the War of Texas Independence*. London: Osprey Publishing, 1986.

Henson, Margaret Swett. *Juan Davis Bradburn*. College Station: Texas A&M University Press, 1982.

Heroes of Texas. "James Bowie" (biography) by J. Frank Dobie. Waco: Texian Press, 1964.

Holley, Mary Austin. *Texas*. 1836. Reprint, Austin: Texas State Historical Association, 1985.

Hopewell, Clifford. *James Bowie—Texas Fighting Man*. Austin: Eakin Press, 1994.

Hoyt, Edwin P. *The Alamo—An Illustrated History*. Dallas: Taylor Publishing Company, 1999.

Huffines, Alan C. *Blood of Noble Men—The Alamo Siege and Battle*. Austin: Eakin Press, 1999.

Huston. Cleburne. *Deaf Smith—Incredible Texas Spy*. Waco: Texian Press, 1973.

Jackson, Ron. *Alamo Legacy—Alamo Descendants Remember the Alamo*. Austin: Eakin Press, 1997.

James, Marquis. *The Raven*. New York: Blue Ribbon Books, 1929.

Jenkins, John H., editor. *The Papers of the Texas Revolution, 1835-1836*. Ten volumes. Austin: Presidial Press, 1973.

Kilgore, Dan. *How Did Davy Die?* College Station: Texas A&M University Press, 1978.

Lack, Paul D. *The Texas Revolutionary Experience*. College Station: Texas A&M University Press, 1992.

Lane, Walter P. *The Adventures and Recollections of General Walter P. Lane, a San Jacinto Veteran*. 1928. Reprint, Austin: Pemberton Press, 1970.

Linn, John J. *Reminiscences of Fifty Years in Texas*. Austin: State House Press, 1986.

Lochbaum, Jerry. Editor. *Old San Antonio: History in Pictures*. San Antonio: San Antonio Express and San Antonio Evening News, 1965.

Long, Jeff. *Duel of Eagles: The Mexican and U.S. Fight for the Alamo*. New York: William Morrow and Company, Inc., 1990.

Lord, Walter. *A Time to Stand*. New York: Harper & Brothers, 1961.

Lozano, Ruben Rendon. *Viva Tejas: The Story of the Tejanos, the Mexican-born Patriots of the Texas Revolution*. 1936. Reprint, San Antonio: The Alamo Press, 1985.

Mason, Herbert Molloy Jr. *Southern Living: Missions of Texas*. Birmingham: Oxmoor House, Inc., 1974.

Matovina, Timothy H. *The Alamo Remembered: Tejano Accounts and Perspectives*. Austin: University of Texas Press, 1995.

McAlister, George A. *Alamo: The Price of Freedom*. San Antonio: Docutex, Inc., 1988.

McDonald. Archie P. *Travis*. Austin: Jenkins Publishing Company, 1976.

McHenry, J. Patrick. *A Short History of Mexico*. Garden City: Doubleday & Company, Inc., 1962.

Menchaca, Antonio. *Memoirs*. San Antonio: Yanaquanna Society Publications, 1937.

Montaigne, Sanford H. *Blood Over Texas: The Truth About Mexico's War with the United States*. New Rochelle: Arlington House Publishers, 1976.

Myers, John Myers. *The Alamo*. Lincoln: University of Nebraska Press, 1948.

Nelson, George. *The Alamo: An Illustrated History*. Uvalde: Aldine Press, 1998.

Nofi, Albert A. *The Alamo and the Texas War for Independence September 30, 1835—April 21, 1836*. Conshohocken: Combined Books, Inc., 1992.

O'Conner, Kathryn Stoner. *Presidio La Bahia*. Austin: Von Boeckmann-Jones Co., 1966.

Olivera, Ruth R. and Liliane Crete. *Life in Mexico Under Santa Anna 1822-1855*. Norman: University of Oklahoma Press, 1991.

Ornish, Natalie. *Ehrenberg—Goliad Survivor—Old West Explorer*. Dallas: Texas Heritage Press, 1997.

Petite, Mary Deborah. *1836 Facts about the Alamo & the Texas War for Independence*. Mason City: Savas Publishing Company, 1999.

Potter, Reuben. *The Fall of the Alamo*. Reprint, Hillsdale: The Otterden Press, 1977.

Rios, John F. editor. *Readings on the Alamo*. New York: Vantage Press, 1987.

Rosenthal, Phil. *Alamo Soldiers: An Armchair Historians Guide to the Defenders of the Alamo*. A-Team Productions, 1989.

Rosenthal, Phil and Bill Groneman. *Roll Call at the Alamo*. Fort Collins: The Old Army Press, 1985.

Santa Anna, Antonio Lopez de. *The Eagle: The Autobiography of Santa Anna*. Edited by Ann Fears Crawford. Austin: State House Press, 1988.

Santos, Richard G. *Santa Anna's Campaign Against Texas*. Waco: Texian Press, 1968.

Scharwz, Ted. *Forgotten Battlefield of the first Texas Revolution: The Battle of the Medina, August 18, 1813*. Austin: Eakin Press, 1985.

Shackford, James Atkins. *David Crockett: The Man and the Legend*. Lincoln: University of Nebraska Press, 1956.

Smithwick, Noah. *The Evolution of a State or Recollections of Old Texas Days*. 1900. Reprint, Austin: University of Texas Press, 1983.

Sowell, A.J. *Rangers and Pioneers of Texas*. 1884. Reprint, Austin: State House Press, 1991.

Sutherland, John. *The Fall of the Alamo*. San Antonio: Naylor Co., 1936.

Thompson, Frank. *Alamo Movies*. Reprint, Plano: Republic of Texas Press, 1994.

Thorp, Raymond W. *Bowie Knife*. Albuquerque: The University of New Mexico Press, 1948.

Tinkle, Lon. *13 Days to Glory*. New York: McGraw-Hill Book Company, Inc., 1958.

Todish, Tim J. and Terry S. *Alamo Sourcebook*. Austin: Eakin Press, 1998.

Tolbert, Frank X. *The Day of San Jacinto*. New York: McGraw-Hill Book Company, Inc., 1959.

Travis, William Barret. *The Diary of William Barret Travis*. Edited by Robert E. Davis. Waco: Texian Press, 1966.

Turner, Martha Anne. *Texas Epic*. Quanah: Nortex Press, 1974.

Walraven, Bill and Marjorie K. *The Magnificent Barbarians*. Austin: Eakin Press, 1993.

Weddle, Robert S. *The San Saba Mission: Spanish Pivot in Texas*. Austin: University of Texas Press, 1964.

Wellman, Paul I. *The Iron Mistress*. (Novel) Garden City: Doubleday & Company, Inc., 1951.

Wharton, Clarence R. *The Republic of Texas*. Houston: C.C. Young Printing Company, 1922.

Wlodarski, Robert and Anne Powell Wlodorski. *Spirits of the Alamo*. Plano: Republic of Texas Press, 1999.

Wortham, Louis J. LL.D. *A History of Texas: From Wilderness to Commonwealth*. Five volumes. Wortham-Molyneaux Company, 1924.

Zuber, William Physick. *My Eighty Years in Texas*. Austin: University of Texas Press, 1971.

Magazine Articles:

Anderson, Chris. "How Did Davy Die?" *Blackpowder Annual*. 1992. p. 30.

Chemerka, William R. "The Alamo Remembered." *Muzzle Blasts*. October 1986. p. 9.

Crisp, James E. "The Little Book That Wasn't There: The Myth and Mystery of the de la Peña Diary." *Southwestern Historical Quarterly*. October 1994. p. 261.

Davis, William C. "How Davy Probably Didn't Die." *Journal of the Alamo Battlefield Association*. Fall 1997. p. 11.

Davis, William C. "Remember the Alamo!" *American History Illustrated*. October 1967. p. 4.

Hamilton, Allen Lee. "Pathway to Retreat Ignored." *Military History*. October 1988. p. 18.

Hardin, Stephen L. "The Felix Nunez Account and the Siege of the Alamo: A Critical Appraisal." *Southwestern Historical Quarterly*. July 1990. p. 65.

Hart, Lianne. "The Daughters of Texas Have a Curt Rebuke for a Yankee Who Remembers the Alamo—Forget It." *People Weekly*. June 4, 1984. p. 46.

Hutton, Paul Andrew. "The Alamo—An American Epic." *American History Illustrated*. March 1986. p. 12.

_____. "Continuing Battles for the Alamo." *American History Illustrated*. March 1986. p. 52.

_____. "Davy Crockett—Still King of the Wild Frontier." *Texas Monthly*. November 1986. p. 122.

McDowell, Bart. "Sam Houston—A Man Too Big for Texas." *National Geographic*. March 1986. p. 310.

Nevin, David. "'Fight and Be Damned!' said Sam Houston." *Smithsonian*. July 1992. p. 82.

Patterson, Gerard A. "Sam Houston—A Personality Profile." *American History Illustrated*. August 1967. p. 20.

Paul, Lee. "The Alamo—Thirteen Days of Glory." *Wild West*. February 1996. p. 36.

Ramsdell, Charles. "The Storming of the Alamo." *American Heritage*. February 1961. p. 30.

Randle, Kevin D. "Santa Anna's Signal." *Military History*. April 1985. p. 35.

Schmidt, Erich von. "The Alamo Remembered—from a painter's point of view." *Smithsonian*. March 1986. p. 54.

Steely, Jim. "Remembering the Alamo." *Texas Highways*. March 1985. p. 22.

Walden, Janice. "A Monumental Task." *Texas Parks and Wildlife*. February 1997. p. 26.

Dissertations:

Williams, Amelia. "A Critical Study of the Siege of the Alamo and the Personnel of Its Defenders." Ph.D. dissertation, University of Texas, June, 1931.

Texas History Online:

The Alamo: www.thealamo.org/

Alamo de Parras: www.flash.net/~alamo3/adp.html

Handbook of Texas Online: www.tsha.utexas.edu/handbook/online/

Links to some Texas history primary source documents on the Internet: www2.austin.cc.tx.us/rgriffin/1693intprimdocs.html

Sons of the DeWitt Colony: www.tamu.edu/ccbn/dewitt.htm

Texas history links (Texas State Historical Association): www.tsha.utexas.edu/history-online/index.html

Texas history resources (formerly "Red Neck Tex's Texas History Resources"): lonestar.texas.net/~dwatson/blanco/tx_hist.htm

The Texian Web: www.flash.net/~alamo3/texianweb/texweb.htm

Index

A

acequia, 18, 322, 329
Adams, John Quincy, 53
Adams-Onis Treaty, 54
Aguayo, Jose de Azlor, Marques de San Miguel de, 15-16
Aguirre, Captain Pedro de, 8-9
Agustin I, 67-69, 71
Alamo battle casualties, 408-410
Alamo battle survivors, 407-408
Alamo capture by Southern sympathizers, 415
Alamo Cenotaph, 418
Alamo Company, 29, 31-32, 44-45, 53, 71, 137, 208
Alamo de Parras, Second Flying Company of San Carlos de, *see* Alamo Company
Alamo flag, 235, 244, 260, 303
Alamo monument, 417
Alamo Wall of History, 424
Alamo well, 127, 329
Alamo, 46, 256-258
    beginning of siege, 306
    diagram of, 323
    mission compound, 47
    shape of, 46-47
    size of, 48
Alarcon, Martin de, 13-14
Allen, James, 360
Almonte, Juan Nepomuceno, 191-192, 307, 382
Alsbury, Horace, 284, 301, 337
Alsbury, Juana, 107, 301, 347, 369
Amangal, Francisco, 29
Anahuac, colonist attack on, 155-158
Anahuac, establishment of, 146-148
Apache Indians, 18-22
Archer, Branch T., 231
armistice, offer of, 335-337
Armstrong, Robert, 113-114
Army of Operations, 288-289, 304
Arredondo, General Joaquin de, 41-44, 52, 55
Austin, John, 154-155, 167, 176

Austin, Moses, 56-59
Austin, Stephen Fuller, 59-60, 64-65, 67, 72-75, 104, 160, 163, 192-193
    arrest, 185-186
    at siege of Bexar, 225-231, 234, 236
    colony, 70, 72-75, 78, 80-81
    commanding army, 220-221
    convention at San Felipe, 172
    departing Mexico, 184
    election as general, 214
    in Mexico City, 61-65, 70
    in Mexico with colonist's petition, 178-180
    release from prison, 203, 207
Autry, Micajah, 261, 361

B

Barradas, Isidro, 78-79
Barrera, Melchora, 318
Bastrop, Felipe Enrique Neri, Baron de, 58, 60
Battle of Concepcion, 221-224
Battle of Rosillo, 38
Battle of San Jacinto, 384-386
Battle of the Medina, 40
Baugh, John J., 277-278, 362
Becerra, Francisco, 322
Becerra, Maria Josefa, 51
Beramendi, Josefa Navarro, 43
Beramendi, Juan Martin, 38, 43, 53, 60, 105-107, 171
Beramendi, Maria Ursula, 43, 53, 105-107
Bexar, siege of, 225-236
Bexar, Texian attack on, 239-244
Blanchard, Alfred, 100-101
Blondel, Philippe, 14
Bonaparte, Napoleon, 30
Bonham, James Butler, 139, 254, 342, 348, 393
Boone, Daniel, 87
Bowie knife, 84-85, 100-102, 104, 121-123, 174, 222
Bowie Sr., Rezin, 86-87, 92
Bowie, Elve, 87, 102

Bowie, James, 82-104, 163-165, 171-172, 174-176, 199, 202, 205, 216, 219-221, 233, 252, 256, 278, 284, 307, 311, 368
  at battle of Concepcion, 221-224
  at siege of Bexar, 227-229
  children of, 291-292
  death of, 397-399
  description of, 82-83
  drinking, 293
  exploration of Trinity, 195-196
  fight with Norris Wright, 82-84
  heading militia force, 200
  illness of, 296
  in Mexico, 105-106
  in Texas, 89, 102-104, 107-117, 123-124
  land speculation schemes, 91-94
  life in Louisiana, 102-103
  malaria, 175-176
  marriage to Ursula, 106-107
  myth, 118-120
  San Saba expedition, 107-117
  sandbar fight, 96-101
  slave smuggling, 89-91
Bowie, John Jones, 118-119
Bowie, John, 89
Bowie, Rezin Pleasant, 86-88, 102, 107-108, 110-111, 113-116, 123, 174
Bowie, Stephen, 102
Bowie, Ursula, 171-172, 174, 176, 291-292
Bradburn, John Davis (Juan), 145-161
Breece, Thomas H., 235
Brent, William L., 93, 101, 103
Briscoe, Andrew, 230
Brooks, John S., 346
Buchanon, David, 111
Buffalo Bayou, 383
Burleson, Edward, 215, 236, 241-242
Burnet, David G., 150, 380-381
Buschbacher, Frank, 127
Bustamante, Anastacio, 76, 78, 134, 165

C

Cadillac, Antoine de la Mothe, Sieur de, 10
Calderon, Jose, 162
Candelaria, Madame, 392
Carey, William R., 234, 243, 251
Caro, Ramon, 286, 288
Casas rebellion, 34-35
Casas, Juan Bautista de las, 34
Castaneda, Francisco, 208, 211
Castrillon, Manuel, 386

casualties of Alamo battle, 408-410
Cato, Rosanna E., *see* Rosanna Travis
Cherokee Indians, 166, 169
"Chicken War," 14
Childress, George Campbell, 345
cholera, 175-176
Cloud, Daniel W., 260-261
Coleto Creek, 379
Collingsworth, George, 213
Comanche Indians, 21-23, 58, 74, 108-117
"Come and Take It," 210
Consultation, 232-233
Cordero, Colonel Antonio, 32
Coronado, Francisco Vazques de, 4
Cortez, Hernan, 3
Coryell, James, 113
Cos, Martin Perfecto de, 199-200, 202, 213, 216, 218, 227, 237, 244, 287-288, 349, 356
  invasion of colonies, 207
Crain, Robert Alexander, 94-101
Crockett, David, 262-274, 317, 331, 373, 420
  as legislator, 270-274
  coonskin cap, 294-295
  death of, 368-369, 399-401
  early life, 262-265
  enlistment in militia, 266-267
  lost in woods, 268-269
  marriage to Elizabeth, 268
  marriage to Polly, 266
Crockett, Elizabeth, 268
Crockett, Polly, 268
"Cry of Dolores," 33
Cummings, Rebecca, 184, 187-190, 201
Cuny, Richmond Edmond, 94-95, 99
Cuny, Sam, 94-95, 99

D

Darst, Jacob C., 208, 339
Daughters of the Lone Star State, 416
Daughters of the Republic of Texas, 416, 423-424
De Leon, Alonso, 4-5
De Soto, Hernando, 4
De Zavala, Adina Emilia, 416-417
Deguello, 362
Delgado, Captain Antonio, 39-40
Dellet, James, 141-144
Denny, James A., 96-100
Departments of Texas, 189-191

Despallier, Bernardo Martin, 36, 42, 92
DeWitt, Green, 73-74
Dickinson, Almaron, 208, 245, 303, 338
Dickinson, Susanna, 245, 377
Dimmitt, Philip, 219, 241
Doyal, Matthew, 113
Driscoll, Clara, 416-417
Duque, Francisco, 357

E

Edwards, Haden, 73-74
Ehrenberg, Herman, 235, 239-240, 245, 347
Elizondo, Lt. Colonel Ygnacio, 34-35, 41-44
empresarios, 73
Esparza, Ana, 309
Esparza, Enrique, 309, 311-312
Esparza, Gregorio, 301, 308-309, 360
Espinosa, Father Isidro Felix de, 8, 11, 15
Evans, Robert, 371

F

Fannin, James Walker, 216, 280-282, 324, 333, 378
Farias, Valetin Gomez, 177, 185, 193
filibuster, 32
Filisola, Vicente, 286-287
Finley, Mary (Polly), 265-266
Flanders, John, 359
Forsyth, John, 358
Fort Defiance, 328
Fort St. Jean Baptiste, 10
Fort St. Louis, 4
Francia, Jose de la, 93
freemasonry, 76

G

Gaston, Sidney, 209
Goliad massacre of prisoners, 379-380
Gonzales, 208-213
Gonzales cannon, 209-210, 215
Gonzales Ranging Company of Mounted Volunteers, 338, 340
Goodrich, Benjamin Briggs, 358
Goodrich, John C., 358
Grant, James, 198, 249, 280, 344
"Grass Fight," 237-238
Grenet, Honore, 415-416
Groce, Jared, 103
Guerrero, Brigido, 371-372
Guerrero, Vicente, 70, 76, 78-79, 134

Gutierrez de Lara, Jose Bernardo, 34-36, 39-40, 71

H

Hall, Warren D.C., 88-89, 150
Ham, Caiaphas, 83-84, 92, 103, 108-109, 115-117, 119
Hasinai Indians, 5-6, 8, 12
Henry, Miss E., 183
Herrera, Governor Simon de, 31, 36, 38-40
Hidalgo y Costillo, Father Miguel, 33-34
Hidalgo, Father Francisco, 3, 6, 10-11, 15-16
Highsmith, Benjamin Franklin, 343
Holly, Ely, 181
Houston, Eliza Allen, 169
Houston, Sam, 216-217, 252-254, 376, 380
    adoption by Cherokees, 166
    arrival in Texas, 165-166
    as Indian agent in Washington, 169-170
    at New Orleans, 168
    at San Jacinto, 383-388
    convention at San Felipe, 172
    early life of, 166
    election as commander-in-chief, 232
    in Creek Indian war, 166-168
    marriage to Eliza, 169
    marriage to Tiana Rogers, 169
Hugo and Smeltzer Company, 416

I

"Immortal Gonzales Thirty-two," 209
Iturbide, Agustin de, 64-67, 146

J

Jack, Patrick Churchill, 148, 151-153
Jackson, Andrew, 52-53, 88, 168-170
Jackson, Louisa, 209
Jackson, Thomas, 208-209
Jameson, Green B., 250, 256, 257-258, 282, 329
Jarvis, Pen, 222
Jefferson, Thomas, 30
Jennings, Charles, 359
Jennings, Gordon C., 359
Johnson, Francis W. (Frank), 154-155, 198, 206, 248-249, 280

K

Karankawa Indians, 74
Karnes, Henry, 222
Kellogg, John Benjamin, 209, 339

Kemper Insurrection of 1804, 36
Kemper, Reuben, 92-93
Kemper, Samuel, 36-39
Kent, Andrew, 339
Key, Francis Scott, 169
Kimble, George, 338
King, Amon B., 379
King, William P., 359

L

La Bahia, 15, 213-214
La Bahia presidio, 36-37
La Mora, 51
La Salle, Rene Robert Cavelier, Sieur de, 4-5
La Villita, 17
Labadie, Nicholas, 147, 150, 154
Lafitte, Jean, 54-55, 88-91
Law of April 6, 1830, 134, 136
Leal, Joaquin, 39, 44
line in the sand, 360, 394-396
Lion of the West, 272
Livingstone, Robert, 30
Logan, William, 149
Long, Dr. James, 54-55, 60-61, 65
Long, Jane Wilkinson, 55, 60-61, 63, 182
Losoya, Domingo, 43, 70
Losoya, Toribio, 43, 71, 135, 137, 258
Louisiana Purchase, 30
Louisiana Territory, 4

M

Maddox, Thomas, 95-96, 98-100
Magee, Augustus, 36-37
malaria, 175-176
Malone, William T., 359
Margil de Jesus, Father Antonio, 3, 7, 14-16
Martin, Albert, 209, 314, 320-321, 338-339
Martinez, Governor Antonio, 58, 60-61, 63
Massanet, Father Damian, 5-6
Matamoras expedition, 248-249, 325
Matamoras, 247-261
McCaslin, Thomas, 113, 115
McNeill, Angus, 102, 106, 171, 175
McWhorter, George C., 97-100
Medina River, 8, 40-41
Melton, Eliel, 137
Menchaca, Colonel Miguel, 41-42
Mexia, Jose Antonio, 160
Mexican casualties, 409-410
Mexican politics, 76-78
Mexican revolution 33-45

Mexican War, 413
Mexico, invasion by Spain, 79-80
Mier y Teran, Manuel de, 76, 133-137, 146-148, 154-155, 158
Milam, Benjamin Rush, 199, 213, 242-243
Miller, Thomas R., 209, 339
Millsaps, Isaac, 339
Mina, Francisco Xavier, 146
Mission Espada, 220
missions, closing of, 26-27
missions,
    Nuestra Señora de Guadalupe de los Nacogdoches, 12
    Nuestra Señora de la Purisma Concepcion, 17
    Nuestra Señora de Loreta, 15
    Nuestra Señora del Espiritu Santo de Zuniga, 15
    San Antonio de Valero, 14-15
    San Francisco de los Tejas, 3, 5-6, 12
    San Francisco Solano, 6-7, 13
    San Jose y San Miguel de Aguayo, 16, 24
    San Juan Bautista, 6-7
    San Juan Capistrano, 17
    San Saba de la Santa Cruz, 21
Mississippi River, 30
Mobile Grays, 254-255
Monroe, James, 30, 54
Montgomery, Lemuel P., 167
Moore, John Henry, 209, 211, 228
Morales, Colonel Juan, 357
Morgan James, 150
Morris, Robert C., 235
Muldoon, Father, 73, 153, 186
Musquiz, Ramon, 163, 172, 197
Musso, Joseph, 118

N

Nacogdoches, 12
Natchitoches, 10
Navarro, Jose Antonio, 38, 43, 105, 176, 347
Navarro, Juana, 284
Neill, James Clinton, 210, 250, 252, 256, 276
Nelson, Edward, 359
Nelson, George, 358-359
Neutral Ground, 31, 35
Nevitt, John B., 97, 100-102
New Orleans Greys, 234-236, 239-240

New Orleans Greys flag, 374
Nolan, Philip, 32
Nuestra Señora de Guadalupe de los
    Nacogdoches mission, 12
Nuestra Señora de la Purisma Concepcion
    mission, 17, 23-25, 222
Nuestra Señora de Loreta mission, 15
Nuestra Señora del Espiritu Santo de
    Zuniga mission, 15

O

Old Three Hundred, 63
Olivares, Father Antonio de San
    Buenaventura y, 3, 6-9, 13-16
Onis, Luis de, 53

P

Palm Sunday, March 27, 379
Patrick, George, 299-304
Payaya Indians, 9
Peace Party, 231
Pedraza, Gomez, 76-78, 165
Peña, Jose Enrique de la, 355, 364, 370
    diary of, 402-405, 421
    manuscript auction, 422
Perez, Colonel Ignacio, 55, 61
Piedras, Jose de las, 157-159, 164
Pike, Zebulon, 32-33
Pizzaro, Francisco, 3, 395
Plan de Casa Mata, 69-70
Plan of Iguala, 64
Plan of the Provisional Government,
    232-233
Plan of Vera Cruz, 162
Point Bolivar, 55, 63

Q

Quinta, 44

R

Ramon, Captain Diego, 3, 7, 11
Ramon, Captain Domingo, 12, 15
Rebellion of 1810, 36
red flag of death, 305
Republic of Texas, birth of, 39
Republican Army of the North, 36-37, 51
Rider, Nicholas, 149-150
Ripperda, Baron de, 28
Robinson, Governor James, 250-251,
    280-281
Rogers, Tiana, 169
Romero, Jose Maria, 357

Rose, James M., 358
Rose, Louis "Moses," 360, 394
Ruiz, Francisco, Antonio, 38, 43, 52-53,
    70-71, 74, 135-137, 156, 347
"Runaway Scrape," 380
Rusk, Thomas Jefferson, 380

S

Salcedo, Governor Manuel Maria de, 34,
    36, 38-40
San Antonio de Bexar, 57
    founding of, 14
    settlement of, 17
San Antonio de Valero church construction,
    23-26
San Antonio de Valero mission, 15-16
    acequia, 18
    convento, 18
    expansion of, 18
    fortification of, 23
    founding of, 14
    Indian raids on, 19-20
    Indians of, 17
San Fernando de Bexar, 20, 27-28
    Apache raid on, 20
    military reinforcement of, 29
San Francisco de los Tejas mission, 3, 5 6,
    12
San Francisco Solano mission, 6-7, 13
San Jacinto, battle of, 384-386
San Jacinto corn, 388
San Jacinto monument, 418
San Jose y San Miguel de Aguayo mission,
    16, 24
San Juan Bautista mission, 6-7
San Juan Capistrano mission, 17, 23
San Patricio, 327
San Saba de la Santa Cruz mission, 21
    Comanche raid on, 21
San Saba Indian battle, 109-117, 125-127
San Saba presidio, 22, 75
San Saba River, 23
San Saba silver mines, 124-125
Sanchez Navarro, Jose Juan, 243-244,
    401-402
sandbar fight, 96-101
    location of, 120
Santa Anna, Antonio Lopez de, 45, 66-69,
    71, 77, 133, 162, 184-185, 193-194,
    310-311, 315, 318, 357, 381
    at San Jacinto, 383-388

capture of, 387
during Spanish invasion, 79-80
early military career, 66-69
en route to Texas, 288-289
inauguration as president, 172
leading army to put down rebellion in Texas, 177-178, 180
mock wedding of, 318
preparing for invasion of Texas, 285-288
putting down rebellion in Zacatecas, 201-202
Schively, Henry, 174
Seguin, 419-420
Seguin, Juan Jose Maria Erasmo, 34, 51-53, 60, 71-72, 105, 219
Seguin, Juan Nepomuceno, 51, 197, 200, 202, 218-219, 301, 319-320, 411-412
Seminole Indians, 53
Shaler, William, 35-36
silver mines, 124-125
Smith, Erastus "Deaf," 218, 240, 242, 279, 384
Smith, Henry, 196-197, 250, 279, 337
Smith, John W., 241, 300, 340, 352
Smither, Launcelot, 211
Smithwick, Noah, 102, 123, 214, 223
Snowden, Lovell, 123
soldaderas, 41
Spanish military uniforms, 29
St. Denis, Louis Juchereau de, 10-12
St. Denis, Manuela Sanchez, 11-12
Stanbery, William, 169
Subaran, Felix Maria, 154-155, 159-160, 162
survivors of Alamo battle, 407-408
Sutherland, Dr., 300, 302

T
Tarin, Juana Isidora Leal, 39, 43, 52, 70-71
Tarin, Manuel, 43, 135, 137, 155, 157
Tarin, Vicente, 29, 34, 39, 43, 52-54, 70-71
Tawakoni Indians, 109, 163
Tenoria, Antonio, 203-204
Tenoxtitlan, 135-137
Teran de los Rios, Domingo, 8-9
Texas borders, establishment of, 30-31
Texas map, first detailed, 32
Texian army, 216-217
The Alamo, 419-420
Toledo y Dubois, Jose Alvarez de, 40
Travis, Alexander, 138-139

Travis, Barret, 128
Travis, Charles Edward, 142, 186-187, 201
Travis, Jemima Stallworth, 139
Travis, Mark, 138-139
Travis, Rosanna, 141-143, 181, 201
Travis, Susan Isabella, 201
Travis, Taliaferro, 139
Travis, William Barret, 139-144, 161, 186-187, 198, 201, 292-293, 319, 361
arrival in Texas, 144
as publisher, 141-142
at beginning of siege of Alamo, 299, 301-303
at siege of Bexar, 227, 229
capture of Mexicans at Anahuac, 203-204
cat's-eye ring, 188, 361
death of, 365-366, 396-397
diary of, 180-183, 186, 188, 190
early life, 139-141
in Anahuac, 148-155, 158-161
in San Felipe, 182-184
letter "To the People of Texas," 312-314
line in the sand, 360, 394-396
marriage to Rosanna, 142
recruiting cavalry, 259-260
relationship with Rebecca, 184, 187-190
temporary command of Alamo, 276-279
Treaty of Fountainbleu, 27
Treaty of Guadalupe Hidalgo, 414
Turtle Bayou Resolutions, 157
"Twin Sisters," 381, 384-385

U
Ugartechea, Domingo de, 149, 157-158, 203, 208
Urrea, Jose, 325, 327, 344-345

V
Veramendi, *see* Beramendi
Victoria, Guadalupe, 76, 133
Viesca, Agustin, 80
Viesca, Jose Maria, 80
Villa de Bexar, 14-15, 17
Vince's Bayou, bridge over, 384

W
Walker, Asa, 225-226, 359
Walker, Jacob, 359, 371-372
Wall of History, 424
War of 1812, 52, 57, 87-88

War Party, 231
Wayne, John, 419
Wells, Cecelia, 94, 102
Wells, Jefferson, 97-98, 101
Wells, Samuel Levi, 88, 94-99, 101
Wharton, John, 386
Wilkerson, Susanna, 208
Wilkinson, General James, 31-32, 65, 73
Williams, Ezekiel, 209
Williamson, Robert McAlpin "Three-Legged Willie," 151-152, 182, 192, 206-207, 342-343

With Santa Anna in Texas, 420
Woll, Adrian 412
Wright, Norris, 82-84, 94-101

Z

Zambrano, Father Jose Dario, 52
Zambrano, Juan Jose Manuel Vicente, 34
Zanco, Charles, 283
Zapadores Battalion, 357
Zavala, Lorenzo de, 71, 76-78, 206, 380
Zuber, William P., 394-385
Zuniga, Marques de Valero Baltazar de, 13

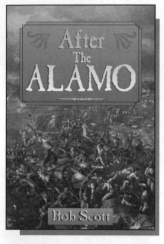

After the Alamo

Bob Scott

Go beyond popular myth and folklore to explore the events and portray the heroes (and the cowards) of the Texas War for Independence. Author Scott examines the battles leading up to Texas' independence and determines that the events at Ft. Defiance, led by James Walker Fannin, inspired Texans more than the Alamo in their struggle to defeat the Mexicans.

Bob Scott developed a passion for Texas history while he lived here. He now lives in Michigan with his son. This is his fourth book.

1-55622-691-8 • $18.95
320 pages • 5½ x 8½ • paper

Exploring the Alamo Legends

Wallace O. Chariton

Did Davy Crockett surrender at the Alamo or did he fight to the very end? Did Sam Houston lie when he claimed he ordered James Bowie to destroy the Alamo? Did Travis really draw the line and did Louis Rose escape to tell the world the story? What happened to the real commander of the Alamo? These and more Alamo mysteries are explored in this fast-paced, hard-hitting, controversial book that may excite patriotism or incite anger.

1-55622-255-6 • $16.95
288 pages • 6 x 9 • paper

Audio tape:
1-55622-133-9 • $15.95

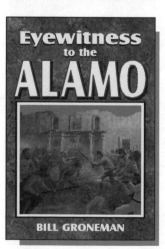

Eyewitness to the Alamo

Bill Groneman

Eyewitness to the Alamo is an actual account of the siege and Battle of the Alamo by those who were present during the attack. Fifty people are believed to have witnessed all or part of one of the most legendary events in Texas and U.S. history.

Did Travis draw his famous line? Was Crockett executed or did he die fighting? Did Bowie fight from his sickbed? Some eyewitnesses claimed to know the true story behind the myths, but were all of these witnesses credible? The origins of and answers to these questions can be found in *Eyewitness to the Alamo*, the first complete accounting of the Battle of the Alamo by one of the country's foremost authorities on the event.

1-55622-502-4 • $16.95
250 pages • 5½ x 8½ • paper

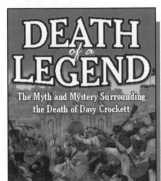

Death of a Legend
The Myth and Mystery Surrounding the Death of Davy Crockett

Bill Groneman

Crockett was one of the most well-known Americans of his time. Today he is still one of the most popular heroes of our history. For years Alamo scholars have been debating whether or not Crockett was taken prisoner and executed after the Alamo battle, or if he went down fighting. *Death of a Legend* traces the roots of our beliefs about his death and updates the reader on the ongoing debate among writers and historians.

Bill Groneman is also the author of *Defense of a Legend: Crockett and the de la Peña Diary*, *Eyewitness to the Alamo*, and *Battlefields of Texas*.

1-55622-688-8 • $18.95
296 pages • 5½ x 8½ • paper

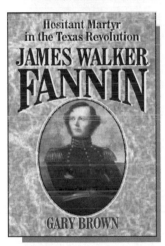

Hesitant Martyr in the Texas Revolution
James Walker Fannin

Gary Brown

James Fannin: illegitimate son of the South, failed businessman, illegal slave trader, and tarnished hero of the revolution. But that was not the whole story. The author delivers a thorough historical analysis and rare insight into the mind of this controversial, misunderstood figure of the Texas Revolution. Included are all of Fannin's known correspondence during the campaign at Goliad.

Gary Brown also wrote *Volunteers in the Texas Revolution: The New Orleans Greys*. Brown resides in Friendswood, Texas.

1-55622-778-7 • $18.95
275 pages • 5½ x 8½ • paper

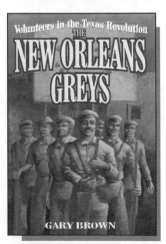

Volunteers in the Texas Revolution
The New Orleans Greys

Gary Brown

In a New Orleans coffee arcade on October 13, 1835, a fighting unit called the New Orleans Greys was born. Within 175 days they had been destroyed as a military unit, and only a few remained alive after the victory at San Jacinto. They were one of the only two units to wear uniforms and carry similar weapons. During the short time they existed, they fought courageously and helped turn the tide of battle in favor of the colonists.

Impeccably accurate but written like a novel with color and drama, this book proves that history doesn't have to be dull.

Gary Brown teaches Texas government part-time at Galveston College and writes Texas history articles for several magazines.

1-55622-675-6 • $18.95
344 pages • 5½ x 8½ • paper